Usability Evaluation of Online Learning Programs

Claude Ghaoui
Liverpool John Moores University, UK

Information Science Publishing

Hershey • London • Melbourne • Singapore • Beijing

Acquisition Editor: Mehdi Khosrow-Pour
Senior Managing Editor: Jan Travers
Managing Editor: Amanda Appicello
Development Editor: Michele Rossi
Copy Editor: Elizabeth Arneson
Typesetter: Jennifer Wetzel
Cover Design: Integrated Book Technology
Printed at: Integrated Book Technology

Published in the United States of America by
        Information Science Publishing (an imprint of Idea Group Inc.)
        701 E. Chocolate Avenue, Suite 200
        Hershey PA 17033-1240
        Tel: 717-533-8845
        Fax: 717-533-8661
        E-mail: cust@idea-group.com
        Web site: http://www.idea-group.com

and in the United Kingdom by
        Information Science Publishing (an imprint of Idea Group Inc.)
        3 Henrietta Street
        Covent Garden
        London WC2E 8LU
        Tel: 44 20 7240 0856
        Fax: 44 20 7379 3313
        Web site: http://www.eurospan.co.uk

Library of Congress Cataloging-in-Publication Data

Usability evaluation of online learning programs / [edited by] Claude Ghaoui.
        p. cm.
    ISBN 1-59140-105-4 -- ISBN 1-59140-113-5 (pbk.)
    1. Internet in education. 2. Computer-assisted instruction. 3. Educational evaluation. 4. Human-computer interaction. I. Ghaoui, Claude.
    LB1044.87 .U82 2003
    371.33'467'8--dc21
                                                    2002014749

eISBN 1-59140-114-3

British Cataloguing in Publication Data
A Cataloguing in Publication record for this book is available from the British Library.

NEW Titles
from Information Science Publishing

- **Web-Based Education: Learning from Experience**
  Anil Aggarwal
  ISBN: 1-59140-102-X: eISBN 1-59140-110-0, © 2003
- **The Knowledge Medium: Designing Effective Computer-Based Learning Environments**
  Gary A. Berg
  ISBN: 1-59140-103-8; eISBN 1-59140-111-9, © 2003
- **Socio-Technical and Human Cognition Elements of Information Systems**
  Steve Clarke, Elayne Coakes, M. Gordon Hunter and Andrew Wenn
  ISBN: 1-59140-104-6; eISBN 1-59140-112-7, © 2003
- **Usability Evaluation of Online Learning Programs**
  Claude Ghaoui
  ISBN: 1-59140-105-4; eISBN 1-59140-113-5, © 2003
- **Building a Virtual Library**
  Ardis Hanson & Bruce Lubotsky Levin
  ISBN: 1-59140-106-2; eISBN 1-59140-114-3, © 2003
- **Design and Implementation of Web-Enabled Teaching Tools**
  Mary F. Hricko
  ISBN: 1-59140-107-0; eISBN 1-59140-115-1, © 2003
- **Designing Campus Portals: Opportunities and Challenges**
  Ali Jafari and Mark Sheehan
  ISBN: 1-59140-108-9; eISBN 1-59140-116-X, © 2003
- **Challenges of Teaching with Technology Across the Curriculum: Issues and Solutions**
  Lawrence A. Tomei
  ISBN: 1-59140-109-7; eISBN 1-59140-117-8, © 2003

Excellent additions to your institution's library! Recommend these titles to your librarian!

To receive a copy of the Idea Group Inc. catalog, please contact (toll free) 1/800-345-4332, fax 1/717-533-8661,or visit the IGI Online Bookstore at: http://www.idea-group.com!

Note: All IGI books are also available as ebooks on netlibrary.com as well as other ebook sources. Contact Ms. Carrie Skovrinskie at <cskovrinskie@idea-group.com> to receive a complete list of sources where you can obtain ebook information or IGP titles.

This book is dedicated to the memory of my beloved Mum and Dad, to whom I owe all that is good in my life.

Fifty percent of the book royalties will be donated by the Editor to orphaned children supported by an international charity.

Usability Evaluation of Online Learning Programs

Table of Contents

Preface

OVERVIEW AND MOTIVATION

In a fair society, all individuals would have equal opportunity to participate in, or benefit from, the use of computer resources, regardless of race, sex, religion, age, disability, origin or other such similar factors.

ACM Code of Ethics

Successful use of information and communication technologies depends on usable designs that do not require expensive training, accommodate the needs of diverse users and are low cost.

There is a growing demand and increasing pressure for adopting innovative approaches to the design and delivery of education, hence, the use of online learning (also called e-learning) as a mode of study. This is partly due to the increasing number of learners and the limited resources available to meet a wide range of various needs, backgrounds, expectations, skills, levels, ages, abilities and disabilities. The advances of new technology and communications (WWW, human computer interaction [HCI] and multimedia) have made it possible to reach out to a bigger audience around the globe.

While "*education for all*" offers new exciting opportunities, it also introduces many new challenges to both providers and receivers of education. Besides delivering customised educational content and linking far-flung professors and students, this mode of study requires a *reengineered vision* of a university's educational process. The benefits of interactive multimedia and the increasing popularity of the WWW open a new paradigm for the authoring, design and delivery of online learning. This introduces a new meaning that emphasises interactivity in learning and an educational cultural change for both teachers and learners. What was once printed on paper and sent through postal mail can now be delivered through the WWW.

While this new electronic approach increases distribution efficiency, it does not exploit the full potential of the technology as an enabler of a reengineering of the educational process itself. The main issues to consider when "implementing online learning for real" are: learning system standards, the necessity to change the culture where the roles of learners and teachers should adapt to the new environment, procurement of systems to deliver and manage online learning, management change (when not changing is no longer a viable option), costing, and roles within the emerging consortia including government, commercial and overseas partners.

However, there is no point in buying a system if the university or consortium cannot change its ways and culture to use the system to best advantage. A few examples of barriers to a successful deployment of online learning are: lack of an in-depth understanding or underestimation of the efforts, time, and resources needed for this change, lack of implementing pedagogy and quality of learning, lack of training in new technologies, and lack of transparent tools and standards. All of these issues have a critical impact on the usability of online learning.

MAIN OBJECTIVE

The primary objective of this book is to bring together two relatively new but important research areas, i.e., "usability and its evaluation" as a practical theme of human computer interaction, and "online learning." By focusing on the issues that have an impact on the usability of online learning programs and their implementation, the book specifically fills in a gap in this area, which is particularly invaluable to practitioners. The book is aimed at researchers and practitioners from academia, industry and government for an in-depth coverage of a broad range of issues on online learning. It aims to raise more awareness of this topic, promote good practice, and share and evaluate experiences (advantages, disadvantages, problems faced and lessons learnt). It promotes both evaluation and research as critical and integral parts of the development of learning and learning tools (rather than supplementary processes). Due to the large number of submissions received, I postponed publishing my chapter to a forthcoming book of mine, which is due to appear in 2004 and is called *E-Educational Applications: Human Factors and Innovative Approaches* (IRM Press, USA).

CHAPTER DESCRIPTIONS

This book includes 21 chapters, grouped into three sections, as follows.

Section I: Using Virtual Learning Environments

Chapter I: ETH World—Implementation of a Virtual Campus Infrastructure and E-learning at ETH Zurich, by *Anders Hagström* and *Walter Schaufelberger*.

This chapter describes the background of a new academic environment called ETH World and its "infostructure." It provides details on its e-learning functionality, using two case studies in architecture and control engineering education.

Chapter II: Implementing Online Delivery and Learning Support Systems: Issues, Evaluation and Lessons, by *J. Bernardes* and *J. O'Donoghue*.

This chapter evaluates an online learning framework called WOLF and concludes with some useful lessons based on evaluating it for the support of students' learning.

Chapter III: Collaborative Learning On-Demand on the Internet Mbone, by *Giancarlo Fortino* and *Libero Nigro*.

This chapter proposes a new online learning paradigm called collaborative learning on-demand (CLoD), which enables a group of workmates to request and watch, on demand, the playback of an archived multimedia session. The chapter also discusses an Mbone-based cooperative playback system called ViCRO and evaluates its usability.

Chapter IV: Improving Usability of an Online Learning System by Means of Multimedia, Collaboration and Adaptation Resources, by *Elizabeth Furtado, João José Vasco Furtado, Fernando Lincoln Mattos,* and *Jean Vanderdonckt*.

This chapter describes an adaptive and collaborative environment which mainly aimed at helping teachers in problem solving. It provides teachers with assistance that adapts to context and students' profiles and allows interaction with other teachers or students.

Section II: Methods, Pedagogy and Theories

Chapter V: Heuristic Evaluation of Web-Based ODL Programs, by *Athanasis Karoulis* and *Andreas Pombortsis*.

This chapter looks into learnability and the overall evaluation of ODL. It then presents a heuristic evaluation method and proves its applicability to evaluating the usability of ODL.

Chapter VI: Coming off the Rails: Evaluation and the Design Process, by *Liz Marr, Dave Randall,* and *William L. Mitchell*.

This chapter addresses methodological issues concerned with the design and creation of computer-supported learning environments. This was based on researching the use of museum environments and artefacts as educational resources for primary-school-age children.

Chapter VII: Developing and Supporting Research-Based Learning and Teaching through Technology, by *Jacqueline Dempster*.

This chapter highlights the importance of developing research-based approaches to learning and teaching and supporting these through the use of IT. It highlights the value of pedagogical objectives and frameworks in evaluating usability of online learning programs in learning and teaching.

Chapter VIII: Online Learning for the Real World: Diploma in Computing Via the Internet, by *Bridget Khursheed*.

This chapter draws attention to the need of evaluating the pedagogical effectiveness of online courses and not just their content and interface. It examines the experience of students in continuing education.

Chapter IX: Usability Inspection of the ECONOF System's User Interface Visualization Component, by *Nadir Belkhiter, Marie-Michèle Boulet, Sami Baffoun,* and *Clermont Dupuis*.

This chapter shows that using a simple, low-cost, but systematic evaluation method called "usability inspection" can alleviate usability problems. This method was tested on a training system called ECONOF, which was proved to be effective.

Chapter X: Issues of Quality in Online Degree Programmes, by *Floriana Grasso* and *Paul Leng*.

This chapter describes the structures and processes developed for quality management and assurance to run an online M.Sc. programme. It emphasises that online discussions play a key role in the quality assurance process and discusses ways in which AI techniques can assist in their evaluation.

Chapter XI: Learning Technologies and Learning Theories, by *Vivien Sieber* and *David Andrew*.

This chapter argues that effective learning can be achieved when an independent and leaner-centred approach is facilitated. It discusses effective learning in relation to learning theory and uses case studies to present some complex learning outcomes.

Chapter XII: Design Cycle Usability Evaluations of an Intercultural Virtual Simulation Game for Collaborative Learning, by *Elaine M. Raybourn*.

This chapter describes a design cycle employed by the author to create a computer-mediated social process simulation called the *DomeCityMOO*. Various evaluation methods were employed to guide usability testing.

Chapter XIII: Computer-Supported Network-Based Learning Environment for the Workplace, by *Joze Rugelj*.

This chapter reports on 10 years' experience in the field of computer-supported network-based learning, from which the author draws conclusions and interesting insights that provide a framework for introducing new learning technologies.

Section III: Managerial and Social Issues

Chapter XIV: Professional to Manufacturing Mode Due to Online University Education, by *Roy Rada*.

This chapter addresses the link between the usability of online education and the pressures of management.

Chapter XV: Changing Roles and Processes in Online Tuition for Higher Education: A Case Study from the UK Open University, by *Gordon Dyer*.

This chapter reports on a case study which compares tutoring a course using normal OU distance teaching methods with the use of computer-mediated conferencing (CMC) and argues that CMC has a major impact on student learning styles and in changing roles within the teaching team.

Chapter XVI: Learnability, by *Philip Duchastel*.

This chapter discusses usability using the concept of learnability by considering three core issues: learning theory, instructional design and curriculum choices.

Chapter XVII: Usability Evaluation of Online Learning Programs: A Sociological Standpoint, by *Bernard Blandin*.

This chapter argues that usability has to be "situated," i.e., it has to take into account "user experience" in its broad sense, which is certainly one of the best design principles. It argues that learner's motivation, organisational learning, culture and environmental factors have a strong impact on the usability of online learning programs.

Chapter XVIII: Security and Online Learning: To Protect or Prohibit, by *Anne Adams* and *Ann Blandford*.

This chapter discusses usability from the security and privacy point of view. It argues that appropriate security mechanisms are essential to prevent unauthorised access to learning material.

Chapter XIX: How Useful Are World Wide Web Discussion Boards and Email in Delivering a Case Study Course in Reproductive Medicine, by *David Cahill, Julian Cook,* and *Julian Jenkins*.

This chapter reports on the experience of using email and Web-based discussion boards to deliver a pilot online course in reproductive medicine to trainee physicians. Evaluation was carried out from tutors' and learners' points of view.

Chapter XX: Ensuring Optimal Accessibility of Online Learning Resources, by *David Sloan, Lorna Gibson, Scott Milne,* and *Peter Gregor*.

This chapter outlines the arguments for taking accessibility into account during design and discusses strategies for ensuring that accessibility plays a core part in the design, development and maintenance of online educational material. Common accessibility problems and solutions are discussed.

Chapter XXI: Online Learning for the Visually Impaired, by *Mirela Arion* and *Marius Iulian Tutuianu*.

This chapter addresses usability from the point of view of visually impaired users, discussing how adaptive technology could and should offer to widen access to users with some disabilities.

CONCLUSION

The 21 chapters included in this book were selected from a large number of submissions received. They cover a wide range of important issues on the subject of "usability evaluation of online learning programs," representing experiences from 13 countries. It was really pleasing to have representations from the following 13 countries: the United Kingdom, Scotland, Switzerland, Greece, Sweden, France, Italy, Belgium, Romania, Slovenia, USA, Canada and Brazil. The chapters report on research, development and real experiences, including theory, practice, techniques, analysis, design, work in progress, and case studies. It is particularly refreshing that authors present new insights and views by reflecting on the inter- and multi- disciplinary nature of this topic, addressing it from different perspectives, e.g., computer science/IT, engineering, psychology, sociology, cognitive science, art, and design. The main contribution of this book is that it specifically focuses on the usability and its evaluation of online learning programs. It promotes evaluation as an integral part of the development cycle, rather than a complementary process, which is most of the time wrongly underestimated, missed or delayed till very late stages. This theme fills in a gap in literature and particularly benefits practitioners who are working in academia, industry or government.

ACKNOWLEDGMENTS

I would like to specially thank Mehdi Khosrow-Pour, the Editor-In-Chief of IGP, for inviting me to edit this book. This has given me a great opportunity to approach experts in this field, who have been very generous in their contributions and participation. Most of the authors of chapters included in this book have also served as referees for articles written by other authors. Many thanks and appreciation go to all those who provided constructive and comprehensive reviews, without such support the project could not have been satisfactorily completed.

Many thanks go to the publishing team at Idea Group Publishing, in particular to Michele Rossi and Amanda Appicello, for their patience and support, despite sometime not being able to keep on schedule.

Finally, I would like to thank all authors for their excellent contributions, and for sharing their invaluable experiences and insights. It has been a great pleasure communicating with you all through email and telephone calls, and sometimes having 'heated but interesting' discussions about issues raised in the chapters submitted. The opportunity to work with so many international professionals like you has truly been a great privilege for me. Thank you for helping me complete this project!

Claude Ghaoui, PhD
United Kingdom, 2002
c.ghaoui@livjm.ac.uk

Section I:

Using Virtual Learning Environments

Chapter I

ETH World— Implementation of a Virtual Campus Infrastructure and E-Learning at ETH Zurich

Anders Hagström
Swiss Federal Institute of Technology Zurich, Switzerland

Walter Schaufelberger
Swiss Federal Institute of Technology Zurich, Switzerland

ABSTRACT

ETH World is a strategic initiative for establishing a new virtual campus at the Swiss Federal Institute of Technology (ETH) Zurich. ETH World will provide services in the areas of research, teaching, learning and infrastructure for the established disciplines in technology and natural science at ETH. The initiative aims to develop the excellence of ETH Zurich, making use of the new facilities and infrastructure instruments and methods that technological development offers. It is an integral part of the university, supporting its academic planning, infrastructure and financing processes. In its first part this paper describes the background of ETH World and an international conceptual competition organized in 2000 to seek ideas for the "infostructure" of this new academic environment. Some results of the competition are presented along with other projects that have been launched as building blocks of ETH World. The second part looks in some detail at e-learning as one of the focal points of ETH World, presenting two cases studies in architecture and control engineering education.

ETH WORLD

Introduction

ETH Zurich, the Swiss Federal Institute of Technology, was established in the tradition of a polytechnic in the mid 19th century. It has since grown from a few hundred people to a community of more than 18,000 students, faculty, researchers and staff, covering the whole range of technical and natural sciences. Its facilities are located in more than 200 buildings in downtown Zurich and on the campus of Hönggerberg eight km from the center.

The university's technical infrastructure is no less complex, with a hugely diverse range of computers and devices, all conceivable operating systems, and many expert users with the broadest range of needs.

In response to the need for adapting this complex organization and its infrastructure to the needs of the information society, ETH Zurich has launched a virtual university project named "ETH World."

The goals have been defined for ETH World (Hagström & Schaufelberger, 2001):

1. to support and augment research facilities with new types of information and communication technologies and offer a platform for collaborative and learner-oriented activities, independent of time and space;
2. to improve access to existing and new scientific and administrative services;
3. to connect virtual and physical space;
4. to provide optimal communication and globally accessible information, not least by breaking down linguistic barriers;
5. to strengthen the different ETH departments and their interdisciplinary collaboration;
6. to create synergies through the integration of advanced research, education and infrastructure;
7. to extend areas of research to accommodate the requirements of the information society;
8. to support students, employees, professors and alumni in their efforts to promote the development and globalization of the ETH community;
9. to provide a forum for cooperation and knowledge transfer for the benefit of business, politics, nongovernmental organizations and society;
10. to enhance the attractiveness of ETH for potential students, cooperation partners and faculty members as well as for sponsors and professional bodies.

The scope of ETH World thus extends beyond mere e-learning to cover all aspects of the university activities: education, research, services and administration.

The first steps towards ETH World were taken in 1999 when the university's executive board decided to finance a number of pioneer projects, putting in place hardware and software infrastructure and developing new concepts.

But this ad hoc approach did not address the broader questions: What physical infrastructure, communication, services and organizational structures should be put in place to achieve the goals of ETH World? A master plan was called for to define the university "infostructure," the merger of information and communication infra-structures, the virtual and physical presence for the ETH Zurich of the 21st century.

ETH World International Competition

To seek new concepts and ideas for this master plan, ETH decided to organize an international conceptual competition, an "architecture competition" for the virtual campus. The competition task was simple: "Imagine a campus, a virtual one. Design this campus!" Entrants were asked to present a conceptual design, an ingenious and realizable concept for the integration of people, new media, research, learning and the existing architecture of ETH Zurich in a global context. The specific competition tasks mirrored the 10 goals of ETH World (ETH Zurich, 2000).

The competition took place in two rounds from June to November 2000. As far as we know, it was the first competition ever launched for this kind of task, and it attracted worldwide attention. Fifty contributions from all over the world were submitted in the first round; seven of these were accepted to the second round.

Many architect teams submitted proposals, which perhaps reflects the fact that architects are familiar with design competitions. But the range of backgrounds of the contributors was very broad: Web designers, computer and software engineers, business consultants, and media and communication specialists.

After careful evaluation and a tight decision, the jury awarded the first prize to the entry "beyond Luxury," submitted by a team of architects, designers and software programmers from Zurich. Three other prizes were awarded and one additional purchase was made.

Results of the Competition

So what made the winners stand out? The jury especially mentioned the winning entry's emphasis on the users and on their access to information as its principal merit and visionary quality.

Indeed, "beyond Luxury" catches the eye with its seemingly simple communi-cation solutions and design. The proposal includes practical ideas for the permanent personal connection to the ETH information network. A smart card with a biometric sensor and built-in radio interface serves as electronic identification and provides wireless access to personalized information. The winners' vision includes Bluetooth and UMTS technologies but goes beyond the already existing: As devices get smaller, the card can be replaced with buttons, wearable screens and other accessories as miniaturized information portals to the world of ETH.

A navigation tool is proposed as a graphical user interface into the information space (Figure 1). Through a personalized pattern, the tool provides quick and easy access to the most frequently used information. Users can also establish links between objects, such as persons, projects, documents and bookmarks. Over time, this grows into a personal dynamic representation of ETH World, filtered for the user.

Figure 1: The ETH World competition winning entry "beyond Luxury" proposes, among other solutions, a graphical user interface for navigating information

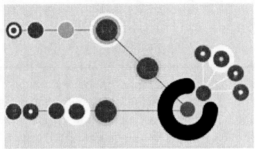

To bridge the virtual and physical worlds, "beyond Luxury" proposes "ETH World grounds": a modular system of lounges where ETH community members can come together. Being transportable, these "grounds" would also allow ETH to establish a presence anywhere in the world (Figure 2).

What is striking in the winning proposal is that it does not contain direct proposals for teaching, learning or research, for example, in the form of a e-learning platform. Instead, it focuses on topics like communication, information and collaboration, i.e., the processes underlying education and research. This focus reflects the approach of ETH World as a basic infrastructure project.

The results of the ETH World conceptual competition have been documented in a book (Carrard & Engeli, 2001) and on the ETH World Web site (http://www.ethworld.ethz.ch).

Figure 2: The "ETH World grounds" represent the "beyond Luxury" vision of physical presence

The competition did not provide a full-grown master plan for the implementation of ETH World as envisaged. But it did provide a wealth of new ideas and refreshing external input into the university's planning and development processes. It also gave access to a talented winning team, with whom ETH is now working to turn the winning ideas into reality.

Other Building Blocks of ETH World

Parallel to the conceptual competition, a large number of individual projects have been launched early on to put in place some building blocks for ETH World. These projects address different areas, such as research tools, community building, information management and infostructure elements, or e-learning.

Some of these projects are financed directly by ETH World, others are funded through a special funding program for e-learning (FILEP), and yet others are undertaken by the various organizational units as part of their regular development activities. Common to all projects is that they all work in the same strategic direction. This bundling of resources, trying to get different parts of the university working towards the same strategic goal, is crucial for the long-term success of the project.

In the following, we will briefly describe some of these building blocks as examples of the multitude of activities in progress on the "building site" of the virtual campus (Schaufelberger & Halström, 2001).

NEPTUN: Laptops for Students

By expanding our view of the computer as a tool for solving specific problems to the computer as a medium that facilitates communication and sharing, we can fundamentally change the way we think and learn (Perrone, Repenning, Spencer, & Ambach, 1996). Recognizing that a personal computer today is an indispensable everyday tool for engineers and scientists, the goal of project "NEPTUN" is to equip every ETH student with a laptop computer as a working tool for learning and research, with wireless LAN to the ETH computer network. The objective is, through permanent, ubiquitous access to computing, to support a fundamental change in the way students communicate among themselves and with faculty and staff. A subsidiary long-term goal is to free the present public student computer workstations for other functions, such as complex calculations and simulations.

Implementation of the laptop project started with a pilot project in the academic year 2001/2002 to gather experiences as to how students can use their laptops. What new methods of working and new competences will emerge? Will there be more contact with teachers, assistants and fellow students? What new forms of teaching will thereby be introduced? How can the user support best be organized?

In the pilot phase, laptops were introduced in four degree programs: architecture, computer science, mechanical and process engineering, and pharmacy. The students of these programs were strongly encouraged but not obliged to buy a laptop with an attractive software package at a discounted price negotiated by the university. ETH

World supported the four departments for putting in place the necessary infrastructure, help-desks, etc. The departments were committed to make sure that the laptops
were used in the education process.

The response from students exceeded expectations. The project is currently
evaluating the experiences and preparing for the next phase with extensions into
further degree programs.

Research Tools

For a research-based university like ETH, research tools and research cooperation are vital for the university of the future. Research interests are also a powerful
motivating factor for faculty and other research staff to get involved in the building
of ETH World.

Two examples of projects are the virtual-real laboratory "Vireal Lab" in
pharmaceutical sciences and the "Chemistry Contact Network." Vireal Lab has
established an environment combining virtual science worlds with the real world.
Researchers and students have access to the virtual world in a specially equipped
room with intelligent "roomware" technology: tables, chairs and whiteboards with
built-in electronic devices, providing easy, collaborative access to 3D-models,
databases and the local computer network.

The Chemistry Contact Network aims to establish time-limited virtual research
clusters around a key research topic such as nanotechnology, catalysis and modern
analytical methods. In addition, tools for research collaboration and cooperation
platforms for cutting-edge fields at ETH are being investigated.

Community Building

Virtual space offers new possibilities for strengthening the university community
and its links with the outside world. Several projects have been launched under the
umbrella of ETH World to support this development. *ETH Life* is a daily Web paper
of ETH Zurich, providing daily reporting on current events at ETH and on matters
concerning the university community. On-line since November 2000, *ETH Life* has
clearly improved internal communication within ETH. Perhaps surprisingly, it has also
contributed to a stronger presence of the university in traditional print media, with
national newspapers regularly monitoring the news from ETH.

An ETH alumni portal is being developed as an access point for former students
into the virtual world of ETH Zurich. The goal is to support the networking among
alumni and between them and their alma mater. Events, contact matching, virtual
meeting points and direct contacts among the alumni create a strong, dynamic
network. An industry portal is under development by the ETH Center of Product
Development.

Information Management and Infostructure Elements

The library is closely affected by the virtual campus. In addition to offering access to a rapidly growing number of electronic journals, the ETH Library is creating its own "e-collection." In addition to doctoral dissertations, this electronic document server allows members of the ETH community to make public digital documents that have not been published through other channels.

Another library project, "ePics," is developing an image database service to serve education and research. The database makes use of a multimedia information search tool developed at ETH, enabling fast on-line searching of images based on the picture content (Schek, Schuldt, & Weber, 2002).

Another infostructure component being put in place through ETH World projects is a streaming video service, which can relay lectures and important events to the whole ETH campus over the Internet. "United Visions" is the name given to a related project, a student-operated on-line television channel for ETH and the University of Zurich.

Questions of data security and privacy are particularly important in an academic environment, where openness and exchange are part of the culture. These issues, along with other questions around health, safety and social impact, are also being carefully considered within ETH World.

E-LEARNING AT ETH ZURICH

Introduction

As for any virtual campus, e-learning is one of the focal points of ETH World. ETH Zurich does not intend to become a distance university; the objective of all activities is to contribute to work on campus.

ETH World supports some projects in the area of e-learning. In addition to these, a large number of development projects are being funded through a new ETH program of support for educational projects (FILEP), many with an e-learning component. Funding for e-learning projects is also available through the national project Virtual Campus Switzerland (VCS). A general support structure for ETH staff wishing to use new media is in place in the form of the Network for Educational Technology (NET).

Funded by these different sources, some 50 projects are currently carried out at ETH, covering a wide range of different approaches of the use of new media in education, from simple and straightforward course material distribution to elaborate interactive learning and cooperation on the Web.

In the following, two courses will be presented in some detail: a first-year course in architecture (arc-line—architecture on-line) and a fourth-year course in electrical engineering. The two courses are very different in nature but have the same common goal: to improve face-to-face teaching by using electronic media, both for project-oriented learning and collaboration. This is also the message of the authors of this contribution to the readers of this book.

CASE ONE: ARC-LINE—
ARCHITECTURE ON-LINE

Objectives

The traditional architectural design course at ETH operates primarily in a physical environment comprised of 10 design studios or ateliers with approximately 200 students and a group of faculty members of the Department of Architecture (Angélil et al., 2000).

The objective of the arc-line project is to develop an architectural design course as a Web-based communication and production network. Rather than replacing current modes of teaching, the objective seeks to enhance the physical realm with the possibilities offered by information technology. The project aims at the superimposition of a physical and a digital space within which students and faculty will interact.

The arc-line projects allows first-year students, while learning about the discipline of architecture, to get involved in actively designing the digital space in which they operate (Figure 3). The students need to identify both the structure and formal properties of this space, and they actively contribute to its growth and evolution. The arc-line platform is thus a dynamic system in a state of continuous transformation. A general framework, a script, identifies the successive steps in the formation of this space. The steps lead from the design of a small architectural artifact to a larger urban conglomerate. Students and faculty are able to navigate through that space and assess the products of their design process.

Figure 3: In the course "arc-line," first-year students learn the basics of architectural design and the most important computer tools while helping to shape the digital space in which they work

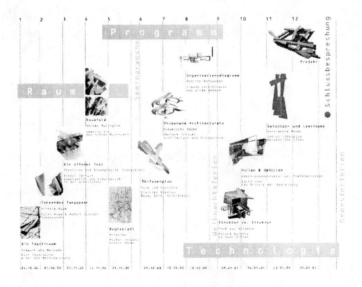

Based on Web technology, this designed space allows connections to various information sources relevant to the teaching of architecture, such as course outlines, lecture notes, bibliographies and readers. A series of communication and navigation tools are integrated within the designed space. In order to heighten interaction, specific portal functions provide transparent, tailored access to digital resources.

The arc-line project will eventually have a social and symbolic function, fostering identification with the academic institution. Its users—students, teachers and researchers—form a collective which arc-line will help to coalesce.

Script for the Design of the Virtual Space

The design of the digital space evolves during the course of the academic year. Following the didactic structure of the curriculum, a series of steps have been identified as benchmarks for the development of the work.

In the first step, the students are given a digitalized cutting pattern, typically used in the garment industry, as a starting point for their design project. The cutting pattern serves as a common territory for the entire studio and introduces an abstract notion of "site" while acting as a frame of reference for subsequent operations. Within this site, students register their email addresses and prepare their home pages, thus starting to occupy the digital space. In the second step, the initial two-dimensional pattern provides the base for inserting three-dimensional objects that are designed using modeling software. The aim is to promote an understanding of space as embodied within an architectural artifact. This object then provides the home base for the individual users. Step three emphasizes communication. Links between the

Figure 4: On the arc-line platform the results of individual and group work are integrated into a common environment, directing the students toward new forms of collaboration

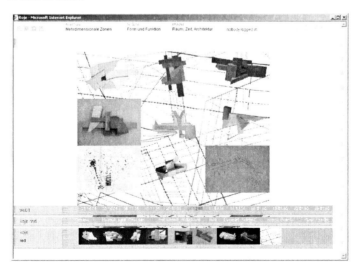

various objects and information pools are defined, including connections to other courses of the department. The digital territory evolves into a multidimensional information architecture. In the fourth step, a spatial field is created, transforming the data structure of the previous stage into a spatial constellation. The emphasis here is on the articulation of architectonic relationships within a collective conglomerate. In step five, a site within the existing city fabric is introduced to address aspects pertaining to complex urban entities. The structure of the digital territory is read analogously to the structure of the physical city. The students collectively identify planning and design strategies for both their digital and urban environments. With this, the students gain experience with the interface between virtual and physical domains (Figure 4).

Adaptation of Navigation Tools

Conceived as an interactive information overlay integrated with the physical reality of the design studio, the arc-line home page presents tailored access to architecture-related resources that are continuously updated by both faculty and students.

The initial development in arc-line has been focused on how to adapt current Web database technology (i.e., Oracle 8i, Microsoft) to meet the specific requirements of the first-year course in architecture and design. The initial buildup uses Web database technology, enabling users to navigate through files and review drawings online using a Web browser. During the design process, student work can be downloaded in a vector-based format. New layers of information (i.e., variations, corrections, commentary) can be added. Furthermore, additional resources, such as chat, email, and project logs for management and administrative services, are provided.

The long-term goal of the arc-line project is to augment the arc-line resources with 3-D modeling software, enabling students to design their own three-dimensional spatial environments.

Building Up Information Pools

The information pools are databases that are compiled according to the specific didactic framework of the architecture curriculum as identified by the current teaching units of the first-year course:

- Architecture and design
- Building construction
- Visual design studies
- Building structures
- Building technology
- Ecology
- Architectural and cultural history

- Sociology
- Mathematics

The arc-line database will include course outlines, selected lecture transcripts, bibliographies, readers, and relevant architectural case studies. In addition to the archival function for material provided by the faculty, additional information pools, such as portfolios of personal work, essays, and process documentations, are created by the students.

In order to promote more effective communication, specific portal functions will offer tailored access to other databases: Arc-line will provide an intelligent offering structure based on the recognition of keywords that will link users with other relevant resources.

Experiences

Arc-line is now on-line. Beginning with the winter semester 2001/2002, the Web database of arc-line has been available as an on-line tool and resource for all first-year architecture students. Initially used by some 50 students out of the 200-student cohort, the number of participants continued to increase steadily throughout the semester, partly due to the successful implementation of the laptops-for-students (Neptun) project. By the beginning of the summer semester 2002, the number of users exceeded 170 students.

The growing number of users has made the further evolution of the digital domain and its relationship to the physical studio environment necessary. Current developments address both difficulties encountered in maintaining a complex, yet accessible structure for an expanded group of users and the possibilities generated by an increased concentration of networked activities. To expedite and optimize the synergies of the dual realms of virtual and physical space, a multitiered strategy is employed.

First, the programmatic structure of arc-line is constantly analyzed and refined to increase usability. Program modules deployed sequentially throughout the semester serve as instruments for the collaborative development of structurally complex territories. These modules allow, in contrast to possibilities of the individual virtual spaces of the winter semester, the simultaneous active inhabitation and manipulation of a larger collective territory and the development of localized, individual interventions. This strategy places emphasis on the qualities of virtual space as a laboratory rather than as an archive.

Second, user log-in procedures have been substantially modified to allow for more immediate access to the virtual workspace, balancing between maximum freedom to establish individual virtual presences and the need for certain common standards for the work. Students are encouraged to explore a wide range of possibilities offered within virtual space for precisely describing individual projects.

Parallel to this is the requirement to establish a collective field of operation through the acknowledgment of the common condition within which work is situated.

Third, students are directed toward the potential of a collective virtual environment to explore new forms of collaboration, both in project teams and beyond. The establishment of active relationships between individual projects is embedded within the didactic structure of the summer semester, where open forms of organization are actively promoted as a strategy to operate effectively within group sites.

Fourth, the increased use of computers by students has made it necessary to further expand the technical infrastructure. Further investment in LAN hardware, electrical infrastructure as well as server and output hardware will be needed.

CASE TWO: ON-LINE CONTROL EDUCATION
Development of the Use of Computers in Control Education

The use of computers has a long-standing tradition at the Automatic Control Laboratory of ETH Zurich. Early work is reported in the references by Mansour and Schaufelberger (1981, 1989), Mansour, Schaufelberger, Cellier, Maier, and Rimvall (1984), and Rimvall, Mansour, and Schaufelberger (1985). Computers were mainly used in the exercises and in project work in the early days. Attempts to distribute software on diskettes are reported in the references of Schaufelberger (1990) and Schaufelberger and Itten (1988). Attempts for the cooperative development of teaching material failed at that time because of the complexity of the development process and because of lack of infrastructure.

Web Site

From this background, it was obvious to use the World Wide Web in control education when this medium became available. Since the first major attempt to use the Web in our courses, there has been some development. After a thorough investigation in 1997, considering especially the authoring systems TopClass and Web Course in a Box, we decided to implement our course directly in HTML on the Web, the main reasons being the small classes (six to 10 students) which allow for easy administration. Our educational home page still has the same appearance as when designed in 1997. It contains the course material but also much additional information, both for staff and for students. The main focus in the course material is on:

- Content
- Exercises and solutions
- Project
- Lecture notes
- Links and additional material
- Administrative questions

Figure 5:   Educational home page of the Automatic Control Laboratory

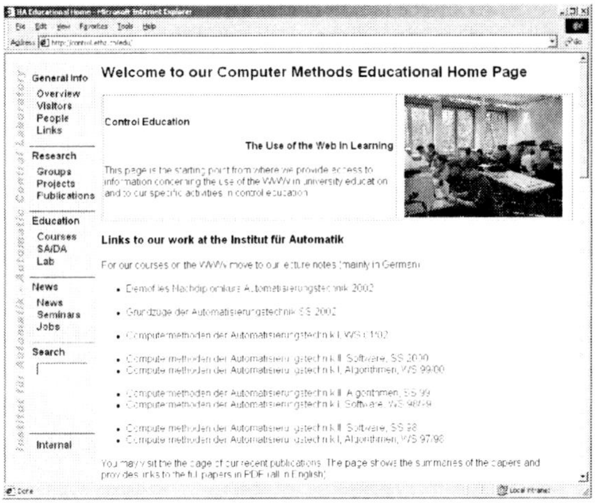

As may be seen from the screen in Figure 5, Computers in Control course material is available from 1997 to 2000. In 2000 we decided to use BSCW (Basic Support for Cooperative Work) as the main tool (OrbiTeam, 2002). The structure of the course has not been changed, only the tool (see Figure 6).

The main advantages of the use of the Web in this setting are:

- course material, exercises and solutions are permanently available;
- the site as information pool: links to tutorials, help, basic material;
- copy/paste from the Web to the individual working station allows very rapid program development; and
- cooperation of students is facilitated by sharing data (BSCW).

Since using the Web, the courses have developed considerably. We are now using about equal time for lectures, exercises and a small project, which is fully integrated into the course. As this is the major development in the education design, we will spend some time to explain these so-called miniprojects.

Course "Computers in Control Engineering"

Computers in Control Engineering is a final/fourth-year course in control engineering with four hours per week (total 112 hours). By taking the course, students earn 10 European Credit Transfer System (ECTS) credit points.

The goal and content may be summarized as follows:

Goal: The use of computers for design and implementation of control systems and their user interfaces. The control system design cycle and its application to case studies. Treatment of the entire cycle and of the numerical properties of the corresponding algorithms.

Figure 6:   Organization of the Computers in Control Engineering course on BSCW

Outline of typical content: Object-oriented programming, introduction to Java, graphical user interfaces, modeling and simulation environments for continuous time- and event-driven systems, control system design cycle, real-time aspects, two miniprojects.

About one-third of the time is spent on each of lectures, exercises and miniprojects.

Projects by tradition play a major role in electrical engineering education at ETH. Three projects are integrated in the education in electrical engineering: two semester projects in semesters seven and eight and a diploma project. These projects have a duration of several hundred hours, while normal exercises and laboratory assignments are scheduled for two to three hours. With our miniprojects we have developed a third approach which lies in between and takes about 20 hours. These projects are carried out in each of the Computers in Control Engineering semester courses. An example is described in the following.

Distributed Control of a Heating System

The goal of this miniproject is to implement a process control system consisting of three computers: a real-time computer controlling the process, an operator station for visualization and manual control, and an engineering station running Matlab. The general outline of the miniproject is shown in Figure 7 (Schaufelberger, Keller, Kraus, & Qiu, 1998).

The main project goals are:
- Learning Java for control and automation applications
- Using the Web for finding information
- Cooperative work
- Distributed computing

Figure 7: Distributed heating control system: in the miniproject the students work in three groups on different parts of the system

Project 2000-2001: 5-6 Weeks
Building a Small Distributed Control System

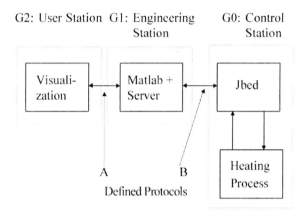

- Defining minimum protocols A and B in order to be able to start implementing independently

From this, the tasks for the three groups of two students were defined as follows:

Group G0 was responsible for the implementation of the control station, namely, control of the physical model process using Jbed, a real-time Java operating system, and for the definition and implementation of interface protocol B. The encountered difficulties were learning Jbed, interfacing with the hardware, and definition of protocol B.

Group G1 was responsible for the implementation of the engineering station, namely, for the Matlab to Java interface for identification/visualization, for the interface protocol for the sending of references, and for the server as a gateway for other visualization clients. The encountered difficulties were learning Matlab and Java and using protocols A and B.

Group G2 was responsible for the implementation of the control and supervision station, namely, for the visualization of the process, for the user interface for process control, and for definition and implementation of interface protocol A. The encountered difficulties were learning Java AWT/Swing (which one to use and how) and the definition of protocol A. Figure 8 shows the simple visualization of the controller action running on the visualization station in Java Swing.

The project went very smoothly, the students being able to carry out the entire development in about 20 hours. Also in this course the use of computers to support the learning process has fundamentally changed the content and the structure of the course.

Figure 8:   Visualization using Java Swing

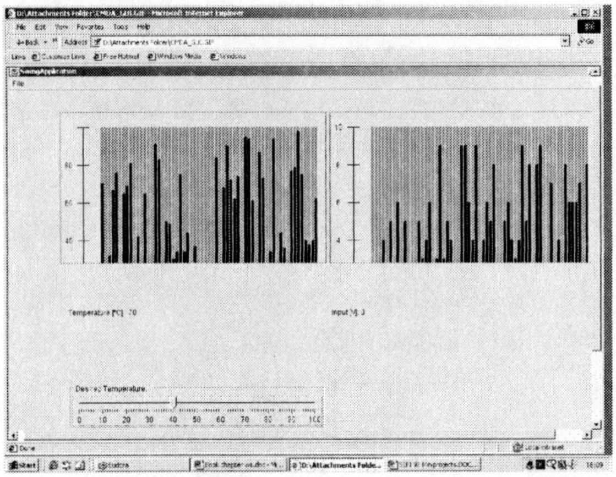

CONCLUSION

ETH World differs from normal university research and development projects as its intention is to influence and change existing structures and processes. The goal of the project is to make itself obsolete: Its successful practices should become normal university activities.

Although conceived from a infrastructure perspective and not specifically as an e-learning environment, ETH World and its related projects already now influence the education at ETH Zurich to a considerable extent. This is shown by two examples from architecture and control engineering. In both cases, the new media are used to improve the education in a classroom or studio environment.

ACKNOWLEDGMENT

The authors wish to thank Professor Marc Angélil and Mr. Cary Siress, ETH Department of Architecture, for their contribution to the arc-line case.

REFERENCES

Angélil, M., Engeli, M., Siress, C., Martin, M., Hollwich, M. & Kellenberg, C. (2000). *Arc-line: Architecture On-Line.* Zurich, Switzerland: Swiss Federal Institute of Technology Zurich, Department of Architecture.
Carrard, P., & Engeli, M. (Eds.)(2001). *Conceptual Competition ETH World: Virtual and Physical presence.* Zurich, Switzerland: gta Verlag.
ETH Zurich. (2000). *Invitation to Tender. Conceptual Competition ETH World.* Zurich, Switzerland: Swiss Federal Institute of Technology Zurich.

Hagström, A., & Schaufelberger, W. (2001). ETH World—Developing a virtual campus infrastructure for education and research. In *Proceedings SEFI Annual Conference 2001* (p. 44 & CD-ROM). Copenhagen, Denmark: European Society for Engineering Education.

Mansour, M., & Schaufelberger, W. (1981). Digital computer control experiments in the control group of ETH Zurich. In *Proceedings IFAC World Congress, 1981* (Paper 63.2). Kyoto, Japan: International Federation of Automatic Control, Vol. XIII, pp. 48-54.

Mansour, M., & Schaufelberger, W. (1989). Software and laboratory experiments using computers in control education. *IEEE Control Systems Magazine, 9*(3), 19-24. Mansour, M., Schaufelberger, W., Cellier, F. E., Maier, G., & Rimvall, M. (1984). The use of computers in the education of control engineers at ETH Zurich. *European Journal of Engineering Education, 9*, 135–151.

OrbiTeam. (2002). *BSCW Home Page.* Retrieved April 2, 2002, from http://www.bscw.de.

Perrone, C., Repenning, A., Spencer, S., & Ambach, J. (1996). Computers in the classroom: Moving from tool to medium. *Journal of Computer-Mediated Communication, 2*(3). Retrieved April 2, 2002, from http://www.ascusc.org/jcmc/.

Rimvall, M., Mansour, M., & Schaufelberger, W. (1985). Computer-aided control systems design in undergraduate education at ETH Zurich. *Transactions of the Institute of Measurement and Control, 7*(2), 90-96.

Schaufelberger, W. (1990). Design and implementation of software for control education. *IEEE Transactions on Education, 33*, 291-297.

Schaufelberger, W., & Hagström, A. (2001). ETH World—Design and implementation of a virtual campus infrastructure for education and research. In *Perspectives in Engineering Pedagogy, Proceedings 30th International Symposium Ingenieurpädagogik.* Klagenfurt, Austria: Internationale Gesellschaft für Ingenieurpädagogik, pp. 244-251.

Schaufelberger, W., & Itten, A. (1988). Low-cost CACSD on the Apple Macintosh. In *Proceedings IMACS World Congress 1988.* Paris: International Association for Mathematics and Computers in Simulation, Vol. II, pp. 586-588.

Schaufelberger W., Keller, D., Kraus, F. J., & Qiu, X. (1998). Miniprojects in control education. In *Proceedings SEFI Annual Conference 1998* (pp. 181-186). Helsinki, Finland: European Society for Engineering Education.

Schek, H.-J., Schuldt, H., & Weber, R. (2002). Hyperdatabases—Infrastructure for the information space. In *Advances in Visual Database Systems, Proceedings of the 6th IFIP 2.6 Working Conference on Visual Database Systems.* Brisbane, Australia: International Federation of Information Processing, pp. 1-15.

WEB LINKS

arc-line—architecture on-line: http://arc-line.ethz.ch

Automatic Control Educational home page: http://www.control.ethz.ch/edu/

CALICE—Computer Aided Learning in Civil Engineering: http://www.calice.igt.ethz.ch

CCN—Chemistry Contact Network: http://www.ccn.ethz.ch

ETH World: http://www.ethworld.ethz.ch

ETH Zurich—Swiss Federal Institute of Technology Zurich: http://www.ethz.ch

NET—ETH Network for Educational Technology: http://www.net.ethz.ch

Vireal Lab: http://www.vireal.ethz.ch

Chapter II

Implementing Online Delivery and Learning Support Systems: Issues, Evaluation and Lessons

J. Bernardes
University of Wolverhampton, UK

J. O'Donoghue
National ICT Research Centre for Education, Training and Employment, UK

ABSTRACT

IT is unlikely to create empty institutions delivering distance learning; it is more likely to create distanceless learning which is potentially more accessible to students. This implies the whole business of delivering teaching and learning will be transformed in a way that has not happened for generations. While it is possible to develop IT-based approaches that, to some extent, mirror traditional methods of remote learning by isolated individuals which has little or nothing to do with lifelong experiences or expertise, most academics will find themselves forced to confront very basic questions about what it is that they are trying to achieve and how they might best go about achieving those desired outcomes. This paper considers some of the practical aspects and ways in which, where possible, they have been addressed. The premise of this work is not about technology but the application of technology in a teaching and learning context.

INTRODUCTION

The UK is constantly developing highly funded acronyms which embrace technology within educational initiatives. Translating the acronyms is difficult enough, but trying to further interpret real sustainable outcomes is even more daunting.

Kearsley (1998, p. 44) writes that "technology is often seen as a quick fix, a siren song" and warns that "educational technology is a distraction … from what matters most—effective learning and good teaching." The approach taken often seems more in the vein of entertainment than education, with television-type material creating an expectation of how information will be presented; the linkup of the Internet and television through streamed video may just exacerbate this.

How does all this affect us as educators? Will we survive? Will we be at worst systematically "robotised," replaced or dispensable? Will our institutions become empty, desolate buildings or computer server hubs?

It is our view that IT is unlikely to create empty institutions delivering distance learning but, to the contrary, is more likely to create distanceless learning which is actually more accessible to all potential students. What this clearly implies, and what few in the academic professions yet understand properly, is the whole business of delivering teaching is likely to be transformed in a way that has not happened for generations. While it is possible to develop IT-based approaches that, to some extent, mirror traditional methods of remote learning by isolated individuals which has little or nothing to do with lifelong experiences or expertise, most academics will find themselves forced to confront very basic questions about what it is that they are trying to achieve and how they might best go about achieving those desired outcomes.

Computing technology is often seen as a "big issue" which will generate change, and discussion is carried at a very abstract and "big issue" level. We need to develop a clearer sense of proportion; while IT has certainly changed our lives dramatically in the last few years, there are inevitable limits to the extent and speed of change in higher education. For example, most British higher education institutes simply do not have resources for the kind of investment needed to get broadcast quality materials for every module at every level; this was true in terms of competing with the Open University and it is true today in terms of a thoroughgoing shift to IT-based delivery. More than this, many commentators have now observed that relatively modest gains have been achieved for quite high levels of investment. While there is a place for "big issue" kinds of articles, what follows is very much a "little issues" study of how useful or usable elements of an online delivery platform have proved to be.

What seems certain is that delivery systems are likely to change the role of academics in higher education. Quite what those changes will be depends upon closely observing current developments and exploring what works and what does not work. What follows is an attempt to pick out some of the issues that arise from the attempt to use one particular IT delivery platform (WOLF—Wolverhampton Online Learning Framework) at one institution in one subject area over four semesters. WOLF exhibits the fundamental components of a virtual learning environment

(VLE), in which learners and tutors participate in "online" interactions of various kinds, including online learning, teaching and delivery. It is not the purpose of this paper to debate the viability or appropriateness of which, if any, VLE to implement. The premise of this particular development is more to do with the application of technology within a teaching and learning context.

THE ROLE OF TECHNOLOGY

One of the major problems we face is that of creating a culture shift in terms of understanding what technology is and what it might achieve in higher education. The shift to focus more on learning outcomes in recent years may make this process less painful but the development of IT delivery platforms requires academic staff not only to rethink what they deliver (Should I amend that lecture since students did not appear to understand the argument?) but also how they deliver their content (What kind of activity will enable students to understand the argument?). In the short term, it is likely that IT-based delivery systems will be seen as the most appropriate alternative means of delivering content, if only because of the Internet and the massive spread of IT-based solutions in our lives.

Higher education is best seen as a process, focused on learning, in which content is combined in some way with some forms of technology, whether they be "chalk and talk," television broadcast, or an IT-based delivery platform. It is our view that the development of technology-based learning *support* structures, that is, technology-based enhancements to formal teaching and learning strategies embedded in the pedagogy, will assist the education and training sector best. In some ways, then, the changes currently going on are compelling us to examine issues about how we support student learning, an issue which many of us might prefer to ignore. The most obvious comment, and one heard quite frequently by the authors, from less IT-committed colleagues is "I simply don't have time to change the way I do my teaching." Behind this statement perhaps there are also a few staff that do not have time or inclination to critically examine or reflect on what and how they do what they do.

Education is a growing industry, driven by worldwide competition between education establishments and by a rising number of consumers who demand an increased amount of flexibility. To survive in this "brave new world," according to a Curriculum Corporation (1994) report for Australian schools, alternative approaches may have to be taken by the traditional providers. Changes in education caused by transformations in the environment are required. Historically education has been a monopoly business (O'Donoghue, Jentz, Singh, & Molyneux, 2000), but with the technological changes and a changing attitude towards learning, new entrants are threatening to overtake the market.

Research suggests that education needs to embrace IT and use it to provide high quality, flexible teaching and learning. In order to be competitive, the organisational structures need to reflect the environment, and this means a change from the present rigid and inflexible internal/stable structure to a more fluid, flexible type. One of the other driving forces is, of course, the need to reduce costs and improve quality. Findings further suggest that technological developments could change the role and position of the teacher/lecturer (O'Donoghue, Singh, & Dorward, 2001).

Over the recent past some naive attempts have been made to address these issues. The most simplistic solution adopted by some institutions has been to invest heavily in technology. It is actually a relatively painless, one-off capital cost to purchase a lot of hardware to introduce technology, videoconferencing, and large labs of PCs with very powerful software. Significant investment has been made in technology within schools, colleges and universities; this has enabled students to use expensive and powerful networked computers to word process assignments and "surf" the Net! While staff have readily taken up email and to some extent the Internet, their "deeper" adoption of the technology in the context of learning delivery has been limited (O'Donoghue, Singh, Caswell, & Molyneux, 2001).

EXPLORING EVIDENCE

In evaluating a series of pilot modules, a very great deal of material has been generated and the authors are faced with the question of how to present this in some accessible fashion while not imposing too much apparent rationality or coherence to the comments themselves. The main strategy used is to review a conceptual schema from Kolb (1984) and Sulla (1999) and add a third category about the nature of institutional challenges. We then attempt to develop summary conclusions in the shape of key lessons.

The Wolverhampton Online Learning Framework (WOLF) is the current version of several years' development within the university (O'Donoghue, Dalziel, Fleetham, & Molyneux, 2000). The focus of this article is upon usability issues, or more simply, whether deployment of WOLF accomplishes either the intended purposes or indeed any purposes at all. We take seriously the note by Wendy Hall and Su White (2001) of the University of Southampton: "It is rather frightening to think that so much money was spent and we are so little further forward." This is an online document available only to ILT members. Rather than focus upon an institutional review, or the views of staff deploying technology, the following draws mainly upon in-class evaluations by students participating in using the technology.

The following material is drawn from qualitative evaluations by students of modules using ICT. Notes are based upon experiences on five level 2 and level 3 sociology modules (around 250 student module registrations) and experiences in collaborating in delivering modules in the subject areas of English, French, Philosophy, and Religious Studies and occasional work in other humanities subject areas as well. This group includes a wide range of different approaches to ICT use; some of these modules were engaging in small "add-on" experiments while others, especially those in sociology, reflected progressive stages of development in using ICT to support learning. In most cases, ICT use was for all students on the module. Points are in no particular order, vary in significance and include positive as well as negative points. It is hoped that simply sharing these points may enable colleagues to avoid the same pitfalls and perhaps benefit from some successful strategies.

THE GOOD NEWS:
THREE SUCCESSFUL INNOVATIONS

Before proceeding to review the detail, we wish to indicate three particular areas that we believe to be of importance. One of the very common requests made of the authors in training sessions for staff considering taking up the delivery platform revolves around what advantages does the platform provide, either in the sense of what will the platform make it easier or quicker to deliver or in the sense of what can the platform do that conventional classroom teaching cannot do. There are three areas we would wish to pick out to highlight. Each depends on ICT for success and would not be possible without a technology and communications infrastructure.

Provision of Streamed Video

Video streaming might appear, at first sight, to be an ideal way to deliver "content"; indeed we intend to undertake some experiments in this area with a delivery of summary lectures. In the first case, interest was in modifying the learning process and developing and delivering something not possible by conventional methods; the chosen area was the evaluation of modules by students.

The provision of streaming video combined with easy-to-use digital video cameras enables staff and students to capture evaluations of the learning process to be repeatedly reviewed at later dates (Figure 1). Students developed "key points" in

Figure 1:   The WOLF screen showing the embedded streamed video

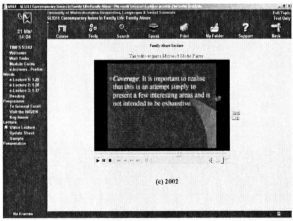

mid-module and end-of-module evaluations in workshop groups without tutors present; the conclusions were then videoed by students themselves. Since the evaluations were put online within a few days of creation, students could see that their evaluation work has been taken seriously and has been presented as they wished: The edited video clips are presented to the whole class for approval before upload. This also means that subsequent student cohorts can review earlier evaluations. Students were very enthusiastic about this process and many chose to see the tutor involved to report how refreshing they found the openness around module evaluation.

There are, of course, minor challenges to be confronted. Lighting conditions, even with the latest digital video cameras, can be a problem, and students need to be advised to use good lighting. More difficult, in a group situation, is adequately capturing sound; because students handling the cameras tended to use the zoom facility, they were simply too far away from the subject to capture good quality sound. Again, this was a matter of advising students beforehand of the need to be within 1 to 2 m of whomever was speaking.

While of course this form of evaluation needs handling with sensitivity and care, it has proved to be one of the areas that impresses students, colleagues and delegates at conferences, etc. We are sure that the whole business of evaluation is treated in very different ways by different colleagues and that many colleagues would find the inclusion of evaluation somewhat frightening. In the present context, the use of streaming video for module evaluation reflects, we believe, a shift in the learning model and a shift in the power relationship between teacher and learner, a shift we thoroughly endorse.

Extensive Asynchronous Discussions

For many years, the authors have adopted a resource-based approach to learning which avoids a set text or limited number of articles but seeks instead to give students a very rich diet of materials along with the key skills and the relevant intellectual or conceptual frameworks with which to make use of those resources. One common feature of this approach is a particular focus upon the concepts, forms of data and definitions. The authors have been keen to see what kind of new resources can be generated by way of collaborative online learning. We had particular success in generating forum discussions around particular very narrowly defined issues, (Figure 2), such as (i) locate a particular definition of family abuse and add this to the forum and (ii) make constructive critical comments on one or more definitions added by other students.

On the negative side, it took some time to find a way of encouraging the majority of students to participate in this exercise; success came with linking the exercise to a small component of assessment. It must also be said that, as is always the case, some students undertook the task in a very mechanical fashion and perhaps did not learn very much. The particular examples yielded hundreds of items on the forum in three days.

Figure 2:   A typical forum (names blacked out)

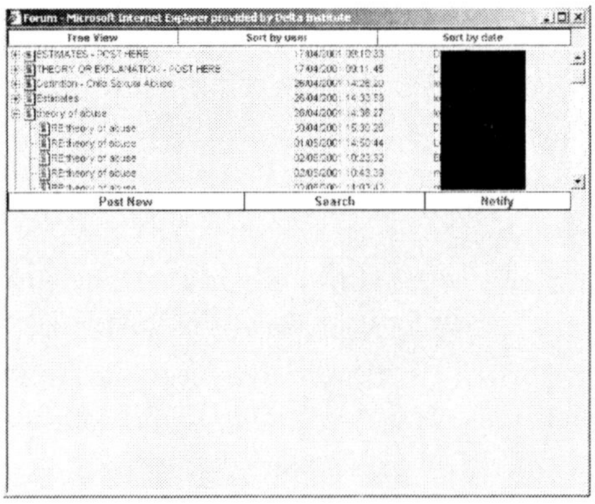

On the positive side, this model generated a wide range of valuable material and some very high-quality critical comments that all students could review. This turned out to be a way in which weaker students could see "what the point was" of particular debates and hence contributed to some quite rapid progress in learning. The feature that seems to be particularly important then is the public and permanent nature of the debate, which would not be possible in conventional techniques. In reviewing end-of-module assessments, it was clear that many students had made use of this forum debate generated several weeks before.

Listing of Shared URLs

One of the long-standing challenges for many staff is to get students to "do the reading." With mass teaching it is generally impractical to personally check that the student has done an adequate amount to work; with asynchronous chat rooms and lists of URLs it is actually very easy to check that each individual in a given work group or module has contributed the required number of items; WOLF "tags" contributions with the registered student name. Of course, students vary in the diligence of undertaking tasks and some weaker students may find themselves disadvantaged. One remedy to this is to generate tasks which require students to undertake work of some kind but do not necessarily have outputs that can be qualitatively ranked; one successful approach has been getting students to add relevant URLs to a list. Linking this, again, to a very small element of assessment meant that in excess of 100 generally relevant URLs were gathered by students themselves in a matter of days. One of the benefits of using WOLF to generate the list of shared URLs is that users do not need to master HTML but simply copy a browser address into an input box; the list generated can also be edited easily and quickly.

Of course, very few students could review all of these URLs but it became clear in the final assessment component that many students had reviewed many of URLs, and this seems to have been a much better approach compared to simply asking students to use conventional or specialist subject search engines.

In future, it is intended to use the same facility to get students to submit brief reviews of the material on reading, and we are optimistic that this will improve work undertaken by students in two senses: firstly, more students will actually "do some reading"; and secondly, students will have access to summaries of all of the reading of a given subject area.

Summary

To be clear at this point, the adoption of a virtual learning environment enabled students to achieve three tasks which were of value to their learning and which would not be possible, or so easy, to achieve within conventional classroom situations. The technology under these three achievements is currently reliable, and while digital video may be a little challenging (especially editing), the use of forums and lists of URLs is straightforward.

EXPLORING THE LEARNING CYCLE

Kolb's work (1984) on the reflective learner suggests that learning is a social process based on carefully cultivated experience. Within this development structure Kolb shifts the learning away from the exclusivity of the classroom (and its companions, the lecture theatre or laboratory) to the workplace, the family, the carpool, the community, or wherever we gather to work or play or love. The significance for educators is profound because, among other things, it leads us away from the traditional concerns of credit hours and calendar time towards competence, working knowledge, and information truly pertinent to jobs, families and communities. It leads us into "independent" learner-directed learning at a time, place and pace to suit the learner. Thus, a prime candidate for flexible-delivery or technology-supported learning environment development.

While the Kolb model is an admirable one, it is important to realise that some colleagues may not adopt such effective methods; this can be seen in the limited use of mid-module and end-of-module evaluations. In institutions under pressure, reflecting on how well or poorly a given class went might be an activity for which tutors simply do not have time. Even if there is time to reflect upon the success of a module, it may not be possible to link activities to "theory" or even consider radical shifts in delivery style.

Among the variety of strategies used to encourage staff to take up a virtual learning environment, one that has been made use of here is the development and dissemination of successful exemplars. This is critically linked to issues of personal investment by staff in learning new technologies and skills; until you can demonstrate to staff that a given technology enables you to do something better, more quickly, or achieve better results, it is unlikely that they will spend a lot of time picking up the technology.

The "Reflective Learner" or "Active Learner" Model?

It is very easy to get carried away with the hyperbole common in discussions about online learning; many of these discussions have at their centre a single model of the learner or the learning process. The most common assumption made is that modern higher education in the United Kingdom has at its heart "active learners" or "reflective learners," that is, individuals committed to high levels of participation and willing and ready to engage in high levels of interaction with other students and staff. It is very easy to begin developing flowcharts of the transfer of information (surface knowledge) and means of facilitating or developing understanding (deep knowledge).

One of the things that actual practical experience in teaching in a modern university brings home is the enormous variation and diversity of students, variation of students between different subjects (for example, nursing students are rather different to drama students or business students), and the dynamic and changing nature of the student population (for example, many commentators accept that the levels of paid work that full-time students engage in has risen dramatically over recent years), which is itself dependent upon the history and nature of the institution (those universities with very high levels of participation from lower social economic groups have quite different characters to more traditional institutions). A further important error made across a great deal of literature is to assume that what worked for one member of staff for one set of students in one institution in one subject area is likely to work for other groups of staff and students in other institutions and in other subject areas.

Efforts will be made to identify the disparity between classical models of the learning process and actual experience in a review of student evaluations. Before proceeding, however, it is useful to pick out a couple of important points to make about the nature of the contemporary student body in the particular institution. It is important to bear in mind that these comments relate to an institution with a very large student population drawn, in large part, from socio-economic groups and ethnic minorities which do not traditionally make use of higher education. Many institutions are observing the worrying trend of a growing "tail" of low achievers; it is tempting to locate the causes for this trend in declining unit resource or poorer teaching delivery. There may however be very different explanations: for example, one of the authors is familiar with students who do not set out to "do their best" nor even to obtain a "good degree," but who make a realistic decision to cope as best they can and try only "to survive." For many students in adverse financial circumstances, there is the inevitable burden of fairly high levels of full-time paid work. At an anecdotal level, one of the authors has surveyed recent level 3 students and found that out of groups of 40 and 60 students only three or four did not have paid work at all. Indeed the majority of students in both groups claim to work full time, at least 35 hours a week, through term time and vacations. In the light of these findings, a certain "drop-off" in attendance and lectures is perhaps not as surprising as it might otherwise be.

In a similar vein, it can be quite revealing to see which areas of technology students make use of. Many academic staff will be familiar with walking into an open-access student computer laboratory and observing that many students are involved in chat rooms and email. One of the surprises in initial experiments in the delivery of online learning was to discover that students were extremely reluctant to make use of discussion forums in which their identity was clear and in which it was known tutors would view their comments. It took some 18 months to devise ways of enabling students to feel comfortable about participating in discussion forums, and one of the key strategies, as used elsewhere, was to link participation to assessment.

IMPLEMENTATION: CONCRETE EXPERIENCE

Training and Preparation

Before anyone can engage in using IT it is important to bear in mind that they are likely to require varying levels of training. Training may need to involve general IT training, Windows-specific IT training, and training specific to the platform—for students, academic staff and support staff.

Embedding Task Orientation

By way of trial and error, it would appear that by far the best means of encouraging adoption by students is class-based "hands–on" workshops with specific tasks. In the present examples, three introductory lectures were delivered online (e-lectures delivering brief pieces of content followed by multiple-choice questions to reinforce the learning), and it was made clear that the rest of the module would make little sense unless these were studied. The first three teaching slots are then used for IT workshops in which students undertake the e-lectures with tutors on hand to help. This not only encourages high levels of participation but ensures that students undertake the necessary training in a very rapid and relatively painless way. It is important to do this work in classroom sessions rather than leaving students to do the work at their leisure to accommodate the very different skill deficits of students from a wide range of backgrounds and previous occupations.

Access: Where and When Chosen

It is plainly important for some students to study off-site, and some of the most enthusiastic are home users. Paradoxically, such students also commented that it helped decrease isolation that they often found when "popping in" for lectures (Figures 3 and 4). It is a common mistake for staff to believe that bringing groups of students together is a means of combating isolation in the learning experience. In fact, for some students, being seated amongst students who obviously "know what's going on" can actually be quite intimidating, whereas taking part in asynchronous discussions where students make clear that they are puzzled by particular issues can be quite

Figure 3: Kolb learning cycle modified to show the process of effective learning (Cox & Pattinson, 2001)

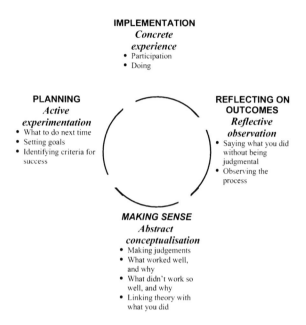

reassuring. At one point in institutional development debates, dial-up access seemed to be dismissed as less important; from the log files the most intense users are those by dial-up. This may be due to having very old PCs in some labs and/or the readiness of IT-aware students to tackle what other students find intimidating, or the ease of use from a remote location, i.e., no travel. In terms of timing, staff often see learning as progressive, but the usage pattern of e-lectures suggests that some students actually return to the beginning elements when about to complete a module.

Reliability

Like any major piece of software, WOLF has suffered a range of reliability problems—some due to the software, some due to aging hardware in student IT laboratories and some due to the environment (Windows 2000 authentication created havoc). A major improvement in 2001 was achieved by integrating fault reporting into an IT services call centre strategy; this has facilitated the rapid identification of key problems and their speedy resolution.

We have also had to consider the scheduling of delivery of learning. Like many universities, most of our facilities used to close down over the weekend; a range of pressures have been moving us towards weekend and even bank holiday opening for our learning centres. With the inevitability of server crashes it is becoming clear that we also need to have IT support available 24 hours a day, seven days a week.

Figure 4:   Some samples of e-lectures

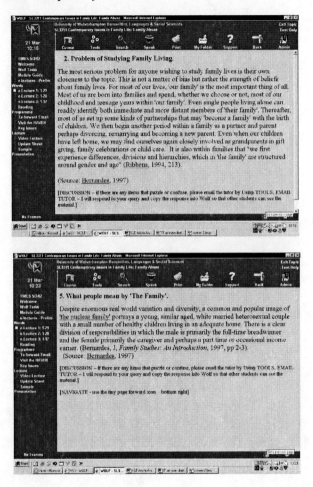

IT Work Is Time-Consuming

The general student complaint about learning being time-consuming is probably familiar to many who teach in higher education. Early experimental work with IT delivery platforms is almost inevitably additional to the existing work of a module rather than a straightforward replacement of tasks. The comment about excessive time is also pertinent to the staff members tasked with the creation of new ICT-based learning experiences. The senior management team all too often regard the use of technology as a cost-effective and time-saving attribute. This is not the case, however; certainly when materials and resources are developed well, the relationship of input to output is daunting (Conole & Oliver, 1998). When added to difficulties around training and access to computing technology, this can mean that IT is seen by students and staff as simply increasing the workload, at least in terms of time commitments.

Hopefully, as development work proceeds and staff become more confident to abandon or delete some of the conventional methods, the issue around time might be reversed. Again, once one feels more comfortable with the technology, it is possible to develop some exercises which students themselves find highly rewarding and judge to be a good investment time; for examples, see the three successes above.

REFLECTING ON OUTCOMES: REFLECTIVE OBSERVATION

Detailed and Careful Module Evaluation

There is a need for close continuous evaluation (this in itself modifies the learning cycle), integration and adaptation of approaches to learning. We make extensive use of module evaluations undertaken by students to enable us to reflect upon the way in which IT delivery systems change the learning cycle.

These evaluations had three elements: firstly, without tutors present, students made video recordings reporting good features, bad features and suggested changes; using the same formula, student groups developed reports (usually of half a page or a page length) for a plenary class discussion; and these reports are then reviewed in plenary sessions, and the module tutor reviews all points made in an attempt to get further detail. One small but important point about those plenary discussions is that the tutor goes to great lengths not to be negative about any point made or at all defensive but rather accepts comments made at face value and seeks clarification as necessary.

Technical Issues

It is no accident that some of the more enthusiastic staff around IT delivery are technically able. One thing that technically able staff can do is recognise a technical problem and give students some explanation (even if it is not very helpful). For example, evaluations revealed an issue around the "reliability of URLs": this relates to copying details from browser address windows into WOLF when Web sites were initially located using Jeeves and similar sites that do not point to the real address but cache a version of the page in the host site. For some colleagues experimenting with WOLF, the fact that some URLs would work and others did not was a cause of immense frustration.

Steepness of the Learning Curve

While you can achieve a great deal in a short time with careful "step-by-step" instructions, this does not solve all problems. WOLF permits students to create word processor files and then upload these for tutor marking. This generated some complaints: many students had real problems opening a Word window, saving the file, then using the browse button in WOLF to upload files; the level of assumed skill and understanding is actually quite high. This kind of problem led to more intensive training in the early weeks of modules and moves to request software development to make such processes easier for students to manage.

MAKING SENSE:
ABSTRACT CONCEPTUALISATION

Integration of a VLE Into Coherent Teaching and Learning Strategies

A high level of teaching enthusiasm is a key to success: With a committed member of staff, students are likely to see WOLF as relevant; where WOLF is an "add-on" supported by an "outside" member of staff, generating students' enthusiasm is more challenging. Hence, simply instructing staff to adopt technology is not a good idea; staff need to be encouraged to rethink their teaching and assessment and adopt technology-supported learning strategies rather than see a VLE as an "add-on." One of the other points about the usability of IT which has become clear to the authors is the way in which it is an enormous mistake to regard IT as an additional or add-on component of a conventional course. It is, of course, very tempting to put a "toe in the water" by experiments with just one element of an online delivery system. Indeed, one of the authors is a learning fellow and had little choice but to commence staff development in this way; it does however have an enormous drawback in that the staff are not compelled to critically reexamine and remodel their teaching strategies until some considerable time after commencing to use online delivery. In a wider sense, it is important to place oneself in the position of the student so that any use of IT is likely to be seen to be beneficial in some way, either by reducing effort, or by improving assessment performance for the same given effort, or perhaps by enabling students to access sets of resources that they could not otherwise access.

In this case study, technology-supported learning is central to the teaching and learning strategy: In class, a data projector is used to deliver PowerPoint for lectures, to access WOLF itself, and to reference Web sites and other applications; outside class, WOLF and email are important.

Comprehensiveness Seems To Be Important

WOLF aims to be able to deliver anything needed for teaching and learning, such as direct access to our Learning Centre Online Public Access Catalogue, email directories, etc. The need for such comprehensiveness was brought home when, at one point, embedded email was not working: At this point, email traffic for the module was limited. Once embedded email was working, the ease of emailing tutors with a few clicks meant that use rose significantly.

Supporting, Enhancing and Extending Communication

Better communication between students and staff, and between students is seen as important in evaluations. In a modern university, there is a tacit acceptance that staff are often "busy" when students may be available; email and asynchronous contacts are identified as important by students.

PLANNING: ACTIVE EXPERIMENTATION

Danger of Overenthusiasm

In early stages, there was a temptation to load a lot of passive content into WOLF and expect students to be pleased by this—in some ways, using WOLF may create more work for students than, say, photocopying handouts. Few students responded to such passive content so tasks were developed which began to give online work an assessment weighting

Customisation

Having an in-house VLE means that we can and do respond to what students and tutors report and develop the platform accordingly—2001 has seen the beginning of work on a variety of functionality requests to adapt the VLE to the needs of colleagues across a range of disciplines with very different pedagogical practices. We have also begun work on customising a "special needs" version to be rather more friendly to a range of special needs in terms of visual disability and accepting different input devices.

Costs and Benefits

Like most VLEs, WOLF does not offer immediate savings in terms of staff investment. At least a dozen workshops have been run with staff where one question always emerges: How much more time will adopting WOLF take up? Invariably the response is that WOLF at least doubles module preparation time and may triple this for first-time use. It remains to be seen over the longer term whether this extra effort is balanced by benefits. For students, similar judgements are often made: A few students refused point-blank to use WOLF at all because they did not judge it to be worthwhile. Happily, most such students are "converted" when fellow students report the ease of access or the location of useful material. On the more positive side, the majority of students often view the use of IT, in itself, as a "good thing" and as signalling a concern to be "up-to-date" and "add value" to teaching. More and more students have seen whiteboards and Internet sites used in secondary school environments and expect such systems as undergraduates. On the downside, students rapidly spot the transfer of costs from the university to students, e.g., cost of Internet connections, costs of PCs and costs of printing.

One other thing that has to be grasped by higher education institutions is that the transition to virtual learning environments is far from "cost neutral." The first level here is the issue of the purchase or development of the delivery system itself. Second, there is the development of the infrastructure so that the delivery system can actually be used. We have faced some major issues here in terms of the provision of staff computing and student computing. Third, there is the issue of training staff to the point where they feel able to experiment in the use of the delivery system. Fourth, and probably most importantly, there is the enormous cost of transferring a module from conventional teaching methods to some mix of conventional and IT-based teaching methods. Plainly in an institution facing financial difficulties, this kind of increase in staff costing is not supportable without significant additional investment. Fifth, however, there is a wide range of incidental costs involving the exploitation of new technologies. For example, one of the authors of this article has had to develop skills and expertise around HTML, digital video recording, digital video editing, file manipulation, and a range of other areas. Most of these areas have also represented one-off or capital costs in some way: for example, the purchase of software, hardware and training.

MODELS OF INFUSION

As tutors and students respond to the challenge to utilise computer technology in the teaching and learning process, they must be mindful of an important distinction between using technology and infusing technology. The context of this is based on some research work carried out by Nancy Sulla (1999), who draws a distinct difference between the embedding of technology naturally as another resource and the using of technology as some ethereal overlay.

"Technology provides opportunities never before available to humankind, yet school, college and university departments are in danger of sabotaging—through incomplete and, in some cases, detrimental implementation plans—the power of technology to transform the teaching and learning process. Three popular trends regarding technology use threaten to impede the transformational impact of technology on the instructional environment."

Education establishments are investing large sums of money toward outfitting rooms with computers with the assumption that computer technology will somehow enhance the educational experience. Education and its practitioners and administrators should be considering the consequences on teaching, learning and infrastructure that the utilisation of technology will have. Gosling (1981) makes some major assertions towards technology use within an educational environment, some of which have materialised, but these are largely based on the use rather than infuse model of interaction.

The first trend is an overemphasis on merely building tutors' and students' technology skills (Sulla, 1999).

There is not only the overemphasis on technology skills, but there is the much more serious preceding problem of persuading staff and students to invest in developing skills. One of the authors is the teaching and learning fellow responsible for IT in the School of Humanities, Languages and Social Sciences. Actually persuading staff to attend training sessions in the first place has been challenging. Once you have people in a training session, persuading them that a given piece of IT is useful is a second challenge. Thirdly, and much more importantly, encouraging staff to take ownership and responsibility for the development of IT involves a quite marked culture shift; staff are used to having IT technician support to do the work for them and find it a bit of a shock to discover that the university expects staff to generate material, edited where necessary, download files, and test the files.

The second trend is the belief that tutors' inability to use technology can somehow be overcome by the students' ability in this area (Sulla, 1999).

One of the reasons for resisting the adoption of technological solutions is the fear of making plain one's own incompetence before a group which may include highly skilled students. There is actually a much more serious problem here; it is a serious mistake to believe that students have uniform levels of expertise and skill. Some students will have high-level IT skills, some will have adequate levels of skill, but some may have a positive phobia of technology. This introduces yet more complexity in the delivery of IT solutions in that take-up will vary significantly; those for whom take-up is low may actually be quite difficult to spot because a host of other "excuses" or "reasons" may be given as to why they have not made use of technology for a particular exercise.

This dangerous belief leads to a third problematic trend. Computer use is often seen as an end unto itself (Sulla, 1999).

On the one hand, adopting technological solutions does signal to students some level of concern and investment by the institution, and a fair amount of module evaluations have been positive because of the effort put into the modules. On the other hand, it is important to get very clear that there are some things that cannot be done by way of IT; in advertising a pilot level 3 module with online delivery to current level 2 students, the author was quite surprised to find students approaching him and asking, not as he had expected, "How many classes do we not have to turn up for?" but rather "Will there be en turn up for? but rather "Will there be opportunities for meetings?" It became clear that students valued face-to-face interaction both with tutors and with fellow students.

INSTITUTIONAL CHALLENGES
New Organisational Structures

One of the major problems that many institutions have faced is how exactly to bring about the implementation of IT-based learning.

While there is a common belief in modern universities that management skills are universal, it may well be that management of IT projects require not only IT skills but also participation in the project itself. This was neatly illustrated in our case by a lengthy misunderstanding about the usability of the delivery platform. Staff using WOLF for teaching found that some elements simply did not work and reported this to their representatives on the management committee; at the committee level, the representative of the software developers reported that the complaints were a result of misunderstanding and staff ignorance rather than software failure. The management committee itself, because few members actually used the development platform, was incapable of verifying either story. Those using the software, after some months of making complaints, simply adapted the way in which they used the software to avoid problematic areas and the problem appeared to have been resolved. The final solution was to turn the error reports into a management issue about the quality of managing software performance.

Models of Encouraging Staff Take-Up

At a range of conferences, a very common statement from delegates is that the real problem is persuading colleagues to take up this or that technology or learning strategy. One model in some institutions is the idea of a separately funded (and usually quite expensive) courseware development unit; while this may generate attractive online content, one of the problems is the "distance" generated between the tutor and students by way of the intrusion of courseware developers who might suggest this or that particular idea because it's feasible and might reject other ideas because they are not technologically possible. In another model where funds are too tight to permit this kind of development, reliance has been placed instead upon the development of exemplars, and arranging ad hoc training sessions, and simply trying to encourage individual members of staff to "give it a go." Given that, in all honesty, it has to be said that adopting a virtual learning environment does involve a lot more work at least in the first instance; it is not exactly encouraging for staff when they are given no extra recognition or teaching time allowances for transferring to a virtual learning environment.

It is important to bear in mind that while some colleagues may enthusiastically embrace technology and be willing to change their relationship with students, other colleagues might find this all very threatening and intimidating. It has to be said that some staff go to quite considerable lengths to develop and maintain a particular style of authority and control and find the whole idea of surrendering some elements of control simply unacceptable.

New Learning Methods

One faces a real dilemma when trying to introduce changes in teaching and learning in that there is an inevitable and sensible conservatism on the part of most staff; at the very best, staff want incremental, controllable change.

What this means in practice is that they wish to "dip their toe" in the IT water and experiment with minor changes on existing modules. Paradoxically this actually inhibits the development of new learning methods because the changes made, using IT, are used to support conventional traditional techniques rather than used to rethink approaches to learning methods.

New Delivery Methods

One of the problems facing most British higher education institutes is that of the currency of the IT infrastructure. In developing the modules from which the modular evaluations are drawn for this article, one of the authors has faced two sets of problems. Firstly, it turns out that the delivery system required a particular version of a particular browser which, in turn, required a given level of CPU performance and memory. A good demonstration of the distance between enthusiastic IT staff and their not so enthusiastic colleagues is that it was not until staff familiarisation sessions that we discovered that most of the staff PCs simply could not run the browser! Secondly, the delivery system includes the facility to deliver streamed video and audio; like many universities, our student PC labs are not sound enabled. One immediate solution was to learn the joys of video editing to provide a rolling credit style summary of what was being said.

New Partnerships and Collaborations

In terms of the delivery of humanities, languages and social sciences there are only limited opportunities for collaborations outside the university. However, it has been interesting to observe how "struggling with the technology" has actually generated a range of new partnerships and collaborations across disciplines within one school and across several different schools. For example one of the authors is now working with staff from Schools of Nursing and Midwifery and Computing and Information Technology in developing a "special needs" version of the delivery platform.

The challenge is to develop a curriculum which can emphasise interconnections between learning pathways, and the practical application of knowledge in a variety of contexts and flexible relationships between core and specialist knowledge. It must be based on sound pedagogy. The focus on students and tutors needs to be not only on the training but also on the facilitation of central processes of learning, which is too often interpreted as something which is transmitted to people rather than an activity for which they themselves have responsibility and ownership.

CONCLUSIONS AND KEY LESSONS

What are the lessons here for e-learning and the use of a VLE to support students in an interactive way?

Use e-learning programmes to support and enrich action within the social group. Don't allow it to become an alienating or isolating experience.

Ensure that e-learning programmes allow maximum flexibility because people bring their whole past history with them when they engage with learning.

Ensure that learners can engage with the programme by adopting communication strategies appropriate to their needs.

Ensure that learners do engage by providing an explicit set of goals with which the learner can identify emotionally, i.e., be aroused and motivated.

Establish ongoing exemplars to demonstrate to staff that students will positively evaluate and welcome the adoption of IT. Use these exemplars to demonstrate to staff that IT enables you to achieve things that cannot be achieved in conventional settings, for example, asynchronous discussion of conceptual material, public dissemination of evaluations by streamed audio and video, and the provision of organised, extensive lists of URLs.

Get the technological infrastructure right! It is important that everybody has access to appropriate technology. One of the attractive things in much IT is to demonstrate "gee whiz" technology—this often demands the most powerful processor, graphics capability, or audio. This is a doomed exercise if the student PC labs are not up to the job and even more pointless if the home PCs owned by students cannot cope either.

Integrate the IT-based learning investment in staff appraisal and staff hours calculation.

Provide extensive support networks. At the University of Wolverhampton, there is an informal support network outside of formal committee structures; while this meets infrequently, it does provide a forum where issues "not on the agenda" can be discussed openly. In most institutions, there tend to be situations where it is not "wise" to criticise a particular individual or his or her pet project; this can lead to situations where simple technological failures are just not acknowledged.

While technology inevitably changes the role of teacher or lecturer, it also needs to be recognised that the adoption of technology may also change the role and dynamic of management and management structures.

Clearly the development of the WOLF VLE will need to be incorporated into the wider institution information system, i.e., a managed learning environment (MLE). This will enable the integration of student records and finance into the learning system. MLE includes the whole range of information systems and processes of the college, university or institution (including its VLE if it has one) that contribute directly or indirectly to learning and learning management (Learning and Skills Development Agency, 2001).

Finally, and in other words, use technology to avoid the major drawbacks of the "one size fits all" didactic approach of traditional teaching methods.

REFERENCES

Conole, G., & Oliver, M. (1998). A pedagogical framework for embedding C&IT into the curriculum. *Association for Learning Technology Journal*, *6*(2), 4-16.

Cox, S., & Pattinson, N. (2001). *Principles of learning*. Retrieved October 24, 2001 from http://193.61.107.61/studyskills/ehe/StudWork/Prinlers/prinlers.html.

Curriculum Corporation. (1994). *Statement on Studies of Society and Environment for Australian Schools*. Melbourne, Australia. Curriculum Corporation.

Gosling, W. (1981). *The Kingdom of Sand*. Council for Educational Technology.

Hall, W., & White, S. (2001, July). *Strategic Implementation of Computer-Based Learning at the University of Southampton*. Institute of Learning and Teaching, Members' Resource Area mailing. Accessed on October 24, 2002 at http://www.ilt.ac.uk/redirectportal.asp?article=Hall-White01a.

Kearsley, G. (1998). Educational technology: A critique. *Educational Technology*, *38*(2), 47-51.

Kolb, D. A. (1984). *Experiential Learning: Experience as the Source of Learning and Development*. Englewood Cliffs, NJ: Prentice Hall.

Learning and Skills Development Agency. (2001). *Definitions of Information Learning Technology* (as defined by the JISC subcommittee). Retrieved February 22, 2002, from http://www.learningtechnologies.ac.uk/ilt/levs.htm.

O'Donoghue, J., Dalziel, C., Fleetham, L., & Molyneux, S. (2000). *Network Learning—A Specification for the Setting Up of a Learning Environment*. University of Lancaster Publications.

O'Donoghue, J., Jentz, A., Singh, G., & Molyneux, S. (2000). IT developments and changes in customer demand in higher education. *Asynchronous Learning Networks*, *4*(1). Found at http://www.aln.org/alnweb/magazine/maga_v4_il.htm.

O'Donoghue, J., Singh, G., Caswell S., & Molyneux, S. (2001). Pedagogy vs technocentrism in designing Web based learning environments. *Journal of Computing in Higher Education*, *13*(1).

O'Donoghue, J., Singh, G., & Dorward, L. (2001). Virtual education in universities: A technological imperative. *British Journal of Educational Technology*, *32*(5), 517-530.

Sulla, N. (1999). Technology: To use or infuse. *The Technology Source, February*. Retrieved January 6, 2001, from http://horizon.unc.edu/TS/commentary/1999-02.asp.

Chapter III

Collaborative Learning On-Demand on the Internet Mbone

Giancarlo Fortino
University of Calabria, Italy

Libero Nigro
University of Calabria, Italy

ABSTRACT

The ubiquity of the Internet potentially allows delivering a variety of electronic learning contents to a wide audience. This work proposes a new online learning paradigm, namely, collaborative learning on-demand (CLoD), and its supporting technology. The CLoD paradigm enables a group of workmates to on-demand request and watch the playback of an archived multimedia session for the purpose of collaborating and cooperatively constructing knowledge. CLoD is featured by cooperative playback systems, which are networked infrastructures providing collaborative media on-demand services. The chapter also details our MBone-based cooperative playback system, ViCRO^C, and presents an investigation of its usability.

INTRODUCTION

Nowadays, the technical and cost barriers to high-bandwidth and ubiquitous networking are rapidly falling. The Internet has extended its realm over new strategic network technologies such as DSL, satellite and cellular systems so as to allow people to easily exchange multimedia information and interactively collaborate without being held hostage to physical proximity.

Within this context, electronic learning (e-learning) based on the Internet and WWW has the potential to effectively and inexpensively satisfy the education needs of a large user target. To this purpose, the current trend is the proliferation of portals for Web-based education which offer new online learning programs enabling synchronous and asynchronous education patterns.

Synchronous and collaborative e-learning can be favored by a worldwide exploitation of IP multicast, e.g., MBone (Kumar, 1996). The MBone, which stands for the virtual multicast backbone on the Internet, is a technology which enables scalable many-to-many multimedia communications so as to better support large-scale virtual classrooms than the traditional point-to-point (or IP-unicast) communications. New application models and protocols centered on the MBone have been recently developed and are being standardized to support the implementation of multimedia services and tools such as videoconferencing, whiteboard, multicast chat, etc. (Crowcroft, Handley, & Wakeman, 1999). Such protocols and services are considered the basic middleware for enabling distance learning paradigms that not only mime the traditional distance learning paradigm, i.e., live transmission of standard lecture courses, but also aim at creating highly decentralized, video-mediated and collaborative virtual learning environments. In fact, the educational research area (Cohen, 1994) proved that instructional methods promoting interpersonal discourse and social construction of knowledge (i.e., collaborative learning techniques) are more effective than methods simply relying on the broadcast of information (classroom transmission metaphor). However, collaborative learning is highly dependent on communication, or discourse. Thus, mechanisms such as shared annotations and questioning which compensate computer-based, video-mediating communication breakdowns are to be introduced for supporting the richer social discourse required for collaborative learning.

The main goal of this chapter is to introduce the cooperative playback system (CPS) and describe its application models, protocols and tools. CPSs enable the collaborative learning on-demand methodology over the Internet MBone. Collaborative learning on-demand (CLoD) is an original learning method in which a small group of students cooperatively selects, plays and controls the playback of a remote, archived multimedia session of a lecture or a seminar and exchanges inter-group questions in order to discuss the session contents (Fortino & Nigro, 2000b; Fortino, Nigro, & Pupo, 2001). The learning method is completely self-tutored and self-paced, i.e., it does not have a tutor who is in charge to drive the learning process.

CLoD models are application models used to structure MBone-based collaborative tools (Crowcroft et al., 1999). They encompass the lightweight sessions (LWS), the announce/listen (A/L), and the pattern interaction topologies.

CLoD protocols are of four types: (i) media, for the transmission of archived lectures (or playback); (ii) control, for the description, initiation and shared control of the playback session; (iii) collaboration, for the exchange of information among the group members; and (iv) coordination, for coordinating users' control actions.

Several tools have been developed and are being improved for enabling collaborative learning on-demand environments. Some of the most representative are: the Interactive Multimedia Jukebox (IMJ; Almeroth & Ammar, 1998), the MBone VCR on Demand system (MvoD; Holfelder, 1997), the multicast Media-on-Demand system (mMoD; Parnes, Synnes, & Schefstrom, 1998), the MASH Rover (MARS; Shuett, Raman, Chawathe, McCanne, & Katz, 1998), the J-VCR (Shirmohammadi, Ding, & Georganas, 2003), and ViCRO^C (Fortino et al., 2001). The tools that better exhibit cooperative-oriented features are the MASH Rover, developed at the University of Berkeley, and ViCRO^C, developed at the University of Calabria.

After describing and comparing the above-mentioned tools, the usability of CPSs for online programs is investigated by taking ViCRO^C as a case study.

The remainder of the chapter is organized as follows. First, the chapter presents definitions and concepts about e-learning and distance learning on the Internet. Moreover, it introduces the CLoD paradigm along with a host of tools and projects supporting it. Then there is a brief overview of MBone and its application models. Next, the chapter describes the characteristics, functionality, interaction levels, protocols and communication patterns of a cooperative playback system (CPS). This is followed by a section detailing the architecture, protocols and graphical user interface of the ViCRO^C system. In addition, related systems are reviewed and qualitatively compared to ViCRO^C. The *Usability of a CPS* section elucidates different criteria such as friendliness, quality of service (QoS), and subjective user satisfaction in the context of real CLoD session scenarios. The *Future Trends* section furnishes an outlook at the CLoD paradigm supported by virtual reality technology (e.g., virtual learning spaces) and featured by mobile computing. Finally, conclusions provide a summary of the main thrust of the chapter and some remarks.

COLLABORATIVE LEARNING ON-DEMAND

Training materials and instructional contents that are delivered electronically over the Internet (e.g., the World Wide Web), through an organization's intranet, or via CD-ROM are known as e-learning.

E-learning focuses on the design of instructional information (IMS, 2002), on the planning of online programs and on distance learning modes by which the learning process is instrumented (e.g., synchronous versus asynchronous and self-paced versus collaborative; Steinmetz & Nahrstedt, 1995).

An asynchronous online course is a popular type of distance learning which usually includes test questions. The learner is individually engaged in a self-paced learning process supported by hypermedia documents, which usually contain text, audio, video and pop-up hints and hyperlinks to related topics. Synchronous distance learning is almost synonymous with the transmission of live lectures, but it embraces more diversified forms of learning in which the student is supported by several tools, such as videoconferencing, whiteboard, chat box, etc.

Today in the education research area, virtual collaborative learning environments are of particular interest because they aim at creating computer-based, multimedia learning processes where learners, who belong to an interactive group, cooperatively construct knowledge. The reader can find a state-of-the-art review about virtual collaborative learning systems in Costantini and Toinard (2001).

Collaborative learning on-demand (CLoD) is a virtual collaborative learning method which enables a self-tutored and interactive learning process where a small group of remote students requests, watches and controls playback of a lecture and exchanges questions (Fortino & Nigro, 2000b). CLoD borrows some of the ideas of the tutored video instruction (TVI) and distributed tutored video instruction (DTVI) methodologies and tools (Sipusic, Pannoni, Smith, Dutra, Gibbons, & Sutherland, 1999). TVI is a face-to-face collaborative learning methodology in which a small group of students driven by a tutor goes over a videotape of a lecture. DTVI is a fully virtual version of TVI, in which each student has a networked computer equipped with audio (microphone and headset) and video (camera) facilities to communicate within a group. TVI and DTVI have proven real effectiveness in that the students involved in their experimentation have been shown to outperform students who physically attended the lectures. The main difference between CLoD and DTVI is that CLoD methodology doesn't assume the presence of a tutor who guides students to construct knowledge (Veerman & Veldhuis-Diermanse, 2001). This fact has a profound impact on the technical implementation of CLoD because, while in DTVI only the tutor has control of the videoconference recorder (VCR), in CLoD each participant to the playback session uses a shared VCR remote controller. In addition, being a learning service on-demand, CLoD needs to be supported by a video on-demand system (VoD).

The Internet MBone-related technology (Crowcroft et al., 1999; Kumar, 1996) delivers tools for videoconference recording on-demand and virtual collaborative learning which are the base for the efficient development of multimedia systems supporting CLoD methodology, i.e., cooperative playback systems. Videoconference recording on-demand (VCRoD) systems (Almeroth & Ammar, 1998; Fortino & Nigro, 2000a; Holfelder, 1997; Parnes et al., 1998; Shirmohammadi et al., 2003; Shuett et al., 1998) are VoD-like systems which allow a user to connect to a media server (MS) and request two kinds of services: recording and playback. By requesting a recording service, a user can either select a media session being transmitted over an IP-multicast address or send its own media session directly to the MS. This way, the MS archives the media session in a multimedia repository. The playback service consents to a user to access the list of archived media sessions, select a particular media session and control its playback by a VCR remote controller. In addition, tools for multiparty, collaborative learning (e.g., MASH Consortium, 2002; MBone Tools, 2002; Parnes, Synnes, & Schefstrom, 2000) enable a group of users to interactively exchange audio/video live streams and text-based messages and to cooperatively share whiteboards and document editors.

CLoD methodology is fully enabled by cooperative playback systems (CPSs; Fortino & Nigro, 2000b), which extend a VCRoD system to be exploitable by a group of users equipped with a question board (Malpani & Rowe, 1997) and optionally involved in a multiparty audio/videoconference.

Several international research projects have the development of CLoD systems as their objectives: the MASH Consortium at the University of Berkeley (MASH Consortium, 2002), the MBone Tools at University College London (MBone Tools, 2002), the MLB (Multimedia Lecture Board), formerly DLB, at the University of Mannheim (MLB, 2002), and the ViCRO^C at the University of Calabria (Fortino, Nigro, & Pupo, 2001). Particularly, MASH and ViCRO^C projects aim at realizing a CPS according to the definition given above. Although both are based on the multimedia Internet protocol stack (Crowcroft et al., 1999), MASH uses the TCL/TK script language, its object-oriented extensions, and C++, whereas ViCRO^C relies on Java technology.

MBONE: INFRASTRUCTURE AND APPLICATION MODELS

MBone stands for the virtual multicast backbone on the Internet (Kumar, 1996). It is a hardware and software infrastructure that enables distribution of and access to real-time interactive multimedia on the Internet. The MBone technologies provide a high degree of network scalability, which completely supports large-scale multimedia communities. The key technology enabling such a network scalability is IP multicast (Deering, 1989). IP multicast is based on the class D addressing scheme of IP (addresses in the range 224.0.0.0-239.255.255.255). The IP-multicast model allows sending a packet from one source to multiple receivers with no packet replication at the source. Such a model facilitates multiparty communications since it places less overhead both on the network and on the involved hosts than IP unicast. Packets delivery is driven by the IP-multicast routing, which is performed by multicast routers (mrouters). They take the responsibility of distributing and replicating the multicast data stream to the final hosts. Multicast addresses are not tied to a specific physical network interface at a certain physical site. They are logical group

Figure 1:   An abstract MBone reference topology

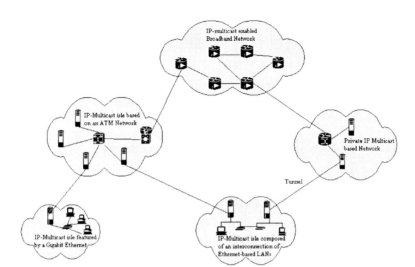

addresses that exist as long as there is a group of hosts interested in sending and receiving multicast packets. A host enters in a group by sending an IGMP (Internet Group Management Protocol) join message. Afterwards, it can send to and receive packets from the joined group. The multicast data delivery tree is formed by the mrouters exploiting routing protocols such as the DVMRP (Distance Vector Multicast Routing Protocol) and the Dense Mode-PIM (Protocol Independent Multicast; Crowcroft et al., 1999). The MBone topology (Figure 1) can be visualized as a tree and a mesh. The tree topology is depicted in Figure 1 near the leaf nodes. The connections between mrouter nodes constitute the mesh topology. A reference MBone map illustrated by Steve Casner can be found at http://www.mbone.cl.cam.ac.uk/mbone/mbone-topology.html.

MBone Application Models

Some design principles for multimedia MBone-based applications have emerged that are very powerful.

1) *The Lightweight Session (LWS) Model* is the base communication and application model (Jacobson, 1994) for building multimedia collaborative applications over IP multicast. This model places no burden on users, has all the scalability, fault tolerance and robustness of IP, accommodates intermittent connectivity, and delivers good performance even when participant link bandwidths are very different. LWS building blocks are as follows: (i) *IP* (datagrams with best effort delivery), (ii) *IP multicast*. It is worth noting that

IP multicast is more than a simple, efficient, robust delivery mechanism. It also greatly simplifies the conferencing problem for users, i.e., if a conference is associated with a multicast address, then users can join the conference without enumerating (or even knowing) other participants; users can join and leave at any time; and the conference has a network visible identity so the network takes care of rendezvous, distribution and membership, not users. This means the group-size-independent scaling of multicast is inherited. (iii) *Timing recovery* via receiver-based adaptation. Unlike normal data traffic, the time structure of real-time traffic has significance. But, since the network infrastructure is shared, competing traffic can distort this time sequence. Thus, the sender puts time stamps in packets so timing is explicit rather than implicit so that the receiver can reconstruct timing before playing out data. This requires a few kilobytes of buffer at the receiver. (iv) *"Thin" transport layer* (according to the application-level framing architectural model). The basic lightweight sessions model is centered on the following keypoints: (i) a session located by a multicast address and a port; (ii) sites which send data; (iii) all sites quasi-periodically multicast 'session' packets containing: identity, reception reports, and synchronization info. All the applications developed over the MBone such as the MBone tools (MBone Tools, 2002) are based on the LWS model.

2)   *The Announce/Listen Model.* A participant in an announce/listen session (Crowcroft et al., 1999; Shuett et al., 1998) periodically announces its state updates, while all other participants listen to and cache these updates. The updates are assumed to be soft states and are eventually aged out, unless overridden by a new update from the announcing client. Announce/listen protocols are robust and can be implemented over an unreliable datagram transport protocol such as UDP. Since no central hard state is involved in such a protocol, it makes the protocol much more resilient to failures. In particular contexts, the use of announce/listen eliminates the need for heavyweight reliable protocols such as TCP or SRM (Floyd, Jacobson, McCanne, Liu, & Zhang, 1997).

COOPERATIVE PLAYBACK SYSTEMS

Cooperative playback systems (CPSs; Fortino & Nigro, 2000b) are video on-demand systems which provide cooperative playback sessions. Cooperative playback sessions are sessions in which a group of users explicitly formed shares both the view and the control of an audio/video playback and collaborates on the contents of the presentation being played by exchanging synchronous questions. Each group member operates on a playback remote controller which is shared by all the others. When a member performs a control operation, this operation is propagated, according to certain rules, to all other members of the group. In order to cooperatively construct knowledge, the group members collaborate to one another by using a

Figure 2: An abstract schema of a CPS

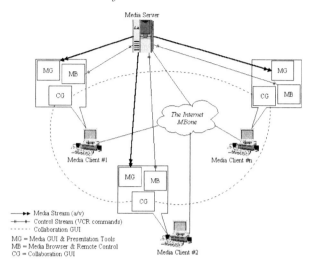

question board, which allows them to send and receive questions. In addition, a member can mark specific instants within a playback session for a discussion proposal (or forum on-the-fly).

Cooperative playback sessions support the concept of WYSIWIS (what you see is what I see), i.e., each member of the group has the same view as the others. Although a precise consistency of the views for all the users is unachievable mainly due to the users' distribution heterogeneity, it must be guaranteed after performing a "pause" or a "seek" command. For instance, after a user pauses a playback, any other user should look at the same frozen image as the one that executed the pause command. In the server-based approach, the view synchronization is always met. In fact, when a user executes a pause command, the reference pausing time is not the one of the user but that of the server, i.e., the instant in time when the server, upon the reception of the pause request, actually pauses the playback.

A CPS is a multimedia distributed system which is structured in two main components (Figure 2): media server (MS) and media client (MC). The MS is the network entity which provides the playback services, i.e., session scheduling, control and streaming. The MC is the network entity which connects to the MS in order to set and/or get into a cooperative playback session. In the next subsection, the functionality, interaction levels and communication patterns of a CPS are presented.

Functionality

A cooperative playback system is equipped with the following functionality: group organization, media streaming, control sharing, joint work, security, and fault tolerance.

Group Organization contains group formation and group management. Group formation enables the creation of a group of users wishing to work on and control the same playback session. Normally, a rendezvous mechanism is employed. A Web-based mechanism provides dynamic Web pages where users can find a list of archived sessions and subscribe to a particular one by filling out a form (Almeroth & Ammar, 1998). Indeed, two mechanisms are currently used according to the Internet multimedia architecture (Crowcroft et al., 1999): Session Directory (SD) and Session Initiation Protocol (SIP). Thus, information about cooperative playback sessions can be obtained by turning on the SD multicast group or by receiving an explicit invitation, via email or SIP notification. The information is normally under the form of an SDP (Session Description Protocol) document (Handley & Jacobson, 1998), which contains the multicast address of the MS, which is needed to locate the playback service, and the title and the description of the playback. Group management deals with issues such as how to share the starting time of a playback session in order for the group members to start and keep synchronized and how to expel from the group a member who interrupts the others using an improper behavior.

Media Streaming delivers media content to the MCs. It is based on a real-time transport protocol (e.g., RTP, Real-Time Transport Protocol), streaming agents and a multimedia archive (Fortino, 1997; Fortino & Nigro, 2000a). The multimedia archive is a media repository which contains both multimedia sessions dumped from the network and media files (e.g., MPEG files). Multimedia content can also be coupled with meta-content which is streamed on a reliable channel. Meta-content is data about content such as information on particular scenes of the multimedia session. An important characteristic of the media streaming functionality is the media flow rate. The media rate should be adaptable (e.g., by using media transcoding servers) in order to accommodate heterogeneous MCs.

Control Sharing allows MCs to share the control of the playback. Normally, this functionality is embedded in the archive control protocol (ACP) on which the MC/MS control interaction relies. Control messages are typical commands of a VCR remote controller such as play, pause, stop and seek (i.e., a play with a time range).

Joint Work is fundamental in the context of a CPS. It is in the form of questioning and annotation. Questioning means that the members of a group can send questions about the content of the playback session and possibly receive answers. Annotation allows tagging a particular point in the session for a discussion proposal, which can be started at the end of the playback. Additional virtual collaborative tools can also be used.

Security provides mechanisms, e.g., authentication and key distribution (Crowcroft et al., 1999), to keep cooperative sessions private. Private cooperative sessions are sessions which cannot be joined and spied by intruders.

Fault Tolerance is an important property of an Internet service which is subjected to frequent network connectivity problems and a pacing introduction of new and not debugged protocols and software. Fault tolerance includes detection, which deals with the discovery of failures at both server and client sides, and recovery, which involves actions the server and/or the clients have to carry out in order to cope with detected failures.

Interaction Levels

CPSs are characterized by four levels of interaction: data, control, collaboration and coordination.

Data involves unidirectional multicast media-stream delivery from the MS to MCs.

Control entails bidirectional control messaging from the MCs to the MS and vice versa. This level is based on a protocol which maintains a shared state table between MCs and the MS and defines the format and the semantics of the control commands. Shared state maintenance is primarily devoted to managing the exchange of control streaming parameters between the CPS server and the clients. These parameters include at least: the server's current position in time on the stream; data, control and collaboration addresses; and control and collaboration session identifiers. On the basis of these parameters, server and clients construct a shared state table, which is dynamic and modifiable during the playback session lifetime. Control encompasses messages that can be transmitted from MCs to the MS and vice versa in order to fill and change the shared state table and control the data transmission. Thus, the control messages are grouped in a shared state table affecting commands (presentation description, presentation setup and shared table updating) and presentation control commands. Presentation description commands allow a user to receive both a list of multimedia sessions archived in the server and the description of a particular presentation. A presentation description should contain at least the presentation title, media types and related data formats in the presentation, and the presentation duration. These parameters are used by the clients to correctly set up the media presentation tools. Optional information such as the presentation creator and its email and Web addresses can also be included. Presentation setup commands are used to request a presentation. A media server, after receiving a presentation request, begins a negotiation phase with the client in order to establish the media stream channels. After this phase, the server launches a player agent on the data channels. Presentation control commands include VCR-like commands, which directly affect the transmission of data. Shared table updating messages consist of replies to requests and messages such as the server's current playtime beaconing.

Collaboration comprises interaction among MCs. Several forms of interaction including questioning, annotation, shared whiteboard, and audio/videoconferencing can be used.

Coordination regulates and coordinates MC's control actions. Control policies are needed to regulate the access to shared resources such as the VCR remote controller. For instance, a user who wishes to seek in the presentation can do so only according to certain rules dictated by the chosen control policy. Three kinds of basic policies have been envisaged: (i) moderation-free, each group participant can perform a command whenever he/she wants; (ii) floor-based, in order to send a command a user needs to get the floor; and (iii) voting, a group member submits a command to the approval of the others, who can acknowledge or refuse it according to a majority vote. Different actions on the VCR remote control can be constrained by different control policies. For instance, the effect of the pause command is different than that of the seek. The former results in a temporary data stream stop, which has to happen as soon as the user presses the pause button. Thus, the pause command can be subjected to the (i) or (ii) policy. Conversely, a seek results in a temporal displacement from the current position in the presentation and not only can occur within a certain tolerance range but also has to be approved by the group, which is usually concentrated on watching the presentation and doesn't want to jump from one point to another in the presentation. The (iii) policy seems to be the most appropriate for this case.

Interaction levels are not independent; in fact, actions performed at certain levels can affect directly or indirectly other levels. For instance, a pause command at the control level has the effect to stop the media transmission at the data level. A voting mechanism at the collaboration level can disable a seek command at the control level.

Communication Patterns

Interactions within a CPS occur through communication patterns. By considering the advantages to exploit multicast, media streams are multicast relayed, i.e., transmitted to a multicast group. The other interaction levels can be mapped onto unicast connections, multicast groups or a hybrid combination of both. The use of multicast versus unicast is strategic for improving efficiency and scalability. On the other hand, the exploitation of Internet standard protocols, which are already standardized, such as RTSP on TCP, can simplify the implementation of the control interaction. The unicast, hybrid and fully multicast approaches to the implementation of the communication patterns have been envisaged. In particular, the data level relies on the Real-Time Transport Protocol (RTP; Schulzrinne, Casner, Frederick, & Jacobson, 1996). The control level is based on a variant of the Real-Time Streaming Protocol (RTSP; Schulzrinne, Rao, & Lanphier, 1998). The collaboration and coordination level centers on custom protocols, e.g., qb protocol (Malpani & Rowe, 1997), on top of a reliable transport protocol (e.g., TCP or SRM-like).

The Unicast Multi-Connected Approach

The multi-connected approach is based on RTSP on top of TCP. A media client that wishes to join a collaborative playback session connects to an MS. Once the RTSP connection is established, the MC is served by a front end (FE), which is encapsulated in a logic controller managing all the FEs of the other MCs attached to the same session. When an MC issues a control command, the MS, after accepting and processing it, replies to all the MCs. By using this infrastructure an MC not only can send a command to an MS but also can transmit questions to the other MCs.

Thus, the MS behaves like a message reflector. This mechanism is achieved by sending an RTSP SET_PARAMETER request, which contains a predefined content type referring to the group interaction channel and the message to be delivered. As soon as an FE receives a request, the logic controller copies the received message to each of the other MCs. Although the approach is not scalable and introduces a heavy load on the server, which has to spawn as many FEs as the number of the group members, it has the advantage of using RTSP/TCP, which is well specified and its implementation is widely available. In addition, if the group size is small the approach can be affordable.

The Hybrid Approach

In this approach, only one group member, called the session initiator media client (IMC), is connected to an MS according to RTSP/TCP. All the members are grouped on a multicast group channel (MGC) based on LRMP (Lightweight Reliable Multicast Protocol; Liao, 1998). LRMP is a multicast transport protocol which allows the user to reliably send a message (LRMP packet) from one sender to many receivers. The IMC can directly send a control command to the MS. The other MCs wishing to send a control command have to transmit a control message to the MGC. This message is captured by the IMC, which encapsulates it in an RTSP request and sends it to the MS. Once the MS has processed the request, it replies to the IMC which in turns reflects the response to all the other MCs. The collaboration messages are also sent onto the MGC. In order to ensure a certain degree of fault tolerance in case the IMC fails or wants to leave, RTSP has been enhanced in Fortino and Nigro (2000a). Two new methods were introduced: PASS and CONTINUE. The method PASS is performed by the IMC when it wants to pass the session control to another MC and leaves. When the MS receives the PASS, it disconnects the IMC and waits for another connection by freezing the FE which was handling the connection with the IMC. The FE is kept alive till a time-out expires. The method CONTINUE is invoked by the new IMC to take control of the session. When the MS receives the CONTINUE request, it connects the new IMC to the frozen FE. If the IMC fails (e.g., leaving without sending the PASS or losing the connection with the MS), the MS behaves the same as if it received a PASS request.

The Fully Multicast Approach

The fully multicast approach is based on an adaptation of RTSP on top of LRMP. An MS is located by a multicast address whereas a playback session is identified by means of a multicast URL. The fully multicast approach is employed in the ViCRO^c system (see next section).

The ViCRO^c System

ViCRO^c is a cooperative playback system implemented according to the fully multicast approach. The architecture of ViCRO^c is portrayed in Figure 3.

The media server (MS) consists of MACπ (multicast archive control protocol) server and player components. The service entry point is the MACπ server, which allows a group of media clients (MCs) to request a playback service according to the MACπ protocol. It is composed of a manager and front ends. The former performs load monitoring and admission control. For each cooperative playback session, the manager spawns a front-end thread which directly dialogs with the MCs. The front end starts, manages and terminates the player under the MCs' control. The component player reads media files consisting of previously archived RTP-based multimedia sessions and streams them back onto the media multicast group (MMG). The player is borrowed from the ViCRO system (Fortino & Nigro, 2000a), which is also equipped with the recording functionality for creating a multimedia archive (MMAr). The data, control and collaboration/coordination levels are based, respectively, on RTP, MACπ and COπ (collaborative protocol).

The media client consists of the MACπ client, a media browser, a collaborative board and media presentation tools. The MACπ client implements the client part according to the MACπ protocol specification. The media browser allows the user to start, control and tear down playback sessions. The media presentation tools currently used are the MBone Tools and the JMF RTP Player. The collaborative board, which is based on the COπ, supports the exchange of questions and related answers, shared annotations, and a flexible voting mechanism. In the following subsections, MACπ and COπ protocols are overviewed and the media clients' GUI detailed.

MACπ: Multicast Archive Control protocol

The primary goal of MACπ is to allow explicitly grouped MCs to access an MS, request a recorded multimedia presentation, and share the control of the chosen presentation playback. MACπ is a multicast variant of the Real-Time Streaming

Figure 3: The architecture of ViCRO

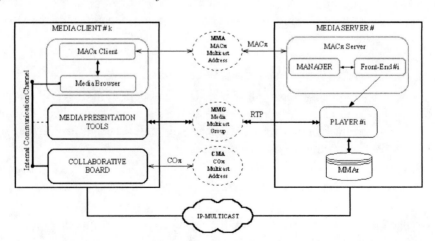

Protocol (RTSP) adapted on top of the Lightweight Reliable Multicast Protocol (LRMP). However, a MACπ session is not strictly bounded to an LRMP transport session. In fact an MS creates for each playback session a *SESSION ID*, which identifies a MACπ session and represents a shared state between the MCs and Ms. The *SESSION ID* is inserted in the body of each exchanged message. An MS is located on an IP-multicast address. An archived multimedia session is identified through a URL as follows: *macp://multicast_address:port/abs_path,* where *multicast_address* is the MS's multicast address, *port* indicates which port the messages should be sent to, and *abs_path* identifies a presentation. MACπ control messages are categorized into requests, responses and notifications. A request is sent from MCs to the MS and is considered provisional in the sense that an MC waits for the response before changing state. A response is transmitted from the MS to all the MCs of the group as a result of an accepted request. It synchronizes the behavior of each MC. A notification is sent either from MCs to the MS or vice versa and does not imply a response. MACπ control messages are structured as RTSP messages in a header, split in several subheaders, and a message body. The request and notification messages include the request line, which contains the request URI, specifying the resource (i.e., the presentation) subject to the request, and the method or command to be executed. The response message embodies the status line, which contains the status code, indicating the result of the command execution carried out in the previous request, and the method executed.

The defined standard methods are: DESCRIBE, SETUP, PLAY, PAUSE, and TEARDOWN, which are used in MC-to-MS requests. The methods LEAVE and BEACON, purposely introduced, are used in notifications. DESCRIBE serves to obtain from the MS the description of a presentation to be played back. SETUP causes the MS to allocate resources for a presentation and starts the MACp session. PLAY starts the presentation streaming. PAUSE temporarily halts the data streaming without freeing MS resources. TEARDOWN frees resources associated with a presentation so that the MACπ session terminates. LEAVE signals an MC's abandonment to the MS. BEACON updates states. A MACπ session is mapped onto an LRMP session. LRMP (Liao, 1998) was implemented in Java under the form of a reusable library. After opening

Figure 4:   MACπ stack and request packet format

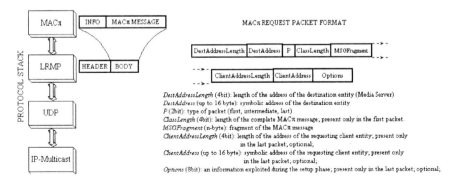

an LRMP session, the MACπ control messages are to be first encapsulated in LRMP packets in order to be transmitted. Since the maximum transmission unit (MTU) at the LRMP level is fixed to 1,400 bytes, it is possible that a MACπ message spans more LRMP packets. In order to minimize the occurrence of a spanning which would result in efficiency degradation, the message is first compressed by using a *Gzipper* block and then, if it fits the MTU, put in one LRMP packet; otherwise, it is fragmented in more packets at the sender and reassembled at the receiver. Since an LRMP packet is multicast to all the session members, a header containing the message sender and target (MS or broadcast-to-MC) and the fragment number is associated to each fragment of a MACπ message (see Figure 4).

COπ: Collaborative Protocol

The collaborative protocol (COπ) was purposely implemented to support both questioning on the playback session contents and synchronization on the control commands among the media clients. Its main characteristics are as follows. (i) It centers on the concepts of the CCCP (Conference Control Channel Protocol; Crowcroft et al., 1999). It does not have a master application which controls the conference and maintains data consistency; instead, each application is responsible of sending and receiving its own data on a common multicast channel. (ii) Messages are based on the LRMP protocol. (iii) Inter-client communication takes place onto a known multicast group. The main COπ functionality encompasses the following.

1) *Identification of media clients.* COp uses a "soft state" approach based on announcement message exchanges for the conference members' identification. A client introduces itself through an announcement message. Every client involved in a cooperative playback session stores in a state table the identity <Username, Host> of the known announced members. The state table is periodically refreshed: At a timer expiration (Dt) the presence/absence of a message announcement from a member in the state table is verified. If a member didn't send an announce message (called also "heart beat" message), the member is considered left. A member can explicitly decide to leave the session by sending a LEAVE message.

2) *Voting mechanism.* The voting mechanism allows handling of the remote control commands play, seek and teardown. Since such commands are shared among the clients, they can be issued only if the majority of the playback session members agrees. When a client wants to execute a shared command, he/she sends a command proposal message and waits for answers from the other participants within a deadline of 5 s. The answers can be positive or negative. In the case of a play or a seek command, the total positive answers are to be the majority with respect to the total number of members. In the case of a teardown command, the total positive answer must be equal to the total number of members. A not sent answer is considered a negative answer.

3) *Interactive remote questioning.* The COp protocol makes possible the interactive remote questioning among the playback session members. Ques-

Figure 5: Media GUI

tions can be directed to all the participants (public question) or to a specific client (private question). It is also possible to hide the identity of the questioner.

Media Client's GUI

The media, control and collaboration windows constitute the graphical user interface of an MC. The media window (Figure 5) allows for presenting the playback (e.g., an audio/video session). Two versions are available based, respectively, on the MBone Tools and on the RTP Player of the Java Media Framework (JMF, 2002).

The control window (Figure 6) makes available the following functions: connection to an MS, browsing the media archive, and selection and control of a playback session. Figure 6 portrays the VCR control panel inside the control window. The VCR control panel shows that the playback session identified by the URL *macp://228.114.228.114:30000/Lecture10_4_2001* was paused at 30 min and 11 s, with 1 hr, 10 min and 15 s being the overall duration.

The collaboration GUI permits the user to monitor the membership of the cooperative playback session, visualize the result of a command voting, and send/ receive questions. In order to describe the collaboration GUI, snapshots from a real cooperative playback session, which is about a research group internal talk focused on "Multimedia Internetworking" given by Giancarlo Fortino on April 10, 2001, are shown and discussed. Each participant was placed on its own computer and located

Figure 6: Media browser and VCR controller

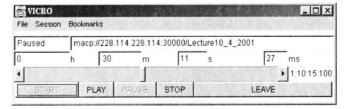

Figure 7:   The attendees panel

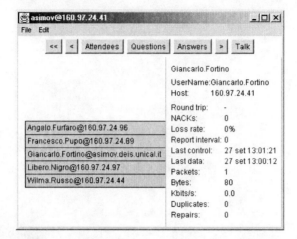

in a separate room. The computers were connected through a 10 Mbps Ethernet departmental network.

The collaborative GUI consists of a main window which contains four panels: attendees, questions, answers and talk. The panels are made visible by using either the buttons corresponding to the names of the panels or the buttons "<" and ">" which allow circular panel scrolling.

The attendees panel (Figure 7) lists the CNAME (canonical name) of the playback cooperative session members. For each member, information about the date of the last control, loss rate, transmitted packets, duplicates, repairs, etc. are reported. As shown in Figure 7, the members of the session are five: Giancarlo Fortino, Angelo Furfaro, Libero Nigro, Francesco Pupo and Wilma Russo.

Figure 8:   The questions panel

Figure 9:   The talk panel

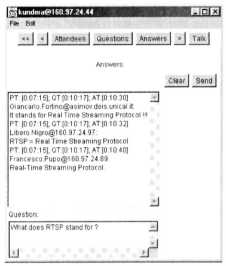

The questions panel allows sending questions to the session attendees. Questions can be directed to all the members (public), to a particular member (private), and anonymously (anonymous). The panel also shows the multicast group (228.114.228.110/44444) on which the collaboration is taking place and the scope of the session (TTL=1, i.e., local). As depicted in Figure 8, the attendee *Wilma.Russo* on the host kundera@160.97.24.44 sends the question What does RTSP stand for? As soon as the question arrives at an MC's host, the answer dialog is displayed. Figure 10 shows the answer dialog, which contains the question sent from *Wilma.Russo* and the related answer replied by *Giancarlo.Fortino*. Of course, an MC can either answer or ignore the question. A threaded sequence of answers related to a proposed question is visualized in the talk panel. In Figure 9, all the answers to *Wilma.Russo*'s question are listed. Each answer is formed as follows: time tags, identity of the member who answered, and answer message. The time tags are: (i) PT (presentation time), the time of the playback when the question occurred; (ii) QT (question time), the time in the cooperative playback session when the question was sent; and (iii) AT (answer time), the time in the cooperative playback session when the answer arrived at the questioner.

Figure 10:   The answer dialog

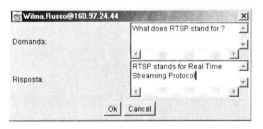

Figure 11:   The voting dialog

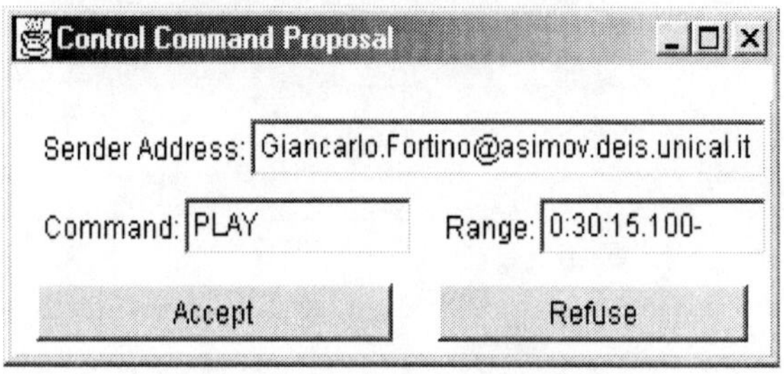

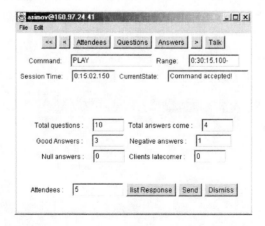

Figure 11 shows the voting dialog by which a media client can accept or refuse a control command within the playback session which was raised by a session member, i.e., *Giancarlo.Fortino@asimov.deis.unical.it*. If the media client presses the button Accept, a positive answer is expressed; else, if he/she presses the button Refuse or doesn't press any button within a certain deadline (e.g., 3 s), a negative answer is issued. Each member of the session can control the voting process by using the answer panel.

The answer panel (Figure 12) reports the command proposal (play), the session time (0:15:02.150), i.e., the time in the playback when the command proposal was issued, the number of attendees (5), and the vote counting. The vote counting entails the total answers come (4), the good answers (3), the negative answers (1), and the null answers (0). As one can see from Figure 12, the result "*Command accepted!*" of the voting process is reported in the text field CurrentState.

Related Work

The following summarizes some research projects and tools which are representative of the state-of-the-art of multimedia systems enabling some form of collaborative learning on-demand environment.

Figure 12:   The answer panel

Interactive Multimedia Jukebox—IMJ

The Interactive Multimedia Jukebox (Almeroth & Ammar, 1998), developed at the Georgia Tech Institute, is a system which implements a distributed video jukebox. IMJ uses the Web as a means to gather requests and present play schedules. Users may request playback but have no means to interact with the server to control the resulting schedule, cancel playback or perform seek or pause operations. Control is performed only on buffered, per-client replicated data of the session.

MBone Video Conference Recording on Demand—MVoD

The MBone Video Conference Recording on Demand (Holfelder, 1997), developed at the University of Mannheim, is a client-server system for interactive remote recording and playback of MBone sessions. It is based on open standards (e.g., CORBA), making it possible for other applications to interface it. The MVoD service consists of three basic components: the manager and the videopump, which form the logical unit called the MVoD server, and the MVoD client. The interaction between the system components is regulated by four protocols: the VCR Service Access Protocol (VCRSAP), the VCR Stream Control Protocol (VCRSCP), the VCR Announcement Protocol (VCRAP), and the VCR Client Message Protocol (VCRCMP). The manager and the client are implemented in Java. The videopump is implemented in C++. The MVoD client can be started either as a Java applet within a Java-enabled browser or as a stand-alone Java application.

Multicast Media-on-Demand—mMOD

The multicast Media-on-Demand (Parnes et al., 1998), developed at the CDT of the University of Luleå, is a system for recording and playing back MBone sessions. mMOD can be controlled by using a command-line interface or a WWW-based interface. The system consists of three separate parts, the VCR, the data translator and the Web-controller. The VCR is a stand-alone program for recording and playing back IP packets on either UDP or RTP level. The data translator translates the traffic in various ways (recoding, mixing and switching techniques) to allow users with different bandwidths to access the service. The Web-controller is a program that acts as a Web interface of mMOD. It is through this interface that a new session can be started and controlled and information about running sessions viewed so that a user can join them. mMOD is completely written in Java 1.1.

MASH Rover—MARS

The MASH Rover (Shuett et al., 1998), developed at the University of Berkeley, is a client/server system for remote media browsing. The media server is implemented by using the TACC (transformation, aggregation, customization and control) toolkit. An RTSP-like protocol is used to remote control media streams. Mechanisms of advertising and discovering new contents are implemented such as rich-description hyperlinks to the archived sessions and automatic detection of significant instants during a session. The client part consists of the MASH streaming player that can operate as media browser or as helper application within a Web browser. It allows the user to bookmark specific sessions and specific instants within a session. The bookmark file can be shared among several participants. The client is implemented in C++ and TCL/TK.

Java Video Conference Recorder—J-VCR

The Java Video Conference Recorder (Shirmohammadi et al., 2003), developed at the University of Ottawa, is a videoconferencing tool capable of recording live multimedia collaborative/conferencing sessions and playing back archived, SMIL- (Synchronized Multimedia Integration Language) -compliant multimedia sessions. J-VCR can capture, process, store and play back collaboration content, i.e., RTP-based streams and whiteboard messages produced by JETS, a multimedia collaboration system. The architecture consists of the J-VCR client, the J-VCR server and a data repository. Any SMIL player (e.g., RealNetwork's RealPlayer tool) can be used to play back an archived multimedia session.

A Comparison of VCRoD Systems

Table 1 collects some useful information about the VCRoD systems mentioned in the previous section and the ViCRO[c] system. The examined properties are the following: paradigm, record and playback services, communication, control protocol, media protocol, cooperative mechanisms, presentation tools, media server platform and programming language. The main differences are on the control protocol, cooperative mechanisms and languages. Each system employs a different control protocol: mMoD uses a Web and applet-based custom protocol; MVoD is based on

Table 1: Comparison of VCRoD systems

SYSTEM	PARADIGM	RECORD	PLAYBACK	COMMS	CONTROL PROTOCOL	MEDIA PROTOCOL	COOPERATIVE MECHANISMS	PRESENTATION TOOLS	MEDIA SERVER PLATFORM	PROG. LANGUAGE
mMoD	MoD	R/L	R/L	U/M	Web-based (P)	RTP/UDP	N/A	MBone Tools	Win95/NT, Solaris	JAVA and CGI
MVoD	MoD	R/L	R/L	U/M	VCRSSP (P)	RTP	Messages	MBone Tools	UNIX	C−− and JAVA
IMJ	Jukebox	L	R	M	N/A	RTP	N/A	P	UNIX	C
MARS	MoD	R/L	R/L	U/M	RTSP-like	RTP/Wb	Shared control and annotations	MASH Tools	UNIX, Windows NT	C−− and Tcl/Tk
J-VCR	MoD	R	R/L	U/M	P	RTP/JETS	N/A	J-VC	Java-enabled	JAVA
ViCRO[c]	MoD	R	R	M	RTSP	RTP	Shared control and questioning	MBone Tools, JMF RTP Player	Java-enabled	JAVA

MoD	Media On Demand
R	Remote and Distributed
L	Local
U	Unicast
M	Multicast
P	Proprietary

the proprietary VCRSCP (VCR Stream Control Protocol); IMJ doesn't have a control protocol; MARS's control protocol is RTSP-like but it isn't RTSP-compliant; J-VCR uses the control protocol of the adopted SMIL player; and finally, ViCRO^C uses a multicast version of RTSP. Cooperative mechanisms such as shared control, annotations and questioning are available in MARS and ViCRO^C. It is worth highlighting that RTP is the media transport protocol utilized by all the systems.

USABILITY OF A CPS

Cooperative playback systems (CPSs) support an original type of synchronous Net-based learning called collaborative learning on-demand (CLoD) which has the potential to be an effective e-learning methodology for small/medium groups of students. However, the usability of a CPS is mainly influenced by general factors (Synnes, Soderstrom, & Parnes, 2001), which are related to the network, desktop hardware and environment, and by specific factors, such as media on-demand service availability, easiness to set up a cooperative playback session, and degree of appeal and simplicity-of-use of the graphical user interface.

One of the issues regarding Internet-based desktop videoconferencing tools is network quality. Without sufficient network resources (bandwidth) and reliability (a "no-lossy" network), it is practically impossible to make a cooperative playback work. Thus, before planning to set up a cooperative playback session, it is necessary to make sure of having the availability of sufficient network resources, or the session (in particular its media part) can result unsatisfactorily and end quickly as a failure. In fact, even using a low-rate media stream (e.g., 128 Kbps for an H.261-based video and 13 Kbps for a GSM-based audio), a network with low reliability (high traffic and frequent losses) will quickly render the reception media quality unacceptable. Loss rates of more than 2% can make the audio tiresome to listen to. Although techniques for repairing and/or for introducing redundancy at the source can be exploited, it is important to have from the network the necessary quality of service in terms of bandwidth and loss rate. Even if the use of IP multicast can dramatically reduce the network resources utilized, it is complex to set up and maintain on a large scale because network maintenance can be multi-organizational and can involve firewalls and security policies. In addition, multicast is not available on the commercial Internet, making unfeasible a home connection. For these reasons, a CPS is well suited to be deployed on academic and company networks. Another issue regards computer hardware and environment. Videoconferencing tools suffer of the problem that audio hardware is practically hard to set up without risking echo feedback or noise. This is the main cause why people find it difficult to use these environments. It simply requires experience to successfully set up the audio levels to avoid problems. Of course, if users are expert this problem doesn't exist. For what concerning with the video, a common reaction to the video quality used in low-bandwidth configurations of videoconferencing tools (typically maximum 128 Kbps of video) is that it looks awful. People compare the video quality to that of the TV. The result is often a loss of interest. The audio quality suffers from the same comparison. The only way to overcome this problem is to increase the perceived quality by sending more data or using a more effective compression. Another important factor to keep under control is the lip synchronization, which can really disturb the viewer. The issues introduced and discussed are general and belong to all the PC-based multimedia environments on the Internet. Over an intranet which supports IP multicast, everything can be set up (statically or dynamically) so as to minimize such issues and deliver to the users a negotiable degree of quality of service.

Peculiar issues arising from cooperative playback systems on which usability can be evaluated involve (as previously mentioned): service availability, easiness to set up a cooperative playback session, and degree of friendliness of the GUI.

1)   A CPS service should be timely available upon users' request. The availability and the access to the service depends on the load of the media server. The chance to obtain more valuable media streams, i.e., streams with a higher quality of service, relies on several factors including media server's load, media server's capability to transcode media streams, and media format of the session to be played back. For instance, if a lecture was archived as a raw RTP file obtained from an RTP stream of 200 Kbps, it isn't possible to improve its quality. In order to increase availability, media servers should be clustered and media gateways are to be exploited.

2)   In order to be appealing for the users, a cooperative playback session has to be easily configured. The CPS functionality of group organization should deliver easy mechanisms to create a group and synchronously start a cooperative playback session. In fact, complex mechanisms drive the users who don't have the necessary expertise to use the system to give up at the first trial.

3)   The main requirements of the graphical user interface are friendliness and intuitiveness. Although one of the main breakdowns is the size of the monitor being used, designing appealing and easy-to-use GUIs can minimize such a drawback. Of course, training on the GUI is needed in order to really exploit all its functionality. Another issue is whether to structure the GUI as a monolithic block or to develop the GUI as a toolset. Besides the GUI of the CPS system, it is possible to use virtual collaborative tools such as multiparty video tools and shared whiteboards to augment the sense of presence within a group. Instead, the use of an audio tool (even if the hardware consents its use) is really discouraged because it can interfere with the playback.

Usability of ViCRO^C

ViCRO^C is being tested by different groups of users in different scenarios. Each user group is small (about four to five persons) and is formed, respectively, by professors and researchers, graduate students and students. The first group is involved in sessions which regard talks about computer science research topics. The second group gets in cooperative playback sessions about doctoral seminars. The third group goes over archived course lectures. Groups operate at different time schedules so as to minimize breakdowns due to network congestion. The media archive is equipped with audio/video sessions constituted by RTP streams with the following characteristics: video rate about 500 Kbps; video format: H.261; and audio format: PCM. Currently few sessions are made available on the media server which is installed on an Ultra Sparc 10. Quality of service of the media streaming was considered good by the users. Thus, the investigation of the usability of cooperative playback sessions featured by ViCRO^C rests on the control and collaborative GUIs and on the handling of the three separate GUIs (media browser, audio/video tool, and collaborative board). The three GUIs fit well a 17-inch monitor with a resolution of 1024 x 768. On the contrary, if the group wants to use further virtual collaborative tools (e.g., the MBone tools *vic* for the video and *wb* for a shared space), the space becomes an issue, because it is hardly unfeasible to arrange all the GUIs in such a way to have everything under control. The control GUI (Figure 6) was considered really intuitive and simple to use. After having set up the cooperative session, the control panel is displayed and can be easily used by the group members to send control commands. The collaborative GUI (Figures 7-12) is the most crucial because a little bit of training is necessary to efficiently use it. In order to have useful feedback by a user, a simple questionnaire is required to be filled out at the end of the playback session experience. The questions are about: (i) the perceived *media quality*, including video and audio quality and the quality of the lip synchronization; (ii) the perceived *interactivity* fluidity when playback control is applied and questions are sent to and received from companions; (iii) *friendliness* and *look and feel* attractiveness of the graphical user interface; (iv) the *degree of breakdown* due to (a) the lack of monitor space to layout all the GUIs and (b) the frequent pop-ups of the answer and the voting dialogs. The analysis of the statistics (see Table 2) resulting from the filled-out questionnaires aimed at extracting qualitative usability information. Results of the analysis carried out show that when the interaction among the users increases and the users' control actions are more frequent, the users shift their attention from the playback session to the interaction with the dialogs, e.g., the

Table 2:   The questionnaire results

point grades: {1..5}	Media Quality			Interactivity		GUI		GUI Drawbacks		
	Video	Audio	Lip Sync	Playback Control	User Questioning	Friendliness	Look & Feel	GUIs Layout	Answer Dialog Pop-ups	Voting Dialog Pop-ups
1st Group (mean values)	3.7	4.2	4.0	3.8	3.8	4.0	4.3	4.0	4.0	4.1
2nd Group (mean values)	3.3	4.0	4.0	3.5	3.7	4.1	4.2	4.1	4.2	4.4
3rd Group (mean values)	3.4	3.9	3.9	3.2	3.6	4.1	4.2	4.1	4.3	4.3
averages	3.5	4.0	4.0	3.5	3.7	4.1	4.2	4.1	4.2	4.3

answer dialog (Figure 10) and the voting dialog (Figure 11), which suddenly and frequently appear on the monitor. In a certain sense, the users feel overwhelmed by too many visualizations and interactions.

Thus, new mechanisms (selective filters and time-outs) are being introduced in ViCRO^C (and should be also introduced in any CPS) which aim at limiting too frequent and undesired interactions, so improving usability. Selective filters block questions sent from "too active" users so as to allow limiting the number of answer dialog pop-ups. Limiting users' control actions is not so easy and the filter-based strategy can be anyway exploited, but the only significant result would be a lot of voting processes terminated unsuccessfully. The mechanism proposed centers on time-outs which temporary inhibit the control activity of a user who performed a control action.

FUTURE TRENDS

MBone-based CPS environments can greatly benefit from advances of the Internet technology in the direction of bandwidth availability, quality of service guarantee and worldwide multicast exploitation. Thus usability from a network point of view can increase. Appealing research opportunities are geared at (i) coupling a virtual-reality-based environment with a CPS so as to deliver a collaborative distributed virtual environment and (ii) creating personal and lightweight interfaces to CPSs so as to allow a client using a handheld (or personal digital assistant) or a 3G mobile phone to get in a cooperative playback session.

Virtual cooperative playback systems (VCPSs) are virtual learning spaces (Ferscha & Johnson, 1999; Georganas, Petriu, Cordea, & Ionescu, 1999) where student avatars (virtual alter egos of students) meet and plan to organize or join a cooperative playback session. A VCPS is accessible and exploitable through a dynamic virtual world (e.g., VRML-based) which mimes a multimedia-equipped classroom where a user can enter in and wait for the others in order to start a cooperative playback session. Virtual reality features merged to multimedia can improve sense of presence and deliver a more appealing virtual collaboration environment.

Cooperative playback systems can be also deployed in mobile environments where users have mobile appliances such as personal digital assistants (PDA) and UMTS phones. The two main issues are: an efficient streaming architecture and lightweight GUIs. New streaming architectures (Dutta & Schulzrinne, 2001) for mobile and ubiquitous networking are being proposed within the Next Generation Internet (NGI) framework. A careful design of flexible and lightweight GUIs for PDAs and 3G phones is required in order to make mobile cooperative playback sessions really exploitable.

CONCLUSIONS

Collaborative learning on-demand (CLoD) is an original learning methodology presented in this chapter which enables a group of students to jointly work on and share a playback session. Cooperative playback systems (CPSs) are multimedia networked infrastructures which support CLoD by delivering cooperative playback sessions. Goals, functionality, interaction levels and communication patterns of CPSs have been described. ViCRO^C, a cooperative playback system developed in the Department of Electronics, Informatics and System Science at the University of Calabria, has been proposed as a case study. In addition a comparison between ViCRO^C and other CPS-like systems has been presented. The comparison shows that only ViCRO^C currently is a true CPS and has the capability to deliver usable cooperative playback sessions. Usability of CPSs is investigated. General and peculiar factors which make a CPS more or less usable and effectively exploitable have been identified. General factors belong to all the computer-based, multimedia networked environments and involve network (e.g., bandwidth and reliability), hardware (e.g., sound) and audio/video quality. CPS peculiar factors encompass easiness to form a group and use the GUI for productive cooperative work. In particular, the usability of ViCRO^C has been investigated on the basis of some differentiated group tests. Media quality was considered good and the GUI easy to use. However, under conditions of high frequency of interactions (questions and control commands), the session participants' attention shifts from the playback to coping with the interactions, i.e., managing too many window pop-ups. Based on this experience, ViCRO^C is being upgraded for embedding selective filters, which limit undesired questions, and time-outs, which regulate control command transmissions. In addition the development of virtual CPSs and mobile CPSs, as outlined in the *Future Trends* section, can offer new opportunities to further exploit the collaborative learning on-demand paradigm.

REFERENCES

Almeroth, K.C., & Ammar, M.H. (1998). The Interactive Multimedia Jukebox (IMJ): A new paradigm for the on-demand delivery of audio/video. *Proceedings of the Seventh International World Wide Web Conference*, Brisbane, Australia, (14-18 April, 1998). Also appeared in Computer Networks and ISDN Systems, 30(1-7), 431-441.

Cohen, E. (1994). Restructuring the classroom: Conditions for productive small groups. *Review of Educational Research*, 64(1), 1-35.

Costantini, F., & Toinard, C. (2001). Collaborative learning with the distributed building site metaphor. *IEEE Multimedia*, 8(3), 21-29.

Crowcroft, J., Handley, M., & Wakeman, I. (1999). *Internetworking Multimedia*. San Francisco, CA: Morgan Kaufmann.

Deering, S. (1989). *Host Extensions for IP Multicasting.* Request for Comments, No. 1112, Internet Engineering Task Force. Available at the World Wide Web: http://www.ietf.org/rfc.html

Dutta, A., & Schulzrinne, H. (2001). *A streaming architecture for next generation Internet.* Conference Record of the International Conference on Communications (ICC), Helsinki (Finland). June 11-14.

Ferscha, A., & Johnson, J. (1999, October). Distributed interaction in virtual spaces. *Proceedings of the IEEE Workshop on Distributed Interactive Simulation and Real-Time (DiS-RT'99)* (pp. 5-13) GreenBelt, MD.

Floyd, S., Jacobson, V., McCanne, S., Liu, C., & Zhang, L. (1997). A reliable multicast framework for light-weight sessions and application level framing. *IEEE/ACM Transactions on Networking,* 5(6), 784-803.

Fortino, G. (1997). *Java Multimedia Studio* (Report No. TR-97-043). Berkeley, CA: International Computer Science Institute.

Fortino, G., & Nigro, L. (2000a). ViCRO: An interactive and cooperative videorecording on demand system over Internet MBone. *Informatica—An Int. Journal of Computing and Informatics,* 24(1), 97-105.

Fortino, G., & Nigro, L. (2000b, August). A cooperative playback system for on-demand multimedia sessions over Internet. *Proceedings of the IEEE Conference on Multimedia and Expo,* (pp. 41-44) New York.

Fortino, G., Nigro, L., & Pupo, F. (2001). An MBone-based on-demand system for cooperative off-line learning. Proceedings of the Euromicro Conference (Workshop on Multimedia and Telecommunications), (September 4-6, pp. 336-344) Warsaw, Poland.

Georganas, N.D., Petriu, E.M., Cordea, M., & Ionescu, D. (1999, May). Distributed virtual environments for training and telecollaboration. *Proceedings of the 16th IEEE Instrumentation and Measurement Technology Conference (IMTC),* (Vol. 3, pp. 1847-1850) Venice, Italy.

Handley, M., & Jacobson, V. (1998). SDP: Session Description Protocol. Request for Comments, No. 2327, Internet Engineering Task Force, Apr. Available at the World Wide Web: http://www.ietf.org/rfc.html

Holfelder, W. (1997). Interactive remote recording and playback of multicast videoconferences. *Proceedings of Interactive Distributed Multimedia Systems and Telecommunication Services (IDMS'97),* Darmstadt, LNCS 1309, (September, pp. 450-463) Springer Verlag, Berlin.

IMS (Instruction Management System). (2002). *Global Learning Consortium.* Documentation at the World Wide Web: http://www.imsproject.org/ Retrieved on Oct. 2002.

Jacobson, V. (1994). Multimedia Conferencing on the Internet. Tutorial 4, presented at ACM SIGCOMM'94. University College London, London, August.

JMF (Java Media Framework). (2002). *Documentation and software at the World Wide Web:* http://java.sun.com/products/java-media/jmf/ Retrieved on Sept. 2002.

Kumar, V. (1996). *MBone: Interactive Multimedia on the Internet.* Indianapolis, IN: New Riders Publishing.

Liao, T. (1998). *Light-weight Reliable Multicast Protocol.* Documentation and software at the World Wide Web: http://webcanal.inria.fr/lrmp/ Retrieved on Dec. 1999.

Malpani, R., & Rowe, L. (1997). Floor control for large-scale MBone seminars. *Proceedings of The Fifth Annual ACM International Multimedia Conference (ACM'97),* (November, pp. 155-163) Seattle, WA.

MASH Consortium. (2002). *Mash streaming media toolkit and distributed collaboration applications based on the Internet MBone tools and protocols.* University of Berkeley (CA). Software and documentation at the World Wide Web: http://www.openmash.org/ Retrieved on July 2002.

MBT (MBone Tools). (2002). Department of Computer Science, University College London. *Software and documentation at the World Wide Web*: http://www-mice.cs.ucl.ac.uk/multimedia/index.html Retrieved on April 2002.

MLB (Multimedia Lecture Board). (2002). Documentation and tools at World Wide Web: http://www.informatik.uni-mannheim.de/informatik/pi4/projects/mlb/ Retrieved on Sept. 2002.

Parnes, P., Synnes, K., & Schefstrom, D. (1998). *mMOD: The multicast Media-on-Demand system.* Retrieved in November 2001 from the World Wide Web: http://www.cdt.luth.se/~peppar/progs/mMOD/

Parnes, P., Synnes, K., & Schefstrom, D. (2000). *mSTAR: Enabling collaborative applications on the Internet.* IEEE Internet Computing, 4(5), 32-39.

Schulzrinne, H., Casner, S., Frederick, R., & Jacobson, V. (1996). RTP: A transport protocol for realtime applications. Request for Comments, No. 1889, Internet Engineering Task Force, January. Available at the World Wide Web: http://www.ietf.org/rfc.html

Schulzrinne, H., Rao, A., & Lanphier, R. (1998). *Real Time Streaming Protocol (RTSP).* Request for Comments, No. 2326, Internet Engineering Task Force. Available at the World Wide Web: http://www.ietf.org/rfc.html

Shirmohammadi, S., Ding, L., & Georganas, N. (2003). An approach for recording multimedia collaborative sessions: design and implementation. *Journal of Multimedia Tools and Applications,* 19(1). To appear.

Shuett, A., Raman, S., Chawathe, Y., McCanne, S., & Katz, R. (1998). A soft state protocol for accessing multimedia archives. *Proceedings of the 8th. Intl. Workshop on Network and Operating Systems Support for Digital Audio and Video (NOSSDAV '98),* (July, pp. 29-40), Cambridge, UK.

Sipusic, M.J., Pannoni, R.L., Smith, R.B., Dutra, J., Gibbons, J.F., & Sutherland, W.R. (1999). Virtual collaborative learning: A comparison between face-to-face Tutored Video Instruction (TVI) and Distributed Tutored Video Instruction (DTVI) (Report No. SMLI TR-99-72). Sun Microsystems Laboratories, Palo Alto (CA), USA.

Steinmetz, R. & Nahrstedt, K. (1995). *Multimedia: Computing, Communications and Applications*. Upper Saddle River, NJ: Prentice Hall.

Synnes, K., Soderstrom, T., & Parnes, P. (2001). Learning in Desktop Video-conferencing Environments. *Proceedings of World Conference on WWW and Internet (WebNet'01),* Orlando, FL.

Veerman, A., & Veldhuis-Diermanse, E. (2001). Collaborative learning through computer-mediated communications in academic education. *Proceedings of the 1st European International Conference on Coputer-Supported Collaborative Learning (Euro-CSCL'01),* (March) Maastricht, The Netherlands.

Chapter IV

Improving Usability of an Online Learning System by Means of Multimedia, Collaboration and Adaptation Resources

Elizabeth Furtado
Universidade de Fortaleza, Brazil

João José Vasco Furtado
Universidade de Fortaleza, Brazil

Fernando Lincoln Mattos
Universidade de Fortaleza, Brazil

Jean Vanderdonckt
Université Catholique de Louvain, Belgium

ABSTRACT

This paper describes an adaptive and collaborative environment for helping problem solving. The main user of the environment is a teacher, here called teacher-student, who accesses the environment aiming at solving difficulties he/ she encounters in the classroom. In order to improve the usability of the system during the problem-solving process, the environment provides the teacher-student with adaptive assistance by identifying what information should be provided and how it should be shown on the screen according to characteristics of the teacher-student, domain and context of use. Moreover, the teacher-student has a collaborative support that allows him/her to interact with other teacher-students.

INTRODUCTION

The usability of an interactive system refers to how easy it is to use and learn the system. In online learning system contexts, the pedagogic usability is also related to how easy and effective it is for a student to learn something using the system. An attempt to ensure usability is to take into account characteristics of the user (such as preferences, language, culture and system experience) and of the context of use (such as easy accessibility and good luminosity of the environment) during the development of a system. This allows the adaptation of the interfaces to the user's needs, varying, for instance, the kind of assistance that is to be offered to the user and the way it is to be shown in order to cope with individual differences. Adaptability improves handling and learning of the interface (Benyon, Crerar, & Wilkinson, 2001). Another way to ensure pedagogic usability is to make it possible for the user to reflect about his/her difficulties on his/her own and with others. Several educational theories claim that learning depends on the individual's knowledge being built by social interactions (Bourne, McMaster, Rieger, & Campbel, 1997; Vygotsky, 1984). We have identified some problems to a successful deployment of online learning:

- Lack of learning quality—Many online learning systems don't bring users to reflect about their problems since they simply present predefined solutions.
- Lack of adaptive tools and guidelines—Learning tools are very useful, but most are not adaptive (Schön, 1987) or else the user model is predefined (Gomes & Viccari, 1999). In addition, user interfaces (UIs) of such tools are generally specified without taking into account guidelines (Eleuterio & Eberspacher, 1999).
- Lack of training in new technologies—Any teacher (our teacher-student), as part of his/her professional development, needs continuous training. Teachers' training is often carried out by using old technologies that cannot deal with adaptive and collaborative processes. It is necessary to fulfill these needs by adopting an integrated pedagogical-technological content (Perrenoud, 2001).

All of these issues have a critical impact on the usability of online learning. Thus, we developed a collaborative and adaptive distance learning environment called Tele-CADI that helps a teacher-student solve his/her difficulties during classes by offering adaptive assistance. Tele-CADI aims:

- To increase the quality of learning—Tele-CADI is supposed to do this by adopting a collaborative problem-based solving strategy. The basis of this strategy is the use of case-based reasoning methods (Aamodt & Plaza, 1994).

A case is a didactic situation that represents the difficulties found by a teacher during his/her classes. Thus, a case study is used to help the teacher-student both to identify and formalize a problem he/she faces and to express a possible solution using reflective techniques. This includes both technical and practical knowledge that the teacher acquires through experience in the classroom.

- To increase the UI usability—UI plays a vital role in improving the communication between the user and the system. The UI is not a complement for the software itself, but an integral part of its contents. Because of this, increasing user interface usability is crucial to the results in the solving of problems by teachers. Tele-CADI can do this by adapting case studies, considering human factors and guidelines. Depending on the adaptation process, a case study can be shown on the screen in different ways.

The remainder of this chapter is structured as follows: in the next section, we explain the main pedagogic principles studied that help us to understand the development of the practical-reflective teacher. Then, we provide the basic concepts used in Tele-CADI with a focus on the usability issue. The Tele-CADI architecture is described in the subsequent section. Then, the process of modeling and representing case studies is described, followed by a depiction of the adaptive process of user interaction and the collaborative process. The technical aspects of Tele-CADI are shown next. Finally, we discuss future developments and summarize the main points of this chapter.

BACKGROUND

Nowadays, many online learning systems are based on the problem-solving method (Pozo, 1998). This is due to the fact that many theories show that learning must be a collaborative constructive process (Schank, 1994) to be followed through problem solving in order to develop the users' capacity for reflection (Dewey, 1959). This inspired us to build a system that provides assistance to the teacher in a collaborative situation of solution of problems. In order to do that, we have studied both the cognitive models of problem solving and the reflective process in the development of the teacher.

Among the models of problem solving (Hoc, 1996; Rasmussen, 1983), John Dewey (1959) defined that, when solving a problem, the student executes the following phases: identification of the problem to be solved, problem evaluation, decision making, execution of the actions taking part in the solution and evaluation of the solution. In a problem-solving situation, varied assistance can be offered during each phase. Such assistance can be of three types: (i) procedural, which refers to the strategies that a student can use; (ii) content-related, which refers to the information and knowledge involved; and (iii) attitudinal, which refers to strategies of the student's motivation to solve the problem.

Concerning the development of the teacher, our studies of the reflective thought and of the practical ways to express this thought (Dewey, 1959; Schön, 1987) helped us to understand the development of the practical-reflective teacher. The *practical-reflective teacher* notion refers to the professional who has competence associated to "a knowledge placed in action, which is holistic, creative, personal and constructed; a knowledge that depends, among other things, on the professional's capacity to appreciate the value of his/her decisions and the consequences of them" (Alarcão, 1996).

According to Schön, in order for a teacher to solve a problem in a practical way, he/she must first understand it very well. From the analysis and reflection of case-study characteristics, it is possible to understand a problem as well as to visualize its consequences. During the examination of a problem, the teacher-student can access a set of case studies that describe similar problem situations. These will induce him/her to ask himself/herself questions like What caused this problem? How can I prevent this problem from occurring again? and How can I break down this problem into simpler problems? When we ask ourselves questions, we integrate new information into our memory, tie old information together in new ways and correct our faulty generalizations (Schank & Cleary, 1995).

Case studies represent real and detailed situations that are interpreted and discussed by an expert. In the case studies, knowledge about a specific event is represented, as well as the theoretical knowledge of the expert who is responsible for the narrative of the situation.

Each case study represents a situation and is composed by the following features:

- Case-study name, which identifies the case study being described;
- Case-study goals, which specify the implicit intentions of the expert when he/she presents the case study;
- Case-study description, which represents a story characterizing a situation composed of problem and solution;
- Case-study orientation, where the assistance to understand the situation and to solve the problem is described; and

Figure 1:   Concepts of Tele-CADI (modified from Hix & Harston, 1993)

Quality of the User (eg., Training the user in new technologies, allowing the user to collaborate and communicate with other users)	Usability through Interaction Devices Video and microphone	Usability of the User Interface Guidelines Human Factors Adaptive User Interaction	Quality of the Learning Application Cases Ontology Scenarios
	Usability of the Computer-Based System		
Usability of the Overall On-line Learning System - TeleCADI			

- Results, which are critical reports describing the consequences of the application of the orientation.

The Tele-CADI system proposed here aims at the development of the practical-reflective teacher, taking into account the following concepts related to the usability of this system.

BASIC CONCEPTS RELATED TO USABILITY IN TELE-CADI

Many concepts studied in different areas (interaction human-computer, cognitive sciences, ergonomic, artificial intelligence and pedagogy) have been considered in order to assure Tele-CADI's usability. We have used these concepts to develop each Tele-CADI component (see Figure 1). Tele-CADI's usability is assured when its components have been built with quality and when the teacher-student's knowledge of interaction with the system has been developed. Quality of a component means the following: (i) Quality in application, which corresponds to a good specification of noninteractive information of the system. In Tele-CADI, the noninteractive information of pedagogic domain is related to the development of the practical-reflective teacher, the assistance provided, the case-study representation, etc. (ii) Usability in the user interface, which refers to a good specification of the interactive information of the system (its windows, its buttons, etc.). (iii) Quality of the interaction device, which makes possible the interaction with different media (sound, text, image) through devices as cameras, microphones and so on. The quality of the user refers to his/her ability to use new interaction devices and technologies, experience with computer-based systems and acquaintance of the domain in question.

The concepts related to usability in Tele-CADI are the following:

- Utilization of ontology to domain model, particularly, to represent case studies. The ontology notion comes from the artificial intelligence area where it is identified as the set of formal terms with one knowledge representation, since the representation completely determines what "exists" for the system (Gruber, 1993). The advantage of using this representation is that the ontology can be defined once and used as many times as necessary. When it is necessary to consider more information in models, such as in the user model, this ontology can be updated accordingly. In online adaptive learning systems, such a flexible user modeling approach is important because there is no predefined information on the users to ensure that interactive applications yield high quality of interaction to a stereotype of all users. In addition, the ontology is useful to create generic representations for case studies representing the problems that the teacher-students have faced. Moreover, as we will show in this chapter, such a representation plays a very important role when the case-study-retrieving phase is executed.

- Utilization of guidelines and human factors to assure the adaptive interaction since Tele-CADI determines which case study should be shown and how it should be shown on the screen. Human factors, such as the teachers' beliefs, and guidelines related to graphic aspects and characteristics of the user and his/her context of use are considered. Guidelines are suggestions about the ergonomic aspects of the interfaces, such as showing only the necessary information or letting the user control the system dialog (Bastien & Scapin, 1993; Bodart & Vanderdonckt, 1993). Taking into account guidelines in the interface design of a system allows the designer to determine the best way in which information is to be provided to the user during his/her interaction with the system.

- Utilization of multimedia resources to improve interaction. The approach adopted to provide a multimedia environment for an online learning tool was the use of different interaction devices to improve interaction (microphone and video camera). Our proposal to specify a multimedia supporting system derives from the great worldwide call for non-textual information. Non-textual information characterizes the systems that use different channels and codes in their interaction with the user.

- Utilization of collaboration and communication mechanisms to assure the quality of the user. Tele-CADI has a module, called TELE (Neto, Raimir, Bezerra, & Sarquis, 2000), which implements the collaborative aspect by allowing a teacher-student to share an application. In addition, Tele-CADI is integrated to another online learning system, called CadiNET (Furtado, Silva, Alves, & Távora, 2001), in order to allow the teacher-student to be trained in new technologies, mainly concerning the Web application. The CadiNET system enables a teacher-student to obtain texts, to perform online activities and to interact with others by means of a forum and chats.

DESCRIPTION OF TELE-CADI

Figure 2 depicts the architecture of Tele-CADI including five main components (Furtado, Mattos, Furtado, & Holanda, 2001):

- The assistance module, which coordinates the recovering of assistance (case studies, texts or links) that is to be presented to the teacher-student.
- The TELE module, which allows the collaboration and communication over the Web by chat and the sharing of any application, such as the scenario editor, with which the teacher-student can appreciate already existing scenarios and build new ones with others.
- The user interface (UI), which is used by the teacher-student to interact with the environment.

Figure 2:   Tele-CADI architecture

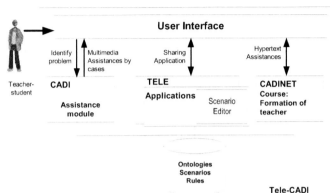

- CadiNET, which offers administrative support to the courses and hypertext assistance to show texts and links.
- Knowledge base, which gives support to the greatest part of the problem-solving process through models (such as the user model and the case-study model) and rules which express the teacher's beliefs.

The cooperation between the main components is the following: The teacher-student requests the analysis of a case study that expresses his/her problem. During this analysis, the UI component provides the teacher-student with some assistance. The teacher-student is provided with case studies retrieved from the knowledge base by the assistance module. The case studies are shown in different ways. If the teacher-student wants to communicate with other teacher-students who have gone through similar problem case-studies and create a scenario together as a possible solution for the identified problem, the UI component calls the TELE module. If the teacher-student wants to read some text, suggested by the assistance module, the UI component calls the CadiNET module. The teacher-student solution is validated by a pedagogic specialist before being effectively stored and made available to others.

In the next section, we will describe the ontology and the tools used by the expert teacher to define and represent the different models stored in the knowledge base. These models are mainly built through two editors: the ontology editor and the scenario editor.

MODELING AND REPRESENTING CASE STUDIES

The ontology is explicitly structured into three separate levels: metamodel, model, and instance. Each level can be considered as a different abstraction level as represented in Figure 3.

Figure 3:   The different levels of the ontology (adapted from Furtado, Futado, et al., 2001)

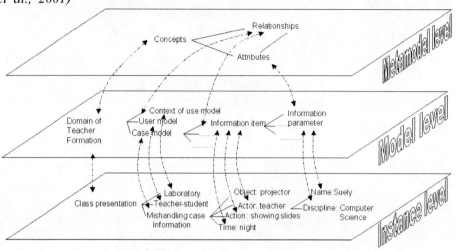

The domain basic concepts are defined in the model level from the instantiation of more general concepts defined in the metamodel level. In the instance level, the concepts related to a specific situation are defined. The example in Figure 3 shows a way to model a situation involving a teacher presentation during a class. The teacher, named Suely, mishandles a projector during a computer science night class. In the model level, concepts about the teacher-student domain are modeled while in the meta-model, we can make the modeling of the basic and general concepts related to any domain as relations, attributes, entities, and so on.

For the simplicity of this paper, we focus on describing the ontology of the case-study model, but the ontology editor is also used to describe the ontology of the user model in order to describe the user's characteristics.

To create the case-study model, the expert teacher models (or defines) the structure of the case study, then instantiates it. During the modelling process of a case study, he defines the information item and its information parameters. We have already predefined some attributes of the case-study model, e.g., a case study representing a problem (called problem case-study) is composed of scenes. One scene represents one specific situation occurring within this generic problematic situation. Modelling a scene, the expert can define the following information items: actor (student, teacher), actions (saying, showing, complaining), objects (table, projector, slides) and environment (place, time, lighting condition). He also defines the information parameters of the *teacher* actor participating in a scene, such as name, discipline and identification. During the instantiation process, the expert teacher instantiates each information item instantiating its parameters.

To facilitate the instantiation and modelling process of an ontology we have built an ontology graphic editor. Figure 4 depicts how the ontology graphic editor can be used to instantiate a scene of the case study "nobody wants to write." In this scene,

Figure 4:   The instantiation of a scene of the case-study "nobody wants to write"

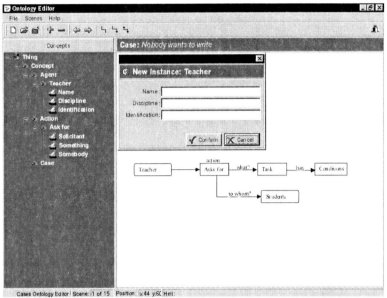

the teacher asks the students to perform a task under certain conditions. On the left side of Figure 4, information items are instantiated, with the parameters of the scene being specified on the right side. In addition, multimedia files, generated by the graphic scenario editor, can be associated with a scene. The graphic nature of the editor improves the legibility and the communicability of information, while information that cannot be represented graphically is maintained in text properties. In the pop-up window, the parameters of the *teacher* actor can be instantiated, for instance, the name of the teacher who asks the students to perform the task, his/her discipline and identification.

THE ADAPTIVE ASSISTANCE PROCESS

The assistance process is carried out by the assistance module and addresses the tasks of retrieving and showing a case study.

Case-study retrieving.   The case-study retrieving is done in an adaptive way by taking into account the ontology and the beliefs of the teacher-student. During the analysis of a problem case-study, the assistance module tries to retrieve similar past case studies stored in the case-study base. The search for similar case studies considers concepts represented on the ontology in order to improve the heuristic function used by the algorithm. This function computes the similarity between case studies by measuring the similarity between the case study's characteristics and those of the case studies in the database. During this computation, it navigates into the ontology in order to identify generic concepts that are common to the characteristics being compared. Thus, the similarity computation is based on the characteristic hierarchical position. For instance, if a teacher-student has a problem related to the mishandling of the blackboard and pencils during the class presentation, the assistance module can retrieve case studies related to the mishandling of a projector.

This is possible because the projector and the blackboard are represented in the ontology as being didactic equipments, then the algorithm attributes a degree of similarity to them. In addition to the use of the concepts defined in the ontology, the assistance module takes into account a set of rules representing the beliefs of the teacher-student. The assistance module instantiates the conditions of these rules with the characteristics of the problem case-study in order to deduce new characteristics of the problem case-study or to increase the relevance of the ones already detected that are associated to implicit beliefs the teacher-student may have. For example, when a teacher-student faces a problem of relationship with students during a night class, the assistance module can recover from the base of rules the following belief: "Teachers believe that students of night classes are uninterested in doing homework during the day." In that way the assistance module can retrieve past similar case studies where this belief is presented.

Case-study showing. To define how a case study must be shown, the adaptation process takes into account the characteristics of the teacher-student and of his/her context of use. After these characteristics are identified, the assistance module chooses the best view to show a case study. For instance, a view that is a combination of sound and image of a case study cannot be appropriate if the context of use of the user (a laboratory, for instance) is very noisy. The views are predefined according to guidelines. These guidelines allow us to determine the best way to divide a screen, to show many media at the same time, to give the user the option of hearing a story about a case study in a quick or slow way, or to repeat a story.

Figure 5 shows a view combining a graphic scenario and a textual story that corresponds to a scene of the case study "nobody wants to write." In this scene, the students complain because they do not want to perform the required task. Figure 5 depicts some buttons that express the assistance available for the teacher-student. These types of assistance are as follows:

- To see reflective questions (*reflective questions* button), which refers to some questions the teacher-student puts to himself/herself, in order to help him/her recognize the problem and reflect about it.
- To obtain specifications of concepts describing the problem case-study (*see more* button).
- To obtain didactic material (*didactic material* button), which suggests some text to be seen in CadiNET, for instance.
- To see the case-study orientation and results of the case study which he/she thinks has some similarity with his/her problem (*found my case* button). The case-study orientation and results refer to a procedural strategy that can help the teacher-student decide what to do, taking into account what other people did

Figure 5: One scene of the case study "nobody wants to write"

(their solutions). It should be stressed that case-study solutions were not presented at first, since it is desirable to instigate students' reasoning and creativity in finding their own solutions.

*   To obtain the list of teacher-students who are using the system and that can collaborate (*Cadi online users* button).

The collaborative assistance process will be described in the next section.

THE COLLABORATIVE ASSISTANCE PROCESS

In this process, emphasis is given to collaborative features among teacher-students through the integration of CADI with CadiNET and TELE. The CadiNET environment helps the teacher-student discover when and with whom he/she can collaborate.

TELE allows the teacher-student to have access to some functions which will, in turn, make it possible for him to establish synchronous interaction with colleagues (such as videoconferences and chats) or to share applications. This collaboration process is characterized by four sequences of operations, namely: the "access request," the "creation of a videoconference," the "entrance to work together," and the corresponding "exit from a videoconference." A practical example of the advantages of such integration is the possibility of performing a task in a collaborative fashion, with several colleagues interacting straight from home.

In the CadiNET environment, teacher-students of a given study group can book a conference to enable the performance of a task or the collaborative solution of a

Figure 6:   The agenda in CadiNet

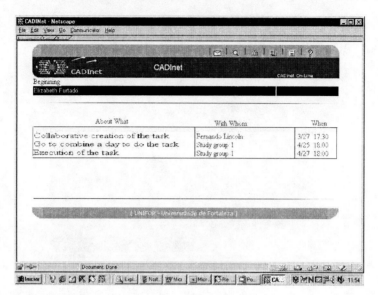

problem. The reservation is automatically included in the list of conferences, which can be seen in Figure 6.

On the day and at the time set for the conference, the students enter the environment and look for their colleagues to start the conference. This is quite a simple procedure: Press the *CadiNET online users* button and select the student, whose name appears on the pop-up window.

The system will provide the means to establish synchronous communication. When the student who was summoned answers the call he will appear on screen (Figure 7). Once they are in conference, the students will wait for the other members of the team to arrive so that the session can be actually held.

When all the members of a group are in conference, they start the work proper, using the features of the TELE environment, where they can talk among themselves (using the TELE chat), send one another new files that may be necessary (using an email), use blank areas to exchange ideas, and even open any application in order to share it.

The screen of the shared application will be shown on the computer of every student in conference, and any alteration performed by one of them will automatically reflect on the other teacher-students' screens.

In Figure 8 the scenario editor is shared. It is useful when some reflection on problems relative to the contents of the course is required, because teacher-students can, for instance, build one possible solution together. When the solution is ready, a teacher-student can send it to the expert through CadiNET.

Figure 7: At TELE, waiting for the "arrival" of the other members of the group

IMPLEMENTATION ASPECTS OF THE TELE-CADI

The environment presented here was implemented using different programming languages and technical solutions.

The ontology, scenario and rule editors were built in Borland Delphi 5.0. They access the knowledge base, whose internal representation is done by using SQL tables. The scenario editor makes it possible to construct the graphic scenarios through the GLScene component, which uses graphic objects built by the 3D Studio tool.

The case-study-based reasoning module was also implemented in Borland Delphi 5.0. The Web pages seen by the teacher-student use the Microsoft Component Object Model (COM) technology to run the reasoner. Even though the graphic case studies are shown in 3D, we intend to use the VRML programming language in order to allow the teacher-student to manipulate the 3D virtual graphic scenarios in the Web.

CadiNET is composed of approximately 100 pages programmed in Microsoft ASP and it also accesses the SQL tables that contain information on the user and the course as well as texts.

In the TELE implementation, two premises were initially established. The first one concerns the adoption of patterns established by such organisms as ITU (International Telecommunications Union) and IETF (Internet Engineering Task Force); and the second one refers to the needs in adopting the Internet-based environment as basic infrastructure. We used some ActiveX controls of Microsoft NetMeeting. The interface was worked through the use of a group of parameters that

Figure 8:   The scenario editor

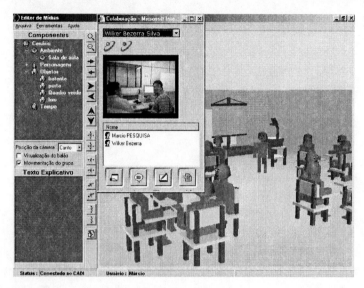

control the objects that will be presented in the user interface. Among the different patterns that NetMeeting supports are the following: ITU H.323 for audio conference and video, ITU T.120 for multi-point conference of access for data, and IETF LDAP for directory services.

FUTURE WORK

The multidisciplinary dimension of this work is characterized by the studies done in divers areas of knowledge, from human-computer interaction and artificial intelligence to pedagogy.

Distance learning adheres to a vision where online learning applications are developed for the widest population of users in the most varied contexts of use by taking into account individual differences. One way to assure universal access to distance learning is to develop learning applications with adaptive user interfaces. These interfaces, able to *adapt* themselves to the user and contexts of use characteristics, are called user interfaces for all. Existing design methods do not necessarily support designing such user interfaces. New design methods have been proposed since then.

Even though we have not yet implemented a method for designing such user interfaces, we have described one method based on an ontology structured into the three levels defined here (Figure 3). The main goal of this method relies on its ability to exploit instantiations captured in individual models to produce multiple UIs, possibly for different computing platforms, development environments or programming languages. The major advantage of the method is that change operated at any level is instantly propagated to subsequent levels: When the ontology changes, all possible models change accordingly; when a model changes, all possible specifications change accordingly and so the set of all possible UIs that can be created.

A relatively new field being studied in artificial intelligence and business is the learning organization (LO). LOs are organizations that are constantly expanding their capacity to create and re-create their respective futures. Such organizations, also named "knowledge-creating" companies, will therefore be those that systematically create new knowledge, disseminate it throughout the entire organization, quickly incorporate it into new technologies and products, and provide a means to store it, thus insuring against loss.

We are integrating the Tele-CADI environment in a computational architecture called MC2 (Furtado & Colera, 2000) that brings together a set of tools that support the process of the learning organization by allowing the creation and maintenance of organizational memory. MC2 has a *participative space*, which makes computerized procedures available that seek to contribute to the development of better relationships between the people and sections of an organization. Tele-CADI has important features for achieving this goal because it provides tools to improve individual learning within an organization by collaboration during problem solving.

Not only can Tele-CADI be used with MC2 to improve the creation and maintenance of an organizational memory, but also to open the possibility of creating a corporate universe. In doing this, it is possible to reach the employee through the Internet in order to motivate him/her to improve his/her knowledge in interesting subjects proposed by the company.

As we have described previously in this article, the didactical approach we follow is strongly influenced by two new concepts: (i) teaching must take into account the students' goals and (ii) problem-solving methodologies are the best alternative to achieve this.

Teaching is essentially a social task that involves a very strong component of dialogue. The interaction between teacher and students becomes a fundamental element in the learning process. Moreover, the collaboration among teachers is established as a central factor in the learning process. This collaboration leads an individual to reflect about the situations he/she encounters.

However, the teacher's development is not limited to the contact with students and colleagues. It includes built-in social and historical experiences, which should also be taken into account during the processes of educational problem solving. Therefore, the teacher's knowledge does not just result from his/her educational experience, but from the wider experience gathered during his/her life.

A collaborative and adaptive teacher's development, therefore, should take into account these wider aspects of the individual. Therefore, besides case studies, Tele-CADI needs to improve its representational and inferential capacity to work with narratives that include social and historical components.

CONCLUSION

This chapter presented an environment which can be considered essential for transporting the teacher-student into a usable system for the following reasons: (i) the teacher-student can explore many kinds of multimedia facilities for the solution of problems according to guidelines and his/her own beliefs, preferences and autonomy; (ii) the teacher-student's reflection on these problems and the possible consequences of the solution he/she proposes can help him/her improve his/her classes and adopt an integrated pedagogical-technological content; and (iii) the collaborative support of assistance through case studies can help the teacher-student find a possible solution from the experiences that collaborators have had in their classes.

Our work is still at an early stage; however, the evidence encourages us to believe that the overall environment being developed has considerable possibilities. The knowledge base is based on concrete experiences, obtained from discussions with a group of 36 teachers. During these discussions, the groups debated and shared their didactic practice and the underpinning knowledge mobilized in this practice. These discussions helped us to discover 25 teachers' beliefs and 80 case studies. In the whole process, the method of problem solving guided us, but we were very privileged by the cooperation we received from the group. At this point, we are searching for solutions that fit the new educational paradigm we believe is evolving at the present time.

ACKNOWLEDGMENT

We wish to thank Cnpq and Unifor, who have sponsored this project, and extend a special thanks to our team, who have supported us in this effort with so much competence that we have come to think of them as a real research group. Our deepest thanks go to: Leandro da Silva Taddeo, Daniel William T. Rodrigues, Wilker Bezerra Silva, Francisco José Alves, Felipe Távora and Márcio Maia Silva.

REFERENCES

Aamodt, A., & Plaza, E. (1994). Case-based reasoning: Foundation issues, methodological variations and system approach. *AI Com Artificial Intelligence Communications*, 7(11).

Alarcão, I. (1996). Formação reflexiva de professores—Estratégias de supervisão. Porto: Porto Editora.

Bastien, J. M. C., & Scapin, D. L. (1993). *Ergonomic criteria for the evaluation of user interfaces* (Rep. No.156). INRIA.

Benyon, D., Crerar, A., & Wilkinson, S. (2001). Individual differences and inclusive design. In C. Stephanidis (Ed.), *User interfaces for all—Concepts, methods, and tools* (pp. 21-46). Mahwah, NJ: Lawrence Erlbaum.

Bodart, F., & Vanderdonckt, J. (1993). Expressing guidelines into an ergonomical style-guide for highly interactive applications. In S. Ashlundn, K. Mullet, A. Henderson, E. L. Hollnagel, & T. White (Eds.), *Proceedings of InterCHI'93* (pp. 35-36).

Bourne, J. R., McMaster, E., Rieger, J., & Campbell, J. L. (1997). *Paradigms for online learning: A case study in the design and implementation of an asynchronous learning networks (ALN) course.* Retrieved from http://www.aln.org/alnweb/journal/issue2/assee.htm.

Dewey, J. (1959). Como pensamos. São Paulo: Companhia Editora Nacional.

Eleuterio, M., & Eberspacher, H. (1999). A knowledge management approach to virtual learning environments. In *Conference International WISE, International Workshop on Virtual Education*, Fortaleza: Demócrito Rocha Editora, (pp. 55-61).

Furtado, E., Furtado, V., Bezerra, W., William, D., Taddeo, L., Limbourg, Q., & Vanderdonckt, J. (2001). An ontology-based method for universal design of user interfaces. *Proceedings of Workshop on Multiple User Interfaces over the Internet: Engineering and Applications Trends.* Retrieved from http://www.cs.concordia.ca/%7Efaculty/seffah/ihm2001/program.html.

Furtado, E., Mattos, F. L., Furtado, J. J. V., & Holanda, R. (2001). Um sistema de aprendizagem colaborativa de didática utilizando cenários. *Brazilian Review of Learning Systems, 8*, April (pp. 52-61), Santa Catarina.

Furtado, E., Silva, W., Alves, J. J., & Távora, F. (2001, August). Um ambiente de ensino e colaboração a distância para formação e atualização de professores da unifor. Congresso Internacional sobre Educação a distância. Retrieved from http://www.abed.org.br/trabalhos.

Furtado, J. J. V., & Colera, C. (2000). Integrating information systems and knowledge engineering to improve learning organization. *Americas Conference on Information Systems, AMCIS 2000, Long Beach*, (pp. 84-93).

Gomes, F., & Viccari, R. (1999). Uso de Heurísticas no projeto de interfaces inteligentes. In *International Congress WISE, International Workshop on Virtual Education,* Fortaleza: Demócrito Rocha Editora, (pp. 103-109).

Gruber, T. R. (1993). Toward principles for the design of ontologies used for knowledge sharing (Tech. Rep. No. KSL-93-04). Stanford, CA: Stanford University, Knowledge Systems Laboratory.

Hix, D., & Hartson, R. (1993). *Developing User Interfaces*. New York: John Wiley & Sons.

Hoc, J. M. (1996). Supervision et contrôle de processus , La cognition en situation dynamique. Sciences et Tecnhologies de la Connaissance. France: Presses universitaires de Grenoble.

Neto, H., Raimir, H., Bezerra, W., & Sarquis, O. (2000). Especificando o tele-ambiente no contexto da educação a distância, *Anais do SBIE'2000, Simpósio Brasileiro de Informática Educativa.* Alagoas: Universidade Federal de Alagoas Editora, (pp. 120-132).

Perrenoud, P. (2001). Formando professores profissionais: quais estratégias? quais competências? Porto Alegre: Artmed.

Pozo, J. (1998). A solução de problemas. Porto Alegre: Artes Médicas.

Rasmussen, J. (1983). Skills, rules, knowledge: Signals, signs, symbols and other distinctions in human performance models. *IEEE Transactions on Systems, Man, and Cybernetics*, *SMC-13*(3), (pp. 257-266).

Schank, R. (1994). Dynamic memory: A theory of learning in computers and people. Cambridge, England: Cambridge University Press.

Schank, R., & Cleary, C. (1995). *Engines for education*. USA: Paperback.

Schön, D. (1987). *Educating the reflective practitioner*. New York: Jossey-Bass.

Vygotsky, L. S. (1984). A formação social da mente. São Paulo: Martins Fontes.

Section II:

Methods, Pedagogy and Theories

Chapter V

Heuristic Evaluation of Web-Based ODL Programs

Athanasis Karoulis
Aristotle University of Thessaloniki, Greece

Andreas Pombortsis
Aristotle University of Thessaloniki, Greece

ABSTRACT

In this chapter we describe the evaluation of Web-based open and distance learning programs in a more technical manner. First of all we discuss some general theoretical issues that are of importance regarding Web-based ODL environments, such as the communication channel between the participating entities, the issue of learnability and the overall evaluation of such an environment. Then we introduce the principles of educational evaluation, of interface evaluation in general and of expert-based approaches in particular, and we compare the empirical and expert-based methodologies. Finally we present the heuristic evaluation, in its initial form as well as in its Web-adapted variation. The main objectives of the chapter are to prove the applicability of the method in the Web in general and in ODL environments in particular and to investigate the appropriate heuristic list, which can assess the usability and the learnability of such an environment.

INTRODUCTION

The rapid establishment of third-generation distance learning environments, the so-called Web-based or tele-teaching environments, brought some problems with it. The main means for the delivery of the new educational approach is the World Wide Web, and there are some good reasons for it: It is easily accessible by many groups of learners. It supports multiple representations of educational material and various ways of storing and structuring this information. It is powerful and easy to use as a publishing medium. Additionally, it has been widely accepted that the hypermedial structure of the Web can support learning. Some researchers characterize the Web as an active learning environment that supports creativity. In addition to this, the Web encourages exploration of knowledge and browsing, behaviours that are strongly related to learning. The associative organisation of information in the Web is similar to that of human memory, and the process of information retrieval from the Web presents similarities to human cognitive activities (Tselios, Avouris, Dimitracopoulou, & Daskalaki, 2001). However, a hypermedial space, like the Web, cannot be considered, only by these features, as an effective tutoring environment. It is rather more appropriate to think of the Web as a powerful tool that can support learning, if used in an appropriate way. This is because learning is a process that depends on other features, such as learner's motivation, previous experience and learning strategies that the individual has been supported to develop, etc. Effectiveness of any educational environment cannot be considered independently of these aspects.

BACKGROUND

The theoretical foundation and the basic principles of distance learning, of open learning and of adult education are not within the scope of this chapter. In this chapter we preassume the knowledge of these principles, and we are mainly interested in examining evaluation methodologies that concern the Web-adapted form of ODL, the so-called distance learning environments of the third generation. However, in order for an inexperienced ODL reader to be able to follow the chapter, we provide the principles of ODL, in a very concise form, with very few comments:

1. An ODL environment has to provide students with spatial freedom, temporal flexibility and the possibility to "tailor" the educational shape to one's own needs. In addition, it has to be flexible enough so that every student may profit by his/her own skills and abilities, utilise his/her previously developed idiosyncratic characteristics (cognitive, social or emotional) and apply his/her previously gained experience and expertise.

2. The instructional material needs ad hoc preparation: Targets and expected results must be stated, keywords must be provided, and a review must be present at the beginning and the end of every chapter. Knowledge units must be small and concise, explanation of difficult and important parts must be

present, examples and/or case studies must exist in sufficient numbers and "parallel" material and references are needed.

3.   A tutor and some tutorial sessions are inevitable. The preparation of the sessions and the role of the tutor and the students during them is a separate chapter on its own.

4.   A communication mode must be established between tutor and students, synchronous (telephone, meetings, etc.) and asynchronous (mail, bulletin boards, etc.).

5.   Assessment of the acquired knowledge is important. The tutor can assess students' progress, yet it is more important that the student performs self-assessment exercises to gather evidence about his/her own progress.

Apart from its theoretical foundation as a research field, open and distance learning still carries its "childhood diseases": the isolation of the student and the following inactivity and loss of interest, mainly due to the aforementioned isolation and due to the prolongation of the study time as well.

Yet, we believe the roots of this problem lie with an issue that almost any researcher of the field pinpoints: The transition of the traditional class to its distant counterpart breaks the personal contact between the participating parts and leads to the isolation of the student. This isolation in its turn cuts off any remaining social interaction, apart from personal contact, between the learner and the teacher as well as between the learners themselves. However, the interaction between the members of the class has been proved to be of paramount importance in every educational environment and must not be underestimated.

Nevertheless, the assessment of the success rate of the established communication channel is one of the greatest challenges an evaluation approach has to take into consideration. The main goal a well-established communication channel has to confront is to facilitate the exchange of knowledge between the participating parts. If this goal is fulfilled, then the student has an advantage over his aim, which is "to learn"; so the notion of the "learnability" of the interface emerges here and starts to play its role.

USABILITY VS. LEARNABILITY

To define the notion of "learnability" we must firstly answer the question What makes the (instructional) content of an environment easily learned? The answer to this question defines in general the learnability of the environment. A more formal definition attempt would be the statement that it is the set of the methods, the modes and the tools of the environment which facilitate the acquisition of knowledge. This work assumes that the notion of learnability embeds de facto the notion of the communication channel; it is impossible for someone to gain knowledge if the environment lacks the means to offer it. So, an evaluation of the learnability of the environment evaluates hence the success rate of the established communication channel. Continuing on, the next question that emerges is the relation between usability and learnability and in how far one affects the other, which is a central question in this chapter. In more detail, we are interested in whether a usable environment facilitates the acquisition of knowledge or the opposite, if a less usable environment sets certain obstacles. And finally, this question transists in the question of whether one can heuristically assess the learnability of an educational environment. Heuristic evaluation, as described initially by Nielsen and Molich (1990) and subsequently by Nielsen (1992, 1993, 1994), is a well-established expert-based interface evaluation method for the evaluation of the usability of a particular interface. A set of interface experts is asked to judge the interface based on a set of a few criteria, the heuristics. However, the application of the method in the Web is very new. The first studies report a good integration with slight modifications in the heuristics, yet its application in open and distance learning environments has just begun.

What do we mean by the term "usability"? According to the ISO-9241 ("Ergonomic requirements for office work with visual display terminals") (ISO, 1998) standard, we have the following definition: *Usability of a system is its ability to function effectively and efficiently, while providing subjective satisfaction to its users.*

Usability of an interface is usually associated with five parameters (ISO, 1998; Nielsen, 1993) derived directly from this definition:

1. *Easy to learn*: The user can get work done quickly with the system.
2. *Efficient to use*: Once the user has learned the system, a high level of productivity is possible.
3. *Easy to remember*: The casual user is able to return to using the system after some period without having to learn everything all over again.
4. *Few errors*: Users do not make many errors during the use of the system, or if they do so they can easily recover them.
5. *Pleasant to use*: Users are subjectively satisfied by using the system; they like it.

Two important conceptions regarding the usability of an interface are "transparency" and "intuitiveness" (Nielsen, 1993; Preece et al., 1994). Transparency refers to the ability of the interface to fade out in the background, allowing the user to concentrate during his work on *what* he wants to do and not on *how* to do it, in our case not interfering with the learning procedure; while intuitiveness refers to its ability to guide the user through it by the use of proper metaphors and successful mapping to the real world, e.g., by providing him with the appropriate icons, correct labeling, exact phrasing, constructive feedback, etc.

What exactly is "learning"? Conceptions of learning were first described in 1979 by Säljö, who interviewed 90 people in Sweden ranging in age from 18 to 70, asking them the basic question, *What do you mean by "learning"?* The analysis of their responses led to five categories of description of learning, as follows:

1: increasing one's knowledge,
2: memorising and reproducing,
3: applying,
4: understanding, and
5: seeing something in a different way.

In 1982, Säljö claimed that there was a relationship between conceptions of learning and the approach to learning adopted by the students, and this was confirmed in Holland by Van Rossum and Schenk (1984). Then, using a different methodology, Giorgi (1986) also verified the existence of these conceptions of learning. In 1993, a longitudinal study of Open University students in the United Kingdom by Marton, Dall'Alba, and Beaty (1993) again confirmed Säljö's five conceptions and added a sixth:
6: learning as "changing as a person."

Traditionally, the contrast between deep versus surface approaches to learning is based on the learner's intention to understand or lack of such an intention. These two different approaches are expressed through a focus on the text itself, which the learner intends merely to reproduce (in the surface approach), contrasting with a focus on the underlying meaning of the text, which the learner intends to comprehend (in the deep approach). This contrast implies that memorisation, which the learner uses in order to reproduce, is by definition incompatible with understanding. But Kember (1996) cites a number of studies of Asian learners which contain evidence to the contrary. Kember and Gow (1990) identified a "narrow orientation" in students who systematically go through sections of the material to be learned, seeking to understand first and then memorise. Hess and Azuma (1991) found that understanding in Japanese schools is achieved through repetition and memorisation, memorisation being used as a technique to understand. Marton et al. (1993) similarly found memorisation used as a strategy to reach or enhance understanding. In terms of a chronological relationship between the two processes, this means that two patterns are found: understanding, then memorisation (Kember & Gow, 1990), memorisation, then understanding (Hess & Azuma, 1991) and both (Marton et al., 1993).

What is the relation between understanding and learning? Landbeck and Mugler (1994) argue that students learn with two quite distinct meanings, one to describe the acquisition and storage of knowledge (which they call Learning1 [L1]), a process which does not necessarily imply understanding, and a second which referred to coming to an understanding of the material that had been acquired (which they call Learning2 [L2]). The knowledge of level L1 normally has to be thought about before it can be understood. Once it is understood, then what students themselves call "real" learning has taken place. The progression from L1 to L2 is illustrated by one student's words: "Well, learning is something that you get into your mind that's something new to you in the first place, and you keep it there, you get to understand it and then later you come to use it. I mean it's always there; it doesn't go away" (Landbeck & Mugler, 1994).

The variable of learnability is considered in the literature as of paramount importance for ODL environments. There has been much discussion recently about the relationship between the usability of an instructional environment and its learnability, namely, the ability of the environment to transfer knowledge. This is a more complicated issue than it seems since some cognitive aspects must be considered as well, for example, the learning styles of the participants, individual student characteristics, such as age and cognitive abilities, or content and nature of the instructional material. Some studies (e.g., Squires & Preece, 1999; Tselios et al., 2001) argue that there is a very close relationship between the aforementioned notions, while others (e.g., Jones et al., 1999; Mayes, 1996) state that the augmented usability of an environment does not affect its learnability or vice versa. Duchastel (2001) prefers to completely separate the two notions in the case of ODL, claiming that the usability of online learning programs can be broken down into two distinct issues: the usability of the site and the learnability of the course content.

In this chapter we assume that usability and learnability are correlated terms and that the usability of the educational environment affects its learnability in a positive way. Squires and Preece (1996) emphasise that thinking of learning and usability as independent issues, which tends to be the usual way of considering them, leads to superficial evaluations of educational software. The design of an interface supports certain cycles of interaction which may or may not support the intended learning tasks. Especially for ODL environments, there are some other aspects that contribute to this conclusion as well, such as the time variable or the presence of novice users. Learning is a process (Duchastel, 2001) and so is instruction in the sense of manipulating the situation so as to facilitate learning. So a usable site adds to this direction, not only by becoming "transparent" to the user, allowing him to concentrate on his goal (Preece, Rogers, Sharp, Benyon, Holland & Carey, 1994; Shneiderman, 1998), but also by becoming "intuitive," supporting thus exploration and experimentation, two important features for every instructional environment (Jonassen, 1992; Laurillard, 1987). When the synergy between usability and learnability occurs, the use of the software can be thought of as "integrated," in that a seamless union develops between the use of the software and the learning process (Squires & Preece, 1996).

THE EDUCATIONAL EVALUATION

In the field of the applied evaluation approaches for educational software, Bates (1981) describes some *experimental* evaluation methods—however, the environment of these approaches is artificial, so it does not provide enough information on its real use with users—while Tergan (1998) provides some checklists to evaluate educational software, an approach that is broadly used. Yet, the ability of checklists to predict educational issues in all but a naive and superficial way has been questioned by several researchers, e.g., MacDougall and Squires (1995). They argue the checklists to be seriously flawed in principle because they do not encompass a consideration of learning issues, and more particularly they fail to take account of the widely accepted view of learning as a socio-constructivist activity, as already stated. They also cite a number of authors who identify problems which evaluators have found with the use of checklists as predictive evaluation tools to select educational software.

The evaluation methodologies applied in the field usually utilise questionnaires in the classroom; however, most questionnaires embody closed-type questions, so they lack the opportunity to clarify some other aspects that could be of interest and have an impact on the environment and on the involvement of the software on learning. Moreover, closed-type questions do not take into consideration the individual differences of the students in learning. In general, quantitative approaches to evaluate an educational environment have been strongly debated as monosemantic approaches that must be supplemented by qualitative ones, which focus on *how* and *what* the student learns.

Other studies in the research field of the evaluation of a distance learning environment are the studies of Holmberg (1977), Saba and Shearer (1994), and Garrison (1993); however, none of them deals absolutely in the field of evaluation of Web-based environments, as it is in the case of Makrakis, Retalis, Koutoumanos, and Skordalakis (1998) and Koutoumanos, Papaspyrou, Retalis, Maurer, and Skordalakis (1996). A questionnaire-based tool has also been produced as a collaboration of seven European universities; it is called EONT (Experiment in Open and Distance Learning using New Technologies) and is described in detail in Papaspyrou, Koutoumanos, Maurer, and Skordalakis (1996). These are all user-based evaluation approaches since they utilise, more or less, questionnaires that have to be answered by users.

It is easy to elicit from the aforementioned studies that there are controversial claims about what must be mainly evaluated or what has greater impact on the overall performance. In addition to this, there are certain known difficulties in the evaluation of educational environments in general, such as the difficulty to anticipate the instructional path every student will follow during the use of the software (Kordaki, Avouris, & Tselios, 2000) or the fact that such environments usually expand as they are used by the students. Nevertheless, in general, it is acclaimed to study the usability of an educational piece in relation to its educational value (Kordaki et al., 2000; Squires & Preece, 1999).

In this chapter we do not concern ourselves with the full spectrum of evaluations that must be performed. We rather focus on the usability aspects of the environment, so we are concerned mostly with the interface of the environment in a way that it is supporting the aforementioned communication channel and through it materializing transfer of knowledge, namely, the learnability of the environment.

EXPERT-BASED VS. USER-BASED INTERFACE EVALUATIONS

What exactly is "interface evaluation"? Interface evaluation of a software system is a procedure intended to identify and propose solutions for usability problems caused by the specific software design. The term "evaluation" generally refers to the process of "gathering data about the usability of a design or product by a specified group of users for a particular activity within a specified environment or work context'" (Preece et al., 1994, p. 602). The main goal of an interface evaluation is, as already stated, to discover usability problems. A usability problem may be defined as "anything that interferes with user's ability to efficiently and effectively complete tasks" (Karat, Campbell, & Fiegel, 1992, p. 399).

We distinguish two major evaluation categories: *formative* and *summative* evaluations. The former is conducted during the design and construction phase, while the latter is conducted after the product has reached the end user. The results and conclusions of the former are used mainly for bug fixing and improving the characteristics of the interface (detecting problems and shortcomings), while the results and conclusions of the latter are used to improve the interface as a whole and meet more user needs in a following upgrade.

The most applied methodologies are the expert-based and the empirical (user-based) evaluations. Expert-based evaluation is a relatively cheap and efficient formative evaluation method applied even on system prototypes or design specifications up to the almost ready-to-ship product. The main idea is to present the tasks supported by the interface to an interdisciplinary group of experts who will take the part of would-be users and try to identify possible deficiencies in the interface design.

However, according to Lewis and Rieman (1994, ch. 5, p. 1), "you can't really tell how good or bad your interface is going to be without getting people to use it." This phrase expresses the broad belief that user testing is inevitable in order to assess an interface. Why then, don't we just use empirical evaluations and continue to research other approaches as well? As we may see further on, the efficiency of these methods is strongly diminished by the required resources and by some other disadvantages they provide, while, on the other hand, expert-based approaches have meanwhile matured enough to provide a good alternative.

The first main disadvantage of the empirical studies is the personal bias of the subjects. It's important to understand that test users can't tell you everything you might like to know and that some of what they will tell you is useless. This is not done on purpose; for different reasons users often can not give any reasonable explanation for what happened or why they acted in a certain way. Psychologists have done some interesting studies on these points.

Maier (1931) had people try to solve the problem of tying together two strings that hung down from the ceiling too far apart to be grabbed at the same time. One solution was to tie some kind of weight to one of the strings, set it swinging, grab the other string, and then wait for the swinging string to come close enough to reach. It's a hard problem, and few people came up with this or any other solution. Sometimes, when people were working, Maier would "accidentally" brush against one of the strings and set it in motion. The data showed that when he did this, people were much more likely to find the solution. The point of interest for us is, what did these people say when Maier asked them how they solved the problem? They did NOT say, "When you brushed against the string that gave me the idea of making the string swing and solving the problem that way," even though Maier knew that's what really happened. So they could not and did not tell him what feature of the situation really helped them solve the problem.

On the other hand, expert-based evaluations are perhaps the most applied evaluation strategy. Why this? Because they provide a crucial advantage which makes them more affordable compared to the empirical ones: it is in general easier and cheaper to find out experts eager to perform the evaluation than users. The main idea is that experts from different cognitive domains, anyway at least one from the domain of HCI and at least one from the cognitive domain under evaluation, are asked to judge the interface, everyone from his own point of view. It is important that they are all experienced, so they can see the interface through the eyes of the user and reveal problems and deficiencies of the interface. One strong advantage of the methods is that they can be applied very early in the design cycle, even on paper mock-ups. The expert's expertise allows him to understand the functionality of the system under construction, even if he lacks the whole picture of the product. A first look at the basic characteristics would be sufficient for an expert. On the other hand, user-based evaluations can be applied only after the product has reached a certain level of completion. In this chapter we concentrate on expert-based evaluations. One of the most popular and theoretically well-defined approaches is the heuristic evaluation, which we are going to describe below.

THE HEURISTIC EVALUATION

Maybe the most frequently encountered evaluation method, of any entity, is the provision of a list of criteria relative to this entity followed by questioning in order to express peoples' opinions. These people can be users or experts in the particular domain. However, a number of problems arise from this approach.

1.   It provides all the disadvantages of the expert-based evaluations (Karat et al., 1992; Nielsen, 1994).
2.   The axes and criteria list may become very long (Lewis & Rieman, 1994). For example, the full interface usability criteria list suggested by Smith and Mosier (1986) includes 944 criteria.
3.   The evaluators' expertise plays a major role (Lewis & Rieman, 1994; Nielsen, 1993). We discuss this issue in detail later.

To handle these problems Jacob Nielsen and Rolf Molich started their research in 1988, and in 1990 they presented the "heuristic evaluation." The basic point was the reduction of the set criteria to just a few, at the same time being broadly applicable and generally agreed; simultaneously augmenting the evaluators' expertise and consequently their reliability. These "heuristic rules" or "heuristics" derived from studies, criteria lists, on-field observations and prior experience of the domain.

The core point to evaluate in the initial approach is the usability of the interface. Based on the ISO principles about usability (ISO, 1998), Nielsen (1994) stated the following heuristics, slightly modified and reorganised by us:

1. Simple and natural dialog and aesthetic and minimalistic design.
2. Visibility of the system status—provide feedback.
3. Speak the users' language: match between system and real world.
4. Minimize the users' cognitive load: recognition rather than recall.
5. Consistency and standards.
6. Flexibility and efficiency of use—provide shortcuts.
7. Support users' control and freedom.
8. Prevent errors.
9. Help users recognize, diagnose and recover from errors with constructive error messages.
10. Help and documentation.

The appropriate number of evaluators and their expertise are an issue of great importance. Research up to now (Nielsen, 1992, 1994; Nielsen & Molich, 1990) has shown:

1. *Simple or novice evaluators.* They do not perform very well. We need 15 evaluators to find out 75% of the heuristically identifiable problems. These are problems that heuristic evaluation can point out. As already mentioned and for different reasons, there are problems that are overlooked using this kind of evaluation. The research has shown that five of these simple evaluators can pinpoint only 50% of the total problems.
2. *HCI experts (regular specialists).* They perform significantly better: three to five of such evaluators can point out 75% of the heuristically identifiable problems and among them all major problems of the interface.
3. *Double experts (double specialists).* These are HCI experts with additional expertise on the subject matter, e.g., educators for educational interfaces. The research has shown that two to three of them can point out the same percentage as the HCI experts.

It is obvious that there is no great difference between experts and double experts in seeking the involvement of the latter in the evaluation. However, there is a very distinct difference between experts and simple evaluators. To point out 75% of the heuristically identifiable problems we need 15 simple evaluators, while three expert evaluators bring the same result.

The method refers mainly to traditional formative human-computer interface evaluation, yet a number of studies (Instone, 1997a; Levi & Conrad, 1996; Nielsen & Norman, 2000) have proven its easy adaptability to the evaluation of Web sites as well.

THE ODL HEURISTIC LIST QUESTION

At this point we confront the main question of this chapter, which can be expressed in a very simple way: Which are the appropriate heuristics to evaluate a Web-based ODL environment? The initial interface heuristics by Nielsen have been adapted and commented on by Instone (1997b) for their application in Web-based heuristic evaluations. Our approach here is simple: To proceed towards a heuristic evaluation of ODL environments, one needs to unfold this list, to analyze and specialise again the heuristics into certain criteria, then combine them with the established ODL criteria and the learnability heuristics, and, finally, to enfold the evolved list again in a combined ODL-heuristic list.

Let's undertake the first medial step. A study conducted by us (Karoulis & Pombortsis, 2001a) produced a modified Web-heuristic list. We argue this list to be more Web-centric and more user-centric. Its structure is slightly different than usual: It consists of 6 axes, and every axis contains three to six criteria (not presented here):

Axis 1: Visible system status and in correspondence to what the user expects.
Axis 2: Flexibility of use and structural integrity.
Axis 3: Efficiency of use.
Axis 4: User control, user-centered design and interaction.
Axis 5: Content and presentation.
Axis 6: Subjective satisfaction, communication and help.

The approach of building the list in axes containing criteria supports its application in two forms, as may be obvious. One is the compact form (only the axis) if there is a shortage of resources (time, money, etc.) or if we have very experienced evaluators available (double experts). The other one is the analytic form (all the criteria) for a more detailed evaluation of the site.

THE LEARNABILITY HEURISTIC LIST

The next step one must perform is the construction of the heuristics for learnability. A good starting point provides the socio-constructivist view of instruction. Some studies in the field (e.g., Kordaki et al., 2000) argue that an expert evaluator cannot predict the students' performance, although he can assess heuristically the learnability of the environment, however with mediocre results. The authors base their claims on the constructivist approach for open learning environments, also known sometimes as microworlds. Their study concludes by presenting a set of learnability heuristics, as follows:

a1 Does the system facilitate the active interaction of the user?

a2 Is the development of personal problem-solving strategies by the learners possible?

a3 Are tools available, corresponding to the way he/she learns and to his/her cognitive level?

a4 Are the available tools of alterable transparency, so that it is possible to express differentiations between students as well as intrinsic differentiations of every student?

a5 Does the environment afford experimentation with the acquired knowledge?

a6 Are there multiple representations and multiple solutions that students can explore?

a7 Is there adequate system feedback and progress feedback, so that the student can reconsider his/her strategies?

a8 Is there the possibility for the student to assess his/her activities on his/her own?

The authors claim that the usability heuristics do not contradict with the above stated learnability heuristics, which derive directly from the basic principles of ODL.

Squires and Preece (1999) proceed one step further: They do not make a combination but a fusion of Nielsen's heuristics with the five socio-constructivist learning criteria (credibility, complexity, ownership, collaboration and curriculum), providing thus a new list, which they claim to be a versatile tool to predictively evaluate educational pieces by their usability and simultaneous learnability. They install this approach advocating that the underlying socio-constructivist theory of nearly every contemporary educational environment is to a high degree compatible to the stated Nielsen heuristics:

1. Match between designers' and learners' mental models.
2. Ensure navigational fidelity.
3. Provide appropriate levels of learner control.
4. Prevent peripheral cognitive errors.
5. Understandable and meaningful symbolic representation.
6. Support personally significant approaches to learning.
7. Build strategies for the cognitive error recognition, diagnosis and recovery cycle.
8. Match with the curriculum.

The on-field validation of the list they propose could result in a powerful evaluation tool. Nevertheless, we think that, in the current research context on the field, a fusion of usability and learnability in a learning environment presents a rather overstated simplification and a fairly diminished evaluation framework, arguing thus to utilise a slightly longer list, yet more lucid and compatible to contemporary needs. We shall present this list later.

We conducted another study (Karoulis & Pombortsis, 2001b) following a different approach to investigate the application of the heuristic evaluation in ODL environments. As a reference for the criteria list we used the proposal of the Greek Open University (Hellenic Open University, 1998), according to open and distance learning criteria, assuming that they were in accordance with the constructivist point of view, already presented. This list has been used for the evaluation of ODL environments of the second generation, so we wanted to examine its applicability in Web-based ones. We proceeded to a reorganisation of the axes and criteria, so a new list emerged, consisting of 80 categorised criteria, which we used throughout our evaluation.

A PROPOSAL FOR A NEW LIST

We are now at the next step of our approach, the reconstruction of the list into a smaller number of axes and criteria, however more Web-adapted. In order to construct a smaller and more versatile list, one must make a compromise. Regarding the great variations of ODL environments, this list has to consist of rather generally expressed criteria, to be flexible in its adaptation to every particular ODL instance, yet it must not contain vague or equivocal heuristics or difficultly assessable ones, which may hamper the evaluators. To achieve this equilibrium is a hard task. Learning issues are complex and highly context-sensitive (Squires & Preece, 1996), so we believe that any further specialisation of the criteria in this phase would threaten their applicability. The list we propose here follows this point of view. As research proceeds, the appropriate form of the list and the correct phrasing of the criteria should improve. In addition to this, we make the assumption that the principles of ODL are well defined, that is, for example, that the student MUST experience spatial freedom and time flexibility. Obviously, due to the great variety of the existing ODL applications, this is a point for discussion. Nonetheless, to proceed here, we follow this assumption too.

We follow the approach to construct the list in the way we already proposed in 10 axes and 42 criteria. The proposal for the new list is as follows:
1.   *Content*
1.1. Self-sufficient educational module (structural integrity)?
1.2. Quantity (coverage of the subject matter)
1.3. Quality (appropriateness, style, language, up-to-date information)
1.4. Scientific value (accuracy, validity)
1.5. Clear student-centered format
1.6. Open to everybody

2.   *ODL adaptation and integration*
2.1. Matching the curriculum
2.2. Spatial freedom

2.3. Temporal flexibility
2.4. Targets, expected results, keywords, review
2.5. Small and concise units
2.6. Explanation of difficult and important parts
2.7. Examples and/or case studies
2.8. Parallel material and references

3.   *User interface*
3.1. Visibility of system status, effective navigation
3.2. Simple and natural dialogs, aesthetic and minimalist design
3.3. User control and freedom
3.4. Consistency and standards
3.5. Error prevention, good error handling and provision of help
3.6. Minimalisation of user's cognitive load, recognition rather than recall

4.   *Use of technologies*
4.1. Full usage of the system's capabilities
4.2. Proper equilibrium between old and new technologies
4.3. The technologies support the instructional environment (not self-targeted)
4.4. The technologies support the management of the environment
4.5. The technologies support the communication channel

5.   *Interactivity with the instructional material*
5.1. Navigational fidelity
5.2. Multimedia components
5.3. Multiple kinds of exercises
5.4. Adaptable environment
5.5. Facilitation of the active interaction
5.6. Support for collaborative work and group dynamics

6.   *Students' support*
6.1. Guidance and encouragement of the student from the instructional material
6.2. Guidance and encouragement of the student from the communication channels
6.3. Accessibility to the supporting elements (tutor, instructional organisation, etc.)
6.4. Assessment of the inactivity feeling

7.   *Communication channel*
7.1. Tutorial sessions (presence and efficiency)
7.2. Tutor (presence and efficiency)
7.3. Synchronous communication channel
7.4. Asynchronous communication channel
7.5. Assessment of the feeling of isolation

8.   *Acquisition of knowledge*
8.1.   Ease of access and understandability of the instructional material
8.2.   Support of personally significant approaches to learning
8.3.   Tools corresponding to cognitive styles and to cognitive levels of the students
8.4.   Does the environment afford experimentation with the acquired knowledge?
8.5.   Multiple representations and multiple strategies that students can explore

9.   *Projects and "learning by doing"*
9.1.   Summarizing exercises
9.2.   Extension activities
9.3.   Exploratory learning (e.g., simulations)
9.4.   Learning through action (e.g., constructions)

10.   *Assessment and self-assessment*
10.1. External assessment exercises and/or examinations (quantity and quality)
10.2. Self-assessment exercises
10.3. Instant-assessment exercises (multiple-choice, yes/no, etc.)
10.4. System feedback on students' progress

Concerning the way the criteria must be applied, we propose the following approach: The evaluator has to ask him/herself if the particular criterion (a) is present at all and if it is, then (b) to what grade it is fulfilled. The assessment can be recorded either in a Likert scale or an open-ended questionnaire, where he/she could note his/her opinion. Below is an example:
1.   *Communication channel*
1.1.   Tutorial sessions (presence and efficiency)
        Yes, there are tutorial sessions; however, only two sessions take place during the semester and their organisation is mediocre. The student doesn't profit from them.
1.2.   Tutor (presence and efficiency)
        No, there is not a tutor at all. However, in the particular context of the course, he is not necessary.

We would like to make some more comments on this list. Firstly, we believe that one issue of paramount importance in ODL is the form of the communication channel, as already mentioned, so there is an axis-heuristic on this topic. Also, the heuristics of the interface assessment by Nielsen are incorporated in a more concise form as Heuristic 3: interaction with the student, so there is no more need to perform a double evaluation, one for the interface and one for the ODL environment. Obviously, this approach means that it is no longer about an interface evaluation, but more about an educational environment evaluation.

Secondly, the greatest threat for an ODL student is the feelings of isolation and the consequent inactivity, which leads in many cases to the suspension of the study (HOU, 1998), as already stated, so we consider them as separate criteria in our list.

We are now finally able to reduce this list to a set of heuristics, with some explanations on every one. Let us emphasise at this point that we do not give extended explanations, and we do not provide guidance on how they could be applied. There are two good reasons for it: On one hand, these are "heuristic rules," which derive from prior experience, studies and reports of researchers in the field, so they must be applied as such. On the other hand, ODL environments provide such a great variety in form and shape, as already often stated, that any attempt to specialise these heuristics would lead to misinterpretations. So, this list is expressed in rather broad terms to provide a wide scope, and there is not any advice on how they could be applied in order for them to be flexible.

The proposed final heuristic list for usability/learnability expert-based evaluation of Web-based ODL environments:

1. *Content:* Is the quantity, quality and value of the content acceptable? Can one characterize it as "student centered" and "open"?
2. *ODL adaptation and integration:* Does the program provide spatial freedom and temporal flexibility? Are the principles of ODL concerned?
3. *User interface*: Are Nielsen's usability heuristics concerned?
4. *Use of technologies*: Does the environment make full use of the potential of the underlying system without hampering the students' performance in any way?
5. *Interactivity with the instructional material:* Are there navigational fidelity and correct multimedia elements? Is the environment adaptable, and does it support collaborative work?
6. *Students' support:* Is there guidance and support of any kind for the student? Are the supporting elements easily accessible?
7. *Communication channel:* Is synchronous and asynchronous communication possible? Are there tutorial sessions and a tutor?
8. *Acquisition of knowledge:* Easily acquired knowledge and support of personal styles and cognitive levels. Support of authentication of the knowledge.
9. *Projects and "learning by doing":* Are there enough exercises and hands-on practice? Is exploratory learning supported?
10. *Assessment and self-assessment:* Is the student assessed according to the principles of ODL? Are there self-assessment tools?

DISCUSSION AND CONCERNS

The general impression from the literature survey we presented in this chapter and the studies we've conducted is that the method is applicable and provides some great advantages as well. These advantages are those of the heuristic evaluation in general: It is cheap, fast and easy to apply; the experts, despite the difficulty in locating them, are more easily brought together than the users; and it is very efficient, according to the problems it discovers in relation to the effort and the resources needed (Levi & Conrad, 1996; Nielsen, 1990, 1992).

However, there are some important concerns regarding the applicability of the method one has to keep in mind when working with it.

Maybe the most important concern is that the heuristic approach may sometimes not allow for usability issues that occur for specific tasks and users groups. It is also not able to identify and to take into consideration socially relevant issues (Hess & Azuma, 1991), such as the individual characteristics of ODL students, financial categorisation, minorities and cultural differentiations, or the well-known problem of the harmonisation of the ODL class, due to the observed student diversity. These issues could lead the evaluation of the usability and the learnability of the system to the edge, in the sense that any opinion of an evaluator could be rejected by an opposing statement of a second one; the paradox being in this case that both are right. This problem occurs in empirical evaluations as well; we presented it briefly as we mentioned the antagonistic studies published up to now on the domain. So, it is obvious that one has to make an assumption on the harmonisation of the ODL class—a common profile of the students, which however has to be broad and flexible more than usual—to enclose as many of the characteristics of the "common ODL student" as possible, even if some researchers advocate that "the common user" doesn't exist.

Locating the appropriate evaluators proved to be very difficult. HCI specialists are very rare, compared to other specialists, and geographically dispersed, a fact that is also true for the ODL experts. This fact eliminated one strong advantage of the expert-based approaches, namely, the obtaining of easily located experts. A tentative approach we propose here is to split the heuristics. HCI experts should perform the usability part of the evaluation, ODL experts should evaluate the learnability issues, and only in the case where one can afford real double experts is it advised to utilise the complete proposed list. Obviously, in the case where one uses simple experts, it is wiser to use the unfolded form of the list, in order to obtain more accurate results.

The issue of the impact of usability on learnability seems to us to be clarified: Concerning ODL environments, there is a clear impact, which could contribute to some undesired side effects as well. Tselios et al. (2001) argue that contemporary computer environments are less neutral, since they inevitably seem to play a significant role in the educational process. Educators and developers of software tools, especially those with high degree of complexity, should therefore be concerned about determining this role and develop adequate techniques for diminishing any negative influence of the tool on the educational process. They suggest that techniques that permit design of software tools with these characteristics should also be defined. This objective becomes more difficult in cases when the task and context of use of the software are far more complex, as it is often in the case of integrated ODL environments.

Another question that remains unanswered and concerns the learnability of the environment is whether the experts are really able to predict the problems experienced by the learners, regarding the cognitive domain of the environment. According to Dimitrova, Sharp, and Wilson (2001), these problems are categorised as *learning support* problems, *comprehension* problems and *missed interactions*. *Learning support* problems deal with how much explanation of the material the students required. The *comprehension* problem category describes which parts of the material the students had problems understanding, while finally *missed interactions* are situations where the students did not perform an interaction which is considered important for achieving their learning tasks.

Another ambiguous point concerns the combination of the heuristic approach with other methods. MacQuaid and Bishop (2001) found that solely applying the heuristic approach could provide some limitations, such as a lack in addressing how much it will cost the developers to fix the problems, or that it does not adequately capture the distinction between high-level (global) and low-level (specific, screen-level) problems. However, combining heuristic evaluation with other methods provided significantly better results. We also suggest the combination of more than one method, preferably an expert-based and a user-based (empirical) approach. However, the combination of heuristic evaluation with other methods to assess Web sites have not yet been examined enough.

FUTURE TRENDS

Concerning the delivery of information over the Web and the collaboration of many people over a network, socially relevant issues arise as well, such as the preservation of privacy (Bellotti & Sellen, 1993). Information technology can store, transmit and manipulate vast quantities and varieties of information. ODL environments are extremely prone to intrusions due to their structure, and a clear way to be protected against intrusions has not yet been found. Future research about evaluation methodologies in a holistic manner should take this point of concern into consideration as well.

CONCLUSION

We claim that expert-based methodologies in general and the heuristic evaluation in particular can be successfully applied in the evaluation of Web-based open and distance learning environments. Generally, many problems of the site under evaluation can be discovered, and the general impression is that, with the results of the heuristic evaluation, one could propose many concrete improvements to the site under consideration, which finally is the aim of every evaluation.

Levi and Conrad (1996) argue that the final assessment of every system must be made according to its usability. Myers and Rosson (1992) calculated that 48% of the total code of every software concerns the interface; Avouris (2000) augments this number to 70% while Myers (1992) claims that in many cases the interface is the system itself. We don't entirely agree with this position: We rather believe that the heuristic methodology provides a powerful tool to evaluate the usability and the learnability of a particular interface; however, in the case of complex environments, like ODL environments, it must be combined with on-field evaluations. There is, more or less, a coincidence of the researchers on the field over this issue (Kordaki et al., 2000; Lewis & Rieman, 1994; Preece et al., 1994; Squires & Preece, 1999). So, we consider the heuristic approach as a powerful tool for the formative evaluation of the first design stages of the environment; however, as the system matures, it should fade out in favor of more user-centered approaches, which can provide an in-depth analysis of the system's usability and learnability. Yet, one must be aware of the constraints of the empirical evaluations, as already discussed, and, most of all, the problem in finding *real users* to evaluate the system under *real circumstances*.

REFERENCES

Avouris, N. (2000). *Introduction to human-computer interaction*. Diavlos, Athens, Greece.

Bates, T. (1981). Towards a better research framework for evaluating the effectiveness of educational media. *British Journal of Educational Technology*, *12*(3), 215-233.

Bellotti, V., & Sellen, A. (1993, September). Design for privacy in ubiquitous computing environments. In *Proceedings of ECSCW'93, The Third European Conference on Computer Supported Cooperative Work*. Kluwer Academic, The Netherlands.

Dimitrova, M., Sharp, H., & Wilson, S. (2001). Are experts able to predict learner problems during usability evaluations? *Proceedings. of EDMEDIA 2001 conf.,* (June 25-30, pp. 419-424) Tampere, Finland. AACE, Charlottesville, VA.

Duchastel, P. (2001, September 15). *Learnability*. Preprint article retrieved from http://home.earthlink.net/~castelnet/info/learnability.htm

Garrison, D. R. (1993). Quality and access in distance education: Theoretical considerations. In D. Keegan (Ed.), *Theoretical principles of distance education* (pp. 9-21) London: Routledge.

Giorgi, A. (1986). A phenomenological analysis of descriptions of concepts of learning from a phenomenological perspective. *Publications from the Department of Education,* Gosteborgs university, Sweden, 18.

Hellenic Open University. (1998). *Open and distance learning: Institutions and functions. Vol. A.* HOU Publications, Patras, Greece.

Hess, R. D., & Azuma, M. (1991). Cultural support for schooling: Contrasts between Japan and the United States. *Educational Researcher, 20*(9), 2-8.

Holmberg, B. (1977). *Distance education: A survey and bibliography*. London: Kogan Page.

Instone, K. (1997a, October 10). *Site usability evaluation*. Retrieved from http://www.webreview.com/1997/10_10/strategists/10_10_97_1.shtml

Instone, K. (1997b, October 10). *Site usability heuristics for the Web*. Retrieved from http://www.webreview.com/1997/10_10/strategists/10_10_97_2.shtml

International Organization for Standardization. (1998). *ISO 9241: Ergonomic requirements for office work with visual display terminals (VDTs)*. Part 10, Dialogue Principles.

Jonassen, D. H. (1992). Designing hypertext for learning. In E. Scanlon, & T. O'Shea (Eds.), *New directions in educational technologies* (pp. 123-130). Berlin, New York: Springer-Verlag.

Jones, A., Scanlon, E., Tosunoglu, C., Morris, E., Ross, S., Butcher, P., & Greenberg, J. (1999). Contexts for evaluating educational software. *Interacting with Computers, 11*, 499-516.

Karat, C., Campbell, R., & Fiegel, T. (1992, May). Comparison of empirical testing and walkthrough methods in user interface evaluation. *Proceedings of ACM CHI '92*, (May 3-7, pp. 397-404) Monterey, CA: ACM.

Karoulis, A., & Pombortsis, A. (2001a, October). Heuristic evaluation of Web sites: The evaluators' expertise and the heuristic list. *Web-Net Conference*.(October 23-27) Orlando, FL. Charlottesville, VA: AACE.

Karoulis, A., & Pombortsis, A. (2001b, June). Heuristicaly evaluating distance learning Web-based environments. *EDEN 10th Anniversary Conference*. (June 10-13) Stockholm. Budapest, Hungary: EDEN.

Kember, D. (1996). The intention to both memorise and understand: Another approach to learning? *Higher Education, 31*, 341-354.

Kember, D., & Gow, L. (1990). Cultural specificity of approaches to study. *British Journal of Educational Psychology, 60*, 356-363.

Kordaki, M., Avouris, N., & Tselios, N. (2000, October). Tools and methodologies for evaluation of open learning environments. *Proceedings of 2nd Panhellenic Conference With International Participation. Information & Communication Technologies in Education* (October, pp. 371-381) University of Patras, Greece).

Koutoumanos, A., Papaspyrou, N., Retalis, S., Maurer, H., & Skordalakis, E. (1996). Towards a novel networked learning environment. In *Proceedings of World Conference of Web Society (Web Net '96)*, (pp. 267-272) San Francisco, CA: AACE.

Landbeck, R., & Mugler, F. (1994). Approaches to study and conceptions of learning of students at the University of the South Pacific: A pilot study. *Research and Development in Higher Education, 16*, 285-289.

Laurillard, D. (1987). Computers and the emancipation of students: Giving control to the learner. *Instructional Science, 16*, 3-18.

Levi, M. D., & Conrad, F. G. (1996, July/August). A heuristic evaluation of a World Wide Web prototype. *Interactions*, *3*(4), 50-61. ACM Publ. Retrieved from http://stats.bls.gov/orersrch/st/st960160.htm

Lewis, C., & Rieman, J. (1994). *Task-centered user interface design: A practical introduction.* Retrieved from ftp.cs.colorado.edu/pub/cs/distribs/HCI-Design-Book

MacDougall, A., & Squires, D. (1995). A critical examination of the checklist approach in software selection. *Journal of Educational Computing Research*, *12*(3), 263-274.

MacQuaid, H., & Bishop, D. (2001). An integrated method for evaluating interfaces. *Proceedings of Usability Professionals' Associations Conference,* (June 25-29) Las Vegas, UPA, Chicago, IL.

Maier, N. R. F. (1931). Reasoning in humans II: The solution of a problem and its appearance in consciousness. *Journal of Comparative Psychology*, *12*, 181-194, Washington, DC: APA Press.

Makrakis, V., Retalis, S., Koutoumanos, A., & Skordalakis, E. (1998). Evaluating the effectiveness of an ODL Hypermedia System and Courseware at the National Technical University of Athens: A case study. *Journal of Universal Computing Science, 4*(3), 259-272, Berlin: Spring Verlag.

Marton, F., Dall'Alba, G., & Beaty, E. (1993). Conceptions of learning. *International Journal of Educational Research, 19,* 277-300.

Mayes, T. (1996, December). Why learning is not just another kind of work. *Proceedings on Usability and Educational Software Design.* London: BCS HCI.

Myers, B. A. (1992, August). Demonstrational interfaces: A step beyond direct manipulation. *IEEE Computer*, *25*(8), 61-73, New York: IEEE.

Myers, B. A., & Rosson, M. B. (1992, May). Survey on user interface programming. *Proceedings of ACM CHI '92* (pp. 195-202).

Nielsen, J. (1990). Evaluating hypertext usability. In D. Jonassen & H. Mandl (Eds.), *Designing hypermedia for learning* (pp. 147-168). Berlin, Heidelberg: Springer-Verlag.

Nielsen, J. (1992, May). Finding usability problems through heuristic evaluation. *Proceedings of ACM CHI '92.*

Nielsen, J. (1993). *Usability engineering.* San Diego, CA: Academic Press.

Nielsen, J. (1994). Heuristic evaluation. In J. Nielsen & R. L. Mack (Eds.), *Usability inspection methods.* New York: John Wiley & Sons.

Nielsen, J., & Molich, R. (1990, April). Heuristic evaluation of user interfaces. *Proceedings of Computer-Human Interaction Conference* (pp. 249-256).

Nielsen, J., & Norman, D. (2000, February 14). *Web-site usability: Get the right answers from testing.* Retrieved from http://www.useit.com

Papaspyrou, N., Koutoumanos, A., Maurer, H., & Skordalakis, E. (1996). An experiment in ODL using new technologies. In *Proceedings of World*

Conference of Web Society (Web Net '96), San Francisco, AACE, Charlottesville, VA.

Preece, J., Rogers, Y., Sharp, H., Benyon, D., Holland, S., & Carey, T. (1994). *Human-computer interaction.* Reading, MA: Addison Wesley.

Saba, E., & Shearer, R. (1994). Verifying theoretical concepts in a dynamic model of distance education. *American Journal of Distance Education, 8*(1), 3659.

Säljö, R. (1979). *Learning in the learner's experience. 1. Some common-sense conceptions* (Rep. No. 76), Gothenburg, Sweden: University of Göteborg, Department of Education.

Shneiderman, B. (1998). *Designing the user interface*, (Third ed.) Reading, MA: Addison Wesley Publishing Co.

Smith, S. & Mosier, J. (1986). *Design guidelines for designing user interface software.* The MITRE Corp. Retrieved from ftp://ftp.cis.ohio-state.edu/pub/hci/Guidelines

Squires, D., & Preece, J. (1996). Usability and learning: Evaluating the potential of educational software. *Computers and Education, 27*(1), 15-22.

Squires, D., & Preece, J. (1999). Predicting quality in educational software: Evaluating for learning, usability, and the synergy between them. *Interacting with Computers*, 11(5), 467-483.

Tergan, S. (1998, February). Checklists for the Evaluation of Educational Software: Critical Review and Prospects. *Innovations in Education and Training International,*35(1), 9-20.

Tselios, N., Avouris, N., Dimitracopoulou, A., & Daskalaki, S. (2001). Evaluation of distance-learning environments: Impact of usability on student performance. *International Journal of Educational Telecommunications, 7*(4), 355-378.

Van Rossum, E. J., & Schenk, S. M. (1984). The relationship between learning conception, study strategy and learning outcome. *British Journal of Educational Psychology, 54,* 73-83.

Chapter VI

Coming off the Rails: Evaluation and the Design Process

Liz Marr
Manchester Metropolitan University, UK

Dave Randall
Manchester Metropolitan University, UK
Blekinge Institute of Technology, Ronneby, Sweden

William L. Mitchell
The British Council, UK

ABSTRACT

This chapter addresses methodological issues concerned with the design and creation of computer-supported collaborative learning environments. It draws on the work of a group of sociologists and computing scientists who together, and independently, have been researching the use of museum environments and artefacts as educational resources for primary-school-age children (six to 11 years old). This work has in part focussed on requirements elicitation for interactive, computer-based collaborative virtual environments (CVEs) and has included a range of techniques including interaction analysis, ethnography, conversation analysis and participative design strategies. Evaluation work carried out with children using and developing Web-based CVEs suggests that no single requirements elicitation technique is adequate in this context and participative design techniques might benefit from insights afforded by a grounded ethnographic approach. We argue that knowledge of context, awareness of educational goals and practice, and an understanding of the nuances of interactive activity are vital for the design and development of useful and useable online educational resources and that evaluation should be integrated with the design and development strategies.

INTRODUCTION

The recent enthusiasm for production of online learning environments for school-aged children raises some important issues associated with the design and development of such systems, their usefulness and usability, as well as the means by which all these processes and characteristics are evaluated. For primary-school children (K-6), in particular, the resources must not only be accessible and attractive but must offer more than a means of entertaining or keeping children occupied—they must also have "educational value." Such a feature may be identifiable through evaluation techniques, for example, by measuring learning outcomes or monitoring children's development, but approaches like this presume much about usefulness and usability and are, furthermore, grounded in the idea that online interaction is simply a re-creation or extension of human interaction.

A defining characteristic of any educational resource must be the process by which it comes into existence. Traditionally, educators have goals in mind and draw on contemporary knowledge and ideas to find ways of achieving these goals. Theories about the way in which children learn are a necessary component of this part of the process. Thus situated learning approaches (Lave & Wenger, 1991) which suggest that knowledge needs to be presented in authentic contexts and that learning requires social interaction and collaboration may prompt the development of systems which replicate the real world or components of it and allow virtual interactions to take place. Constructivist approaches (Bruner, 1986, 1990) that stress experience, context and design may, for example, result in models which allow students to build their own learning environments. However, the resources which are adopted are created within the material and physical constraints in which they are to be used. Thus, anything which cannot be easily and cheaply replicated and made readily available to those at whom it is aimed will not gain currency, and this holds true as much for online resources as for paper-based or other physical materials.

The intention in this chapter is to focus on the evaluation of production processes through an exploration of two approaches to requirements elicitation, one ethnographic and the other involving user participation. In this way we will be addressing methodological issues concerned with the design and creation of computer-supported collaborative learning environments, referring specifically to the development of interactive, computer-based collaborative virtual environments (CVEs). We draw here on work which has been carried out by a group of sociologists and computer scientists who together, and independently, have been researching the use of museum environments and artefacts as educational resources for primary-school-age children in the UK.

The choice of museum environments and artefacts in this work has been driven in part by recognition within the international museum community that the development of information society technologies (ISTs)[1] has given them renewed potential within the educational arena. In particular, they have the potential to be key content providers for learning networks, but a major obstacle to achieving this is the lack of technical and design skills in developing Web sites. However, even when these production skills are available, the resources developed by the museums may still fall short of the requirements for the education sector. The fundamental problem is the difficulty of identifying education requirements for the Web-based resources, as we discuss below. Without a means of identifying requirements, we would argue, it is impossible to identify suitable means for evaluating the effectiveness of the resources.

The work we describe draws on projects conducted in collaboration with a number of UK schools and museums with the specific intention of informing the development of online learning resources. A range of methods has been used including, for example, interaction analysis, ethnography, conversation analysis and participatory design strategies. Our findings suggest that no single requirements elicitation technique is adequate in this context and that participative design techniques might benefit from insights afforded by a grounded ethnographic approach. We will argue that knowledge of context, awareness of what we mean by educational goals and practice, and an understanding of the nuances of interactive activity are vital for the design and development of useful and useable educational resources. Further, we will suggest that usability evaluation techniques may also benefit from these insights.

BACKGROUND

For the last 10 years at least, the use of information society technologies has become increasingly significant for education policy, and this trend has spawned a range of initiatives in the development and implementation of new tools for learning environments. In the UK, the National Grid for Learning, for example, aimed to provide a mosaic of information networks based around the Internet to enable schools to share resources wherever they are located (Department for Education and Employment, 1998). The Computers in Teaching Initiative (CTI) was launched in 1989 to "maintain and advance the quality of learning and increase the effectiveness of teaching through the application of appropriate learning technologies." The 1999 UK government green paper "The Learning Age" suggests that there are positive educational outcomes of interactivity—a key feature separating computers from other media in enhanced learning. These initiatives have been accompanied by recognition that the technology can improve and extend accessibility, facilitate lifelong learning and complement flexible learning programmes. Within the European Community this has given rise to initiatives which will provide personalised access to e-learning and the development of advanced learning environments.

Other examples abound and such initiatives have been complemented by the activities of museums in the UK and elsewhere, which are repositioning themselves within the "local and national pedagogical landscape" (Hemmings, Clarke, Francis, Marr, & Randall, 2001, p. 97). That is, having a long tradition as educational and information institutions, they are not only keen to exploit the potential of new technologies to further integrate themselves as resource providers but have actively been enjoined to do so in the UK by a Department of National Heritage report, "A Common Wealth" (Anderson, 1997), and across Europe by a range of funded programmes such as Raphael. Their activities range from a simple Web presence through the development of technically supported hands-on experimentation and discovery zones to the provision of virtual environments (Archimuse, 1999).

One common denominator of these approaches is the concept of interactivity, which, to reiterate, is claimed to have positive educational outcomes in that "hands-on" involvement results in more meaningful activity and thus greater understanding than the didactic instructional model of teaching and learning. Interactivity has therefore become a buzzword in educational thinking and is closely intertwined with another well-used term, virtual reality. In line with Hughes, O'Brien, Randall, Rouncefield, and Tolmie (2000), we take the notion of the virtual to rest on the assumption that electronic technologies might enable users to interact with elements and spaces which have been engineered by technology and need not bear any relationship to our embodied experiences. The enthusiasm for such projects has resulted in a plethora of attempts to emulate the imaginative creations of cyber-punk and science fiction writers, an irony not lost on William Gibson, who, it is claimed, has publicly criticised pundits in the VR industry on these grounds!

One of our concerns here, then, is that the teaching and learning strategies inherent in the work of education are in danger of becoming peripheral to the visions engendered by the technology. Whilst interactivity through virtual environments may well have educational advantages, we argue that unless these advantages can be identified, understood and captured at the design stage, such environments may provide little more than something else to keep children occupied. Effective evaluation techniques are, of course, vital in this context.

A second and equally important concern lies in the nature of debates about teaching and learning goals. A number of themes characterise more recent contributions to the literature, including those which emphasise "communities of practice" and the notion of "situatedness," which in turn give rise to arguments about optimal contextual conditions for learning. Seely Brown, Collins, and Duguid (1989), for instance, make the point that "inauthentic" settings (the classroom) tend to lead to practices of abstraction which may result in learning failure. This breach between learning and use, which is captured by the folk categories "know what" and "know how," may well be a product of the structure and practices of our education system, and as a consequence, methods of "didactic" education supposedly assume a separation between knowing and doing, treating knowledge as an integral, self-sufficient substance, theoretically independent of the situations in which it is learned and used (Seely Brown et al.). To use a simple example, knowing the underlying workings of a combustion engine does not necessarily equip one to drive a car.

Such arguments also stress the significance of practices, of becoming full participants in appropriate communities of practice. Thus, Lave and Wenger (1991) argue that:

> *Newcomers develop a changing understanding of practice over time from improvised opportunities to participate peripherally in ongoing activities of the community. Knowledgeable skill is encompassed in the process of assuming an identity as a practitioner, of becoming a full participant, an old-timer. (p. 68)*

In other words, under normal circumstances, the longer one is involved as a participant, the more expert a player one becomes.

This would suggest that the educational value of technologies such as virtual environments lies in the need to present "authentic" settings which allow users to participate as practitioners (either as teachers or as learners) in educational contexts. We want to suggest, however, that the appropriation of ethnomethodological insights in work of this kind has led to something of a conflation of, on the one hand, a legitimate concern for the politics and morality of educational practice and, on the other, an equally legitimate concern for the ordinary, everyday practicalities of doing education. Below, and in the context of our own work, we emphasise that there is a need to keep these things analytically separate. The design of VEs and other technologies for education may well depend on theoretical and moral/political assumptions about the nature of education, but they will equally depend on our attention to the simple business of getting teaching and learning done.

These requirements give rise to some methodological issues and problems. Traditionally, requirements capture for computer systems development has been overwhelmingly driven by the potential and constraints of the technology. That is, what it is believed the hardware can do imposes its own limitations on the final products, with users as secondary considerations. However, work in the field of computer-supported co-operative work (CSCW) and, more latterly, in computer-supported collaborative learning (CSCL) has shifted the emphasis towards the complex relationship of goals, practice and technology. Participatory design practitioners, in particular, now regularly look to the fields of sociology, anthropology and cognitive science and borrow techniques from these disciplines to bolster understandings of context and practice. Thus ethnography, interaction analysis and conversation analysis have become candidate methods alongside participatory design techniques in the design, implementation and evaluation of educational systems. Nevertheless, and in our view, the emphasis on both the technology in question and the conflation of theoretical and moral issues with the notion of "practice" precisely leads us into a largely unexamined acceptance of "authenticity." That is, the concept of "practice" can come, ironically, to elide a relevant focus and one which has important consequences, and that is the moment-by-moment practical character of the work of "doing" education.

Recently, however, we have seen some attempts to specify the relationship between various commitments and the practical problem of understanding how work is done. Simonson and Kensing (1994) and Crabtree (1998) have, for instance, written about the complementarity of participatory design stances and ethnographic studies and made suggestions as to how they can be integrated. In keeping with arguments that have informed debates on ethnography for several years, however, we want to revisit what it means to see things "from the point of view of the actor" here. In a nutshell, we borrow the idea of "ethnomethodologically informed ethnography" so as to reposition our understanding of "practice" much as indicated by Crabtree and by others as no more or less than "members' methods"; that is, in the context of what they know and assume about their work and the organisational knowledges they deploy, how they go about deciding upon "what to do next." Such descriptions are rigorous and precise and, in our view, form a part of the work of assessing new technologies. In adopting analytic choices of this kind, we are not trying to suggest a single effective informing strategy for the design of educational technologies but that a comprehensive and multifaceted approach might be necessary.

The reasons for this lie in removing confusions about what various approaches can and cannot reveal. Thus it has been suggested that ethnography in the context of education may be useful in telling us about the "current forms and context of schooling on which society has agreed" (Griffin, Belyaeva, Soldaotova, & the Velikhov-Hamburg Collective, 1993, p. 124) but tells us little about what educational goals might be because they are not directly visible. Such a vision of ethnography, whereby it explores the foundations of consensus at the expense of visions of alternative futures and focuses only on the directly visible, seems to us rather odd. To reiterate, ethnography (in our version) seeks to explicate members' methods—no more and no less—on the assumption that revealing them in detail may carry with it indications of some of the problems that might be encountered when designing educational change. Members' methods are, of course, subjectable to what Garfinkel (1967) called the documentary method. In other words, a visible method stands proxy for a set of knowledges, expertise, and so on that are carried by members. There is no great problem here in deploying common sense to identify warrantable conclusions about what these things might be. Knowledges and expertise may not always be immediately visible but are always reportable. The task of ethnographers is to be familiar enough with the character of organisational life that the business of accounting and reporting becomes possible and is made sensible. The problem of the "educational goal" does not, for us, lie in its "invisibility" but in firstly its presumed "mentality" and relatedly in the degree to which it has a normative character (Searle, 1995). Our point is that we must be careful to separate these matters out.

In the main, requirements gathering and evaluation of museum-based online educational resources to date have taken four distinct approaches, as Sande Nuttall (2001) outlines. The first of these can be characterised as "identifying heuristics" by interviewing teachers and students about how they currently use Web sites and which features they find most useful. Such heuristics can be categorised as educational (for example, having a clear explanation of aims, having up-to-date information, having information that matches the needs of education professionals), presentational (having clear layout, good mix of text and pictures) and navigational. A second approach is the observation of classroom use of resources but we would argue that this approach appears to presume some level of effectiveness and an acceptance of assumptions about how teaching and learning are achieved in the classroom. As we discuss below, seeing requirements gathering and evaluation as pre- and post-development activities may prevent recognition of the significance of practical classroom management for usability.

The final two categories are evaluation by piloting and evaluation by teachers. The former is not yet well developed, although some recommendations have been made for formal measures, but the latter has made some headway in the UK. One example is Teachers Evaluating Educational Multimedia (TEEM)[2], where evaluation is carried out analytically by expert users against a set of heuristics. However, few of the resources evaluated here have been museum generated.

Despite these initiatives, there are still hurdles to be faced in developing online educational resources using museum artefacts. As Nuttall (2001) summarises:

While it is clear that museum resources can have a distinctive contribution to make in terms of the learning that they can generate, it is not clear whether this distinctiveness is appreciable in classroom use of Websites or whether there are different expectations and different criteria involved in judging educational Web resources generated by museums. We do know that while there may not be many established benchmarks for good educational sites, Website use in the classroom is likely to increase dramatically and with this increase we can expect that teachers will be more vociferous in their opinions and more sophisticated in their needs and expectations. The need for Web developers to ask, listen to and understand needs in the classroom will remain crucial to their ability to meet those needs.

We do not claim to have all the answers here, but in what follows we draw on our experiences in two separate projects to highlight the significance of these methodological issues for the design and evaluation of educational resources. Both projects involve ongoing work with museums which is being conducted by sociologists and computer scientists at Manchester Metropolitan University in the UK. Some of this work has been conducted separately and independently within the auspices of our particular disciplines whilst some has been collaborative. Our intentions here are twofold: to show how it might be possible to uncover real practice as opposed to just teachers' accounts and secondly to examine other aspects (such as the school visit or children's expectations) rather than just what goes on in the classroom. In this chapter we combine some of our findings and, to reiterate, focus on two pieces of ethnography, one concerning the work done in managing interaction with an artefact during a school visit and the other on managing outcomes in work done in designing a virtual environment in a school classroom. In both instances we were concerned with the mechanisms by which schoolchildren and teachers define what it is to participate in an educational experience.

Our descriptions of the projects are necessarily brief as the detail and analysis have been rehearsed elsewhere (Hemmings, Randall, Marr, & Francis, 2000; Mitchell, Economoou, & Randall, 2000). They are introduced merely as a vehicle for our discussion of the methodological issues.

WHEELS ON RAILS

This particular study arose from a two-year ethnography of the work of museum staff and the activities of visitors at two institutions, both of which were in the process of introducing new information systems of varying application. Some of these were intended to support administrative and curatorial procedures, some to improve accessibility and others to extend educational facilities. Our view with regard to that last was that the effectiveness of such systems would largely depend on the extent to which they were informed by an understanding of what kind of information-related educational work was being undertaken and by whom and how this work was organised. One frequently recurring component of the work done by educators, curators and others is the organisation of the school visit, and here we discuss an instance of this at the National Railway Museum (NRM) at York in the UK.

The NRM contains a gallery of interactive exhibits dealing with aspects of railway technology, entitled the Magician's Road, which is intended primarily, though not exclusively, for the use of school parties visiting the museum. These displays are designed to encourage hands-on experimentation by the children in what is a clearly structured and organised environment. The exhibits are of the "press this button" or "move this lever" type and each is accompanied by a set of instructions for its use, an explanation of the purpose of the exhibit and the actual "solution" to the problem. It occurred to us that, given the link between text, images, objects and interactivity in play here, much could be learned from observation of the use of such artefacts about the potential of hypertext applications (and, by extension, virtual environments) as educational media. In effect we could evaluate potential virtual environments through observation of the "real."

Furthermore, we have here the opportunity to consider the value of authenticity for educational aims as well as the potential value of participation in design when children are "leading" or "guiding" their own investigations. In other words, we are in the position here to say something about how educational practices might be accomplished when oriented towards a representational structure which reflects real-world environments and practices. However, one factor which stood out about the experience in the Magician's Road was the level of organisation which supported visits. These are "scripted" in the planning of the site, in the way the text was presented alongside each artefact, in the preparation provided by the host and in the activities of the explainers present. We shall also see that what we have termed "teacherly" intervention was a significant factor in the educational experience.

One exhibit, Wheels on Rails, consists of some model railway track, sloping downwards with a right-handed curve towards the foot, and six sets of wheels of varying shape. The experiment here is to try and identify the set of wheels which can successfully negotiate the track to the foot without falling off. Our observations, conducted in person and through analysis of several hours of videotaping, provided us with some useful insights into the advantages and disadvantages of the scripting we identified and are detailed below.

First and foremost, the textual descriptions and the instructions for use were peripheral to the children's interaction with the artefacts. The only occasion on which children were observed to read the text were when directed to do so either by teachers with the groups or by the "explainers" who were circulating within the location. This was surprising as the text not only detailed the experiment to be carried out but also gave the correct solution and an explanation. In all the instances we witnessed, the children gravitated first to the actual equipment and, when undirected, only looked to the instructions when unable to find a "solution" to what they perceived to be the problem, finding a set of wheels that didn't fall off. The text, therefore, seemingly took second place to an assumption that they would intuitively identify these things.

Secondly, because there was a time limit placed on their presence within the resource location, there appeared to be a competitive element to unguided access to the artefacts. Several groups almost raced from one exhibit to the next and on some occasions the constituent members seemed to be intuitively organising themselves in optimum fashion for finding a solution in the shortest possible time. That is, when numbers allowed, each member would take one or two sets of wheels and test them until the correct set was identified, at which stage they would fly off to the next exhibit. It was never clear in these unguided instances whether the children actually learned the lesson that was intended by educators. In other words, though they might have found the right set of wheels, they may not have known why it was the right set. When an explainer attempted to draw the attention of children to the shapes of the wheels it was not evident that the children had done more than feign listening.

On one occasion, however, a teacher had imposed further structuring on the visit and had guided the children to read, act, read again, listen and then give feedback on what was happening, as the following extract from the interaction between the teacher and six pupils illustrates:

Teacher: OK, why did it win? Why did this one manage to go round the corner?

Pupils proffer explanations. One pupil takes the "right" set to the bend and shows the teacher.

Pupil: That stops it.

Teacher: "What do you mean, it stops it?

Pupil: Well, when it goes that way ... in there ... it pushes against the rail.

Teacher: Right ... and it works, doesn't it? You always find it works. Where's the other one? ... Surely this one would work as well, wouldn't it? So why doesn't it?

Teacher rolls set of wheels.

Teacher: Why is this one coming off?

Pupil: Oh, I know. ... I know.

Teacher rejects explanation.

Teacher: Right, back to your shape ... why does this one stay on? (gesturing with "right" set, shows nearly right set of wheels)

Teacher: As that one comes off (pointing to left-hand wheel), why doesn't this one (points to right-hand wheel) keep it on?

Pupil: It can't turn.

Teacher: Pardon? ... Pardon?

Pupil: It can't turn.

Teacher: It can't slide up and down. This one can. It can't slide up and down. This should, shouldn't it? But it can't ... because it can't slide up and down.

This was the only time when we could be reasonably certain that the "desired" outcome—an understanding of *why* one particular set of wheels stayed on the rails right to the end of the track—had been attained.

The "designed" character of the setting and the formal instructional elements of the Magician's Road clearly embody some "theory" of educational achievement in so far as instructions for use are designed to accompany the activities, relevance of historical and scientific issues is established, and both the visits and the exhibits themselves are structured with a view to "time to completion." However, and separately from this, we can establish what children and adults actually do in this designed environment. Our conclusions had to do with the timely and expert way in which teachers were able to judge what question to ask and when to ask it so as to arrive at a lesson to be learned. That is, the teachers and explainers were able to identify the appropriate point at which intervention is required if an explanation is to be proffered.

The implications of these conclusions for the design of electronic interactive educational resources are clear. Simply providing a context for discovery does not in itself ensure that "desired" lessons are learned, even if we can agree, theoretically and morally, on what is to be desired. Our analysis points to the interrelatedness of problems of timeliness, the structuring of questions and responses, and the design of artefacts as being the significant issues here. They are indicative, that is, of what it looks like in an educational context to report on members' methods. *Assuming* that lessons have been learned is risky, for, as with any medium for curriculum delivery, there is simply no way of verifying absolutely that understanding has occurred. What we could observe is that teachers and explainers appeared to assume that a lesson had been learned when the children were able to verbalise their knowledge in response to appropriate prompts.

USING VIRTUAL ENVIRONMENTS IN THE CLASSROOM

Our second example returns to the problem of "visibility" in ethnography, and we here make the point that, unless we know "what to ask" or "what to look for," neither as participants in design nor as observers of practice will we be able to reveal goals, educational or otherwise. Somewhat serendipitously, some of us were able to follow up the work we had done on structuring, intervention and interaction during museum visits of schoolchildren to examine kinds of pre- and post-visit work which are done in classrooms. This gave us the opportunity to observe children making use of virtual environments, to discuss with teachers some of the practical constraints on this type of delivery and to involve children as participants in a design process. In this way we were able to build on the insights afforded by the naturalistic techniques of observation and interaction analysis used in the museum visits and combine them with insights from the contributions the children themselves were able to make. In effect, we were once more eliding the divide between requirements elicitation and evaluation.

As a result of work which had been done at Manchester Museum, a number of virtual environments had been built, based around the pyramid builders' town of Kahun, including a virtual walk-through and working models of various Egyptian artefacts. (See Figures 1 and 2 and also www.doc.mmu.ac.uk/RESEARCH/virtual-museum/Kahun.) These had been placed on the Web and contact had been made by a teacher at a school in the South of England who had been using them with children in the classroom. Following some email correspondence, the children (aged about 10-11) were encouraged to design their own paper mock-ups of Web pages with versions of artefacts and text they would like to see. Some time was then spent with the children and the teachers in order to improve our understanding of what was happening and to give the children some guidance in their design. The observations which follow refer to the contributions of the children in small-group discussions, our perceptions of classroom practice and discussions about this with teachers.

Our attempts to assist children in their designs and elicit comment on the sites provided showed an overwhelming concern with the more superficial components

Figure 1:   Virtual walk-through of Kahun

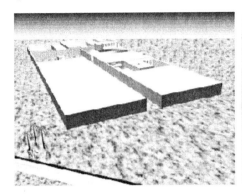 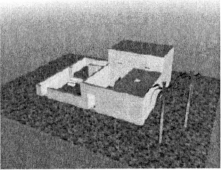

Figure 2:   Virtual model of the shaduf artefact

such as colour and effects and the practical problems of linking images with text, as the following remarks on their own and their friends' efforts illustrate:

"So, you need to give us a basket picture. ..."

Or these comments by the King Tut group about their Web site (see Figure 3):
"We wanted the candles in the background. Can you make the candles flicker? We wanted some stars as well. The sky's like a bluey blacky colour."

The children reported willingly and happily on the matters that they deemed relevant, but what they saw as important reflected broadly a concern with colour and other effects or a concern with "mistakes" they had made in linking text and pictures. Indeed, the children were very good at identifying attractive and immediate features of the interface but showed no disposition to discuss educational content. Thus, they seemed to focus on "surface" issues in design (e.g., what colours to use). It was also

Figure 3: Web site designed by the King Tut group

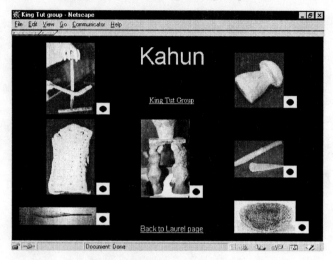

sometimes unclear how much importance children placed on various features of their designs. For example, one group specified the flickering candle but the Web site developed had only a simple, static, dark background, despite which it still met with their approval. In this respect we were identifying what Scaife, Rogers, Aldrich, and Davies (1997, p. 344) had already pointed out about the reporting abilities of children, which is that they

> *"are very good at letting us know what it is that keeps them engaged which is often not what adult designers or their proxies. ... would have expected. We also need to recognise, however, that children cannot design their own learning goals."*

It occurred to us that perhaps the problem was that we were not placing these issues in a context that children would readily understand and that a more narratively based approach might be useful. This, we thought, might resolve the fact that the conceptual designs generated by the children did not make full use of the potential of VE in that they all followed the "traditional" pattern of a set of information pages. One of the exercises, therefore, that children undertook was writing stories in which the various artefacts they had already designed might appear.

This task exploited more of the potential of the VE medium for narration and exploration. At first glance, however, the stories were, for us, disappointing (if entertaining). The children seemed to have difficulty reconciling the two demands of, on the one hand, telling a good story and, on the other, structuring tales in such a way that the salient artefacts could be brought out. In any event, our problem was precisely one of understanding how the meaningful world of schoolchildren related to our own.

Just as we discovered that educational goals were not paramount for the children so too did it seem for the teachers. Observation of classroom practice showed us something we had earlier recognised in the museum visits—that the achievement of an educational outcome is largely a matter of practical management. Issues of relevance for teachers include such things as the amount of time available to them, the numbers with which they are dealing and the structuring of the task at hand. Discussion with the teachers confirmed this perception and revealed some specific ways in which practical issues informed the structuring of tasks. Resource constraints, for example, in the form of access to computers, influenced the way in which computer-related work would be structured in and through the teachers' recognition of the need for everyone to "have a go" and the time available in which to complete the task. Thus, reference to resources included the following observation:

"We're lucky ... three computers (!). ... We allow the children on the computers in twos and generally everyone gets a turn."

And, regarding allocation of time:

"The biggest problem is organising the day, especially with compulsory literacy and numeracy. You can get things going really well ... and then you've got to stop because its numeracy hour ... and then try to pick it up again another time."

Additionally, teachers have to structure activities on the basis of assumptions they make not only about the competence of children, but also about the competence of their colleagues. Here, for instance, we discovered one feature of group working online that we had not previously considered:

"Actually, using the Net fits really well with group work. You've got to organise the class, of course, because we don't have the equipment to have everybody doing it at the same time. But the groups work really well with it—there are always suggestions about what to do. Maybe that's why there isn't any problem with navigation."

Expertise on the part of staff, however, was more problematic:

"We've been doing Egypt with year five and six. Five of us have been working on the project, in a team. We meet once a week and myself and [the IT coordinator] basically run through what we want to do. We provide all the resources the people in the team will need. The big issue is technophobia. **Several staff really don't feel confident using the technology.**" *(our emphasis)*

What we were seeing here is that the competencies of the children and of fellow staff were seen as affordances and constraints in this type of work. Group work with children was seen to work particularly well as they could help each other in navigating through the systems to arrive quickly and economically at appropriate solutions. This reflected what we had observed in the "wheels on rails" setting—that children seemed to intuitively organise themselves to get the task in hand, as they perceived it, out of the way. For some teachers, however, a lack of familiarity with the technology and a degree of technophobia constrained what they were prepared and able to get involved with.

One final point worthy of mention here is that teachers carry with them a view of what is worth learning and what is not. Thus one teacher told us:

"We don't encourage the kids to 'surf' for sites themselves. I spent some time looking around, which is how I found your site. And then I told the kids, right, this is where you're going. The kids can't discriminate between useful and less useful material. Like, with the Egyptians, there's all this 'God was an alien' stuff, and I don't want them going there."

This notion of what is useful is constructed from experience. Thus the teacher who had made the initial contact revealed that she had come across the Kahun sites whilst looking for material to direct children to. It is her belief that children are unable to discriminate between what is useful and what is not and that there is much on the Web which might appeal to children but which has little if any educational value. There are many attractively presented Web sites but the content is often flawed and the presentation may not always be appropriate. The experience of teachers allows them to determine what is good and what is not and at what level the material, especially text, needs to be pitched. Being able to describe the features of something which is just right for 10- and 11-year-olds is difficult to do but long experience in "trying things out" with those age groups makes it immediately possible to identify the "right" content.

CONCLUSIONS

We began our discussion with reference to some of the problematic issues associated with the design and use of electronic interactive technologies as educational media. These issues are primarily concerned with, firstly, the best way to collect data to understand the educational process and whether knowledge of what happens now can tell us anything about what might happen in the future. That is, we are concerned here with the move from description to prescription. Second, they are to do with the degree to which participants in the educational process can effectively be involved in the design of educational resources. We have established that naturalistic approaches to educational practice can be helpful in that they can contribute to understanding of the situation in question, that is, the context which we are observing. But the extent to which it is possible to generalise from the "here and now" is less certain.

One of the reasons for this, it was suggested, is that educational "goals," while they may be acknowledged by participants as being present, are not visible.

However, this problem with visibility, we have argued, is not a problem at all so much as an elision of the significance of practice. Teachers can tell us what they hope and expect that a child will learn in a particular situation and a child may be able to verbalise their understanding of what they have been doing, but these only emerge as a result of "knowing what to look for" or "knowing what to ask" rather than being evident in the activities we are observing. In other words, it is only the moment-by-moment practical character of the work being done that we can hope to identify.

Hitherto, we had believed that an amalgam of approaches, a multifaceted approach, to requirements elicitation and design would produce a set of rich and useful results. We are still convinced of this but the seeming complementarity of methods is more complex than would first appear. Our interactions in the classroom with children and teachers as participants in the design process were informed to a considerable extent by what we already knew from observation of museum visits. In other words, our understanding of the arrangements pointed to "what to ask." Through involvement of teachers and children in design we were able to identify the importance of practical management of learning experiences. Thus, we could return to our video recordings with a new analytical focus. Subsequent shadowing of school parties in other museums has drawn on this knowledge in informing us "what to look for." In other words there is an interdependence between the two methods, and the complexities of this relationship require a better understanding.

This is important because of the assumption that naturalistic approaches provide us with no more than rich and potentially useful descriptions. Without analytical focus, it would appear that their contribution to prescription is limited. As we have argued elsewhere (Mitchell et al., 2000), design in education rests on far more than a mutual understanding of a particular domain; it includes a range of moral, political, cognitive, theoretical and practical assumptions, all of which are held to a greater or lesser extent by participants in and informants of the design process.

Problems ensue because our endeavour here is less to do with what we are trying to find out than why we are trying to find it out. The relationship between practice and goals is not something which observation alone can achieve precisely because this is to do with the relationship between description and prescription. What is relevant for the ethnographer in producing a description of practice may differ from the significant issues for the participatory designer looking for prescription of design. These complexities cannot be resolved merely by adding in other techniques. We believe that design of effective educational resources is not simply about ensuring user participation, taking into account real-world context or studying interactions but that a variety of methods need to be closely interwoven and their interdependence recognised. Technology may offer considerable potential for the delivery of educational processes, but for it to replicate or produce "ideal" conditions for acquiring knowledge it needs to be informed by a thorough understanding of the particular and varied circumstances in which knowledge acquisition can occur, be it in classroom, museum or any other real-world context. This would seem to indicate for us that the distinction between requirements gathering and evaluation is an artificial one (Randall, Twidale, & Bentley, 1996). The notion that these are pre- and post-design activities is misleading, and evaluation should be seen as enveloping all aspects of design, development and usability testing.

Our own current work in this field is intended to take these ideas further. It is clear that virtual collaborative environments offer a range of potential benefits to learners both through providing simulations of authentic settings and in allowing users to construct their own environments, thus building on prior learning. However, little is yet known about how children might react to virtual interaction. Usability evaluation of CVEs must therefore focus on observation of children experimenting in such settings, and future endeavours will attempt to incorporate such techniques within the development process.

ENDNOTES

[1]   We have here adopted the terminology employed within the next Framework programme (VI) of the EC in place of the previous standard, ICTs (information and communication technologies).
[2]   See www.teem.org.uk.

REFERENCES

Anderson, D. (1997). *A common wealth: Museums and learning in the United Kingdom*. Report for the Department of Culture, Media and Sport. London: HMSO.

Archimuse. (1999). *The best on the Web: Museums and the Web 99*. Retrieved from http://.archimuse.com/mw99.index.html

Bruner, J. (1986). *Actual minds, possible worlds*. Cambridge, MA: Harvard University Press.

Bruner, J. (1990). *Acts of meaning*. Cambridge, MA: Harvard University Press.

Crabtree, A. (1998). Ethnography in participatory design. In *Proceedings of the Participatory Design Conference* (pp. 93-105) Seattle, WA: ACM Press.

Department for Education and Employment. (1998). *Open for learning, open for business: The government's national grid for learning challenge*. Retrieved from http://www.dfee.gov.uk/grid

Garfinkel, H. (1967). *Studies in ethnomethodology*. Englewood Cliffs, NJ: Prentice Hall.

Griffin, P., Belyaeva, A., Soldatova, G. & the Velikhov-Hamburg Collective. (1993). Creating and reconstituting contexts for educational interaction, including a computer program. In E. Forman, N. Minick & C. Addison Stone (Eds.), *Contexts for learning: Dynamics in children's development* (pp. 120-152) Oxford, England: Oxford University Press.

Hemmings, T., Clarke, K., Francis, D., Marr, L. & Randall, D. (2001). Situated knowledge and virtual education: Some real problems with the concept of learning and interactive technology. In I. Hutchby & J. Moran-Ellis (Eds.), *Children, technology and culture* (pp. 97-113) London: Falmer Press.

Hemmings, T., Randall, D., Marr, L. & Francis, D. (2000). Task talk and closure: Situated learning and the use of an interactive museum artefact. In S. Hester & D. Francis (Eds.), *Local educational order: Ethnomethodological studies of knowledge in action* (pp. 223-244) Amsterdam/Philadelphia: John Benjamins.

Hughes, J., O'Brien, J., Randall, D., Rouncefield, M. & Tolmie, P. (2000). Virtual organisations, organisational knowledge and the customer: How "virtual organisations" deal with "real" customers. *Information Systems Review, 1,* 43-58.

Lave, J., & Wenger, E. (1991). *Situated learning: Legitimate peripheral participation.* Cambridge, England: Cambridge University Press.

Mitchell, W., Economou, D. & Randall, D. (2000, November). *God is an alien: Understanding informant responses through user participation and observation.* Paper presented at PDC 2000 6th Biennial Participatory Design Conference, New York.

Nuttall, S. (Ed.). (2001). *Building digital content: A study in the selection, presentation and use of museum Web content for schools.* Retrieved November 14, 2001, from http://www.mda.org.uk/bdc_intro.htm

Randall, D., Twidale, M. & Bentley, R. (1996). Dealing with uncertainty— Perspectives on the evaluation process. In P. Thomas (Ed.), *CSCW requirements and evaluation.* London: Springer-Verlag.

Scaife, M., Rogers, Y., Aldrich, F. & Davies, M. (1997). Designing for or designing with? Informant design for interactive environments. In *Proceedings of CHI '97: Human Factors in Computing Systems* (pp. 343-350). Atlanta, GA: ACM Press.

Searle, J. R. (1995). *Construction of social reality.* London: Allen Lane.

Seely Brown, J., Collins, A. & Duguid, P. (1989). Situated cognition and the culture of learning. *Educational Researcher, 18,* 32-42.

Simonson, J. & Kensing, F. (1994). Take users seriously but take a longer look: Organisational and technical effects from designing with an ethnographically inspired approach in PCD '94. In *Proceedings of the Participative Design Conference* (pp. 47-58). Chapel Hill, NC: Computer Professionals for Social Responsibility.

Chapter VII

Developing and Supporting Research-Based Learning and Teaching Through Technology

Jacqueline Dempster
University of Warwick, UK

ABSTRACT

The chapter draws on the work of two national projects concerned with developing research-based approaches to learning and teaching and supporting these through technology. A pedagogic framework underpinning the design and delivery of such courses is outlined. In exploring the usability of online environments (programs) for research-based learning and teaching, the chapter discusses issues and needs in the context of operational usability. Factors relating to educational and technological usability are presented in the light of development of pedagogic principles for research-based learning, analysis of existing online systems and tools to support such courses, and evaluative case studies considering approaches in specific subject areas. The solutions to technological support implemented and evaluated through the pilot courses are discussed and generic educational good practice is highlighted throughout.

INTRODUCTION

The chapter draws on the work of two national projects concerned with developing research-based approaches to learning and teaching and supporting these through the use of technology. A pedagogic framework underpinning research-orientated approaches to the design and delivery of courses is outlined. Specific approaches to the selection of learning activities are discussed in the light of disciplinary variances in research processes. The solutions to technological support, implemented and evaluated through the work of two national teaching development projects, are discussed. A range of case studies is presented, which serves to illustrate course approaches across a number of subject areas that support students online in developing high-order learning capabilities. Generic lessons learned are highlighted throughout.

In exploring the usability of online environments (programs) for research-based learning and teaching, this chapter deals with two key educational objectives:

(1) supporting inquiry, debate and creativity though sharing and review of work using Web publishing and discussion programs and

(2) augmenting student collaborative learning by accessing and networking with remote experts using Web-mediated videoconferencing and other communications programs.

Issues and needs for both aspects are discussed in the context of operational usability. Factors relating to educational and technological usability are presented in the light of development and evaluation work in the following areas:

• pedagogic principles for research-based learning underpinning the course approaches;

• analysis of existing online systems and tools to support research-based courses; and

• case studies illustrating the use of technological systems across a range of subject areas.

BACKGROUND

The term "research-led" is widely used in the UK higher education sector to describe universities that demonstrate a high capacity for good quality research whilst claiming that their research informs and enhances their teaching. A link between research and teaching has been both supported and contested for many years (Brew & Boud, 1995, p. 262; Centra, 1983; Entwistle, 1998; Robbins, 1963). For a recital of this highly politicised debate, see Ramsden and Moses (1992, p. 274), Hattie and Marsh (1996, p. 511), and Roach, Blackmore, and Dempster (2001). It is true to say that in research-led universities, staff are highly research-orientated and teaching programs are often strongly informed by staff research interests. The former vice chancellor at Warwick asserts that "if our graduates are to lead and shape this ever-changing world, they need to see their own disciplines as being alive and dynamic, with values being challenged and altered continuously by new discoveries" (Follett, 1994, p.4).

Research activity by its nature fosters innovation and debate and can therefore provide a valuable model for student learning. Buckingham, Shum and Sumner (2000, p.138) describe such activity as the "cut and thrust of debate between peers" and suggest this "is a core skill that we seek to foster in students, and ... within scholarly communities." Educational development in many research-led institutions therefore aims to bring the benefits of a research environment into teaching and learning processes (Boyer Commission, 1998) by considering those working processes inherent to both research and learning (Roach et al., 2001). In their disciplinary research or professional work, academic tutors use evaluative, collaborative and creative processes, drawing on high-level thinking and understanding capabilities to do so. This can provide a valuable model for curriculum design since such capabilities are generally transferable and valued not only in research, but also in employment and broader lifelong learning pursuits. If we wish to strengthen links between research and teaching, we might therefore consider the extent to which development in students of these "research capabilities" is supported and assessed in our courses.

The research process can directly influence the nature of courses taught only if the intended "research capabilities" are emphasised and explicitly developed in the students. The absence of suitable pedagogic frameworks in this area means that the nature and effects of such research approaches are, however, hard to evaluate (Barnett, 1984; Dempster & Blackmore, in press; Elton, 1986; Roach et al., 2001). This is at odds with the increasing requirement in the HE sector for explicit descriptions of learning outcomes. The QAA benchmarking process is promoting an outcomes approach to learning in which the results of learning are expressed in a form that permits their achievement to be demonstrated and measured. Such explicitness and indeed the assessment of research-based learning are difficult areas. The capabilities we seek to develop and assess challenge the value of criterion-led objectives-based and competency-based approaches to learning. The use of prespecified criteria is not useful in defining creative and innovative learning outcomes. There are enormous difficulties if these are to be "measured" against a grade or percentage scale. One might argue that judging the extent to which such learning outcomes have been met requires the use of more "expressive objectives" (Eisner, 1985).

The issue is further complicated when seeking to make use of online learning programs to assist or enhance traditional practice or provide new opportunities. Given the high cost of IT infrastructures, institutions are increasingly forced to demand tangible benefits from online learning programs in the absence of clear frameworks for judging effectiveness and success. In order to evaluate the usability of online systems that might support research-based learning, a framework is required that makes more explicit statements about the capabilities we seek to develop in students. The framework should inspire as well as guide the use of ICT tools to support these specific objectives and to do so in a cost-effective manner.

Through the work of two national projects, the Centre for Academic Practice at the University of Warwick has been exploring and developing the relationship between teaching, learning and research through the use of technology. We have sought to evaluate the needs of a research-led institution with respect to educational strategies and the benefits offered by ICT. This has implications for the staff who teach and the capabilities developed by the students. The work has resulted in a set of pedagogic principles that provide a model for the design of research-based courses, learning activities and assignments (Roach, Blackmore, & Dempster, 2000, 2001). These are grounded in educational theories of how we learn as well as presenting practical ways forward for lecturers, academic developers and institutional managers alike. Implementation of the models applied to courses across a range of disciplines has led to the identification of key usability issues and a framework for evaluation.

The two projects are TELRI (Technology-Enhanced Learning in Research-Led Institutions) and ANNIE (Accessing and Networking with National and International Expertise). Both are led by Warwick, but work collaboratively with staff and departments in a number of other research-led institutions, namely, the universities of Oxford, Southampton, Birmingham and Durham for TELRI and Kent at Canterbury, De Montfort, Exeter, Plymouth, Lancaster and Manchester for ANNIE. The projects are funded by the UK's Higher Educational Funding Council in England (HEFCE), respectively, under the Technology in Teaching and Learning Programme (TLTP) and the Fund for the Development of Teaching and Learning (FDTL).

The TELRI project is concerned with developing the creative and collaborative capabilities of students through the use of ICT that supports the sharing and discussion of work. The case studies presented span a range of subject disciplines. Predominantly, the role of online learning programs is in supporting critical thinking and debate that is focussed on the students' own work (or work in progress). Learning activities may also draw on primary resources, including current research, for which online learning environments can provide highly flexible access. In TELRI, the approaches developed tend to support exchange and commenting on document-based material. The ANNIE project is complementary to this in that it aims to develop online learning approaches that engage students in creative and collaborative activities in the highly visual and practice-based disciplines of theatre and drama by augmenting access to teaching and workshops led by scholars and practitioners of national and international standing through integration of online learning programs. Case studies focus on effective approaches for students to interact with experts in distant locations.

PEDAGOGIC PRINCIPLES FOR RESEARCH-BASED LEARNING AND TEACHING

A fundamental premise in both TELRI and ANNIE is that research-based learning and teaching involves not just subject matter, but the development of the kind of investigative techniques that encourage high-order thinking. In other words, we encourage learning that is based on knowledge construction—the "imaginative extension of scholarship"—rather than merely its acquisition. In this way, highly productive collaborative learning may be developed, adding an extra dimension to the exchange of views and increasing understanding of the course concepts. Students learn not so much the content of the subject as the process—"in particular the creative cognitive process of offering up ideas, having them criticised or expanded on, and getting the chance to reshape them (or abandon them) in the light of peer discussion" (Rowntree, 1995, p. 207).

One of the most valuable outcomes from the TELRI work is the knowledge and understanding gained in how to design courses which make the learning outcomes and assessment criteria explicit and provide students with the necessary skills and capabilities for life beyond higher education. This is of particular value to research-led institutions with the increasing need to define in more explicit terms the concept of research-led teaching and learning. It is equally of value to the wider range of courses that rely on the concept of "scholarship" as the key learning process.

TELRI has used the terms "adaptive" learning and "adoptive" learning to distinguish the capabilities that research-based courses aim to develop in students (Table 1). Like research, adaptive learning is inherently a creative, generative and reflective process. In novel and open situations, it requires and develops higher cognitive processes. Adaptive learning differs from its counterpart, "adoptive" learning, which is best described as the application of well-understood knowledge and the mastery of tools, techniques and procedures in bounded situations (Roach et al., 2001). The extent to which the development of adaptive capabilities is balanced against adoptive learning outcomes in a course design is likely to determine a student's ability to respond effectively to undefined and unfamiliar situations within and beyond the discipline context (Roach et al., 2000).

Table 1: Adoptive and adaptive learning outcomes (from Roach et al., 2001)

ADOPTIVE LEARNING	ADAPTIVE LEARNING
Knowledge and Practice of...	**Formation and Generation of...**
Facts, Assertions, Rules and Laws	Personal Interpretation and Meaning
Terminology, Language and Protocols	Evaluation and Decisions
Techniques and Procedures	Arguments, Reasoning and Justification
Organisation and Structure	Synthesis and Conceptualisation
Established Principles and Relationships	Originality, Creativity and Innovation

In establishing a framework to inform the design of appropriate course activities and assessment approaches, TELRI has used generic terms to describe learning outcomes of research-based courses that essentially borrow from constructivist theories (particularly, Kuhn, 1981; Dreyfus & Dreyfus, 1986; Boud, 1988). The discipline-specific aspects of adaptive learning are problematic. The terminology used by educational developers to describe research-orientated "processes"—which may include "authentic," "open," "interpretative," "analytic," "expressive," "inventive"—and the descriptions of learning from subject experts can be difficult to define. For example, what does it mean to be inventive in biology as opposed to history? How is an interpretative piece of work in mathematics different than one in law or literature? The absence of meaning in generic descriptions brings us back to the same foundation. What does it mean to be an expert in each individual subject field? What does a successful researcher in any given field do in terms of their thinking process? The TELRI course design guidelines (Roach et al., 2000) use a generic framework to assist academic tutors to think through such questions and make explicit statements about the capabilities of experts in their discipline that can be used as meaningful learning outcomes. From this, the type of learning activities (assignments), course resources and methods of delivery that will support and assess the development of such capabilities can be more effectively planned, implemented and evaluated.

Research-based courses essentially centre on research-driven tasks, which encourage the students to engage with key issues in the course, as well as to explore their own interests in the topic. The requirement to comment constructively on the work of other members of the group helps students to see each assignment in a wider perspective than would otherwise be the case from their own engagement with each task. This offers them insights into approaches to and criteria for assessment. In terms of learning outcomes, students not only acquire new insights into the subject area through their own research but also, when supported by online learning programs, learn how to use IT-based techniques as a tool for the investigation and interrogation of primary materials relevant to the discipline. Students are active partners in all the case studies and pilot projects and have a significant role to play in shaping the learning outcomes of the courses.

Assignments for research-based courses are designed to reward originality, risk taking, creative thought, critical inquiry and analysis, evaluation and decision making. Assessment is therefore strongly dependent on the expertise of the tutors. In our case, these are highly active and proficient researchers in their discipline. However, it is true to say that the use of online learning environments widens the gap between how students learn and how they are assessed (Salmon, 2000, p. 93) when assessment procedures remain locked into traditional examination modes.

It is claimed that making explicit the more ineffable and subjective criteria for assessment of a research-based course by providing access to previous course work will lead to standardisation of students' work. It is interesting, however, that it is felt that the students are in fact able to identify a common "standardised" content or "formula" for a high grade. This suggests that there is one, when, indeed by definition, original and creative work precludes this. It would be interesting to see how the publishing of highly graded work from open (and possibly closed) questions for students to access might influence a tutor's assessment criteria, particularly if, even in the absence of plagiarism, all work submitted deserved a first-class grade.

The most successful uses of online programs in research-based learning have been in courses where assessment has been flexible and taken place alongside the learning using the same online environments. The most common approaches have been student publishing of assessed work or work in progress to a shared Web area with the facility to view and comment on each other's work. Development in assessment for online and open learning environments is still new territory (Cann & Pawley, 1999). The features of good scholarly peer review and debate have been proposed by Buckingham Shum and Sumner (2000, p. 139) in relation to peer review in journals: open, informed, dynamic, carefully constructed, cumulative, preserved. These may provide an equally useful guide for assessment of student work in relation to research capabilities. Guidance for the design of assignments for research-based learning has been produced as part of the TELRI work (see Roach et al., 2000). From a pragmatic perspective, tutors have shifted the focus of assignments from the individual student contributing to group activities and debate to the submission of a piece of written work reflecting the students' own approaches to planning, justification, decision making and undertaking of the "research" task.

Since these issues have a critical impact on usability of online learning programs to support such "scholarly" activities, we believe the approaches identified here as appropriate for research-led institutions are equally of value across the broad context of higher education.

OPERATIONAL USABILITY

The potential benefits of online learning programs in courses have been shown over the years to be difficult to demonstrate unless the types of learning the course intends to support are made explicit. Cost-effectiveness of using technology above traditional methods can only be properly evaluated when the intended aims of the ICT intervention have been identified. There are two main considerations. Firstly, a clear overview is needed of the learning processes required for the students to achieve specific learning outcomes and develop specific capabilities. Without this pedagogical framework, there is a tendency for ICT methods and use of materials to be "bolt on" or time-consuming to develop or implement, and the learning gains often remain unclear or dubious. With or without technology, a clear purpose in terms of the capabilities being developed, assignments, support and resources assists in ensuring the quality and cost benefits of the course are maintained or enhanced. Secondly, the overall cost benefits of integrating ICT depend on practical factors that are mostly specific to each organisational context (Dempster & Blackmore, 2002). These may include the level of existing IT infrastructure, IT training needs, staff development and support, the need for remote access for some or all students and tutors, availability of course resources, time-tabling and marking limitations, feasibility of distributing work, and so on.

Evaluation methodologies with which to assess different online learning programs from a pedagogical perspective have been limited (Britain & Liber, 2000; Conole & Oliver, 1998). Institutions mostly tread new territory regarding the limitations of particular packages until their own evaluation of implementation is well underway. This can be a costly approach if the system invested in proves unsuitable for its academic needs. Operational frameworks can help to reveal the underlying pedagogical assumptions and orientation of online environments. They aim to provide institutions and their academic and supporting staff with a basis upon which to choose a VLE package according to how they want to teach and wish their students to learn.

There is a great deal of software available to support learning and teaching online. Most of the benefits of online learning programs lie in their potential to support styles of learning that are especially time-intensive for university teachers using traditional methods (Britain & Liber, 2000). Student-centred, resource-based, discussion-led and collaborative learning have always formed a core part of a university education, but are not always as straightforward to implement as the lecture and other traditional methods. As Laurillard (1993) states, "it is not that teachers want to teach this way any more than students want to struggle to learn in this manner, both parties are constrained to operate within a university system over which they have limited control and which is barely capable of withstanding external the pressures currently being exerted upon it." Those supporting staff to develop new skills and competencies must therefore take a strategic approach to the integration of e-learning into teaching practices (Oliver & Dempster, in press).

In the case of research-based learning, evaluation of appropriate forms of ICT was based on the need to emulate environments that support the natural creative and collaborative practices of researchers. For the TELRI project, we interviewed tutors in research-led universities across a range of subjects to ascertain the preferred ways of sharing and commenting on work and collaborative debate for themselves and their students. We have surveyed and tested a number of applications on usability issues specific to supporting and augmenting research-based learning for either campus-based or dispersed classes. Technological support for research-based courses may require established facilities such as publishing for both lecturers and students, structured virtual forums, help guides for set tasks, email, feedback facilities for the tutor and so on. Despite their popularity, early online tools such as these have not had the impact on teaching and learning that may have been expected.

One likely reason is the lack of cohesion between the various online tools. In pedagogic terms, principally, it is essential that the course, the technologies and student assignments provide a coherent system where each component is dependent on the others. After all, the educational system experienced by the students is inherently integrated. A number of packages have emerged over recent years that claim to provide integrated environments for using the range of these information and communication tools. The user interfaces traditionally associated with online communications programs have been replaced with the more intuitive interface of the Web (often referred to as virtual learning environments or VLEs; see a review by another TLTP3 project, TALENT, at http://www.le.ac.uk/TALENT/book/c4p9.htm). However, the continuing absence of cohesive pedagogical frameworks in many cases has resulted in development in the use of online learning programs (or VLEs) that fail to produce cost-effective and long-term change. Success is often evaluated on the basis of adoption rather than pedagogic viability and the educational benefits therefore remain unclear or dubious.

Regardless of the level of integration of online learning tools, not to mention the costs and training implications, we found significant gaps in interface and functionality in meeting the needs of tutors and students in research-based teaching and learning. In particular, few existing packages (such as FirstClass, WebCT, Blackboard, Fdlearning, WebBoard) allow students to publish work to be viewed by anyone other than themselves or their tutors. Some programs allow submission of documents and media files, usually as attachments sent to a group. However, none were capable of supporting annotation by students of work in progress in any usable form.

The majority of courses with an online component were used to facilitate access to resources, thus contributing to the delivery of the module rather than providing a platform for student learning in itself. While guidance is provided to the course as a group, support and feedback tends to be offered to students as individuals. As such, students learn as individuals rather than collaboratively. We found little evidence of the kind of cohesion between assignments, publishing, sharing and open exchange activities and access to supporting course materials that one would expect for supporting creative and collaborative learning.

EDUCATIONAL USABILITY

A prerequisite to the selection of specific online learning programs for course delivery and/or support is to establish which types and range of learning outcomes can be achieved by which methods. This is true even in the absence of a consideration of ICT opportunities. The pedagogic principles identified for research-based learning assist in establishing clear educational objectives and in making explicit the kinds of generic capabilities to be developed. Within the TELRI and ANNIE projects, two broad kinds of learning activity that students might engage in to develop such research-like capabilities have been piloted in courses that aim to support creative and collaborative learning. These are (1) sharing and discussion of primary materials and students' own work or performance and (2) accessing and networking with discipline experts. Both serve as a reminder that the focus of a research-based course should be on *process* rather than content.

These approaches aim to foster investigative capabilities in the students through contact with the research methodologies of full-time members of staff and expert practitioners. Such courses encourage students to be innovative and creative in their work and in this way provide opportunities for students to create new insights into the discipline rather than simply replicate existing knowledge. Risk taking is an inherent part of the creative process. It has been important in TELRI courses that curriculum design and online learning programs that support the assessment processes encourage this open sharing and debate of "work in progress." In so doing, it aims to allay the misguided expectation of many students that passive adoption and well-presented recital of established ideas are a safe bet to a good grade.

Discussion and debate enable students to explore and test out ideas and form their own meaning. These are central processes in arts and humanities curricula. ICT tools that support and extend this "tutorial" type of environment are valuable, particularly with increasing class sizes and time-tabling problems. In TELRI, tutors commented that technologies that allowed students to submit their assignment work and to view and comment on the work of others provided a clearer stimulus and focus for discussion than in previous traditional modes of teaching or even online discussions loosely associated with the module. They also facilitated additional or alternative ways for students to express their ideas and approaches, to "learn from seeing" and to participate in collaborative group work. This often resulted in increased enjoyment and sense of ownership in their learning. Students were motivated to maintain a steady flow of work from week to week. They acquired a wider perspective of the topic by seeing several different responses to the same assignment. Subjecting the work of their peers to such reflection enhanced their powers of reflection on their own critical practices.

Such approaches are equally valuable in the social sciences, where research capabilities manifest themselves in students' abilities to gather, evaluate and present evidence and construct arguments. These processes rely on discussion and debate as the major forum for learning, in addition to opportunities to apply and try out theories and concepts. Online learning programs that offered a means for students to prepare joint presentations, work through problems and share scarce case study material were used successfully in the pilot courses to support tutorials and small-group work. The approach was most beneficial in developing higher levels of abstraction and evaluation by introducing students to "real world" issues, particularly through the lecturers' academic research and through the use of primary materials rather than textbook sources that could be accessed fairly seamlessly through the online learning environment.

Problem-based classes are a major activity in many science curricula and prompt feedback is essential. A common approach is through "practice with feedback" using increasingly open contexts or problems. Learning activities focussed on the students identifying, evaluating and making use of a wide range of information and data sources, employing methods to interpret data, justify their approaches, make reasoned conclusions and solve problems. The networked environment is most valuable here, mirroring the approaches of scientists in professional practice as well as offering rapid feedback to learners.

In traditional teaching situations, debate and discussion tend to reside within a time-tabled tutorial context or in students' own social settings. The focus for such dialogue ranges from broad topical issues, key primary (research) materials or the students' own assignments or "work in progress." When the shared object of discussion is a document, an email list or Web board will not provide an effective platform for referring to different features or conducting parallel streams of discussion (Blackmore, Roach, & Dempster, 2001; Buckingham Shum & Sumner, 2000). More intuitive systems for publishing and annotating are required. Furthermore, when the shared object of discussion is a more visual piece or indeed a "performance" of some kind, online systems will be required to support learners and tutors in more interactive ways. Little significant work has so far been undertaken in the sector to achieve a fully interactive approach to distance-taught workshops. Accessing remote experts has previously only been achieved as a passive activity using satellite linking or videoconferencing with lectures delivered from remote rooms. Facilitating interaction from visual performances in remotely linked workshops for active and collaborative learning presents a different set of challenges to traditional models of teaching facilitated by the majority of integrated online learning programs.

TECHNOLOGICAL USABILITY

In considering the online learning programs for supporting research-based learning, TELRI uses its distinction of adoptive and adaptive learning to clarify appropriate ways in which online programs might be used to support learning (Blackmore et al., 2001; Roach et al., 2000). Three categories for the application of technology to learning emerge: resources, support and assessment. In the category of learning resources, online tools can be used to enhance the flexibility of access to course content and primary materials. Together with computer-based assessment, such tools generally support the adoptive aspects of learning. Online tools that provide learning *support* can assist in developing adaptive aspects of learning by offering environments for students to share and discuss work (written or visual) and obtain feedback from tutors and experts on their ideas and understanding. The Boyer Commission (1998) report makes a similar distinction in encouraging the use of ICT that "enriches teaching rather than substitutes for it" and wanting students to have tools "with which they can discriminate, analyse and create rather than simply accumulate."

Courses delivered in whole or in part via Web-based approaches have the potential, if in course design a deliberate attempt is made to do so, to encourage discussion and debate. In TELRI, learning activities focussed on research-like assignments, which the students explored as individuals but debated as a group. If adaptive learning is to take place, an online environment must enable students to engage in some kind of activity or communication process that encourages students to generate new ideas. It must also support the students' need to have ready access to feedback related to their personal input or to interact with other students or experts. Online publishing and discussion tools have the potential to support collaborative learning activities and sharing of work and can offer immediate and flexible feedback from both peers and experts. Through the functionality offered by online learning programs, students are provided with the means to contribute to and view a collection of primary materials or class work and associated reflective or critical comments that drew on and developed students' evaluative, justification and decision-making capabilities. The tutor then becomes an instigator and facilitator of research-based learning, rather than the expert who presents and delivers research-led teaching.

The Web has many advantages in delivering networked online courses taught across one or several institutions, amongst them the speed and ease of communication and the visual integration of multiple types of media. Its main pedagogical advantage, however, is that in its open publishing and sharing functions, it is ideal for supporting research-based approaches to learning. Research-based learning courses benefited from the capacity for the Web to provide the requisite immediacy and flexibility of access to two key elements, brought together in the same online learning environment:
(1)   electronic resources (materials, media, databases, work applications and so on) available through hyperlinks and/or search engines and
(2)   student publishing and feedback facilities for sharing and discussion of such materials and, importantly, the students' own work.

At the same time, the Web should not restrict access for any student. Accessibility issues must therefore be incorporated into the design and delivery methods of online activities and resources (see *Interactions* issue on this theme: http://www.warwick.ac.uk/ETS/interactions/vol5no2/).

Interestingly, work on pre-Web hypermedia systems for scholarly publishing at the Open University's Knowledge Media Institute (KMI) formulated similar design principles for an online environment that support document sharing and discourse (Buckingham Shum & Sumner, 2000, p. 140-143). These were (1) avoid overelaborate discussion structuring schemes; (2) integrate document media with discourse; (3) redesign work practices to emphasise discourse; and (4) support the new practices with tools. An example can be seen in the review system incorporated into the Web-based *Journal for Interactive Media in Education* (JIME: http://www-jime.open.ac.uk/).

Many comparative reviews of online learning programs concentrate on features, tools and technical specifications (http://www.ctt.bc.ca/landonline/choices.html) rather than their application in practice. For the TELRI project, we evaluated a wide range of online learning environments specifically for their capacity to support student Web publishing and annotation of work identified as necessary for research-orientated activities. (For a list of links to detailed reviews on specific packages, see http://www.telri.ac.uk/Technologies/.) TELRI approaches have been piloted with a number of existing software and systems, bearing in mind the need of lecturers for simplicity, "fitness for purpose" and cost-effectiveness of technology solutions. Although a number of commercial packages can provide some of the functionality to allow document sharing and discussion, there are several limitations that restricted their use to support research-based learning activities.

- Most discussion tools, either stand-alone (such as WebBoard) or as part of a VLE-type package (such as FirstClass, Blackboard, WebCT), operate at the level of asynchronous communication of textual messages. Although messages are primarily text-based, MIME is usually supported by most browsers, and in online discussion tools, non-text attachments can usually be included in a message. Few programs supported synchronous collaborative exchange in anything more than textual "chat" format. Video-based collaborative activities are often difficult to set up. Leaving aside the logistical challenges of appropriate rooms, firewall protocols and adequate network links, they require software that is rarely provided within standard VLE-type packages.

- From a pedagogic and practical perspective, discussion tools need to integrate seamlessly with other learning tools so that online resources and student-contributed work, which form the focus of debate and discussion, can be accessed in one step from all members of the class group. This is an aim of integrated online learning packages, which handle it to varying levels of satisfaction for research-based work, and is handled less well in discussion boards.

- The online learning programs reviewed varied in the ability to offer tutors a means to set certain presentation aspects of the learning environment or to create hyperlinks to other documents or resources held on a local server or on the Web (such as primary research materials, links to databases, FAQs, reading lists, etc.).

- In all VLE-type packages reviewed, tutors lacked the ability to schedule in advance the opening and closing of a group, which would be a key feature in the use of these tools for student publishing and viewing of assessed work.

- Very few VLE-type packages provided the means to set up publishing and hyperlinking facilities for the *learners* in addition to the tutors (or could do so only in a very clumsy way that restricted its practical use in courses). Work submitted by students as "messages" could be identified as "source documents," but the programs did not provide any facility for these to be displayed alongside the reply so that the student or tutor comments could easily be related to the original work. The only example that came close was the electronic *Journal for Interactive Media in Education* (www.jime.open.ac.uk/), where peer review is facilitated by a commentary that can be displayed in a window/frame alongside that within which the document resides. Even here, annotation against specific parts of the text was not supported, although discussions threading was a feature.

In our selection of online systems to support the document-based publishing and discussion activities in TELRI courses, some compromises were inevitable. It was also apparent that many academic staff did not have ready access to the tools or VLE packages we wished to pilot with them. A simple CGI-based Web publishing tool was therefore produced that enabled submission, viewing and critiquing of work as a group activity. Students could upload work by entering text into a Web form (or copy/pasting from a word-processed document) and/or uploading images or other file types to be displayed in the browser frame. Without such a tool, many interested staff would have been unable to explore the approaches. The volume of interest and uptake achieved is most definitely attributed to the simplicity and ease of use of the ICT. That it was freely available and circumvented the IT training and support usually required for an integrated package of online learning tools (i.e., a virtual learning environment, VLE) added to its popularity. The tool has, therefore, been very attractive to staff who wanted to work in this way without a requirement that either they or their students should develop sophisticated Web publishing skills.

Development of a tool "in-house" provided us with three opportunities:

(1)   to provide an accessible and simple ICT tool for staff and students to use in the pilots;
(2)   to tailor the functionality of the tool specifically to the needs identified for supporting research-based learning activities; and
(3)   to avoid compromising the evaluation of the pilots by technology that was not sufficiently "fit for purpose."

In the ANNIE project, the technological usability evaluation explored the capacity of online learning programs to support collaborative learning centred on visual or performance-based activities (rather than the document-based focus of the TELRI courses and the OU's KMI work). Firstly, a survey of distance teaching across all disciplines in the UK was carried out and secondly an evaluative study was undertaken of software available to enhance work in this area. From a vast review of over 1,000 Web-supported courses and previous work undertaken to capture visual and performance-based activities, there was a disappointing lack of innovation in this area.

> "The majority of courses offered rely on traditional distance teaching methods, which may be adapted for electronic distribution, but essentially preserve traditional distance pedagogy supported by information packs, books, CD-ROMs. In some, a web presence is mostly used for delivery of resources and unstructured or unmoderated discussion and social discourse. The vast majority of computer based distance teaching falls into a small number of subject areas: Business, management, electronics, computing and astronomy. Such subjects

tend to translate well for web delivery, but have an audience for whom the preferred study mode is self-paced distance learning" (Fergusson, 2001).

Any relevant development has focussed on passive capturing of lectures or demonstrations rather than the support of interactive, creative and collaborative learning activities. The areas of greatest value as models for participatory workshops include interactive online performance, mass participatory events (such as national experiments) and virtual rehearsals of plays. In addition to computer-based software solutions, we have also looked into other technologies, principally ISDN videoconferencing. An obvious requirement is for clear, high-quality video contact between individuals or groups, though its use for workshop classes has also been of importance in the ANNIE project. Since videoconferencing suites are rarely in appropriate locations for the purpose of workshop activities, the technology now exists to run good quality video over high-speed networks. This makes videoconferencing facilities much more mobile. In theory, any office, studio or workshop with a network outlet can become a videoconferencing room. The mobile equipment networks to dedicated ISDN lines and from there to the remote institution. This is obviously an important development in the area of distance participation in practical workshops. It has been used with partial success (due to technical failings not pedagogic ones!) in the initial pilots for ANNIE.

The development of the ANNIE case study pilots considered how these kinds of technology might best support the pedagogic aims of the student activities and best meet their learning needs. The rationales for using technology and the effect it had on the students' performances and the learning process were key elements in the overall usability evaluation. In general: "When the aim is solely to broaden the range of activities and expertise available to students, videoconferencing is selected. When changes in the aims for the students' learning is considered, for example developing critical or reflective practice, or collaborative working, then computer-mediated communication and computer-based resources are considered" (Dempster & Childs, 2002).

EVALUATION METHODOLOGIES

Specific evaluations of the implementation of new methods were conducted using a variety of standard methods. We triangulated findings from interviews with course developers/tutors, student questionnaires and the reflective observations of the support team members. In our approach, we compare qualitatively educational effectiveness of the new teaching and learning approaches with previous or possible alternative approaches, including the role played by technological intervention. We considered the intended capabilities to be developed against the extent to which the tutor felt the students had demonstrated the specific learning outcomes attributed to research capabilities, that is, the "adaptive" components. (These are summarised in Table 1 in the section *Pedagogic Principles*.)

In terms of the costs and benefits in the online learning approaches, one would ideally measure learning outcomes of groups making use of ICT against those who do not. This can in most cases be achieved by evaluating outcomes with the previous years' equivalent groups. It is unlikely, given the relatively small timescale of the development projects, that one would have been able to identify major learning shifts. However, we have been able for each intervention to derive qualitative data on changes in student capability and the learning experience.

Many individual academics who have adopted the approaches are clearly convinced of the worth in supporting research-based learning. Promoting factors were the motivation of the students to use the ICT approach and the ease of use of particular online tools. In nearly all evaluations, the students perceived the research-based approach to assignments as adding an extra dimension to the course. Importantly, course tutors were generally convinced that the level of learning and quality of the students' work had increased significantly.

Immediate and longer-term benefits were evaluated in the following areas:

- more explicitness in curricula about learning outcomes and assessment criteria;
- enhanced student achievement in the skills that contribute to research capability;
- improved access to learning opportunities;
- cohesion of teaching and learning processes into a coherent strategy;
- increased ratio of motivators to barriers (leading to increased uptake and success);
- maintenance of quality in courses involving larger numbers of students;
- reducing teaching staff workloads in preparation, delivery, support and marking;
- increasing the quality time that staff can spend with students;
- reducing the overall cost of methods and materials in the longer term;
- more effective use of existing IT infrastructure;
- innovation and potential for new distance learning development and partnerships;
- increased student motivation and satisfaction from creative and self-paced approach;
- reducing the overall costs of using remote experts; and
- staff development.

The cost of each intervention might also be measured in terms of: improved or increased use of existing equipment; provision of new equipment; staff training and learning time; and production of new tools and materials. The intervention cost must be compared with the cost of current or where possible alternative methods. Costs in pilot courses were projected to longer-term benefits of the intervention in terms of maintaining quality and values, staff development, student motivation and achievement, and other factors affecting sustainability (validity and viability).

The use of advanced technology can also enable departments to deliver and support courses in ways otherwise not possible. For example, the close network of scholars and professional practitioners that are exploited in the ANNIE project enable the Warwick and Kent theatre and drama departments to maintain the involvement of experts long after they have physically left the university. The use of distance technologies has the potential to enable such scholars or practitioners to continue to contribute to whole modules or one-off classes to their degree programs from a remote location. Not only is the curriculum enriched as a consequence but the costs are substantially reduced, both to the department in terms of consultancy and travel expenses and to the expert in terms of time, travel and commitment.

USABILITY OUTCOMES FROM EXAMPLES IN PRACTICE

Looking at the complexity of operational, educational and technological issues and needs in the usability and cost-effectiveness of online learning programs, it is understandable that "it is harder to know how to use the technology than to develop it" (Buckingham, Shum, & Sumner, 2000, p. 151). With this in mind, this section provides illustrations of research-based learning approaches in courses spanning a range of subject disciplines. From both formative and summative evaluations, the outcomes are identified in each case study in relation to particular aspects of educational and technological usability outlined above.

The support of students' creative and collaborative learning activities explored throughout this chapter require that online learning programs can, to varying extents, provide students with the means to share and critique materials, particularly their own work, through:

- publishing,
- annotation, and
- discussion.

The priorities and the integration of these functions vary according to the specific purposes and aims of the course involved. There are definite variances in the learning activities and support requirements across the disciplines. From a synthesis of case study evaluations across the projects across the case studies implemented through TELRI and ANNIE, a number of generic elements emerge as successful outcomes of the research-based approaches across all subjects and courses. Primarily these fall into the categories listed in Table 2, the benefits of which were generally felt by tutors to outweigh the costs of the intervention.

Developing and Supporting Research-Based Learning   145

Table 2: Generic outcomes from implementation of research-based approaches in subject-based courses (from TELRI Project: http://www.telri.ac.uk/ Evaluation/Case_Studies)

Outcome	Evidence of
Increased quality of students' work or performance	Enhanced learning
Enhanced conceptual understanding of underlying meaning	High-order learning
Generation of original ideas and expression	Creativity and innovation
Improved search and analysis techniques	Reasoning and analysis
Problem posing as well as problem solving	Synthesis and evaluation
Increased student motivation and sense of ownership of course	Student-led approach
Increased student participation in review and debate	Discussion-led approach
Students working more as groups than as individuals	Collaborative learning

In some cases, in terms of staff time to explore and implement the educational, technological and operational requirements, the actual pilots were rarely cost-effective. However, once the approaches were embedded into the lecturer's own practice or departmental culture, the cost benefits were extremely favourable.

Language Learning

In a course for nonspecialist French language learners in the Language Centre at Warwick, students focus on a single assignment involving research, presentation, discussion and analysis. Two groups of 30 students were asked to choose an image and conduct some background study, then upload the analysis of the chosen image to the Web using the TELRI forms-based publishing tool (see Figure 1).

This work formed the central theme to a presentation, a question and answer session and a written piece incorporating further research suggested by peers. All aspects were delivered in the target language. In so doing, students build up linguistic knowledge and meaning through the creative use of language.

Despite a wide differentiation in the technical expertise of both the students and tutors, very few technology-related difficulties were encountered. It was clear that the transparent use of technology was a success factor. The design of the online program was purposely kept as simple as possible to avoid distraction from the main process of language learning. The technology-based approaches allowed scope within the course schedule for students to reflect more deeply than was previously possible in solely time-tabled groups. A higher degree of focus in face-to-face seminars was also apparent. Linguistic knowledge and fluency of expression in a wider range of communication areas (listening, reading, speaking and writing) were also enhanced. The use of such approaches in subsequent runs of the course and in other courses offered by the Language Centre makes the initial investment in staff time highly cost-effective in the longer term.

Figure 1:   Submission form and student page via Web publishing

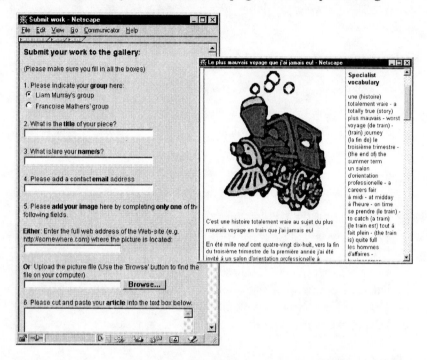

In a module for a third-year cultural course in Italian Studies at Warwick, we took the above approach a stage further to support students' critical analysis of a document translation into Italian through the use of commenting facilities. Previously in the course, there had been a problem with perception versus reality of translation as a practice. The course tended to be grammar oriented. Few new knowledge and critical-thinking skills were developed in translation. A Web site was prepared to enable students to submit drafts as individuals in a group of five. The facility enabled students to compare, contrast, comment on and redraft translations as needed (Figure 2).

Higher-order thinking skills within student discussions, comments, and translations were evident to the tutor. The skill objectives of the course were to develop an analytical and critical view of translations, develop the ability to use a multitude of resources, and develop the practice of drafting and redrafting translations; and finally, language accuracy was a major objective. Perception of the course focus was shifted from grammatical emphasis to professional evaluation emphasis. The site publication produced more direct and intelligent questioning. The translation accuracy improved and grammatical skill levels were maintained or improved.

Comparative Literary Studies

In English and Comparative Literary Studies (Warwick), a module on North American Women Writers aims to encourage in students individual interpretations

Figure 2: Viewing and commenting on student and group translation work through Web publishing

and responses within the frameworks provided by the prescribed critical reading. The objectives of the course program are to study a selection of 20th-century North American Women Writers in depth, within the wider context of North American literary and cultural preoccupations, and with reference to recent critical debates. The course is based around a seminar program. The interdisciplinary backgrounds of the students taking the course meant that it is difficult to support the differing needs and understanding with respect to cultural contexts and critical analysis abilities. In particular, tutorial teaching for such large groups is restricted in the depth of analysis that could be supported by group work and tutor guidance. Some students are part time with work and other commitments so that time-tabling face-to-face sessions is increasingly difficult. There are fewer large seminar rooms and so booking teaching space was also a problem.

In order to alleviate some of these problems, a Web site of notes on course texts and bibliographies was produced along with the use of a simple email list to extend tutorial discussions (Dennis & Dempster, 2000). This has the advantage of not triggering a great demand for training, since most students already use the Web and email. The use of email-based discussion aims to encourage independent learning and group collaboration and to democratise the learning process without precluding the provision of lecturer input and support. In the absence of a more sophisticated online learning environment, a permanent record of the email list contributions was included on the Web site by implementing an archiving system. A student work area was subsequently added using the Web publishing tool developed for TELRI. The

Figure 3:   Integrated Web site for comparative literary studies providing course information, guidance on set texts, email discussion and archives and student web publishing

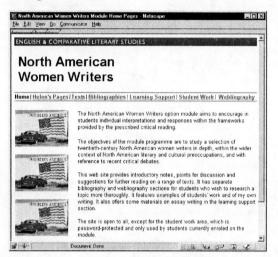

students can submit their non-assessed work, view the work of others and comment on and discuss the critical analysis approaches taken and the ideas generated. The home Web page for the course (Figure 3) integrates a general overview of the seminar structure for set texts, links to assignments, tutor's notes, bibliographies and Web resources, access to the discussion archives, and the student work (publishing) area.

The integration of ICT allows far more in-depth reflection on the critical analysis process than the face-to-face seminar program would otherwise have allowed. With the Web publishing implementation, the Web site provides a far more integrated learning environment. The students are becoming familiar with going to the Web site for all their online activities, i.e., retrieving resources, engaging in discussions and publishing their work. Students are given more freedom and opportunity to experiment with their own ideas and arguments. With emphasis on an open process environment where comments and tutor's remarks are recorded, students' abilities in structuring their argument and expressing reflective reasoning for their ideas are enhanced.

The student contributions to the email discussion and their published work provide an excellent resource for following cohorts of students on the module. There is a need to moderate these and putting them up on the Web site is quite time-consuming, but well worth the effort. Making the high quality work (marked where possible) available provides the students with a sense of purpose and understanding of the assessment criteria. Students used the email discussion list to add or elaborate further on a remark made in the seminar. The mix of different degree courses represented on the module allowed students to share their specific skills and knowledge with other members of the group.

History and Law

The Web and CD-ROM provide students with more access to information than ever before. However, students still need to develop expertise in evaluating the relevance of what they encounter in their researching techniques.

A second-year core module in the Department of History (Comparative American Studies) on North American Themes is based on lectures and seminars. The Web publishing approach was implemented to facilitate students' reflection on their approaches to research and enhance the development of evaluation and critical analysis skills. The students select a book, research article or Web site relevant to the course objectives. Using the Web publishing facility, they submit a critical review of the chosen primary text and can view the reviews of others in the class. This work is used as discussion material for the seminars. Since in the past, original source material was difficult to access, this approach provides a purpose for using Web-based resources. Furthermore, it builds up a resource base of critical analysis that is reusable in future courses. The approach forms an open process learning environment and provides opportunities for originality and risk taking, essential elements for the development of high-level thinking. An online discussion board is currently being integrated into the approach to extend seminar debate. The tutor commented that the approach enhanced the students' motivation to read the texts, their willingness to take risks and exchange ideas and their level of reasoning and abstraction of arguments.

In a similar fashion, an assignment and assessment scheme was developed with the School of Law at Warwick based on making those working and study practices leading to high quality work more transparent to the students. This allows students to approach future assignments and finally dissertations with greater success and originality. The process, not accidentally, reflects the research process practiced by experienced academics. The main failing of a student's approach is often a superficial interpretation of the course information and assignment meaning and depth. This often underlies the inability to design cohesive and effective strategies to allow them to define clearly and tackle each of the individual assignment components. TELRI approaches enable a learning process development to be incorporated into the course without the need for additional tutor support. Nevertheless, feedback on the student contributions may provide a valuable focus for tutorial work or email discussion during the process. Submission of the learning process log was conducted after the piece of assessed work was submitted. The full process and associated best examples are then published (anonymously) to a course Web site. The students benefit from clear examples of best practice and best work for subsequent assignments.

TELRI worked with TALL (Technology-Assisted Lifelong Learning) and the Local History group in the Continuing Education Department at Oxford University to develop and evaluate a Web-based course that aims to develop the student as a confident and proficient researcher of family and community history. The purpose of the course was to develop students' abilities to analyse critically approaches to data search and query techniques appropriate to supporting concepts and arguments. Assessment of the course is based on three set assignments, designed to develop students' analytical and evaluative capabilities.

The need to design a specific online learning environment for the course was a huge cost. However, we felt this was necessary since commercial or HE managed learning environments (MLEs, e.g., WebCT, Blackboard, COSE) did not allow TALL to establish the philosophy in the way they wished. The course is currently run as a mixture of online and offline material. That is, it has a traditional print-based focus (using PDF files for downloading and printing) backed with network support for collaborative work and discussion provided by WebBoard conferencing software. The sense of overview of course structure, content, logic and purpose is easily hidden in an MLE. As such, it does not allow students to take as much responsibility for their own learning as we required.

In responding to the new environment, the tutors were reactive rather than proactive. Students on the other hand were asking for more integration of facilities for voice-based, synchronous conferencing, rather than purely text-based discussions.

Biological Sciences

Research capabilities are developed in science curricula through sophisticated problem-solving and reasoning skills. A course on Bioinformatics has been developed that integrates a problem-solving approach with critical discussion of appropriate approaches and choice of techniques. The focus of the course is on solving a real research problem in the area of genomics. The course consists of seven modules and is driven by problem-solving exercises embedded in each of the modules (Figure 4). The students are given a DNA sequence and are expected to do a series of analyses on it. The course modules are designed to help students to deconstruct this complex task into a set of relatively simple exercises. In doing so, the course has two important aims; one is just to be aware of the techniques in bioinformatics and to teach students how to apply them and the other is that the students gain understanding in the underlying theory.

Students are given access to a publishing area on the course Web site where they can present their findings and discuss their choices with peers (and tutors). The students upload an overview of how they plan to tackle the report write-up that they will eventually submit at the end of the course. A blank notice board input area on the Web site allows students and tutors to add comments.

The need to develop knowledge and techniques is driven by the students' need to work through the problem. The final assessed output is a research report, which emphasises the students' reasoning and justification in deciding the appropriate procedures and resources to utilise. Furthermore, students are expected to develop the ability to think critically about the results they are obtaining and to discuss this in

Figure 4: Bioinformatics resource-based course integrating problem-solving, analysis and reflection exercises and online learning support systems

their report. Through this approach, students also gain understanding of (1) how different programs require data to be inputted in different formats and (2) the importance of this in terms of obtaining a sensible answer to data analysis. These are prerequisites to performing accurate research.

Performing Arts

In theatre and drama modules, online videoconferencing and Web-based programs are used to provide access to research-based teaching and workshops led by practitioners of national and international standing. Interactive activities aim to enhance the students' learning experience and promote student engagement in self-directed learning. Different methodologies have been piloted to evaluate the usability of online tools for meeting these aims.

Videoconference Seminars and Workshops

Students took part in differing mixes of asynchronous preparation work through Web-based discussion boards, attending the videoconference(s) and follow-up asynchronous exercise.

In a course on Performance and Hypertext, the students drew on the skills of an artist situated in a remote location to engage in issues regarding the status of the virtual body and the options it offers for live performance. Four computers with Web cameras were set up in a studio at Warwick. Twelve students engaged in workshop activity with the remote tutor, using cameras and the chat facility available in the chosen iVisit software (Figure 5). The use of Web technology in a course on Virtual Scenography allowed a remote expert in the creation of virtual world in theatre design to interact with a group of around 10 students. He presented his material, set up some

Figure 5: Telematic performance. Remote expert links up with local group of students through videoconferencing and Web-based exercises

exercises and responded to queries. A videoconference was used successfully for the final discussion and feedback.

Web-Mediated Video-Based Exercises

These sessions were successfully supported from a set of pages on the course Web site. The exercises were videotaped using a digital camera and uploaded to the Web site for review by students and the lecturer. One example is a module on stand-up comedy, where the tutor took students through a series of exercises to build up their ability to do stand-up comedy. The students undertook the activities as a class, commenting on each other's performance. The students recorded their feedback and uploaded it, proving an effective means of enabling peer review and tutor assessment.

Software Tutorials

These were distanced learning case studies where students worked offline through software tutorials supported online by the lecturer. There was a limited amount of synchronous work. One example of this is for lighting designers at Kent who received an introduction to and support for lighting design software produced by a professional expert in the field. The module successfully integrated an initial synchronous demonstration, asynchronous use of a support Web site of resources, Web-based discussion and NetMeeting tutorial sessions, culminating in a fruitful follow-up videoconference discussion.

Online Learning Support

Web-based learning materials and use of discussion boards were effective approaches in this area of development. Modules provided both a support for and a demonstration of media- and Web-based aspects of theatre work. In a module at Warwick, online learning programs aimed to provide a "virtual residency" for a theatre company to engage with a group of students on the course. Videoconferencing, Web-based discussion and the use of images and video shared through the Internet followed an on-site visit. The module involved remotely located tutor and students and centred on video and pictorial material presented asynchronously through an interactive Web site. Students annotated the materials online with their own ideas and interacted effectively via a Web-based discussion board.

In evaluating the usability of the online facilities for video-based teaching and learning activities (Childs, 2002), the feedback from students and tutors was enthusiastic. Although many students were apprehensive about using the technology, most found the process of communicating with the remote tutor (expert) far more inclusive than they had anticipated. Although not apparent during the videoconference sessions, during the discussions, tutors and students commented that the lack of visual cues resulted in the communication being more limited and disjointed for the remote work than for the group of students in the local room. The communication was also constrained by the students' self-consciousness at appearing on the projected image. Recommendations for future sessions therefore included the use of a separate monitor, which cannot be seen by the participants, for monitoring the outgoing signal and to ensure echo suppression is used at both ends.

In broad terms, videoconferencing had few advantages over traditional face-to face-sessions, apart from enabling the session to take place. The students felt that delaying the session until an occasion that the remote expert tutor was available to deliver a face-to-face session would have been detrimental to their studies; they felt that continuity of contact with the same lecturer was important. Videoconferencing was an effective substitute but did not provide "added value." In the evaluation (Childs, 2002), the students benefited from a number of the technologies and considered that their use in face-to-face sessions would also be helpful. All the students stated that they would not have any problems with using videoconferencing in the future, and where students had been apprehensive about the first session, there was no longer any apprehension about repeating the experience.

FUTURE TRENDS

It is not coincidental that the capabilities we seek to develop through research-based learning enable a student to develop a "skill of transfer." This encompasses the range of transferable skills considered essential for employability and lifelong learning (Barnett, 1994; Bridges, 1994; Hyland, 1994). Indeed, the research-based framework developed for TELRI was seen as a practical and sound way forward in the development of transferable skills in other learning contexts, as wide-reaching as management training and school-based education.

The strategy adopted in both projects is one of engaging staff across a range of disciplines in dialogue about curriculum design and delivery. This assists in identifying research capability components in the context of specific study programs and disciplinary needs and enables a more insightful exploration of how such capabilities might be further developed through the use of online learning programs.

The online resources, tools, materials and systems developed and implemented by the TELRI and ANNIE projects are being used in different ways. Mostly they are used by academic teaching staff in supporting the delivery of courses and learning, but it is well recognised that this needs to be sustainable in order to bring about some impact on continuing practice at an institutional level. The ideas are increasingly being incorporated into teaching and learning strategies and academic staff development programs of many of the institutional partners involved in the projects. Despite this and the increasing growth and diversity in the use of ICT in learning and teaching, development is often patchy and lacks the coordination of other elements of university management. Some of these operational issues are well known to educational developers and learning technologists across the sector but have rarely been documented. They are usually evidenced on the basis of individual projects rather than generic studies. Future evaluation studies (one such is planned as part of the TELRI project transferability work) should seek to provide useful vehicles for exploring the *processes* of implementation of teaching innovations within particular institutional contexts.

One reason for the lack of embedding of new practice within an institution may lie in the context in which its individual academics must operate. Learning technology still struggles to find an appropriate base and by its very nature challenges the status quo. There is often a significant gap between funding and support provided for IT infrastructure and a central support unit for teaching development. Additionally, there is an element of conflict for academics between their conception of effective learning, which may suggest a research-based and student-led approach, and the pragmatic attitude that academic staff tend to adopt in order to survive within the current parameters of institutional contexts. Institutions vary immensely in their structures and working practices, i.e., the operational context that supports and integrates teaching development into its core academic business (Dempster & Blackmore, 2002). The retention of many existing organisational structures, policies, procedures and staffing arrangements can in many ways undermine or compromise the pace and impact of innovative development. It is therefore essential that these operational contexts are better understood if future educational development projects, particularly external ones, are to be cost-effective and result in enhanced practice and quality. The depth of analysis required of such institutional contexts was unfortunately beyond the scope of the current projects. It is an area worthy of future research.

The application of distance technology in the field of the arts and particularly in practice-based disciplines is virtually nonexistent. The study of distance teaching and learning programs may not offer us much in the way of positive models for development. They may be useful in terms of what not to do, but our remit is to find an entirely different set of principles particularly for subjects that are not obvious candidates for this mode of delivery. This means we have the luxury of starting from first principles and can be confident that we are not duplicating existing research. The pilots undertaken in the ANNIE project pave the way for the development of highly innovative yet practical ways forward to providing online environments to support interactive, creative and collaborative learning activities.

CONCLUSIONS

This chapter has aimed to highlight the value of pedagogical objectives and frameworks in evaluating usability in the main and considering validity and viability of online learning programs within specific learning and teaching contexts. In aiming to harness and exploit online learning programs, the focus of our two projects on research-based learning (and "research-led" teaching) served to re-establish our key educational purposes to the benefit of teaching and learning quality. We believe the research and development involved has had a significant impact on higher education in that it has contributed to a renewal of the debate on supporting the development of higher order thinking and learning in the curriculum. In particular, the projects have evolved at a time when higher education is being asked to improve the thinking and transferable skills of students. The course design framework considers the pedagogical rationale for implementing research-based learning, while the case studies and review of tools offer examples of what to do with the technology to support this. As a result, we hope to have been influential in developing new approaches to curriculum design and the appropriate application of ICT to support creative and collaborative learning.

The cohesion required between educational usability and operational usability, including technological factors, is not to be underestimated. Integrating individual innovation with institutional strategies is essential in the management of change in academic practice. The chapter hopes to have highlighted how institutional factors can both impact on innovation or bring teaching and research closer together to enhance learning. Both TELRI and ANNIE offer ideas that are practical to an extent in most operational contexts. This has had an impact on staff development programs and has been perceived as enhancing professional development by those academics involved.

It is less straightforward to measure the improvements in student learning that have come about through such implementation projects. This is a widespread problem as higher order cognitive skills and their assessment is not well defined. It has certainly been difficult to attribute any student's "capability" to a specific online learning program. Higher education will be keen to evaluate what is and is not appropriate and "fit for purpose" with respect to the usability of online learning programs to support institutional learning and teaching strategies. As institutions commit to buying in or building their own, they will ultimately be looking to judge the cost-effectiveness of that investment against their own goals. Feedback provided from project evaluation suggests that in general the online approaches for sharing and discussion of students' work have led to greater collaboration and communication between staff and students and amongst students. It is therefore valid to conclude that the requisite functionality of online learning programs for supporting research-based learning and teaching activities discussed in this chapter has been seen to enhance comparative and critical evaluation skills and foster an environment in which originality and innovation can flourish.

ACKNOWLEDGMENTS

The author wishes to acknowledge the valuable contributions by the project team in undertaking aspects of the development and evaluation work discussed in this chapter, namely, Dr. Paul Blackmore, Graham Lewis (Centre for Academic Practice), Dr. Mick Roach and Jim Evans (TELRI), and Professor David Thomas, Mark Childs and Cat Fergusson (ANNIE).

Furthermore, academic and support staff in the participating departments provided useful insights into research-based practice and usability requirements. In particular, I wish to thank at Warwick, Hugh Denard (School of Theatre Studies), Abdul Paliwala (School of Law), Trevor Hawkes (Institute of Mathematics), Nick Mann (Biological Sciences), Helen Dennis (Department of English), Loredana Polezzi (Department of Italian), and lecturers in the Language Centre; as well as the Department of Continuing Education at Oxford; the Faculty of Engineering at Southampton; the Staff Development Units at Birmingham and Durham; and the School of Drama, Film and the Visual Arts at Kent.

REFERENCES

Barnett (1984). *Evaluation, Nature and Effects of Research Approaches.*

Barnett (1994). *Transferable Skills,Employability/Lifelong Learning.*

Blackmore, P., Roach, M., & Dempster, J. (2002). The use of ICT in education for research and development. In S. Fallow & R. Bhanot (Eds.), *Educational development through information and communication technologies.* London: Kogan Page, Chapter 12, pp. 133-140.

Boud, D. (1988). *Developing student autonomy in learning.* London: Kogan Page.

Boyer Commission. (1998). *Ten Ways to Change Undergraduate Education Section VI. Use Information Technology Creatively.* Retrieved on November 22, 2002 from http://naples.cc.sunysb.edu/Pres/boyer.nsf/webform/VI.

Brew, A., & Boud, D. (1995). Teaching and research: Establishing the vital link with learning. *Higher Education, 29*(3), 261-273.

Bridges, D. (1994). *Transferable skills in higher education.* Norwich, England: University of East Anglia.

Britain, S., & Liber, O. (2000). *A framework for pedagogical evaluation of virtual learning environments.* Retrieved on November 22, 2002 from the Joint Information Systems Committee Web site: http://www.jisc.ac.uk/jtap/htm/jtap-041.html

Buckingham Shum, S., & Sumner, T. (2000). New scenarios in scholarly publishing and debate. In M. Eisenstadt & T. Vincent (Eds.), *The Knowledge Web: Learning and Collaborating on the Net.* London: Kogan Page, Chapter 8, pp. 135-151.

Cann, A. J., & Pawley, E. L. (1999). Automated online tutorials: New formats for assessment on the WWW. In S. Brown, J. Bull, & P. Race (Eds.), *Computer-assisted assessment in higher education.* London: Kogan Page.

Centra, J. A. (1983). Research productivity and teaching effectiveness. *Research in Higher Education, 18*(4), 379-389.

Childs, M. (2002). Evaluation of videoconferencing sessions in accessing and networking with remote experts. Retrieved on November 22, 2002 from http://www.ukc.ac.uk/sdfva/ANNIE/ie/Outputs/Feedback.htm.

Conole, G., & Oliver, M. (1998). A pedagogical framework for embedding C&IT into the curriculum. *ALT-Journal, 6*(2), 4-16.

Dempster, J., & Childs, M. (2002). Accessing and networking with national and international expertise. *Forum, 20*, 10-11. Retrieved on November 22, 2002 from http://www.warwick.ac.uk/services/CAP/Publications/Forum/Back_issues/Forum_20/forum_20.html#annie.

Dempster, J. A., & Blackmore, P. (2002). Developing research-based learning using ICT in higher education curricula: The role of research and evaluation. In R. Macdonald & J. Wisdom (Eds.), *Academic and educational development: Research, evaluation and changing practice in higher education.* London: Kogan Page, Chapter 11, pp. 129-139.

Dennis, H., & Dempster, J. (2000). Enhancing critical debate through Web-based discussion and publishing. *Interactions, 4*(2). Retrieved on November 22, 2002 from http://www.warwick.ac.uk/ETS/interactions/vol4no2/dennis.htm

Dreyfus, L., & Dreyfus, S. E. (1986). *Mind over machine: The power of human intuition and expertise in the era of the computer.* Oxford, England: Basil Blackwell.

Eisner, E. W. (1985). *The art of educational evaluation: A personal view.* London: Falmer.

Elton, L. (1986). Research and teaching: Symbiosis or conflict. *Higher Education, 15*, 299-304.

Entwistle, N. J. (1998). Conceptions of teaching for academic development: The role of research. In K. J. Gregory (Ed.), *Development training for academic staff* (pp. 23-32). London: Goldsmiths College.

Fergusson, C. (2001). *Evaluating Approaches and Technologies* (ANNIE Project report). Retrieved on November 22, 2002 from http://www.ukc.ac.uk/sdfva/ANNIE/ie/Outputs/CSTechno.htm.

Follett, B. *The University of Warwick teaching and research: The essential partnership*. University of Warwick, Publicity and Publications Office.

Hattie, J., & Marsh, H. W. (1996). The relationship between research and teaching: A meta-analysis. *Review of Educational Research, 66*(4), 507-542.

Hyland, T. (1994). *Competence, education and NVQs*. London: Cassell.

Kuhn, D. (1981). The role of self-directed activity in cognitive development. In I. E. Segel, D. Brodzinsky, R. M. Golinkoff (Eds.), *New directions in Piagetian theory and practice*. Hillsdale, NJ: Lawrence Erlbaum.

Laurillard, D. (1993). *Rethinking university teaching—A framework for the effective use of educational technology in higher education*. London: Routledge.

Oliver, M. & Dempster, J. A. (in press). Embedding the use of ICT through strategic staff development. In P. Blackmore & R. Blackwell (Eds.), *Strategic Staff Development in Higher Education*. Open University Press.

Ramsden, P., & Moses, I. (1992). Associations between research and teaching in Australian higher education. *Higher Education, 23*, 273-295.

Roach, M., Blackmore, P., & Dempster, J. (2000). *Supporting high level learning through research-based methods: Guidelines for course design* (TELRI Project publication). Retrieved on November 22, 2002 from http://www.telri.ac.uk/guidelines.pdf.

Roach, M., Blackmore, P., & Dempster, J. (2001). Supporting high level learning through research-based methods: A framework for course development. *Innovations in Education and Training International, 38*(4), pp. 160-169.

Robbins, L. (1963). *Higher education (The Robbins report)*. Report of the Committee appointed by the Prime Minister under the Chairmanship of Lord Robbins, 1961-63. London: Her Majesty's Stationery Office.

Rowntree, D. (1995). Teaching and learning online: A correspondence education for the 21st century? *British Journal of Educational Technology, 26*(3), 205-215.

Salmon, G. (2000). *E-moderating: The key to teaching and learning online*. London: Kogan Page.

Chapter VIII

Online Learning for the Real World: Diploma in Computing Via the Internet

Bridget Khursheed
University of Oxford, UK

ABSTRACT

This chapter examines usability evaluation in the context of the Diploma in Computing via the Internet offered by the University of Oxford Department for Continuing Education and, to some extent, its on-site course partner. This ongoing online course is aimed at adult non-university (the "real world" of the chapter title) students. The chapter follows the usability evaluation process through the life cycle of course development, delivery and maintenance, analysing the requirements and actions of each stage and how they were implemented in the course. It also discusses how pedagogical evaluation must be considered as part of this process, as well as the more obvious software considerations, and how this was achieved within the course. Finally it draws some conclusions concerning the enhancements to course usability of the virtual classroom and how this atypical evaluation material can and should be integrated into an overall usability evaluation picture.

INTRODUCTION

Teaching computing by distance learning is not a novelty and, in some ways, the subject lends itself to such treatment in its study of logical concepts such as algorithms. However, in others, an isolated student suffers the same difficulties as an occasional home PC user: through the use of software (and programming languages) in a way that can encourage the problematic without support. It is interesting to compare the experience of classroom computing teaching and find that, even with support, students can find actual computer use daunting. The development and practice of usability evaluation within such an online course would therefore need to focus not only on its interface and content presentation but also its pedagogical effectiveness. This chapter examines the experience of adult non-university (the "real world" of the chapter title) students in continuing education. It focuses on an ongoing online course in computing offered by the University of Oxford Department for Continuing Education and, to some extent, its on-site partner.

The Online Course

The Diploma in Computing has been available on-site at the Department for Continuing Education since the early 90s and online (as the Diploma in Computing via the Internet) since 1999.

The course's students come from all walks of life ranging from teachers to the retired, the unemployed, lawyers and even IT professionals. The learning goals for the course centre on a broad familiarity and confidence with all aspects of computing in keeping with a student body that very often has vocational motivation for studying, although this is not always the case.

The course has the following aims:

*   To provide a systematic introduction to modern computing
*   To put students in control of information technology
*   To enhance career prospects in a key skill area
*   To give an opportunity for employers to upgrade staff skills

The course itself:

*   Involves two years' distance learning using the latest Internet technology
*   Includes an Oxford summer school experience
*   Leads to the award of an undergraduate Diploma in Computing
*   Carries CATS credit rating of 120 points at Level 2, meaning that the course can be used to count toward an undergraduate degree if you continue your study at another university (Level 2 is approximately equivalent to the second year of study on an undergraduate full-time degree course at a British university)

The dual status of the course, running face-to-face and through distance learning, provides a unique insight into the respective learning needs of students. Analysis of their learning experience, supported by rich data past and present, has shaped and continues to shape the development of the course itself in both its versions.

The Requirements for Usability Evaluation

When the online course was first mooted, it was seen as a development on the existing on-site course and one that could reflect on its successful reputation.

There were initially two main areas of concern.

1. *Students would not find the course a satisfying learning experience.*

On the first point, the course is delivered to part-time learners outside the university over a period of two years. Such a long period of online study had rarely if ever been attempted within British higher education, with the preference being for shorter courses of weeks' or even days' duration. In comparison to delivery on-site, where the level of interaction and pastoral support is high, these online learners are isolated and disparate and yet dealing with complex materials, including programming, over a long period of time. As the course was developed within the Department for Continuing Education, strategies were both in place and available for the support of part-time learners, addressing the fact that this group of learners may also have had bad experiences with education in the past. For example, the course features a summer school at the end of the year to foster a sense of genuine face-to-face involvement in the course. Such strategies had yet to be tested on online learners.

In addition, online course data (Gardner & Newdick, 1998) shows that students drop out significantly in the early days of such courses with numbers stabilising once they feel established. For example, one of the North American universities studied by the report declared between 35-50% nonstarter rates; that is to say, students who dropped out before even starting the course in spite of paying a deposit. Rapid drop-out was a common experience across all five of the Sloan Report universities. Instant and early drop-out cannot be directly attributed to usability problems, perhaps rather to presentational problems: for example, students may not realise how long they would have to study each week to make a success of an online course in comparison to the scheduled two hours of classes per week. It was clear that the Diploma in Computing would have to address these potential problems to be successful. The course team decided to do so in the following three ways.

a. First, by being as usable as possible for new users, to prevent early drop-out, and for established users; with technical support playing a key role here.

b. Second, user interaction had to be emulated in a virtual classroom to engage students and foster an environment that promoted learning.

c. Third, user interaction had to be monitored by systems and personnel, including tutors in a new online role, to prevent students' drifting away.

2. *Development must run alongside delivery.*

Available time and resources meant that once the pedagogical specification phase of the course was complete, units of materials would be in production as the course was delivered. This potential area of strain was resolved by the development of a comprehensive evaluation plan prior to the course's commencement to test its effectiveness in a range of areas including usability. The unavoidable and tight schedule also encouraged the selection of an evolutionary model of course production allowing different levels of evaluation data analysis to be fed back into the course at predefined key and measurable stages.

The requirements for usability evaluation were therefore to:

1.   Prove the online redefinition of an existing on-site course pedagogically effective and usable.
2.   Provide the usability metrics to confirm, support and improve the delivery of a course in an online environment.

USABILITY OF AN ONLINE COURSE: CONCEPT AND DEVELOPMENT

Usability Definition and Goals

Jared Spool (1997) defines Web site usability in terms of how effective users are at doing what they want to do. A usability definition for an online course and the goals to be developed from that definition must include reference to learning aims and pedagogical effectiveness.

As a starting point, the team worked from three general principles developed by Dix, Finlay, Abowd, and Beale (1993) to support usability in an interactive system. These are:

•   Learnability: the ease with which new users can begin effective interaction and achieve maximum performance
•   Flexibility: the multiplicity of ways the user and the system exchange information
•   Robustness: the level of support provided the user in determining successful achievement and assessment of goals

This concept of usability informed all of the following areas of development:

•   The evolutionary delivery schedule
•   Gathering and decomposition of existing course materials into a usable structure
•   What new materials were added and why
•   Use of the in-house Extensible Markup Language (XML) Authoring Process (XAP)
•   Testing early stages' course usability

Usability metrics, the long-term evaluation of usage, would provide data on whether these pedagogical and usability goals were achieved.

The Delivery Schedule

The course was delivered in Version 1 form for its first three years, including annual maintenance increments: Versions 1.1. and 1.2. These featured some design changes in response to its initial usability evaluation, maintenance and content updates; the latter also saw a move to an XML version of the course.

A new version of the course is planned for the next academic year. This will feature a complete overhaul of the course design in response to larger usability and content issues picked up from evaluation data analysis.

It is important to note also that the course, with the exception only of Unit 0, was developed alongside delivery.

Working With Legacy Materials

One of the most common pitfalls in online course development is the use of existing course materials without adapting them to the online delivery method. For example, in a poorly developed online course, material is often produced in word processor files, such as Word, or Portable Document Format (PDF), all of which must be printed out to be functional, with little consideration given to navigation or the other areas of support required by the student. This results in an incoherent and hostile environment, especially for new users, that does not meet the definition of usability above; learning activity is impeded and problematic. The Sloan Report mentioned earlier found consistent evidence of this kind of course development: For example, one of the courses studied was described as follows,

> *The course seems to consist only of readings of documents plus four exercises and a final exam. ... An example of this lack of guidance is the first exercise. It contained only the message saying, 'Welcome to our first exercise.' That was it. Nothing about 'You should read this or that, or do this or that, or go here or there.'*

To combat this, the course development team analysed the pedagogical elements of the on-site course and their corresponding assessment to produce a course specification. They then brainstormed what else students would require, coming up with functional requirements such as an email and chat forum, and an administration section. This same breakdown of content and function served as the basis of an introductory unit that combined front-end functionality with a refinement of the content; Unit 0's Getting Started materials also help reassure new users. Unit 0 is also the only non-assessed unit in the course and has no corresponding unit from the on-site course as such matters can be dealt with face-to-face in the classroom. This non-assessment allows students to get to grips with the course structure in a non-threatening environment. The system is both learnable and supported.

As far as content went, the units were broken down into three levels:

- A navigational overview of the unit, which usually comprised five sessions
- A session "spine" providing a walk-through menu of the whole session, usually comprising around seven sections

- The section information page or learning object: a single online activity that achieves a pedagogical aim—these are the building blocks of any online course, allowing learning aims, as listed in a specification, to be realised, taught and assessed

Students could thus drill down to section level to perform the study tasks for a particular unit but never lose sight of navigational and other functions. This flexible approach was achieved by presenting learning objects in single secondary windows with no internal navigation function. Behind the section windows, however, the spine page's own navigation can be seen easily as shown in Screenshot 1.

The design hypothesis was therefore underpinned throughout by an apprecia- tion of Dix et al.'s (1993) principles: New users would learn the online course structure in Unit 0 to maximise their efficiency when coming to the first assessed unit; once confident, users could interact with the system in a number of different ways depending on preference, such as Search; and finally, activities were reinforced by easy access to contact information and Help.

The evaluation of these features centres on the results of online forms for each unit. An email survey after Unit 1 gathered more information specifically on the success of the navigation scheme. Other evaluation methods were also put in place, of which more are discussed in the section *Summary of Current Evaluation Methods* below.

Adding New Features: A Usability Rationale

As has been mentioned, alongside the conversion of existing material, the course team was careful to consider the extras that can be grouped loosely under the headings software and administrative functions.

Screenshot 1: Spine page with secondary window showing navigation

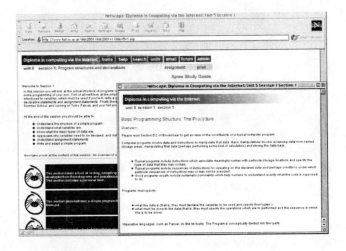

If we consider that an online learning program or course is in itself a piece of software, then to enhance usability we must add features common to software. For example, these might include, if we follow Dix et al.'s (1993) principles further:

- A learnable graphic user interface (GUI)
- Access routes to functions that are suitable for different levels of users—explicit navigation for novices and shortcuts for experts
- A Help file and support service

Add to this a mechanism of support for the user as they are working with the interface; so, for example, an allowance for what Shneiderman calls "user think time." This concept might be described simply as an understanding of how long a user's eye and mind work a screen (Shneiderman, 1998). This in itself presupposes a detailed user study and task analysis stage within the development cycle.

However, an online course is not just a piece of software, to be used in isolation or in groups by the user to achieve certain tasks; it is also both a pedagogical tool and process. Therefore the course production process must also consider how to emulate the environment of a place of learning and the support it provides for its students online. This includes access to the rules and regulations of the course, information on practicalities such as fee payment and summer school accommodation but also a place for students to group and chat and to work over problems with an expert in the subject.

The combination of these extras plus the content, both legacy and new materials, begins to add up to a workable course online.

XML and Reuse

The Technology-Assisted Lifelong Learning (TALL) group within the Department for Continuing Education at the University of Oxford developed a proprietary XML-based production system known as XAP (XML Authoring Process) in response to course delivery requirements. The Diploma in Computing was moved to the XML/Active Server Pages (ASP) development and output method during that year as part of the maintenance increment Version 1.2 changes for a number of reasons.

Although the change was transparent to users, it has allowed much greater control of production and style choices as the XML is rendered through external style sheets. This has meant users have the benefit of a consistent look and feel throughout the whole 12-unit course. It can also provide the basis of a quick, easy and total move to a new version. Branding of the course through scripted headers and footers was also instigated as part and parcel of the ASP output pages that house the XML content. This meant that pages were consistently labelled and version-controlled, something that users had requested in the usability survey described below.

Overall this change has meant much tighter and more efficient handling of the course materials. It has had some downsides, however, in that the XML schemas have at points been strained to keep up with authorial demands; a system for such changes has now been put in place. Usability is enhanced by the ability to respond quickly to student demand.

Testing Course Usability in the Early Stages

Evaluation methods have been integrated within the course from day one but additional testing was considered necessary to test key areas of user response in the early days of the course in 1999. This is not because the course team doubted the validity of the overall evaluation data but more because the first year of course delivery was also the first chance to analyse our unique student body in more depth.

It is worth noting that the team was well aware of the inherent limitation of some methods of data gathering before the course commenced. While online forms, for example, are able to provide a running commentary on course activity, they do not provide all the information. Return rates are consistently poor (and remain so in spite of various attempts to encourage, bribe and cajole students to fill them in—the team has so far stopped short of force). There is more information on the course's use of online forms and other evaluation methods available in the *Summary of Current Evaluation Methods* section below.

In May 1999, as students were completing Unit 2 of the course, an email survey was sent out to provide a check on the design and structural usability. This was administered by direct email to each student, with more information and reminders put up on the forum; it achieved about a 50% response rate (after a second call for replies specifically aimed at those who had failed to answer the first time).

The survey had 14 questions centering on establishing the user's sense of confidence and supported community as they used the course. As a result, obvious usability questions, such as what navigation features were the students using and how long had it taken to master the course structure, are mixed with questions referring to the larger picture; for example, did students have a sense of the course team and how the people on the course related to them and, more significantly, how course team members, especially tutors, could be approached.

The questions are listed in full in Table 1.

Overall the response was positive, with students who answered finding the course usable and enjoyable. The student body, as might be predicted of computing students, had up-to-date and uniform equipment: overwhelmingly Microsoft Windows 95 and above, using Internet Explorer 4 to browse (although the core specification remained at this stage only that the course should be usable for version 3 browsers of whatever variety). Confidence levels were high with one exception; the majority of students referred to a navigational learning curve which, whilst it had not stopped them from mastering the navigation, had slowed them down in the first days of the course. This was noted down as something to be remedied long-term when the course was to be redesigned in its second version. The third-party tools, such as those providing the multiple-choice question (MCQ) facility and the forum,

Table 1: Usability survey questions

1. What browser do you use?
2. What operating system do you use?
3. How long had you used the Internet for before you started the [Certificate]?
4. Do you like the way the course looks? If not, why not?
5. Can you find your way around the course? Now? What about at the beginning?
6. What features do you use mostly for navigation? Spine documents? Units menu? Bookmarks/Favourites? Other?
7. Do you want more links? Inside the course? To external sites? Other?
8. Do you feel confident in the material presented? Why? Why not?
9. Do you know who develops the course?
10. Do you feel confident you can contact the following by email: the course developers? the course director? your tutor?
11. What benefits have you gained from the self tests? If nothing, why? Why not?
12. What benefits have you gained from Webboard? If nothing, why not?
13. Do you find the audiographics useful? If not, why not?
14. Anything else you want to tell us...?

appeared to be sufficiently integrated to also get a positive response; a structural concern of the development team. Team members were identifiable too.

Key results of the survey on a specific and time basis included:

- Short-term changes
  for example, printing
- Medium-term changes
  for example, clearer labelling of learning objects and more effective version control
- Long-term changes
  for example, discarding of redundant navigational features to ease initial learning curve

All in all, the survey provided an endorsement of the course development and delivery that was invaluable as reference over the next year of development.

A summary of the complete range of evaluation methods is included in the next section.

Summary of Current Evaluation Methods

"Evaluation is an analytical process that is intrinsic to good teaching" (Ramsden, 1992, p. 217). Evaluation occurs in all teaching, but in many ways, online evaluation has the scope to outstrip its on-site counterpart in the variety of tests that can be made on student engagement and success.

This section examines the range of evaluation methods used during the course life cycle, focusing particularly on those that are part of the production cycle. These evaluation methods fall loosely into two main areas:

- **Covert methods** that monitor students without them being aware and **overt methods** that engage students in the monitoring process

Pedagogical evaluation covers both these areas and is mentioned in its own section below.

Evaluation methods used on the Diploma in Computing via the Internet are detailed in Table 2.

Students are encouraged to participate in third-party tool activity by the knowledge that doing so could be the deciding factor in deciding a close call of Pass/Fail or, more typically, between Distinction/Pass.

All data gathered by these evaluation methods is stored, monitored and fed back into course production as appropriate (see Figure 1).

Overall this data has shown that student drop-out can be predicted by covert means, usually by a failure to make regular log-ons to the course. However, overt data, including interviewing of students who are dropping out or intermitting or deferring the course, show that students overwhelmingly point to personal life change as the reason they are leaving the course, not to a lack of effectiveness in the teaching of the course and its materials.

TALL IT Help

Queries received through the Help line often centre on more general usability issues, which are logged and then channelled through to the appropriate recipient; for example, the course's internal quality assurance department. For example, students may spot small errors or typos in course materials and these can be instantly corrected.

Table 2: Summary of evaluation methods

Overt/covert	Timescale	Method
Overt/covert	On-going	Tutorial evaluation (see below)
Covert		Server logs
		Third party tool monitoring: e.g., O Reilly Webboard and Questionmark Perception
Overt		Online evaluation forms
	One-offs	E-mail survey
		Questionnaires
	Post-graduation/ (Intermitting and Deferral)	Interviews

Figure 1:   Use of evaluation data

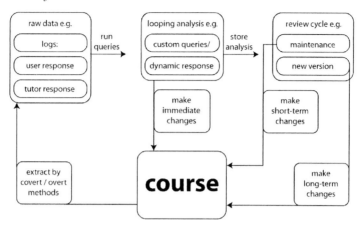

USABILITY OF AN ONLINE COURSE: PEDAGOGICAL EVALUATION

The Virtual Classroom

In spite of all the care to provide a usable interface, without evaluation of the teaching and learning generated by the course, something is missing. From study of the on-site course, it was clear that classroom teaching needed to be emulated in a way that went beyond mere presentation of materials, beyond too the inclusion of dynamic interactive activities within learning objects. It is the role of the tutors and their interaction with students that is seen as the key to a successful online course. Teaching excellence is perceived to be synonymous with study at the University of Oxford. To this end, the course attempts to foster a virtual classroom through its use of forums and also maintains a high ratio of tutors to students.

Strengths and Weaknesses of the Virtual Classroom as an Aid to Usability

This section examines the concept described above, lists its strengths and weakness, and attempts to understand what tutors can and cannot do, making use of existing data gathered by the TALL team monitoring tutor activity.

The virtual classroom concept is seen as essential to the learning activity of students. Activities such as a game included in Unit 0, for example, to promote use of the forum must be considered the key factors in overcoming the instant drop-out factor. This is a true group activity, which means that each member of a tutor group has a unique part to play in the exercise and must then present it on the forum too. Drop-out will still occur, however, with a significant rate of students leaving the course after Unit 0 now being factored into course acceptance numbers.

However, the concept does not work any more efficiently for all students than a real classroom would mean all students were guaranteed to pass a course. To compensate for this, course activities have been developed with the team player and the loner in mind, allowing both to make their contributions. Course participation requirements put some pressure on students to participate and tutors are encouraged to email and otherwise hustle students to contribute. To this end also, the virtual classroom includes a social area or common room to try and generate a feeling of community amongst the students.

Data shows that all of this is largely wasted where the tutor(s) are not actively involved in the forum. In cases where tutors have performed less than effectively for a number of reasons such as illness or pending resignation, the board has suffered and students are quick to raise complaints in this situation. This can be seen in the Year 2 statistics (see Table 4), where the Turing group shows a marked decrease in posted messages compared to other groups. Another example, from the Lovelace group, reveals that two students who showed leadership through initiating threads and chat sessions in the forum gained distinction in the course. This overall enhanced activity may have benefited everyone in Lovelace as all students passed in this group. However, the student who failed to participate actively in the forum gained the lowest pass grade. A tentative analysis might be that those types of students who would like the classroom environment are able to gain something equally valuable from the virtual environment too. More study is needed to decide, however, if these active participators online could in fact be considered part of the same characteristic group of students.

In spite of this possible similarity, introducing academics and experienced teachers to the role of online tutor is not yet a smooth transition. This must centre on the fact that while some parts of the move online are familiar, such as the marking of assignments, much is not. The use of the forum and email as the predominant vehicle for student contact means that tutors, in some respects, require skills honed more in the world of IT support than in the classroom. The ability to visualise a student's problem and to be able to respond effectively on the basis of that visualisation must be considered a learned skill online; in addition, the ability to connect in a pastoral sense with students requires more effort online than the smile or shared words at coffee break that might work well in an on-site course.

Finally, it is worth mentioning the place of live chat within the virtual classroom. Whilst this is available within the forum system that the course employs, it has never been a prescribed part of the course activity for tutors or students. Its operation is somewhat slow and "clunky," with a refresh rate that causes conversations to stutter. Students in some tutor groups, however, still find the facility useful and have developed their own or modified solutions to its slowness. For example, a conversation uses a series of symbols to indicate the different threads being responded too.

+I'm much better. ++Huffman trees. +++I am staying at St. Peters from Friday night.

A better chat facility is a consistent request in evaluation; and "lurkers," students who do not post but will visit the forum, are particularly interested in having access to a floating window listing those active on the forum while they are looking at other sections of the course.

Overall, access to real people through the virtual classroom aids and lubricates student activity on the course; encouraging heightened and more effective usage and ability to interact with the course materials, making the course more usable and robust. However, as has been pointed out, this does not guarantee, but may encourage, pedagogical success for tutor or student. A closer look at tutorial evaluation below helps to clarify this point.

Summary of Pedagogical Evaluation Methods

This section summarises how tutors can evaluate student success on an ongoing basis using the following methods:
- Communicating with students:
  - ➢ The forum
  - ➢ Email
  - ➢ Summer school
- Monitoring and reporting
- Assessment
- Administrative backup

Communicating with Students: The Forum

Tables 3 and 4 show data detailing the number of student and tutor postings per unit for the course forum for the years 2000 and 2001. The data for Year 2 is incomplete as the last unit had not yet been taken by the students.

Table 3: Year 1 of the course forum statistics

Year One								
Tutor Group	Unit 0	Unit 1	Unit 2	Unit 3	Unit 4	Unit 5	Unit 6	Common Room
Babbage	69	60	40	45	35	46	27	97
Boole	122	83	77	122	79	69	29	73
Leibniz	192	62	57	47	77	59	21	144
Lovelace	68	56	47	40	45	47	37	170
Pascal	102	48	25	55	33	133	36	75
Turing	130	47	35	44	29	17	4	44
General (two reported conferences only)	Common Room (known as Admin & Unit Comments in Year One	122		Revision	118			

Table 4: Year 2 of the course forum statistics

Year Two (up to and including Unit 11)							
Tutor Group	Unit 7	Unit 8	Unit 9	Unit 10	Unit 11	Unit 12	Common Room
Babbage	22	18	23	23	18		53
Boole	35	26	23	3	23		31
Leibniz	31	40	11	14	11		106
Lovelace	47	57	50	37	53		71
Pascal	30	48	22	27	25		28
Turing	13	10	1	6	0		2
General	Common Room	318		Revision	58		

As the data shows, there is an obvious distinction between the activity of Year 1 and Year 2. Students appear to be eager to engage with each other and tutors in Year 1. This is evident in the weighting on the introductory Unit 0 and the general board. The game in Unit 0 also encourages use of the forum and a familiarity with what is for many a nonintuitive environment. Tutors are encouraged to coach students in forum use in the early units. As the units progress, the role of the tutor changes to a more specifically educational one up to pre-exam revision live chats and other sessions. In Year 2 such chitchat is cut out, and with student numbers diminishing by about 50%, some tutor groups show little sign of activity at all.

This does not affect the validity of the virtual classroom as an evaluation tool as much as one might think, however, because the drop-out rate is highest in the earliest part of the course. Therefore a tutor can spot noncontributors at an early stage (a weekly data sheet summarises activity to the course team also) and take appropriate action.

Communicating with Students: Email

Some students will not perform well in the virtual classroom any more than they would find a real classroom a comfortable environment. This is a problem of pedagogical usability. These students can be contacted by email directly, and this would also be the case of students identified at risk by their lack of involvement on the forum or through non-completion of assignments. Reporting back to the course team when students are not participating is part of the responsibility of the group tutor; this gives a second and more serious warning that a student may be about to drop out than the bare server log activity figures that the course team receives weekly. It is possible, though not desirable, for a student to go in at the beginning of each unit, print down the course materials, eschew the forum but still be in a chatty and helpful email correspondence with their tutor, who can therefore verify that the student is actively pursuing the course. This is a good example of where tutor feedback is invaluable.

Communicating with Students: Summer School

Students meet their tutors (and the course team) for a face-to-face evaluation session usually the day after they have completed the yearly examination. This allows students a direct channel of communication, which often focuses on usability issues, such as access to course books and the presentation of MCQs. The session is free-form, encouraging students to make their own points rather than the predominantly guided responses of questionnaires and online forms.

The tutor's role is significant, however, as the data gatherer in this situation, and without access to tape recorders, some of the information the course team may have considered useful is invariably lost.

The summer school can also be used to trial new versions of the computing course amongst the existing student body.

Monitoring and Reporting

Student activity statistics are provided to tutors and the course team on a weekly basis. This allows a clear picture of when a student is logging on, but as has been mentioned above, there are occasions when the human factor is vital in establishing whether a student is really at risk. Systems monitoring is highly significant in establishing patterns of course use however. The section *The Future* below discusses further plans for improving the reporting of student activity in a way that exploits this kind of data.

Assessment

Assessment of student activity is done at a number of different levels from learning object to examination, all of which combine to provide a cumulative picture of student success in achieving the specified learning aims. In addition to those assessment methods mentioned, tutors are required to mark student assignments for each unit and an annual summer school assignment. This allows another insight into the performance of students which is a useful complement to forum activity.

Administrative BackUp

If students need extra help outside the scope of the tutorial, the course team and Internet course administrator at the Department for Continuing Education provide extra support. The feeling that students are part of an actual university and not just online appears to encourage participation.

WORKING WITH THE DATA

This section examines how to deliver continuous improvement based on the usability evaluation data gathered in the processes described above. The development process flowchart in Figure 1 shows how changes can be made on a short-term, medium-term and long-term schedule; examples of which have been given in earlier sections.

THE FUTURE

The final section looks at Version 2, including our redesign work in response to students' reported steep learning curve handling the navigation system at the start of the course. As shown in Screenshot 2, the navigation bar has been pruned and grouped according to gestalt rules of human perception (Nielsen, 1993).

In addition, the development team aims to improve our usability evaluation process; for example, better reporting, such as a just-in-time on-page resource that monitors student learning gaps (incompletely accessed materials and so on) and feeds back that information directly to tutors. This identifies what unit sessions or even individual sections have not been accessed by students. Tutors can check this information when dealing with student questions and point out what areas need to be covered. Given the nature of online study and its interruptability for technical and social reasons, students themselves may not be aware of these gaps, which makes this level of reporting especially useful. This development also provides useful data for the development team. If all students are covering a section but tutors are still finding that the concept is not getting through, there is considerable evidence that the pedagogical effectiveness of this learning object is compromised.

CONCLUSION

After three years and course intakes, usability evaluation has proven the Diploma in Computing to be usable and pedagogically effective whilst also providing a foundation for a program of continuous improvement. However pedagogical usability is not limited to interactions with online software and that is the dilemma. It is clear, in the light of the running of the computing course online and on-site, that the online course shares both successes and concerns with the on-site. As a result, it can be argued that to make the course pedagogically usable demands educational interaction over and above mere production of materials, the development of learning objects whose success we are only now beginning to quantify as a result of our more fundamental usage metrics data.

Does the online course do better for distance learners outside an academic institution?

Screenshot 2: Version 2 spine page

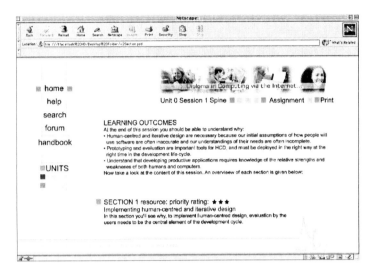

It is true that, for example, the mechanisms for gathering and using data are much more formalised in the online course, but that is not necessarily a significant difference. If we think in terms of the usability definition of Dix et al. (1993), it is possible to reference that data to discover, for example, whether a student is both accessing the course materials and indeed whether they are participating in the virtual classroom. It seems to the author, however, that once again the key question is to refer to the course's learning goals to ascertain whether they are being met by the course for a true determinant of its ultimate usability for the student. In the online course, the metrics for gathering this information must be a combination of the mechanical and human intervention: Has a student learned from this group exercise cannot be judged merely from entry and exit data on a particular page, although that data can and does reinforce tutorial expertise.

The most obvious distinction to be suggested in a computing course is that hands-on experience of working with computers is valuable and will be provided in larger measure by an online course. The typical distance learning student is also well served by a course that can adapt flexibly to their schedule, learning environment and other needs. However, even in this case, without evaluation of both usage and pedagogical effectiveness, this advantage will be lost when compared with an on-site course.

In conclusion, while fully admitting the need for further work, the course team feels that we have to a certain extent met our objectives and concerns. The inclusion of usability evaluation metrics has been crucial to our development path and to online educational quality and will continue to be so.

ACKNOWLEDGMENTS

With thanks to Dr. John Axford, course director, and Dr. Robert Lockhart, staff tutor, from the Department of Continuing Education's Computing Course team for their comments and advice concerning the text of this chapter; to Audrey Cantley, head of design at TALL, for the screenshots, figure and tables, some at very short notice; and to Prudence Hobbs for allowing the author enough child-free time to get this chapter finished during her maternity leave.

Acknowledgments to Dr. Raymond Flood, Jonathan Darby, Sonja Needs, Ang Gilham, Jim Hyndman, Robert O'Toole, the TALL team, course tutors, authors and assessors, whose expertise, patience and hard work have made this course such a success.

The Sloan Report and computing course data is used courtesy of the Department for Continuing Education, University of Oxford.

More information on the Diploma in Computing via the Internet is available from www.tall.ox.ac.uk/computing.

REFERENCES

Dix, A., Finlay, J., Abowd, G., & Beale, R. (1993). *Human-computer interaction.* London: Prentice Hall.

Gardner, N. S., & Newdick, M. (1998). *Sloan report.* University of Oxford, Department for Continuing Education, Oxford.

Nielsen, J. (1993). *Usability engineering.* London: Morgan Kaufmann.

Ramsden, P. (1992). *Learning to teach in higher education.* Routledge.

Shneiderman, B. (1998). *Designing the user interface* (3rd ed.). London: Addison-Wesley.

Spool, J. (1997). *Web site usability: A designer's guide.* User Interface Engineering, MA.

Chapter IX

Usability Inspection of the ECONOF System's User Interface Visualization Component

Nadir Belkhiter
Université Laval, Quebec, Canada

Marie-Michèle Boulet
Université Laval, Quebec, Canada

Sami Baffoun
Université Laval, Quebec, Canada

Clermont Dupuis
Université Laval, Quebec, Canada

ABSTRACT

This chapter is a report on the findings of a user interface evaluation process performed on a decision support system named ECONOF. The issue of properly evaluating the visualization component of a system's user interface is first addressed. Then, the usefulness of the results obtained is shown through the illustration of the improvements made to the ECONOF visualization component. As the user interface evaluation step in most software design and development projects is more often than not neglected, when not totally bypassed, computer professionals need to be more aware of the importance of the user interface design step within any kind of development life cycle.

INTRODUCTION

The usability of the user interface has been recognized as a key success factor to the design and development of interactive systems. This recognition led to the development of evaluation methodologies. This chapter aims at illustrating how the results obtained from a carefully performed evaluation process can lead to the improvement of a user interface. The process that has been used comes from the "usability inspection" method (Molich & Nielsen, 1990; Nielsen, 1993; Nielsen & Mack, 1994; Wiklund, 1994). It is a low-cost, easy to perform, and informal (heuristic) evaluation method that can bring major and significant improvements to a particular user interface.

The system evaluated for the sake of the illustration is named ECONOF (Economie de la Formation). It was developed to provide help and assistance to managers that have to select continuous training activities. ECONOF proposes a set of topics, facets, and criteria that guide managers who perform the analysis of the teaching and learning activities proposed by different providers of online learning programs. More specifically, the chapter provides a description of the initial user interface, then shows how its usability has been evaluated and, finally, illustrates what improvements to the ECONOF user interface have been made.

BACKGROUND

The role of illustrations in the problem-solving process has been addressed by several researchers. Katz and Lesgold (1996), Levonen (1996), Merlet (1998), and Merlet and Gaonac'h (1996) performed a synthesis of the research results concerning the effects of simultaneously using various media on a same device (such as animated text, fixed images, animated images, and sounds). They reported that for the past 20 years, a large number of research results consistently showed that images combined to a text make easier the understanding of the text (Levie & Lentz, 1982; Levin, Anglin, & Garney, 1987). The works of Belton and Elder (1994) concerning visual interactive modeling (VIM) and those from Chau and Bell (1996) regarding the use of VIM as an interface for decision support systems (DSSs) are integrating these findings. As ECONOF refers to DSS domain, i.e., the selection of the online learning program, if any, that best suits the need for continuous training of a particular organization, we were believing that the adding of visual elements to the interface would benefit to the managers using the system. The problem was to find where to integrate the visual elements and doing so, enhancing the usability of the ECONOF system.

Many user interface usability concerns have been addressed by computer and human sciences researchers coming from the multidisciplinary human-computer interaction (HCI) community. One of them is the software life cycle. As example, we can mention the step-by-step design and development process proposed by Mayhew (1999). Its main characteristics are to be centered around usability engineering principles. We can also mention Nielsen's (1992b, 1993, 1999) works on usability engineering and others' works regarding the finding of general design principles for ensuring software product usability (such as Bickford, 1997; Carroll, 1995; Constantine & Lockwood, 1999; Dix, Finlay, Abowd, & Beale, 1998; Dzida, 1989; Gould & Lewis, 1985; Hix & Hartson, 1993; Lynch & Horton, 1999; Mandel, 1997; Mayhew, 1992; Namioka & Schuler, 1993; Shneiderman, 1998; Winograd, 1996). Some researchers such as Hackos and Redish (1998) and to some extent Johnson (1992) propose approaches for performing user and task analysis.

From a system development perspective, the rapid application development methodology (RAD) (Billings, 1996; Liang, 2001; Martin, 1991), which is mainly based on the prototyping principle, is widely recognized as the most suitable methodology for interactive systems development where user interface usability is considered as a key issue by designers.

The design of the user interface has also been addressed from another perspective, being the information visualization one. In addition to the works mentioned above regarding VIM, researchers such as Bergman (2000), Card, Mackinlay, and Shneiderman (1999), Fayyad, Grinstein, and Wierse (2001), Plaisant, Rose, Milash, Widoff, and Shneiderman (1996), Spence (2001), Tufte (1983), and Ware (2000) proposed various ways of approaching the design of effective user interfaces. Their main concern was to productively utilize the powerful human visual faculties. The idea was to provide end users with methods and tools that will facilitate the envisioning of hidden knowledge contained in a particular set of data. Their works address several issues, such as finding ways to:

- deal with a growing number of data as with an increasing number of attributes;
- evaluate information visualization systems;
- measure and understand the benefits of different techniques when tested under various development projects (tasks, end users, data characteristics, data properties, etc.);
- discover and explore new techniques; and
- determine the appropriate application fields.

The need to conduct interface evaluation is there and recognized, but the unfailing evaluation methodology does not exist. Moreover, the user interface evaluation step in software design and development projects is more often than not neglected, when not totally omitted, mainly for time and cost considerations (Mayhew, 1999; Nielsen, 1992b). The resulting products fail to meet the user's needs, especially as regards the human factors. According to the Software Engineering Institute (SEI):

- more than 1/3 of large software development projects are cancelled;
- a project is generally two times longer than initially planned;
- 3/4 of large computer applications have operational defaults and *do not meet functional and usability needs.*

The interface evaluation process, when performed, often relies on an exploratory and intuitive approach (Blesser & Foley, 1982; Redish & Dumas, 1993; Rubin, 1994).

We stated before that an absolutely reliable methodology for evaluating a user interface is not available, but it is nevertheless worth to perform the evaluation mainly because answers to very important questions can be found. Examples of questions are as follows:

- Is the user interface favoring a faster and better decision making?
- Is it easy for the manager who has to interrupt his or her ongoing work on the computer to quickly close the application?
- Is the DSS simple enough that a novice user can easily and intuitively use it even the first time?

The evaluation of a particular user interface can be either formative, i.e., performed on a prototype version during an iterative design process, or summative, i.e., done on the final version of the software product at the end of the development process. The selection of a certain usability evaluation approach also depends on the end users' availability. When end users are not available and so cannot actively participate to the usability evaluation process as proposed by Namioka and Schuler (1993), others' approaches, such as an analytic one like GOMS (which stands for goals, operators, methods, and selection rules; Card, Moran, & Newell, 1980; Gray, John, & Atwood, 1993; John & Kieras, 1996; Kieras, 1997; Olson & Olson, 1990), or cognitive walk-through (Wharton, Reiman, Lewis, & Polson, 1994), or heuristic evaluation (Molich & Nielsen, 1990), can be used. When end users can participate in the evaluation process, traditional empirical approaches that come from different fields of human sciences (psychology, sociology, anthropology, ethnography, etc.), like interviews or acceptance tests (Shneiderman, 1998), passive or active observation via camera recording (Lund, 1985), "thinking aloud" technique (Lewis & Mack, 1982; Nielsen, 1992a), verbal protocols analysis (Ericsson & Simon, 1984; Lewis & Mack, 1982), critical incidents analysis, or surveys (Chin, Diehl, & Norman, 1988; Dix et al., 1998; Hix & Hartson, 1993; Ravden & Johnson, 1989; Root & Draper, 1983; Shneiderman, 1998), are generally used.

Before identifying which evaluation method was used and explaining why we selected it, we give more details concerning the ECONOF system.

THE CONTEXT OF USE OF ECONOF

The SEI's capability maturity model (CMM) is a five-level scale for measuring software capability maturity. The objective of the CMM is to help organizations improve their software process through the progression from an immature, unrepeatable software process to a mature, well-managed software process (Paulk, Curtis, Chrissie, & Weber, 1993a, 1993b). In order for an organization to advance to a higher

CMM level it must focus on improvements in key process areas. Each key process area identifies a group of related activities for reaching a set of goals that will enhance the organization process capabilities. At the first level, named *initial*, the software process is characterized as ad hoc and few processes are defined. At Level 2, named *repeatable*, software development is planned and estimated with a reasonable degree of confidence. At Level 3, named *defined*, the process, with its standard and guidelines, is well defined. It is at this level that a key process called *training program* is identified.

The multicriterion model ECONOF with the related software presented in this chapter concerns the Level 3 key process (training program) of the CMM. ECONOF helps managers to determine whether it is profitable or not to invest in a certain type of continuous training activities. Its elaboration allowed the finding and calibration of different topics and facets. But, when it comes to the way used to present the results, we have many indications that managers would benefit from a more visual and explicit presentation. Moreover, the understanding of the results, which is a prerequisite to the problem-solving process of managers implied in the selection of continuous training activities, would be enhanced by a better visual presentation and an improvement of the user interface usability.

Before addressing the visual and usability concerns, we present, in the next section, the functioning of ECONOF.

THE FUNCTIONING OF ECONOF
The Data Input Component

The current release of the ECONOF multicriterion model with the related software considers four main topics that correspond to the most documented within the literature (Martin, 1998; Turban, McLean, & Wetherbe, 1999):

- training transfer;
- program evaluation;
- cost/benefit analysis;
- training technologies needs.

As these topics are located at the top of the window, a manager can easily see them. In the same way, he or she can intuitively understand that they correspond to a certain set of factors. Each topic was thought to provide help to managers who analyze different related facets. Managers can easily see the list of facets related to a topic; he or she uses the pointing device to position the cursor on the topic. For example, the facets considered under the *cost/benefit analysis* topic are presented at Figure 1.

When a manager, in accordance with Level 3 of the CMM, engages in a process of planning a training program for computer professionals and makes the selection

Figure 1:   Example of facets proposed for the cost/benefit analysis topic

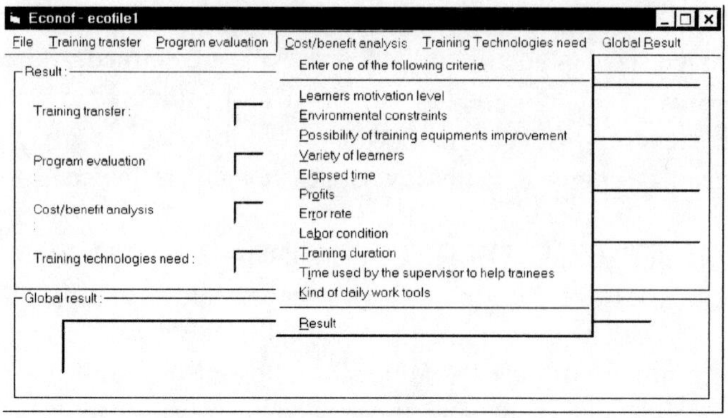

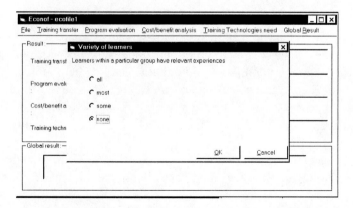

of a facet, sub-windows are used to collect the pertaining information. An example is presented in Figure 2 for the *variety of learners* facet of the *cost/benefit analysis* topic.

As regards the *variety of learners* facet of the *cost/benefit analysis* topic, computer managers have to determine if the learners, i.e., the computer profession-als enrolled in a same training activities, have the same relevant experience. For example, suppose an online learning program that proposes several graded coopera-tive learning activities. If there are novices and seniors in the same cooperative team, the novice and the senior will have to compromise on the level of the practical work they will address. It is possible that the topic selected by the whole cooperative team has nothing to do with the need of the company that pays for the course. When the learners of a same group don't have the same relevant experience, the risk of diminishing the usefulness of the money that a company invested increases.

Under the same facet, computer managers have also to determine to what extent learners of the same group, i.e., the computer professionals enrolled in a

Figure 2:   Example of an aspect to consider for the variety of learners facet

Figure 3:   Example of diagnosis obtained for the cost/benefit analysis facet

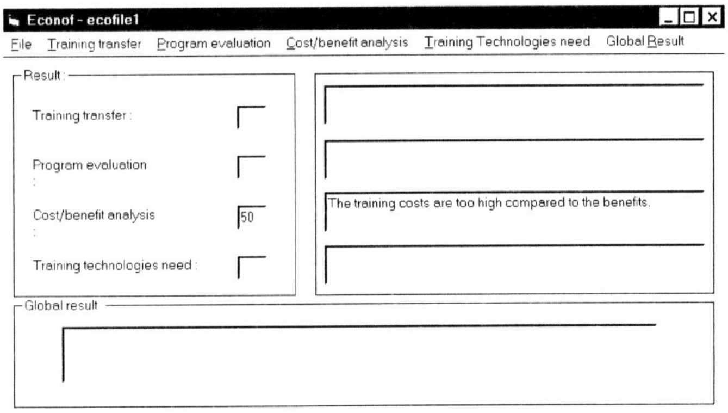

particular training activity, have the same reading capabilities. It is recognized that the benefit of a training session for a person is affected by the way the level and the rate suits his or her own. When the learners of the same group don't have the same reading capabilities, the risk of diminishing the usefulness of the money invested increases for the company or the computer service. This company or service is at risk of failing to reach the CMM's Level 3.

In the following section, we describe what are the results available and how they are currently displayed to the end user.

The Visualization Component

Each item used to assess a facet and then a topic has an assigned weight. For example, a positive action or situation for the business might be worth 10 points while a negative one might be worth 0. The weight assigned to each item was determined through prior research results (Boulet, Ben Jebara, Bemmira, & Boudreault, 2002; Boulet, Ben Jebara, Boudreault, & Guérette, 1998; Boulet, Boudreault, & Guérette,

Figure 4:   Example of global result

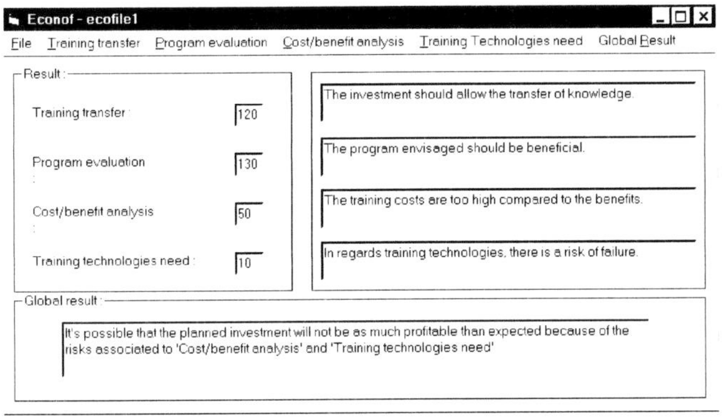

1998a, 1998b). Using the weight assigned to each facet, ECONOF first calculates a result for each topic. To view this result, the manager selects the option *result*, located at the bottom of each topic menu (see Figure 1).

Depending on the value obtained, a short opinion is displayed. Figure 3 shows an example of a diagnosis concerning the *cost/benefit analysis* topic.

At the end of the process, ECONOF displays its general opinion based on the results calculated for each topic. That is the option *global result*, presented in Figure 3. It may consist of an advice to the computer managers of the company or the service to not invest because there is a risk of losing the investment. Figure 4 presents an example.

THE VISUAL INTERFACE CONCERNS

As shown in Figures 3 and 4, the interface for presenting the results is mainly made of fixed text. The numbers that correspond to the total of weights for each topic are simply displayed without any references to their actual meaning. In short, the manager that uses ECONOF does not have any idea of the model behind so he or she can't use his or her good knowledge of the company during the problem-solving process of selecting pertaining continuous training activities.

It can also be seen in Figures 3 and 4 that the layout of information on the screen was not carefully planned. However, Caro and Bétrancourt (1998) mention as a critical factor the layout and the format of any text displayed on a screen; the more the white spaces on a screen are well used, the better the information presented is perceived and handled. According to Coe (1996), the white spaces left on a computer screen should be between 40% and 60%, while on a paper sheet it should be 25% to 40%. These are only some examples of informal and general guideline principles coming from the literature. So, the more we were looking at the interface, the more we were convinced that we needed a systematic approach to assess our user interface visualization component. We needed a systematic approach to discover and then remove as many usability problems as possible. In the following, the method selected for the sake of our study is presented.

THE HEURISTIC EVALUATION

We previously listed several usability evaluation methods. Before identifying and summarizing the characteristics of the one we selected, we comment on the reasons why we have chosen it rather than another one.

We have mentioned in the *Background* section that when the end users are not available to actively participate to the evaluation process, designers have to adopt an analytic evaluation method. Among this kind of method, we have also mentioned that the main ones are the *GOMS* method, the *cognitive walk-through* method, and the *heuristic evaluation* method. *GOMS* is a predictive and formal evaluation method which is recognized as being not appropriate at all for complex interactive systems like a decision support system. ECONOF is a decision support system. *Cognitive walk-through* is a method which is particularly appropriate for applications intended for a large public. ECONOF is certainly not such an application.

The *heuristic evaluation* method was originally proposed by Molich and Nielsen (1990). It is now better known as one of the "usability inspection" methods (Nielsen & Mack, 1994). It consists of an analysis conducted by an impartial usability professionals team. To perform the evaluation, the team uses a variety of informal design heuristics (guidelines). In their method, Molich and Nielsen propose a list of nine design heuristics. It can be noted that others' sets of heuristics exist like the eight golden rules of Shneiderman (1998) or the five DIN standards factors (Dzida, 1989). However, as the *heuristic evaluation* technique was originally proposed by Molich and Nielsen, we decided to refer to their heuristics set. The main goal of their heuristics set is to identify and then to remove the usability problems. The low cost, the easiness of use, and the fact it is a method so intuitive that it can be used at the early stage of the software development process are among the recognized advantages of this type of *heuristic evaluation*. As weaknesses, we can first note it is a method that emphasizes the usability problems rather than the solutions. Second, the method cannot be appropriately iterated in the sense that different usability problems could be identified each time the method is repeated on the same design. Finally, it has been observed that some heuristics can often erroneously confirm usability predictions (Cockton & Woolrych, 2001). As stated before, one of our main goals was to obtain a list of problems the visualization component could cause to the end users. This means the first weakness was not pertaining to our project, and nor were the two other weaknesses listed. On the other side, as the relevance of the method has been established (Nielsen, 1994) through the years with practical cases, likewise its easiness and very low cost, we selected it.

The Usability Inspection of the Visualization Component

In this section, we list all the usability problems that we have identified in the ECONOF system's user interface visualization component after a heuristic evaluation based on the following nine design heuristics proposed by Molich and Nielsen (1990) has been conducted.

Heuristic 1. Use a Simple and Natural Language

a.   The file name ("ecofile1") at the top of the window (see Figures 1, 2, 3 and 4) is not familiar and represents "technical" and useless information for novice users.

b.   The system name ("Econof") at the top of each user interface window can be confusing since it is located just near the file name.

c.   The system name ("Econof") is displayed with the same size and the same character font as the file name.

d.   The four main topics of the ECONOF system are located on the same level as the *file* menu. It can be confusing because the *file* menu is an integrated part of the MS Window interface and consequently not at all related to the ECONOF system.

e.   The four main topics of the ECONOF system are located on the same level as the *global result* option even though it is not a topic menu nor a *file* menu.

Heuristic 2. Provide Clear Ways to Exit the System

a.   There is not any clear button to exit. To exit the ECONOF system, the user must go through the *file* menu and then select the *close* item or click at the right top corner of the window like any Microsoft software. ECONOF is not a Microsoft software.

Heuristic 3. Speak the User Language

a.   The way of displaying the results, i.e., using numerical values, does not have any usual nor understandable meaning for end users.

Heuristic 4. Allow Shortcuts (for Expert Users)

a.   Some shortcuts located in the same menu are made up with the same letter (see *cost/benefit analysis* vertical menu in Figure 1, for example).

Heuristic 5. Reduce the User Memory Load

a.   When the result for one of the four topics is displayed, the user has to memorize all the item values that he or she has chosen for each facet related to the topic.

Heuristic 6. Supply Clear and Informative Error Messages

a.   When the user cancels a *file open* operation, the system displays the useless and unclear warning message reproduced in Figure 5 (French version of ECONOF).

b.   When the *result* option is selected in one of the four topic vertical menus while no criteria has been entered by the user, the system displays the error message illustrated in Figure 6 (French version of ECONOF). This message is neither informative nor clear.

Heuristic 7. Be Consistent

a.   The result calculated for a topic is expressed by and displayed with a numerical value and a short opinion (Figure 3). The content of the global result is only an opinion without any reference to some numerical values. It may be confusing for the user.

b.   In the topic menu at the top of the window, each option has a shortcut which is made up by the first letter of its name. There is no shortcut for *global result*, the last option on this topic menu (see also Heuristic 4a).

Figure 5: Example of a warning message

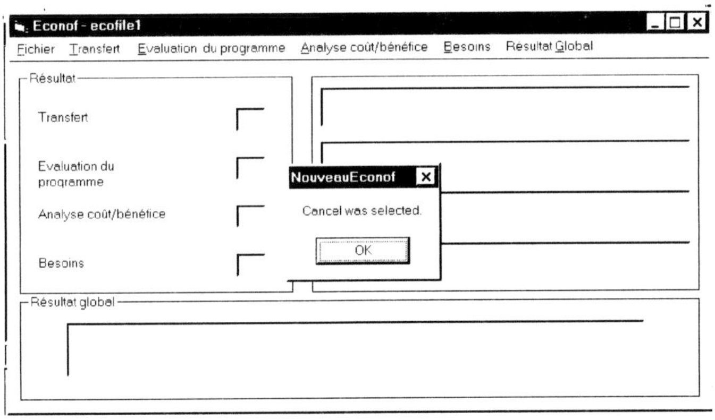

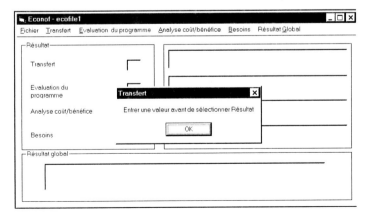

Heuristic 8. Prevent Errors

a.   We can see in Figure 3 that the *global result* option at the top of the window is not grayed (as in Figure 2) although only one topic has been analyzed (i.e., the *cost/benefit analysis* topic). It is unclear which result will be produced if the user clicks on the *global result* option, i.e., the same as the one that is displayed when the user selects the option *result*, located in each topic menu, or another one.

b.   See Heuristic 7b, which also applies here.

Heuristic 9. Supply Informative Feedback to the User

a.   The content of the opinion displayed as the result is not sufficiently informative. For example, in Figure 3, one can ask himself or herself by how much "the training costs are too high compared to the benefits."

b.   Once the result has been displayed for a topic (numerical value at the left side plus opinion at the right side of the window), it is difficult to visualize which

Figure 6: Example of an error message

facets among all the facets can explain this result. It would be useful to be able to have a more detailed view (i.e., for each facet) of the result.

c.   Once the global result has been displayed (general opinion at the bottom of the window), it is difficult for the user to visualize which topics among the four can explain this result. It would be useful to provide users with a more detailed results visualization according to the result of each topic.

d.   Results are displayed as text without any graphics.

e.   Once the global result has been displayed as shown at Figure 4, the user does not know how to print it.

f.   See Heuristic 3a, which also applies here.

The results of this usability inspection process allow us to redesign the visualization component. The resulting implemented new release is presented in the following section. Please note that, in the remaining of the text, the usability problems listed above are referenced by their heuristic number followed by the pertaining letter.

THE IMPROVED RELEASE OF THE VISUALIZATION COMPONENT

Several authors have shown the usefulness of visual representation for human-computer interaction (Horton, 1994; Kobara, 1991; Mullet & Sano, 1995; Ossner, 1990; Pejtersen, 1992). Those findings lead us to use a graphical representation mainly based on named icons. The main screen of the first release (Figure 1) has been replaced by the welcome (usability problem Heuristic 1a) and main menu screen of the new (French) release (see Figure 7).

It can be seen that the initial horizontal topic menu (Figure 1) for entering facet item values has been replaced by four icon buttons located in the middle of the screen (Figure 7) (Heuristics 1b and 1c). The use of icons allowed the suppression of any shortcut ambiguity (Heuristics 4a and 7b). Each flag (i.e., a circle inside a square) at the left bottom corner changes color: When it is green, it means that the criteria of at least one facet have been entered (clear visual feedback), and when it is red, the user knows he or she did not make any input for the facet.

The *file* menu and the *global result* option have been removed from the topic menu (Heuristics 1b and 1c). The icons at the bottom of the screen allow users to easily open, close or save a file, to ask for a results display (textual and/or graphical) or for help, to quit the application, and so on (Heuristics 2a, 9d and 9e).

Figure 8 illustrates the modified textual visualization component. It was redesigned to allow the user to easily go from the visualization of one topic result to another. *Back* and *forward* navigation buttons can be used to go from one screen to another within the same topic, and localization in navigation is indicated at any time

Figure 7: Main menu of the new ECONOF system's user interface (French version)

by the page number information at the right side of the screen (Heuristic 5a). For example, in the screen illustrated in Figure 8, the user can see that the entered criteria for all *transfer* topic facets are distributed along two pages. The global result is displayed at the left bottom of the screen. The button located at the right bottom of the screen can move the user back to the application main menu.

As mentioned in a previous section, the use of visual elements helps any user to get a better understanding of the meaning of the information presented. That is why a button named *indicateur* was added (see Figure 7). When the user clicks it, a

Figure 8: Textual visualization for the transfer topic result and global result

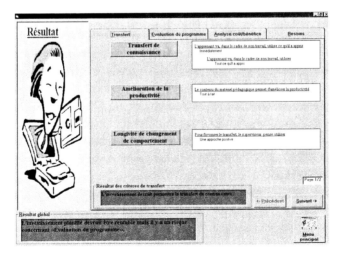

Figure 9: Detailed graphical visualization for the transfer topic result

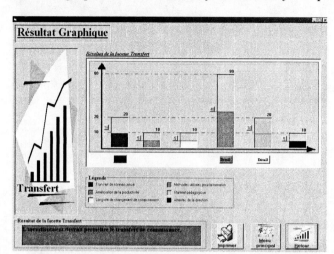

graphical and detailed visualization of the results, either for a particular topic or the
global result, is displayed. Figure 9 illustrates the visualization for the *transfer* topic
result. The manager can easily see to which criteria he or she must pay particular
attention. Then, he or she will be able to negotiate with the training provider in order
to change the estimate. After having entered the new values, he or she will be able
to see the impact of the changes made to some of these criteria (Heuristics 3a, 9a,
9b, 9c, 9d).

When a facet result can be more detailed, a *detail* button is displayed under the
histogram representation (see Figure 9). The selection of this button allows the user
to obtain more detailed results (Heuristics 9b, 9c, 9d); he or she can do it until the
detail button does not appear anymore.

Figure 10: Textual and graphical display of global result

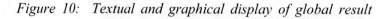
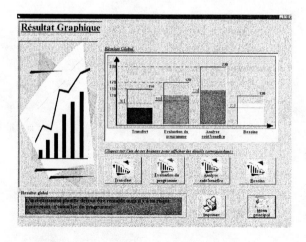

Figure 11: Printing function screen

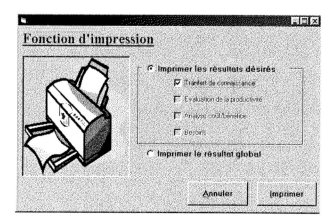

When a manager wants to get a textual and graphical display of the global result, he or she has to come back to the main menu screen. To do so, he or she selects the *menu principal* button located at the bottom of the screen (Figure 9) and then asks for the global result. The screen shown in Figure 10 is displayed.

The use of the topic buttons located under the general histogram representation allows the manager to go through more in-depth, detailed results. In this way, the support to the decision-making process is much more useful and efficient than the one provided in the previous release (Heuristics 9a, 9b, 9c, 9d). Of course, the manager can, at any time, print the global result and each of the detailed ones (Heuristic 9e; see Figure 11).

FUTURE TRENDS

What is next? We have now a user interface that communicates better than the previous one but we have lost the great portability of the software. Before, we were able to move all around the world with ECONOF without any problem. Now, it runs only on computers equipped with powerful screens, so a very recent and far more expensive hardware. It means we will have to focus on this portability issue with a team of computer professionals specialized in this matter.

As regards the life cycle of a computer project like ours, we would not change our approach. It would have been totally impossible to think about working on the user interface at the beginning of the project. In the early stages, nobody in the team of computer professionals has any idea of the product to develop. The first steps of the projects were made of complex statistical analysis of historical data files in order to find factors, criteria, facets, weights, etc. As we did not know what would be found, it would have been useless to hire user interface specialists.

Once we had determined that several criteria were repeatedly existing, we had to produce a model of the relation between each of them. The first implementation was made using macros of a spreadsheet in order to have a prototype that can be easily used by the managers testing the model and its conclusions. So, again, it was too early to think about the design of the user interface. After two years of testing, adjustments, enhancements and enrichments of the model behind the system and, consequently, of the system itself, we had a more complete set of criteria and the reliability and the validity of the model were established. That is where we performed the conceptual modeling of the data and of the treatments. They led to the production of another release where the input function was enhanced; the C programming language was used. We should have had the user interface designed at this point of the project.

What did we learn regarding the user interface design place in the life cycle? In spite of what is repeatedly suggested within the literature, it is our opinion that when a totally new kind of software application is designed, i.e., the problem is not clearly defined and the solution, if there is one, is not even found, it is not useful and productive to address the user interface issues during the first phases of the development life cycle. But, as soon as a working solution has been found and the first implementation of the corresponding system has allowed to confirm the validity and the reliability of the model behind, a careful user interface design should be performed in conjunction with the modeling tasks. By doing so, the problems of portability, which are affecting our system and will force us to have it reprogrammed, would be avoided.

Moreover, during the development life cycle, another issue should be addressed at the same moment as the modeling tasks and the user interface design. It is the issue of designing an effective way to present the written results. For now, it is what is displayed that is printed (WYSIWYG paradigm). It means, for example, that the color indicators that contain important information are not visible when printed. Moreover, the way the results are organized was created not considering the characteristics and the richness of the written paper but taking into account the limitation of a computer screen. It is our opinion that the printed outputs of ECONOF would gain in being carefully designed.

This last comment leads us to propose the adding of a sub-step to the development life cycle, being the printed material design. As mentioned before, it should take place at the same moment as the user interface design and aim at ensuring the printed results' usability.

CONCLUSION

ECONOF aims at assisting the selection process of pertaining continuous training activities for computer professionals (to know more about the software and the model behind, see Boulet et al., 2002; Boulet, Dupuis, & Belkhiter, 2001). To make sure to reach the goal, an emphasis must be put on the design of the interface, particularly the result visualization component. We learned from our experience where this emphasis takes place in the development life cycle, being after the reliability and the validity of the model (multicriterion in our case) has been confirmed. In this chapter, we have shown how much a simple and low-cost but systematic evaluation (also called "usability inspection" method) of a user interface component can be useful for identifying and then removing usability problems. Note that if it is needed, particularly for a system used to help to resolve critical situations (live or death situations, for example), the evaluation process and consequently the user interface usability could be far more refined by performing two others' and complementary successive heuristic evaluation phases; being, first, the eight golden rules of Shneiderman (1998) and, the second, the five DIN ergonomic principles (Dzida, 1989). Even if the illustrative evaluation experience reported in this chapter has been limited to one user interface component rather than covering the overall user interface, it should convince the computer professionals of the need and the efficiency of a user interface evaluation step within the iterative development life cycle.

Finally, it is our belief that further courses on cognitive psychology and user interface design should be included in the curriculum of the university and college computer science training programs in order to highlight the importance of opening interactive software products to cognitive ergonomics concepts. In the same way, courses that address the design of written results that are actually thought and organized for the medium used, being the paper, and not simply the replication of the information displayed, which was summarized and cut out due to the limitations of space of the screen, should be added. Methods and techniques to inspect those written results, say, a "usability inspection" of the written results, should be also developed.

ACKNOWLEDGMENTS

We would like to express our thanks to the referees who suggested to us pertaining enhancements that contributed to the improvement of the initial content of the chapter. Some parts of this project received financial support from the Natural Science and Engineering Research Council of Canada (NSERC).

REFERENCES

Belton, V., & Elder, M. D. (1994). DSS: Learning from VIM. *Decision Support Systems, 11*, 12-21.

Bergman, E. (2000). *Information appliances and beyond: Interaction design for consumer products*. New York: Morgan Kaufmann.

Bickford, P. (1997). *Interface design: The art of developing easy-to-use software*. Chestnut Hill, MA: Academic Press.

Billings, C. (1996). *Rapid application development with Oracle designer /2000*. New York: Addison-Wesley.

Blesser, T., & Foley, J. D. (1982). Towards specifying and evaluating the human factors of user-computer interfaces. In *Proceedings of Human Factors in Computer Systems* (pp. 9-18). Boston, MA.

Boulet, M. M., Ben Jebara, F., Bemmira, F., & Boudreault, S. (2002). A comparison of three delivery systems for teaching an information technology course. *Communications of the ACM, 45* (4ve), pp. 129-135.

Boulet, M. M., Ben Jebara, F., Boudreault, S., & Guérette, L. (1998). Teaching process modeling to undergraduate computer students: Effects of using Lotus Notes and television programmes. In *Integrating Technology into Computer Science Education ITiCSE 98 Proceedings* (pp. 102-108). Dublin.

Boulet, M. M., Boudreault, S., & Guérette, L. (1998a). Effects of a television distance education course in computer science. *British Journal of Educational Technology, 29*(2), 101-111.

Boulet, M. M., Boudreault, S., & Guérette, L. (1998b). Using technology to deliver distance education in computer science. *Journal of Engineering Education, 87*(4), 433-437.

Boulet, M. M., Dupuis, C., & Belkhiter, N. (2001). Selecting continuous training program and activities for computer professionals. *Computers & Education, 36*(2), 83-94.

Card, S. K., Mackinlay, J. D, & Shneiderman, B. (1999). *Readings in information visualization: Using vision to think.* New York: Morgan Kaufmann.

Card, S. K., Moran, T. P., & Newell, A. (1980). The keystroke-level model for user performance with interactive systems. *Communications of the ACM, 23*(2), 396-410.

Caro, S., & Bétrancourt, M. (1998). Ergonomie des documents techniques informatisés: Expériences et recommandations sur l'utilisation des organisateurs para linguistiques. In A. Tricot & J. F. Rouet (Eds.), *Les hypermédias: Approches cognitives et ergonomiques* (pp. 123-138). Paris: Hermès.

Carroll, J. M. (1995). *Scenario-based design: Envisioning work and technology in system development.* New York: John Wiley & Sons.

Chau, P. Y. K., & Bell, P. C. (1996). A visual interactive DSS to assist the design of a new production unit. *INFOR Journal, 21*(5), 30-39.

Chin, J. P., Diehl, V. A., & Norman, K. L. (1988). Development of an instrument measuring user satisfaction of the human-computer interface. In *Proceedings of CHI'88—Human Factors in Computing Systems* (pp. 213-218).

Cockton, G., & Woolrych, A. (2001). Understanding inspection methods: Lessons from an assessment of heuristic evaluation. *Proceedings of the Joint International IHM-HCI Conference* (pp. 171-191). Lille.

Coe, M. (1996). Sensation, perception and user documentation. *Intercom, 2,* 13-15.

Constantine L. L., & Lockwood, L. A. D. (1999). *Software for use: A practical guide to the models of usage-centered design.* New York: Addison-Wesley.

Dix, A., Finlay, J., Abowd, G., & Beale, R. (1998). *Human-computer interaction.* New York: Prentice Hall.

Dzida, W. (1989). The development of ergonomic standards. *ACM SIGCHI Bulletin, 20*(3), 35-43.

Ericsson, K. A., & Simon, H. A. (1984). *Protocol analysis: Verbal reports as data.* Cambridge, MA: MIT Press.

Fayyad, U., Grinstein, G., & Wierse, A. (2001). *Information visualization in data mining and knowledge discovery (Data management systems).* New York: Morgan Kaufmann.

Gould, J. D., & Lewis, C. (1985). Designing for usability: Key principles and what designers think. *Communications of the ACM, 28*(3), 300-311.

Gray, W. D., John, B. E., & Atwood, M. E. (1993). Project Ernestine: Validating a GOMS analysis for predicting and explaining real-world task performance. *Human-Computer Interaction, 8*(3), 237-309.

Hackos, J. T., & Redish, J. C. (1998). *User and task analysis for interface design.* New York: John Wiley & Sons.

Hix, D., & Hartson, R. (1993). *Developing user interfaces: Ensuring usability through product & process.* New York: John Wiley & Sons.

Horton, W. (1994). *The icon book and disk: Visual symbols for computer systems and documentation.* New York: John Wiley & Sons.

John, B. E., & Kieras, D. E. (1996). Using GOMS for user interface design and evaluation: Which technique? *ACM Transactions on Computer-Human Interaction, 3*(4), 287-319.

Johnson, P. (1992). *Human computer interaction: Psychology, task analysis and software engineering.* New York: McGraw-Hill.

Katz, S., & Lesgold, A. (1996). Students' use of textual and graphical advising resources in a coached practice environment for electronic troubleshooting. *Proceedings of UCSI'96 Conference* (pp. 67-72). Poitiers.

Kieras, D. E. (1997). A guide to GOMS model usability evaluation using NGOMSL. In M. Helander, T. Landauer, & P. Prabhu (Eds.), *The handbook of human-computer interaction* (2nd ed., pp. 733-766). Amsterdam: Elsevier Science.

Kobara, S. (1991). *Visual design with OSF/Motif.* New York: Addison-Wesley.

Levie, W., & Lentz, R. (1982). Effect of text illustrations: A review of research. *Educational Communication and Technology Journal, 30*(1), 195-232.

Levin, J. R., Anglin, G. J., & Garney, R. N. (1987). On empirically validating functions of pictures in prose. In D. M. Willows & H. A. Houghton (Eds.), *The psychology of illustration* (pp. 213-237). New York: Springer-Verlag.

Levonen, J. J. (1996). The complexities of newspaper graph. In *Proceedings of UCSI'96 Conference* (pp. 23-31). Poitiers.

Lewis, C., & Mack, R. (1982). Learning to use a text processing system: Evidence from "thinking aloud" protocols. In *Proceedings of Human Factors in Computer Systems Conference* (pp. 387-392). Washington.

Liang, D. Y. (2001). *Rapid Java application development using JBuilder 4/5/6* (2nd ed.). Englewood Cliffs, NJ: Prentice Hall.

Lund, M. A. (1985). Evaluating the user interface: The candid camera approach. In *Proceedings of CHI'85—Human Factors in Computing Systems* (pp. 107-113).

Lynch, P. J., & Horton, S. (1999). *Web style guide: Basic design principles for creating Web sites*. New Haven, CT: Yale University Press.

Mandel, T. (1997). *The elements of user interface design*. New York: John Wiley & Sons.

Martin, J. (1991). *Rapid application development*. New York: Macmillan.

Martin, J. (1998). *Cybercorp: The new business revolution*. New York: Amacom.

Mayhew, D. J. (1992). *Principles and guidelines in software user interface design*. Englewood Cliffs, NJ: Prentice Hall.

Mayhew, D. J. (1999). *The usability engineering lifecycle: A practitioner's handbook for user interface design*. New York: Morgan Kaufmann.

Merlet, S. (1998). Niveaux de traitement et intégrations des informations multimédia: L'exemple de la compréhension orale en langue étrangère. In A. Tricot & J. F. Rouet (Eds.), *Les hypermédias: Approches cognitives et ergonomiques* (pp. 141-156). Paris: Hermès.

Merlet, S., & Gaonac'h, D. (1996). Pictures and listening in a foreign language: Analysis in terms of cognitive load. In *Proceedings of UCSI'96 Conference* (pp. 24-29). Poitiers.

Molich, R., & Nielsen, J. (1990). Improving a human-computer dialogue. *Communications of the ACM, 33*(3), 338-348.

Mullet, K., & Sano, D. (1995). *Designing visual interfaces*. Mountain View, CA: SunSoft Press.

Namioka, A., & Schuler, D. (1993). *Participatory design: Principles and practices*. New York: Lawrence Erlbaum.

Nielsen, J. (1992a). Evaluating the thinking-aloud technique for use by computer scientists. In H. R. Hartson & D. Hix (Eds.), *Advances in human-computer interaction* (Vol. 3, pp. 75-88). New York: Ablex.

Nielsen, J. (1992b). The usability engineering lifecycle. *IEEE Computer, 25*(3), 12-22.

Nielsen, J. (1993). *Usability engineering*. Boston, MA: Academic Press.

Nielsen, J. (1999). *Designing Web usability: The practice of simplicity*. Indianapolis, IN: New Riders.

Nielsen, J., & Mack, R. L. (1994). *Usability inspection methods*. New York: John Wiley & Sons.

Olson, J., & Olson, G. (1990). The growth of cognitive modelling in human-computer interaction since GOMS. *Human-Computer Interaction, 5*, 221-265.

Ossner, J. (1990). Transnational symbols: The rule of pictograms and models in the learning process. In J. Nielsen (Ed.), *Designing user interfaces for international use* (pp. 11-38). Amsterdam: Elsevier Science.

Paulk, P. C., Curtis, B., Chrissie, M. B., & Weber, C. V. (1993a). *Capability maturity model for software* (CMU/SEI-93-TR-24). Pittsburgh, PA: Carnegie Mellon University, Software Engineering Institute.

Paulk, P. C., Curtis, B., Chrissie, M. B., & Weber, C. V. (1993b). *Key practices of the capability maturity model* (CMU/SEI-93-TR-25). Pittsburgh, PA: Carnegie Mellon University, Software Engineering Institute.

Pejtersen, A. M. (1992). The book house: An icon based database system for fiction retrieval in public libraries. In B. Cronin (Ed.), *The marketing of library and information services* (pp. 572-591).

Plaisant, C., Rose, A., Milash, B., Widoff, S., & Shneiderman, B. (1996). LifeLines: Visualization personal histories. In *Proceedings of the ACM CHI '96 Conference: Human Factors in Computing Systems* (pp. 221-227). New York.

Ravden, S., & Johnson, G. (1989). *Evaluating usability of human-computer interfaces: A practical method*. Boston: Ellis Horwood Books.

Redish, J. C., & Dumas, J. S. (1993). *A practical usability testing*. New York: Ablex.

Root, R. W., & Draper, S. (1983). Questionnaires as a software evaluation tool. *Proceedings of CHI '83 Human Factors in Computing Systems* (pp. 83-87). Boston.

Rubin, J. (1994). *Handbook of usability testing: How to plan, design, and conduct effective tests*. New York: John Wiley & Sons.

Shneiderman, B. (1998). *Designing the user interface: Strategies for effective human-computer interaction*. New York: Addison-Wesley.

Spence, R. (2001). *Information visualization*. New York: Addison-Wesley.

Tufte, E. R. (1983). *The visual display of quantitative information*. Cheshire, CT: Graphics Press.

Turban, E., McLean, E., & Wetherbe, J. (1999). *Information technology for management: Making connections for strategic advantage*. New York: John Wiley & Sons.

Ware, C. (2000). *Information visualization: Perception for design*. New York: Morgan Kaufmann.

Wharton, C., Reiman, J., Lewis, C., & Polson, P. (1994). The cognitive walkthrough method: A practitioner's guide. In J. Nielsen & R. L. Mack (Eds.), *Usability inspection methods*. New York: John Wiley & Sons.

Wiklund, M. E. (1994). *Usability in practice: How companies develop user-friendly products*. New York: Academic Press.

Winograd, T. (1996). *Bringing design to software*. New York: Addison-Wesley.

Chapter X

Issues of Quality in Online Degree Programmes

Floriana Grasso
Liverpool University, UK

Paul Leng
Liverpool University, UK

ABSTRACT

Online delivery of degree-level programmes is an attractive option, especially for working professionals and others who are unable to contemplate full-time residential university attendance. If such programmes are to be accepted, however, it is essential that they attain the same standards and quality as conventionally delivered degrees. We describe here the structures and processes developed for quality management and assurance in a programme of online master's level degrees in a UK university. The pedagogical approach places great emphasis on the role of online discussion in the teaching and learning process, and we argue that this also has a key role in the quality assurance process. We discuss ways in which techniques of artificial intelligence can be used to assist instructors and others to manage and evaluate discussions effectively.

INTRODUCTION

It is clear that there is a demand for education and in particular for degree-level courses from individuals for whom full-time university attendance is not a practicable option. The emergence of the Internet offers a new framework for the delivery of such courses. This model is likely to appeal especially to working professionals and others whose career or personal circumstances make it impossible for them to spend a year or more at university, but for whom the opportunity to study and to obtain a high-level qualification is attractive. However, for applicants to an online degree programme, the perceived attractions of the mode of delivery are likely to be offset by corresponding doubts about the quality of the education offered and, consequently, the value of the qualification obtained.

Clearly, a university is the most appropriate organisation to provide degree-level courses, whether via the Internet or otherwise, and the reputation and experience of an established university offers the best assurance to prospective students that the degree programme they pursue will provide genuine value and academic standing. Offering a programme of study over the Internet, however, is very different in many respects from traditional university teaching. There have been, over a number of years, many attempts to develop systems to support a paradigm of online learning (see, e.g., Anderson & Kanuka, 1997; Davies, 1998; Suthers & Jones, 1997). These systems may or may not mimic conventional lecture-room teaching, but will always involve major differences in the way in which teaching and student support are organised. Furthermore, the Internet lends itself naturally to an internationalisation of education delivery, but this too poses challenges for universities that have developed their structures within the framework of national education systems. Finally, the management and marketing of such programmes also involves skills and procedures that are largely unfamiliar to universities, but which belong in the repertoire of commercial organisations.

A key question, then, concerns how and to what extent can the qualities that make university education attractive be preserved in the context of a quite different model of delivery. Our purpose in this chapter is to address this question and especially to consider the corresponding issues of quality assurance. We do so in the context of an examination of a recently introduced programme of online study, which provides the opportunity for students to study for postgraduate degrees of master of science (MSc) and MBA, pursued entirely online. This development arises through a partnership between a "traditional" university in the UK and a commercial organisation with extensive experience in providing and marketing educational services. We describe here the planning and structure of the degree programmes.

As we have suggested, both the online medium and the partnership between a university and a commercial organisation raise serious issues for the delivery of degree-level programmes: issues of academic standards, pedagogic approach, assessment, student support, and quality assurance. Questions that arise include:

- Which of the processes, procedures, and teaching methods used within the university should be replicated in the online context, and how should this be done?
- What new problems arise in the management of online degree programmes, and how can they be addressed?
- Conversely, what shortcomings of conventional university teaching can be mitigated in an online environment?

- What is the appropriate division of responsibilities between the partners involved?
- Finally, and crucially, what organisational and other structures are required to ensure the quality of the education provided and the standards of the degrees offered?

We discuss these questions and how they are addressed in the organisation of the programmes we describe, and the implications for the management and resourcing of online degree programmes.

A key aspect of the pedagogic approach used is an emphasis on a form of seminar-based learning, involving extensive online dialogue within groups of students. We shall discuss the importance of this in the context of the issues mentioned above. We will argue that online discussion and argument are crucial in two respects. Firstly, the approach recreates some of the intellectual atmosphere of a traditional university (often, paradoxically, absent in actual lecture-based teaching) and by doing so mitigates the potential alienation and isolation which can be associated with distance learning. Secondly, the existence of an ongoing recorded dialogue within the classroom provides support for a number of practical issues arising in online teaching, including issues of progress monitoring and assessment.

The central role played in the pedagogy by discussion and argument, however, raises further issues concerning the ways in which these dialogues should be facilitated, moderated, and evaluated. In the latter part of the chapter we present a framework for the analysis of arguments of this kind and discuss its possible application in this context. Our objective here is to suggest a way in which the role we suggest for dialogue in online education can be supported by objective and partially automated systems.

BACKGROUND

The Degree Programmes

We will begin by outlining the principal features of the programmes which are the basis of this case study. The initial targets for the venture were working professionals in the information and communications technology industry, which is now a major employer throughout Europe and, indeed, elsewhere. Because of the rapid and recent growth of the industry, many of those employed are both relatively young and, to some extent, under-qualified for the demands of the career they are pursuing. Obtaining high-level qualifications is likely to be seen as desirable both by these people and by their employers, for whom the shortage of appropriately skilled personnel is a large and growing problem. This demand is apparent in the popularity of the graduate training programmes offered by the University of Liverpool through its CONNECT Centre (Charlton, Gittings, Leng, Little, & Neilson, 1997). CON-

NECT offers postgraduate certificate programmes aimed at skills updating for computing professionals, and the demand for these even within the local region has been sustained at a high level for a number of years.

Most of those working in a professional capacity in the ICT industry in Europe are already graduates or have professional experience sufficient for them to be seen as graduate-equivalent. For these, the appropriate level of qualification to which they might aspire is a master's degree. Taking a career break to obtain such a qualification is, however, an expensive option for a working professional, so the opportunity to study while remaining in full-time employment is likely to be attractive. The employer, also, may be persuaded that facilitating this opportunity will be a way of retaining the services of staff whose skills are in short supply, as well as a way of developing these skills.

To address this perceived need, two programmes have been introduced, leading to an MSc in IT, and to an MBA. The two programmes have a similar, although not identical, structure. We will here focus for illustration on the MSc, although most of the issues raised apply equally to the MBA.

While there are many reasons, social as well as academic, why a student may wish to attend a university, a working professional is unlikely to be attracted to pursue an online degree unless its academic standing is assured. Part of this assurance can be given by mirroring, wherever possible and appropriate, the academic structure of established programmes. Thus, the (online) MSc in IT comprises eight taught modules, each of 15 CAT units, followed by a dissertation project and in this respect follows closely the model used for many conventional MSc programmes, including the one used in the parent University of Liverpool. The academic content of the modules is scarcely relevant to the subject of this chapter, except to note that the academic level of the material is CAT level M, i.e., master's degree level. The programme differs significantly from the "on-ground" MSc offered at Liverpool in that it is targeted more specifically at professionals in the IT industry who already have significant practical experience and sophisticated understanding of the field. We will discuss the implications of this more fully later.

Programme Delivery

The major difference, of course, is in the module delivery mechanism, which will also be discussed more fully below. Each taught module, in general, is delivered entirely online over the Internet over a period of eight weeks. For this purpose, the year is divided into five periods of 10 weeks, allowing for two-week vacation periods between each module. If, as is expected to be the norm, a student pursues only one module at a time, this schedule would enable the full programme, including the final dissertation project, to be completed in about two years, although this can be extended to allow for longer vacation periods.

Module delivery involves the use of proprietary software to support a *virtual classroom* for each module, within which a group of up to 20 students study. This software, the SoftArc FirstClass system, has been widely used for online teaching (Persico & Manca, 2000). In this case it is hosted by a commercial agency, relieving both the university and its commercial partner of the problems of direct management of the server site. The mode of communication is asynchronous, necessarily, given the requirement to enable students to fit the demands of the course into their work schedule and the additional problems of catering for staff and students who may be working in several different time zones. Associated with each virtual classroom is a set of mail folders to which students, teachers, and others involved in the course administration have access. Essentially, module delivery and all other teaching interactions take place via these folders. This deliberately low-technology approach makes the programme available to any student who has use of a PC with Internet access.

Pedagogic Approach

The taught modules of the programme aim to achieve outcomes comparable to those of conventional teaching. However, it is not the intention to provide a replication of a classroom-based module delivery: To do so would fail to take advantage of both the virtues of the medium and the capabilities of the students and would at best provide a debased imitation of conventional teaching. We start, instead, from the standpoint that lecture-based teaching, whatever its merits, is not necessarily an ideal which online teaching must necessarily emulate. The weaknesses of the model are very familiar to all those who have taught or been taught in higher-education establishments in the UK and elsewhere. Students, all too frequently, attend lectures in an entirely passive mode, expecting to listen and receive the information they require while making no positive contribution themselves. Interaction between lecturer and students and within groups of students is low, especially in the large classes which are typical of most modern universities.

This mode of teaching is especially inappropriate for the target group of students, who are, in general, mature, confident individuals with a wealth of personal experience to contribute on their own account. We aim, instead, to create a teaching environment which is closer to the *seminar*-based model, in which discussion of concepts and experiences plays a central role. Two broad principles inform the approach we use: *constructivism* and *collaborative enquiry.*

Constructivism (Wilson, 1996) describes a view of learning in which students construct their own unique understanding of a subject through a process which includes social interaction so that the learner can explain understandings, receive feedback from teachers and other students, clarify meanings, and reach a group consensus. Collaborative enquiry via Internet-mediated communication provides a framework for this mode of learning (Stacey, 1998). The aim is to use the medium to foster the creation of a *learning community* (Hiltz & Wellman, 1997), which will enable dialogue between participants, sharing of information, and collaborative project work. This mode of learning has much to commend it in many contexts, but is particularly appropriate when, as in this case, the students themselves will often bring to the class knowledge and expertise that is outside the experience of the course teacher and which can be shared with the group.

Each module is structured as a series of seminars, usually of one week's duration. Typically, at the start of each week, the module instructor posts a "lecture" (some text, plus possibly graphics, video, etc.) to a folder in the virtual classroom, together with some "discussion questions" for the class to consider and other exercises and assignments (possibly including collaborative assignments) relating to the current topic. During the rest of the week, the students respond to the discussion questions, posting both initial replies and further comments on their colleagues' replies to an open-access folder (to which the instructor may also contribute). Answers to exercises and other assignments are normally posted to a closed folder accessible only to the instructor. Both the assignments *and* the discussion, however, are elements in the assessment of the module; in this mode of instruction, it is vital to require the active participation of students. Research has shown (Klemm & Snell, 1996; Lai, 1997) that involvement in online discussion is rarely wholly effective unless moderated by external facilitators, and in our case, making it an assessed element is part of this.

The moderated discussion (Collins & Berge, 1997) is, in fact, a key feature of the teaching paradigm used and serves a number of purposes. Most obviously, it provides the means by which students may share knowledge and experience, comment on the course materials and assignments, raise questions, and add to the understanding of their colleagues. To a significant extent, the students thus participate actively in the teaching process, augmenting the overall learning experience as well as reducing the load on the instructor (many questions posted by students can in fact be answered by others in the class).

The Partnership

The programmes have been created by a partnership between the University of Liverpool and a commercial organisation, K.I.T. eLearning of Rotterdam, a subsidiary of a commercial provider of educational services. While the potential of online learning has latterly attracted much interest in universities, realisation of the potential has been inhibited by a number of factors. One of these has been the level of investment involved in the context of a financial climate which, for UK universities at least, has been difficult for a number of years. This, however, is only one of the reasons for developing the K.I.T. partnership. For Liverpool, as for most other UK universities, venturing into European-wide or indeed worldwide course delivery is uncharted territory. The partnership brings together the academic experience and standing of an established university with the commercial and marketing experience of an established and successful company also active in the educational field. The university's role is essentially to uphold the academic standards required for the award of the degree, while K.I.T. brings to the partnership, in addition to its experience in marketing, an understanding of the service concept which is vital for the market served by the programme. This collaboration has made it possible to create and market the programme within a timescale which would scarcely have been possible for a university-only venture.

The partnership, in a broader sense, goes beyond that between the principal organisations involved. Also included are the instructors, who are being drawn from across the world. Most are established academics in universities in the US, Canada, Australia and Europe who are engaging in the programme on a part-time basis largely because they are excited by the opportunity it offers to be involved at the start of a new development in education.

QUALITY ASSURANCE ISSUES

It will be apparent that the context we have described poses a number of challenges for a university intent on maintaining its reputation for academic standards and quality of teaching and learning. Issues to be considered include:

- Academic control and management
- Validation and approval procedures
- Defining and maintaining academic standards
- Staff appointment and training
- Monitoring of programme delivery
- Assessment procedures
- Student identity and plagiarism
- Student progression and support
- Student involvement and feedback

All of these might potentially be threatened by conflicts between interests of the parties, by the indirect relationship between the university and some of the people involved in the delivery of the programme, and by the absence of a physical location for the programme. They are issues of usability, in the sense that failure to address them adequately will undermine the reputation and recognition of the qualification awarded and, in the extreme case, will make the programme unusable as an alternative to a conventional campus-based education. We will examine these issues in turn and describe the approach that has been taken towards them.

Academic Control

The MSc in IT offered via this programme is a fully accredited degree of the University of Liverpool, and the university properly insists that the degree conforms to the standards and requirements expected of its other postgraduate degree programmes, within the framework defined by the QAA for the provision of distance learning (Quality Assurance Agency, 2000). The primary requirement, consequently, is that all academic aspects of the programme should remain the responsibility of the parent university and that the university should have structures and procedures that are effective in discharging this responsibility.

This requirement is met principally via the provision of a dedicated unit, the e-Learning Unit, based in the Department of Computer Science and staffed by established academic members of the department with appropriate technical and secretarial support. The role of the e-Learning Unit is to oversee all academic aspects of the course programme and to ensure that the procedures required by the university are followed and appropriate academic standards maintained. Beyond this, the responsibility of the unit is to manage the relationship between the university and the other participants in the programme, including students, with particular reference to the questions of quality assurance identified above.

The management of student admissions provides an illustration of the nature of the relationship. Marketing of the programme and student recruitment are the responsibility of the partner organisation, K.I.T., and might, without other constraints, be driven by financial considerations. However, all recommendations for admission are subject first to the approval of the unit and then by the Admissions Department of the Faculty of Science, using the same procedures and criteria as apply to internal MSc courses. A similar relationship applies in general to all other academic issues.

Defining and Maintaining Academic Standards

A second premise for the management of the programme is that, wherever possible, its organisation and management should follow procedures that can be compared to those established for other degrees of the university. The detailed curriculum for the MSc was developed as a collaboration between staff of the university, K.I.T staff, and part-time instructors appointed to the programme who are based throughout the world. The approval of the curriculum, however, and of other academic aspects of the programme is entirely internal to the university and follows the model created for the approval of all other degree programmes of the university. Thus, a detailed programme specification, including curriculum details, has passed through a series of stages of validation, including approval at departmental, faculty, and university levels, with advice being obtained from external experts. The latter included, in this case, both UK-based and overseas academics, and industrial advisers.

Subsequent development of the programme and continued review of academic standards and other academic issues are the primary responsibility of a Board of Studies established for the MSc. This board includes representatives of the partner organisation, K.I.T, but is chaired by the director of the e-Learning Unit and includes also representatives of the parent academic department, i.e., Computer Science, and faculty, i.e., Science. The board now reviews and validates all curriculum developments and other changes to the agreed programme and its delivery, reporting to the Faculty of Science through the normal university procedures.

In these respects the definition, validation, and subsequent review of the programme exactly mirror the normal university processes. Additional to this, however, is a further review process, carried out initially at six-month intervals and now annually. The purpose of these reviews, carried out by senior university management, is to examine the continued effectiveness of the academic structures established for oversight of the programme and the effective operation of the partnership.

Staff Appointment and Training

Teaching (and, to a large extent, development and continuing enhancement) of the curriculum are principally carried out by *instructors* recruited by K.I.T. These instructors, who are all appointed on a part-time basis, are based throughout the world and are principally holders of academic appointments in other universities (largely in the US). Although recruitment of these staff is the responsibility of K.I.T, all appointments are subject to university approval: first via the e-Learning Unit and then by the Faculty of Science through the same procedures that apply for the approval of non-established staff to teach on internal programmes. In giving this approval, the same criteria are used as would apply for full-time appointments: Instructors are required to have the qualifications and experience required of university teachers, and those involved in curriculum development and/or supervision of dissertations are required to be research-active academics.

All staff appointed to the programme are required to first undertake an (online) training programme, over a period of six weeks, in which they are instructed on the use of the software platform and the methodology and pedagogic approach used in the programme. Further to this, in the first module they teach, the instructor is overseen by an academic *mentor*, whose role is to advise and guide the novice.

Monitoring of Programme Delivery

As we briefly described above, module delivery takes place entirely through the medium of email communications in the "virtual classroom." Perhaps paradoxically, this makes overseeing the operation of the degree programme easier than is the case for "on-ground" teaching. Because *all* significant communications between staff and students—"lectures," assignments, discussions, and personal communications—are made electronically, all are subject to scrutiny as required, by "lurking" in the classroom while the module is being delivered and/or by examining the recorded history of the class subsequently. The teaching materials, of course, are well defined and approved by university procedures, and it is easy to ensure that they are delivered as required when the module is taught. Thus, the academic staff of the e-Learning Unit monitor the delivery of each module to ensure that the agreed syllabus and procedures are followed, and the assessment is fair and of the appropriate standard.

Assessment Procedures

Assessment is made entirely on the basis of work carried out within the virtual classroom, including contributions to the classroom discussion. In general, each element of work is assessed on a weekly basis. The individual grades thus assigned are combined, using a transparent formula, to produce an overall grade for the module. The target qualification is an MSc, which is classified only at Pass and Distinction level, and the grading formulae and criteria reflect this: Essentially, the aim of assessment is to verify attainment of module learning outcomes at threshold levels, rather than to produce a fine-grained classification.

Assessment is carried out initially by the module instructor: However, in this as in other respects, the module is subject to moderation by the *module monitor*, based at the university's e-Learning Unit. Review of module assessment outcomes is an explicit part of the end-of-module procedures, and results are not confirmed (even on a provisional basis) without the agreement of the module monitor, who, of course, has access to all the relevant information contained in the record of the virtual classroom. These provisional results are finally subject to confirmation by the Board of Examiners established for the programme. This board operates in a similar manner to others in the university, with a composition similar to that of the Board of Studies, but also including an external examiner from another university. The external examiner, also, has full access to the virtual classroom and so, in practice, has the opportunity for a more detailed and free examination of assessment processes than is usually possible in on-ground teaching.

These procedures are, in some respects, stricter than those that normally apply in university teaching: There is, in practice, less freedom for instructors to depart from agreed assessment processes and criteria, as everything is open to review both by the e-Learning Unit and by the Board of Examiners. These constraints, which some instructors find irksome, are in our experience essential. Because instructors are drawn from a wide variety of cultures, it is particularly difficult to arrive at a common understanding of the interpretation of a particular assessment grade. The only way to maintain comparability between module grades, therefore, is firstly to define very clear grading descriptors and criteria and secondly to insist that the interpretation of these is moderated firmly within the UK assessment model.

Student Identity and Plagiarism

One of the questions that most exercises organisations considering online learning is that of how to confirm the identity of participants, together with the related question of protecting against plagiarism. In the teaching context we have described, however, we believe these problems are more apparent than real. The key point here is the role played by *discussion* in the virtual classroom. Because participation in discussion is a requirement for students enrolled for a module it provides a means of monitoring their effective involvement and assists in preventing impersonation and plagiarism. Involvement in the programme demands a thoughtful, personal contribution from each student on almost a daily basis, which would be almost impossible to falsify. In practice, the (online) characters of students become very well-known to their instructors, other students and the module monitors.

Of course, it would be naïve to assume that plagiarism cannot take place. However, the fact that all communications take place online and are recorded and preserved for as long as required (i.e., at least until after student graduation) again provides some protection. In particular, it becomes relatively easy to apply programmes that perform comparisons of work submitted in the virtual classroom or use services that perform checks against plagiarism throughout the Web.

Student Progression and Support

The requirement to participate in online discussion also provides an effective means of monitoring student progress. If a student is failing to keep up with the requirements of the programme, this becomes apparent within days, as his/her contributions to the discussion falter. At this point the instructor can intervene (via a private mail folder) to investigate and take action if required.

Outside the virtual classroom, student progress and support are the responsibility of a *programme manager*, who takes on most of the roles of a personal/academic tutor (although again, of course, the role is effected in an online mode). The instructor will report problems and absences to the programme manager for further action.

Student Involvement and Feedback

Close monitoring and review of module delivery are key elements of the programme. Part of this includes monitoring of student reaction. At the end of each module, students attending are asked to complete an online questionnaire on all aspects of the module and its delivery. An anonymised summary of this is returned to the instructor, who is required to complete a structured report commenting on the outcome of the module and issues arising in its delivery or raised in the questionnaires. This report is sent to the module monitor, who adds further comments. Finally, the composite report and questionnaire returns are reviewed routinely by the Board of Studies and are also made available to the Board of Examiners. This process, of course, is not novel but, in this case, is applied rigorously: Module results are not presented for confirmation to the Board of Examiners until these reports are available.

Summary

From the description above, it will be clear that a principal objective in defining the management structures of the programme has been to replicate, as closely as possible, procedures established for use in campus-based programmes. The primary reason for this has been to ensure that the online degrees are demonstrably equivalent in standards and quality to other master's degrees of the university. In fact, however, we need to go further to overcome the likely preconception that online degrees will be inferior in these respects. In campus-based teaching, also, most practical problems can be resolved informally through discussion at departmental level between staff involved, including course directors and academic managers. While this kind of discussion can take place, and does, in an online environment, there are a number of factors which can lead to problems, including the lack of direct managerial control over instructors and cultural differences. To resolve these questions, there is a greater need than usual for very precisely defined procedures that can be called upon. For these reasons, our first conclusion is that it is necessary that the procedures and structures established should be, wherever possible, more stringent, and applied more rigorously than is usually the case for conventional degrees.

The second point that emerges is the key role played by *discussion* in the course programme. The principal reason for this is that it is a central part of the constructivist pedagogy: Students are required to engage in discussions of work introduced in the virtual classroom as a way of leading them towards a personalised understanding of the topics covered. Discussion also, of course, allows students to contribute to the understanding of others and, in the process, creates a learning environment which most students seem to find stimulating and supportive. Beyond this, however, we have pointed to a number of ways in which the classroom discussion is used to assist in the management and quality assurance of the programme: as part of the assessment regime and a key defence against impersonation and plagiarism and as a tool for monitoring progress and identifying students who are experiencing problems. In the model we have described, online discussion is a key aspect of usability. This raises questions about how classroom discussion should be managed and examined, which we will consider in the next section.

PROVIDING INTELLIGENT SUPPORT
TO THE PROGRAMME

We have seen above that discussion has a central role in the programme, underpinning the pedagogic approach and influencing a number of aspects of quality assurance. As contributions to discussion are an important part of the basis for student assessment, major emphasis should be put on how to evaluate them effectively and fairly. At present, this evaluation is dealt with by pragmatic procedures of the instructor and others involved in the programme and its monitoring. This situation, besides being obviously time-consuming on the instructors' side, is naturally liable to inconsistency, both between different classes of the same module and between different modules. On the other hand, the availability of class discussions and indeed the complete record of what happens in the virtual classroom in electronic format offers a unique opportunity for exploitation by information technology that should not be missed, as it can offer a way to facilitate the instructor's job and add guarantees of objectiveness in the judgment.

We introduce in this section a first step in this direction, by describing an ongoing project aimed at finding avenues for improving not only the evaluation of students but also the preparation and delivery of teaching material by means of artificial intelligence techniques. The project, conducted in collaboration with the Intelligent Interfaces Laboratory of the University of Bari in Italy,[1] is still in its initial phases, so we present here only our preliminary thoughts in the various aspects we feel could benefit from such an intervention.

Perspectives of Research

We seek to design and build a tool which would aid the whole process of online teaching and learning: from the preparation of the teaching material, to the conduction of individual deliveries of a module, with the assessment of the students, to, finally, the evaluation of the module itself on the basis of single runnings of it, in order to inform its future deliveries, thus closing the informative cycle.

We should perhaps point out immediately that we by no means envisage a tool that would substitute the human instructors and facilitators. On the contrary, the tool is conceived as an aid to the programme staff: As a matter of fact, we would, as a first instance, see the tool being used exclusively by staff, and not by students. Such a tool would be mainly used to ascertain that the pedagogic objectives of the paradigm have been met. Moreover, though this is currently seen more as a by-product than a principal aim of the system, the tool would be used in the phase of module construction as an authoring aid that would help with the preparation of the teaching material on one hand and of the assessment material on the other, the latter being in some way produced on the basis of the former.

In what follows we will briefly examine the three main areas in which we are conducting our investigations.

Student Evaluation and Virtual Classroom Conduct

As explained previously, the student evaluation process consists of two main activities: the assessment of students' individual pieces of work and the evaluation of the virtual classroom discussion on the topics proposed by the module facilitator. While the former can be compared to the typical on-ground teaching situation of a student handing in exercises for the lecturer to assess, the latter poses big challenges to the module facilitator. Virtual classroom questions are designed to provoke discussion; therefore, they generally do not have a right or wrong answer, but they aim to keep students engaged all week to try and come to an agreement on the topic proposed. This gives rise to both a qualitative and a quantitative issue for the module instructors. Qualitatively, the instructors are asked to deal with very open and diverse responses and have to keep a delicate balance between guiding the discussion to avoid it going off topic and leaving the students the freedom to speculate as they wish. Quantitatively, the instructors are asked to find their way through a huge amount of messages (for some courses it is not unusual to have more than 500 postings per week) while not losing the grasp of the situation, being attentive to students in need of further explanation or encouragement, keeping an eye for students taking the lead too much, perhaps at the expense of others, or even dealing with more or less subtle situations of plagiarism or collusion. Both issues pose a burden on the module facilitators which should not be underestimated, which is even more important as the overall quality of the programme delivery depends so crucially on the instructors' performance.

While perhaps nothing can substitute for the human judgment, we believe that our environment could and should provide valuable help to the instructors by monitoring the classroom and "raising flags" if some situations manifest themselves, in case they go unnoticed. At the same time, we would not undergo excessive changes to the system as it is now: The current environment is sufficiently easy to use and comfortable even for students who are less computer literate, and we would not move to a more sophisticated environment without losing some degree of expressiveness on the students' part. We aim, therefore, at making the most of what we have by designing a tool that could "wrap up" the virtual classroom discussion without being even noticed by the student, a tool that would look over the instructor's shoulders and help in understanding what is going on. Such a tool would benefit the whole online education process from several aspects, as Edwards and Mercer (1987) suggest. The analysis of student responses to discussion questions, when seen in isolation, can help in identifying the level of self-explanation the student has achieved. The analysis of argumentation and negotiation occurring among students in the virtual classroom may help to encourage constructive conflicts and in identifying problematic situations, such as the presence of disruptive students or cases in which the discussion goes off topic. Finally, ongoing models of the students can monitor their inquiry processes as a way to plan interventions aimed at further explaining given topics or correcting misconceptions.

Several paradigms are being investigated towards this aim, and it is perhaps outside the scope of this chapter to analyse them at length; but the principal idea is to see each student as a "conversational agent" (Poesio & Traum, 1997) for which a "mental model" can be constructed, able to represent both knowledge (concepts at various levels of abstraction) related to the module topics and how different pieces of knowledge are related to one another. As this has to be done on the basis of the student replies, which are written as free text, techniques of conversation analysis (Pilkington, 1999) would "contextualise" each of the student messages in a clear way by linking it to other relevant pieces of the discussion, such as the instructor feedback, relevant parts of the lecture material, other students' supporting or antagonistic positions, and so on. In order to produce the student's mental model, we are investigating at the moment the level of expressiveness of the belief network (BN) paradigm (Pearl, 1988). In brief, BNs are a method of reasoning based on probability, whereby one can express whether a causal relationship exists between two states of affair and quantify this relationship in probabilistic terms. In our case, we would use BNs to represent the likeliness that a certain notion is understood by the student, provided that a given set of other notions have been learned. These relationships can help in evaluating single pieces of work, as student responses can be compared to a "canonical model" of the course material: By means of elicitation techniques, the student mental model of the topic under study can be constructed. This will constitute a BN which, when compared to the canonical model, will enable the facilitator to estimate how much has been understood by the student and, by using propagating algorithms proper of the BN framework, to infer which specific notions need further explanation.

This process produces two important results: First, the module facilitator will be helped to achieve a fair, objective "base grade" for each student. This grade is not meant of course to be final, as several factors can influence the instructor's judgment, but it would provide a common ground to assess each student in the classroom. Second, the discrepancies between the student model of the topics and the canonical model will help identify points of intervention and aid the production of personalised feedback. The issue of producing feedback has been raised several times by module facilitators as one of the most time-consuming tasks, if done properly, which at the same time produces a tremendous effect on students. Similarly, in their question-naires, students mention the instructor's feedback as one of the most proficient ways to improve their knowledge. A tool that can at least partially help in such process will no doubt be one of the most welcome improvements to the programme environment.

The process can be scaled up when considering the overall discussion in the virtual classroom. One can think to create a collective model of the whole classroom, much similar to the one of the single students, which in the same fashion contains all that has been put forward within the class discussion. Analysis of the model would enable the facilitator to realise whether the class has collectively formed a misconception that needs to be corrected or if the class is focusing the discussion onto issues that are not answering the question proposed. Moreover, the facilitator may need to enforce some communication protocol among students, to encourage participation from more silent students, or to force more verbose ones to step aside and leave more space to others. A collective model of the class, when compared to the single student models, would enable us to spot such situations. This may be coupled with, for example, formally designed dialogue rules that could act as "traffic lights" in the course of the conversation. Again, students do not necessarily have to be aware of these mechanisms, at least until some pilot study would reveal whether an explicit "dialogue game" (Carlson, 1983) could improve students' discussion and learning, but instructors can use hints coming from the tool to adapt their behaviour.

Improving Modules on the Basis of Feedback

The impressive amount of information that is collected in various moments of the teaching and learning activity should not be wasted. So far, the module monitors, together with the module developers, are asked to perform a quality control on each module delivery and inform, if necessary, future deliveries, a feedback which could in principle lead to some changes in the module material. This is a long and complex process, and it is not always trivial to identify the single causes of problems in a module. Statistical methods can help in this process. If we maintain the various BNs representing what the students have learned in each running of a particular module, algorithms can be used to assess the level of learning that the module material produces. By aptly combining the various BNs, one can estimate what an idealised "average" student learns from the material proposed. This can be compared with the canonical model of the course material to find discrepancies, thus allowing us to quantify the extent to which the learning aims of the module have been achieved. Such feedback may result both in an update of the module structure, by introducing or eliminating important notions, and, perhaps more frequently, in an amendment to the way the module is proposed to students, perhaps changing the style of the presentation, or adding emphasis to relevant sections, or highlighting comparisons with notions learned in other modules. Indeed, by representing quantitative measures of the links among concepts, BNs can also help identify "important" notions, perhaps helping to shape a module's learning objectives.

Improving the Quality of Teaching Material

Despite not being a major objective of our research, undoubtedly one of the scopes for improvement in our programme of study concerns the presentation of the material to students. So far, lectures are prepared by hand by the module developer, included in text files and presented to the virtual classroom at the beginning of each teaching week. The enormous potential of the media is therefore not exploited to the full: The lecture, as it is now, is a rather static object. It has to be modified by hand and only by the module developer, if any situation arises, and cannot be tailored to the need of the specific cohort of students in the class. One way to change this situation could be to provide the module developer with a tool for the semiautomatic production of the module material. One could think of helping the developer to frame a "conceptual map" of the course, which could formalise in some way the knowledge that the module is meant to transmit (a map that can easily be transformed into the canonical model of the course that will inform the BN algorithms). This could be done at various levels in order to represent both the overall vision of the module and the lower-level notions to convey. Authoring tools could then help the module developer to obtain a fair representation of such a map, and, once the module material has been formalised in such a way, techniques of natural language processing (Reiter & Dale, 2000) may be used to help generate the actual material to be proposed to the students. The material could be more similar to a hyper-book than to a simple, static document, and the students will be able to explore it more freely, so that they will hopefully improve their understanding of the connections among concepts. Further developments may include techniques to produce the module material "on the fly," tailored to the particular cohort of students or to the particular facilitator's style: The aim would be to create an environment in which everybody can feel more at ease in order to improve teaching and learning performances.

Summary

We have presented in this section some hints on how the quality of our programme can be improved by arming the staff involved with tools that, by means of artificial intelligence techniques, can aid the whole process of module delivery. We are especially aiming at easing the facilitator's work: Facilitators, or instructors, are the prime contact for students as far as the taught material is concerned, so their performances crucially influence the performances of the whole programme. The particular pedagogic model used, entirely online based and so heavily relying on discussion and collaborative learning, has to guarantee, on the instructor side, full awareness of what happens in the virtual classroom and prompt intervention to solve potential problems. A tool is envisaged that could help in monitoring the situation, without substituting itself for the human being, and, more importantly, would be as transparent as possible to the students, who would not be constrained in their approach to the classroom. Besides this more immediate advantage, such a tool would have the added value of forcing the staff involved in the preparation and delivery of the module to fully and explicitly specify the parameters that have to be accounted for in designing and assessing a module's learning objectives, an issue that is perceived to be of paramount importance for quality assurance (QAA, 2000). Finally, but not less importantly, we believe that an online environment, and especially an educational one, cannot ignore the computer as its prime means for being conceived and conveyed; therefore full advantage should be taken from the media technology, both in terms of human-computer interaction and in terms of information-processing techniques. Improving the quality of the environment and exploiting its potentials to the full will improve the quality of the entire programme.

CONCLUSIONS

We have here described some issues arising in the planning and delivery of postgraduate degree programmes that are taught entirely through the medium of the Internet. What has become immediately apparent to all who are involved is that online learning, in the form that we are using, is not an easy option for anyone. It is demanding on both students and academics, both of whom must recognise that it requires a level of involvement and interaction far beyond what is usually expected in a university lecture room. This involvement brings its own rewards, however: Paradoxically, online learning seems to provide an environment in which students can support each other, and staff and students understand each others' strengths and limitations.

Alongside these advantages, however, there are corresponding problems. We have focused in particular on the questions of *quality assurance* of the programme, which are key to the acceptability and hence the usability of the paradigm. We have argued that the role played by *discussion* in the programme is of central importance in addressing these problems. Our experience, supported by student questionnaire returns, is that students seem to find the online discussion an especially valuable part of the overall learning process, and we have also used the discussions as a key element in the strategies used for assessment and programme monitoring. Using discussion effectively, however, is both time-consuming and in other ways problematic. One of the difficulties we have encountered is in limiting the involvement of students in the discussion. We have found that, usually for the best of reasons, students participate all too enthusiastically in the discussion, so that just to maintain an involvement in the debate requires a substantial commitment of time. This, in addition to the workload created by the weekly assignments, results in many students putting far more time into the programme than was expected. For this reason, the class size is restricted to a maximum of 20. We have found that even this size sometimes leads to too much online discussion, and we are exploring ways to control this so as to limit the workload. We are also investigating whether a slightly more attenuated module timescale may be preferable.

Other issues relate to the need to standardise the teaching and assessment process between instructors and students whose background is from a range of different teaching and learning cultures. For these reasons, also, we are exploring ways in which to provide intelligent computer-aided support for the analysis both of discussions and for other aspects of the virtual classroom, including quality management of module materials. We expect that tools of this kind will assist instructors to manage and evaluate student involvement in online discussions and thus help to do this objectively and uniformly. The teaching and learning context we have described will provide an ideal environment to investigate the applicability of this research.

ACKNOWLEDGMENTS

The authors wish to thank Professor Denis Smith for his helpful comments on a draft of this chapter. We also acknowledge the contribution to this work that is being made by our colleagues at K.I.T. eLearning, especially Yoram Kalman and Emanuel Gruengard.

ENDNOTES

[1]   The project is partially funded by the British Council and the Ministero dell'Università e della Ricerca Scientifica e Tecnologica in the scope of the British-Italian Partnership Programme.

REFERENCES

Anderson, T., & Kanuka, H. (1997). On-Line forums [1]: New platforms for professional development and group collaboration. *Journal of Computer-Mediated Communication, 3*(3). Retrieved November 25, 2002 from http://www.ascusc.org/jcmc/vol3/issue3/anderson.html.

Carlson, L. (1983). *Dialogue games: An approach to discourse analysis.* Dordrecht, The Netherlands: D. Reidel.

Charlton, C., Gittings, C., Leng, P., Little, J., & Neilson, I. (1997). The impact of the new connectivity: Transferring technological skills to the small business community. In F. Neiderman (Ed.), *Proceedings of ACM SIGPR Conference* (pp. 97-103). San Francisco, CA: ACM Press.

Collins, M. P., & Berge, Z. L. (1997, March). *Moderating online electronic discussion groups.* Paper presented at the American Educational Research Association, Chicago. Retrieved November 25, 2002 from http://www.emoderators.com/moderators/sur_aera97.html

Davies, G. (Ed.). (1998). Teleteaching '98: Distance learning, training and education. *Proceedings of XV IFIP World Computer Congress.* World Computer Congress, Vienna (August) Austrian Computer Society.

Edwards, D., & Mercer, N. (1987). *Common knowledge: The development of understanding in the classroom.* London: Methuen & Routledge.

Hiltz, S. R., & Wellman, B. (1997). Asynchronous learning networks as a virtual classroom. *Communications of the ACM, 40*(9), 44-49.

Klemm, W. R., & Snell, J. R. (1996). Enriching computer-mediated group learning by coupling constructivism with collaborative learning. *Journal of Instructional Science and Technology, 1*(2). Retrieved November 25, 2002 from http://www.usq.edu.au/electpub/e-jist/docs/old/vol1no2/article1.htm

Lai, K.-W. (1997). Computer-mediated communication for teenage students: A content analysis of a student messaging system. *Education and Information Technologies, 2*, 31-45.

Pearl, J. (1988). *Probabilistic reasoning in intelligent systems: Networks of plausible inference.* San Mateo, CA: Morgan Kaufmann.

Persico, D., & Manca, S. (2000). Use of FirstClass as a collaborative learning environment. *Innovations in Education and Training International, 37*(1), 34-41.

Pilkington, R. M. (1999). *Analysing educational discourse: The DISCOUNT scheme* (CBLU Tech. Rep. 99/2). Leeds, England: University of Leeds, Computer Based Learning Unit.

Poesio, M., & Traum, D. R. (1997). Conversational actions and discourse situations. *Computational Intelligence, 13*(3), 309-347.

Quality Assurance Agency for Higher Education. (2000). *Distance learning guidelines.* Retrieved November 25, 2002 from http://www.qaa.ac.uk

Reiter, E., & Dale, R. (2000). *Building applied natural language generation systems*. Cambridge, Cambridge University Press.

Stacey, E. (1998). Learning collaboratively in a CMC environment. In G. Davies (Ed.), *Teleteaching '98, Proceedings of XV IFIP World Computer Congress* (pp. 951-960). Vienna, Austrian Computer Society.

Suthers, D., & Jones, D. (1997). An architecture for intelligent collaborative educational systems. *Proceedings 8th World Conference on Artificial Intelligence in Education'97*, (August, pp. 55-62) Kobe, Japan.

Wilson, B. G. (1996). *Constructivist learning environments: Case studies in instructional design*. NJ: Educational Technology.

Chapter XI

Learning Technologies and Learning Theories

Vivien Sieber
University of North London, UK

David Andrew
University of North London, UK

ABSTRACT

Learning technologies can provide a rich learning environment; this chapter explores the relationship between traditional learning theories and technology-mediated learning. Two examples are presented where technologies are used as tools (a) to evaluate and create Web pages and (b) to create learning technology teaching materials. The range of learning outcomes resulting from these projects are discussed in terms of Gardner's (1993) theory of multiple intelligences.

INTRODUCTION

Appropriate use of learning technologies can promote effective learning, in particular by providing an environment that fosters independent, learner-centred experiences. The intention of this chapter is to identify those aspects of learning technologies that promote effective learning and discuss them in relation to learning theory. Case studies are used to illustrate the complex array of learning outcomes that can follow teaching with learning technologies.

BACKGROUND—LEARNING THEORIES

Leaning technologies (LT) may be defined as the use of any technology that enhances the learning experience. Using this definition LT may be considered to range from typewriters, overhead transparencies, and simple audiovisual aids to sophisticated video, DVD, audio displays and computer-aided learning (CAL), multimedia, the Internet and Web pages, or virtual and managed learning environments (VLEs/MLEs). Cullen et al. (2002) widen the definition of a VLE to include any learning involving the application of telematics, information and communications technology (ICT). For practical purposes, during the present discussion LT will be confined to any form of digital media, with particular reference to multimedia and HTML. Ellington, Percival, and Race (1995) detail practical approaches for the successful introduction of these technologies into higher education. More recently, Boyle (1997) and Maier and Warren (2000) provide overviews of learning and teaching for the range of different types of LT. These three books were published within five years of one another, and comparison of both the type of technology discussed and the extent of the discussion demonstrates the rate of change within the computing industry and the increased range and sophistication of the types of LT available to academic staff, with subsequent changes in learning and teaching. The impact of the Internet and intranets in higher education (HE) is recent and already has far-reaching effects. Whilst the Internet is not per se a learning technology, in that it is an unregulated mass of information of variable quality, the World Wide Web does provide opportunities for learning. The mass expansion of materials available from the Internet and the opportunities offered by electronic communication, in the form of email, synchronous and asynchronous discussion, VLEs, etc., have altered the learning experience for most undergraduates. Perhaps the greatest emerging opportunity offered by the Internet is that of increased communication via email, bulletin boards, and discussion groups and the possibilities for peers to comment on work in progress.

There is considerable variation between individuals in the way they learn, and an individual may well learn in different ways at different times. A further aim of this chapter is to consider whether or not learning technologies promote different types of learning from conventional didactic teaching and to account for these differences. The case studies presented are examples of projects where students use LT as creative tools and show that engagement with the subject matter is deep and occurs over a wider range of levels than normally follow traditional didactic teaching, in that students use and demonstrate multiple intelligences (Gardner, 1983, 1993).

Educationalists frequently attempt to use hierarchies to describe the learning process, for example, the taxonomic hierarchy of Bloom (1972) and Bloom, Krathwohl, and Maisa (1979)(Figure 1A), where skills are divided into lower cognitive skills (comprehension, application) and higher cognitive skills (analysis, synthesis, evaluation). Biggs (1999) relates higher learning outcomes to "deep" and "surface" approaches to study, arguing that students must undertake appropriate

Figure 1A: Bloom's taxonomic hierarchy showing higher and lower order cognitive skills

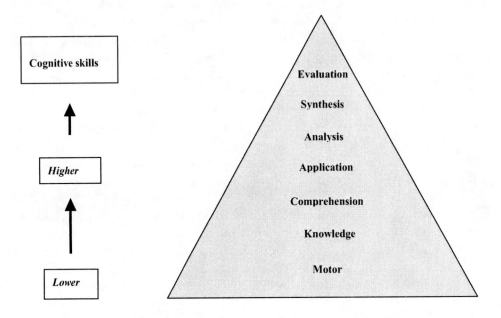

activities which promote deep learning if high-level outcomes (reflection, application, hypothesis) are to be achieved.

A number of theories describing the process of "learning" have been developed, and are summarised, with commentary, by Cullen et al. (2002). It is often difficult to separate the theoretical basis (behaviourism, cognitivism, etc.) used to describe how learning occurs from the practical processes (didactic, problem-based or computer-mediated) involved in promoting the learning itself. Table 1 summarises the key elements of the three learning theories, along with their main protagonists and examples of learning technologies that support these approaches to learning.

Andragogy, the facilitation of adult learning, differs from learning in children, as adult learners are capable of self-direction problem-solving and can apply their knowledge and experience. The teacher acts as a facilitator and mentor rather than adopting a didactic role. Both the context and environment of learning are important. Cullen et al. (2002) carried out a bibliographic review of post-compulsory education in the UK and were able to distinguish three categories of education: (a) didactic, (b) andragogic (learner-directed, learner-centred, problem- or work-based learning), and (c) a mixture of (a) and (b). Where didactic learning is traditionally centred on delivering subject content to the student(s). Didactic learning might be represented by simple DOS text-based computer teaching materials with linear programming and

Table 1:   Main focus and key concepts of educational theories, the primary authors associated with developing these theories, and examples of learning technologies

FOCUS OF THEORY	THEORISTS	LEARNING TECHNOLOGY
Behaviourism		
• Stimulus/response • Learning induced through sequencing and reinforcing desired objectives (changes in behaviour), e.g., programmed learning (step-by-step mastery) • Emphasis on predetermined aims, systematic activities, practice, and feedback • Learner role tends to be passive	**Pavlov:** patterns of association **Skinner (1968):** learning by reward and punishment **Gagné (1977):** neo-behaviourist also draws on constructivism	• "Do and review" • MCQs, quizzes, jigsaws • Linear presentation of information • Navigation choices restricted
Cognitivist/Constructivist		
• Learning is an active, goal-oriented process of constructing knowledge/meaning/understanding via interaction with environment (social as well as individual process) • Knowledge stored in mental structures (e.g., linguistic, logic, mathematical, conceptual schemata) • Learning occurs in developmental/progressive stages • Emphasis on active participation and making transparent the elements of knowledge and practice in the subject/profession (e.g., key concepts, theories, methods, writing, and other forms of communication) • Conversational framework between student/tutor	**Piaget (1970):** stages of psychological and cognitive development; level of *development determines learning* capacity **Bruner (1966):** concept development: from concrete to abstract thinking; concepts as key tools of learning **Bloom (1972):** taxonomy of levels of cognition **Vygotsky (1978):** *learning precedes development* as the learner shifts through the "zone of potential development" **Perry (1970):** phases of ethical development **Gardner (1993):** multiple intelligences **Laurillard (1993):** knowledge built from dialogue between tutor/student **Prosser and Trigwell (1999):** learning situated in student experience	• Multimedia CAL • Simulations • Virtual worlds
Experiential "discovery" learning		
• Importance of experience as a resource for learning by self and others • Key role in learning of feelings, identity, motivation/curiosity • Emphasis on the learning/knowledge-making processes (not just content and product) • Task/problem-centred rather than subject-centred • Learning a collaborative process which encourages independent study • Learning not isolated, built on previous experience	**Friere and Shor (1987):** education for liberation **Lowyck and Knowles (1984):** andragogy/adult learning **Kolb (1984):** learning cycles **Maslow;Rogers (1969):** humanistic psychologists; education should aim at the development of the whole person	• Web page evaluation • Creating Web pages • Creating multimedia learning materials • Electronic discussion groups • Computers as tools

limited interactions that were created in the 1980s. Answers are acknowledged to be right or wrong but the user must proceed through the material in preordained steps. This largely represents traditional behaviourist instructional design systems (Gagné & Briggs, 1979), as behaviourists conceive learning as induced through association (classical conditioning) or rewards and punishments (instrumental conditioning). In LT these are represented by simple "do and review," multiple-choice questions (MCQ), and linear navigation with limited user choice; where in practice, teaching materials are presented in a systematic, programmed, step-by-step manner with practice and feedback. To some extent most LT materials may provide a degree of user centredness in that the student may choose when and how fast to work through the materials.

Cullen et al. (2002) identifies a "new pedagogy," based largely on constructivist theory and practice, with four main types of pedagogical method: expository, interaction, conversational, and experiential. Cognitivism places the learner at the centre of an active, goal-orientated process. Learning is believed to occur as a progressive series of developmental changes as the learner constructs meaning from the materials presented. Academic discourse is an important part of constructing a theoretical framework as the learner acquires and uses knowledge. Laurillard (1993; and cited by Draper (1994)) extends constructivism to include student/tutor interactions, placing learning within a "conversational framework." The learner is not in a vacuum, as learning is influenced by and dependent upon the learner's previous experiences (Prosser & Trigwell, 1999). Jonassen, Mayes, and McAleese (1993) and Perkins (1991) present a theoretical basis for a constructivist rationale of learning during use of learning technologies.

"Learning by doing" provides the student with an opportunity to do something, obtain feedback, and learn from their mistakes. It places the learner at the centre and in control of the learning experience. The two case studies presented in this chapter are both examples of how effective use of LT can promote this type of learning. Experiential learning is implicit in Kolb's (1984) learning cycle, where experience is the starting point for reflection and abstract thinking, from which new understanding arises, to be tested against experience again.

Learning does not take place in isolation, as each student has their own history, experience, culture, and society. Intelligence is frequently seen and assessed by the ability to apply learned factual information to solve problems. But this does not account for the context where learning takes place. Intelligence may be seen as the result of interaction between innate potential and opportunities and constraints arising from society (Gardner, 1993). It is, perhaps, simplistic to consider learning in isolation. Bloom's taxonomic hierarchy does, for example, not include affective domain: feelings, curiosity, identity, and motivation, which are also an important part of the process of learning. Gardner (1983, 1993) presents a theory of multiple intelligences, recognising seven different forms of intelligence: verbal, musical, spatial, logical, interpersonal, intrapersonal, and kinaesthetic. Lave and Wenger (1990) recommend a practice-based theory of learning where separation of knowledge and practice is unsound, as learning is not only acquiring abstract knowledge and the transmission of that explicit abstract knowledge.

Learning is a complex process that differs from individual to individual, and descriptions of learning therefore tend either to oversimplify the process or to result in broad generalisations. In addition, individual learning normally falls within a continuum of styles (Honey & Mumford, 1992). VARK assesses learning styles in terms of visual, aural, read-write and kinaesthetic ways of processing information (http://www.active-learning-site.com/cgi-bin/vark-explanation-script.pl). Generally, people use a mixture of several styles and may indeed find different learning styles more appropriate to particular tasks. There is a complex relationship between factors that promote deep versus surface learning, the learning cycle, and individual learning styles. Honey (2000) used an online questionnaire to investigate the existence or otherwise of e-learning styles and found that there was no relationship between preferred learning style and likes and dislikes during e-learning.

A multimedia environment provides the opportunity for text, graphics, video, and sound which stimulate the user, apparently acting as intrinsic motivators for further use. Boyle (1997) discusses the issues associated with conceptual and presentational design of multimedia teaching materials which may be used to support innate human perception and the constructive process. There is, increasingly, less distinction between multimedia, CAL, and Web-based materials, as many programmes now utilise HTML or XML. However, transmission speeds experienced by distance learners may still make CD-ROM more practical than online Internet connections, especially where large graphics files are included in the material. The development of hypertext and multimedia provides the learner with a rich environment, freedom of navigation, and a range of types of interaction. The extent and type of interaction that a learning tool provides between the user and the LT is one of the main determinants of how effective that tool will be in promoting learning. In educational terms, the student must be at the centre of the learning experience and interact with the materials if they are to achieve "deep" learning (Biggs, 1999). One of the major factors that promotes learning is feedback and the use that learners make of the information that they are given. Multimedia can provide a rich learning experience (Grabinger & Dunlap, 1995). Multimedia environments fulfil some requirements of constructivist theory; in particular, the use of graphics stimulates and motivates learners to form their own construct of the information presented (Boyle, 1997). Information may be presented in pictures, sound, or animation, with a reduced emphasis on text. Douglas (1998) suggests that the relationship between reading, writing and thinking skills has been radically altered as visual images from television and video games have largely replaced reading in mass culture. Multimedia learning materials have the advantage that students are presented with a learning environment similar to the entertainment environments they have experienced, are comfortable with, and choose to spend time in. During his construction of a systematic theoretical basis for educational multimedia design, Boyle (2001) distinguished between cognitive and interactional layers of explanation, with the latter being the more appropriate for multimedia learning environment design.

Although multimedia can present subject content vividly with sound, graphics, animations, and video, the range of types of interactions is limited by technical possibilities. With ingenuity, rich learning experiences have been created despite programming restrictions. Interactions typically available include: identify the correct answer, multiple-choice questions (MCQ), drag and drop, simulations, and fill in the gap. Academic staff, learning technologists, and multimedia programmers have used considerable imagination to produce the variety of learning materials that is currently available. Indeed, once a programme template is available, the subject content that can be presented through that template is not restricted. Examples of successful multiple-choice quizzes can be found in most subject disciplines, and examples are available from the ELICIT module "Developing computer aided assessment" (http://www.scotcit.ac.uk/) and the Computer Aided Assessment Centre at the University of Luton (http://www.caacentre.ac.uk/).

Computers are ideal at marking MCQ tests and quizzes, providing various degrees of formative feedback or indeed summative assessments. More complex feedback routines are possible. A programme may be written which, following an incorrect answer, makes a student return to revise the point that has not been understood so that they must get the answer correct before continuing through the programme. In general, graphics and animations replace text in multimedia programmes, and only a small proportion of these packages attempts to deal with the complex alternatives offered by written language. For example, much English language tuition offered via the Internet provides little more than pretty ways of learning vocabulary. More complex materials situate the material in the social context of Britain and offer a series of exercises or comprehension tests following a paragraph of spoken text, for example, http://www.britishcouncil.org/english or http://www.halfbakedsoftware.com, which are still based on MCQ, fill in the gap, crosswords, or drag and drop. By contrast, Digital Education online courses (http://www2.actden.com/writ_den/index.htm) appear to some extent to overcome the limitations of MCQs by presenting ingenious, complex questions that require deep levels of thought and understanding to identify the correct answer. Computers can provide unique tests for individual candidates and create "adaptive" tests where the programme responds to a wrong answer by asking further questions on that topic until the candidate can demonstrate appropriate expertise.

Simulations range from complex mathematical calculations, for example, the relationships between predators and prey in natural populations, to the algorithms used to produce sophisticated simulation games like Sim World and Sim City.

Simulations encourage deep learning and are particularly effective where case studies and systems can be modelled effectively, for example, in medicine, management, biology, hard sciences, and engineering (Maier & Warren, 2000). Simulations reflect the process of interactions between the structures when certain parameters are manipulated, causing a change in behaviour. Many simulations ask the user to enter values representing one of the variables in the model, in effect to predict the effect of the change. The learner needs to understand and apply the underlying model to make an effective prediction and is both interacting with the programme and getting feedback on the result of their intervention.

An immediate example of a drag and drop exercise is the solitaire game which is normally included in Windows. Using the mouse button the player selects and moves a card to its appropriate position in the game. Inappropriate moves are not allowed. Rich learning materials have been constructed using these programming routines, for example, to add the correct labels to a diagram or to arrange human chromosomes in accordance with the standard pattern ascribed to the human karyotype. Educationally, this type of interaction engrosses students and provides instant feedback, as wrong moves are not allowed, forcing the student to make a further selection. It is also relatively easy to provide a score of the number of correct or incorrect moves and the time taken to complete the exercise. This type of information may motivate an individual student to try harder or produce a competitive element between students. Highly sophisticated programmes can be designed to

Figure 1B: Types of learning technology which might be associated with stages in Bloom's taxonomic hierarchy

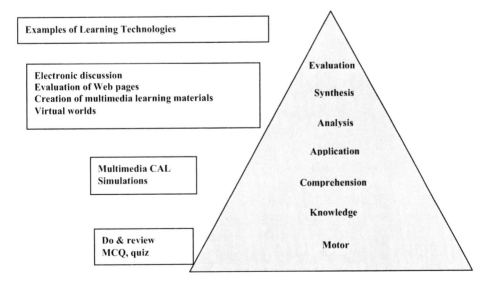

provide useful feedback in terms of subject content by explaining why a move was the wrong choice. Figure 1B shows the relationship between types of learning technology and stages of Bloom's taxonomic hierarchy.

Multimedia and the Internet are rich learning resources. The Internet, in particular, provides the opportunity to develop the higher order cognitive skills of searching, evaluation, and synthesis. These skills are essential for Internet users and many students recognise implicitly the variation in quality of materials on the Web. Sixty percent of a class of first-year life sciences undergraduates (2000), who had received no previous formal teaching on the Internet, cited "variation in quality" as the main problem they found with the Web. As increasing amounts of information become available from the Internet, "information overload" is becoming an increasing problem. Students need to be able to find, evaluate, and use materials relevant to their studies. The first case study describes a collaborative Internet project for first-year life science undergraduates at the University of East London that was carried out as part of a compulsory second semester first-year skills unit.

CASE STUDY 1—INTERNET ASSIGNMENT FOR 1ST-YEAR UNDERGRADUATES

The aims of the project were to teach students about the Internet and search engines, to use search engines effectively, to find and evaluate information, and to write simple Web pages. As the majority of students had not previously used the Internet, they were given an introductory large-group lecture that described the Internet, its origins and limitations followed by an IT workshop which introduced the Netskills Tonic tutorial on the Internet (http://www.netskills.ac.uk/TonicNG/cgi/sesame?tng). Students were given a detailed description of the project, learning outcomes and marking scheme at the start of the module. Tutorial groups (four to six students) were facilitated by personal tutors who might have limited interest or expertise in ICT. Tutors were also given detailed descriptions of the process students would be expected to follow and marking criteria. The topic for each group was set by the tutor, sometimes following consultation with the group, and was generally one intended to raise general interest in current issues in biology (for example: "genetically modified food" or "gene therapy"). Two voluntary practical workshops were available, (a) search engines and (b) writing Web pages in Netscape Composer or MS Front Page and FTP, but only half the class chose to attend these sessions. The projects were structured, and it was made clear when students should collaborate and when they should work alone.

Projects followed the following stages:
1.   Internet search to identify and select the three most relevant Web sites.
2.   Individually submit a 500 – 1,000 word report evaluating these Web sites and abstracting the information from these Web sites.

3.   Construct an individual "home" Web page containing details and personal introduction.
4.   Work as a group to produce Web site linking individual "home pages" and pages presenting the group view of the topic researched.

The intended learning outcomes for this project were: understanding search engines, evaluating Web pages, cooperating with others in a group project, and writing simple Web pages. The majority of students appeared to enjoy the project and were motivated to spend time using the Internet and evaluating Web sites. Students developed important evaluation skills which they then transferred to more traditional sources of information (books, newspapers). During the course of this assignment, students gained a range of technical and motor skills in that many improved their keyboard skills and learned how to construct simple Web pages. Social and group skills were developed throughout the project. Small groups of students actively discussed, negotiated, and frequently taught one another through all stages of the project. This relatively simple group project resulted in a complex learning experience as the students engaged deeply with the materials. Development of evaluative skills was an implicit part of the assignment. Students were forced to engage with the subject content as they tried to explain the material to their colleagues, either in informal discussion or presented on their Web pages.

CASE STUDY 2—CREATION OF MULTIMEDIA LEARNING MATERIALS BY FINAL-YEAR PROJECT STUDENTS

Final-year biology undergraduates frequently have to submit a research project which may account for 30% of their final-year marks. Replacing conventional laboratory- or library-based projects with the development of multimedia learning materials has proved highly effective in promoting higher-order learning outcomes. Students engaged deeply with subject content and gained advanced IT skills.

There were distinct structured stages to these projects in that the student had to choose a subject-specific topic that would be suitable for development as a CAL programme for future students (Sieber, 2001). Projects followed the following stages:

1.   Agree the subject-specific topic that will form the basis of the LT material.
2.   Find and evaluate available multimedia teaching materials (CAL, Web sites, etc.).
3.   Evaluate available authoring tools: (PowerPoint, HTML, Dreamweaver, Flash, Authorware, etc.) and identify appropriate tools for project.
4.   Library and Internet literature searches to collect subject-specific content.
5.   Written summary of the subject content.

6.   Specify programme content, navigation, and design appearance.
7.   Construct programme.
8.   Evaluate LT materials.
9.   Produce final written report summarising all stages of the project and the results of the evaluation. (Assessment was of the final report and the LT materials produced.)

This process of specification, design, evaluation, and modification is similar to process of developing any new LT materials and follows the stages identified by the EFFECTS programme (http://sh.plym.ac.uk/eds/effects/). These different phases also resemble the stages of Kolb's learning cycle. In terms of learning theory, students are researching and presenting subject-specific materials in their own way and creating their own interpretation of the information. Students engage in a dialogue with the tutor during the development of these materials and the projects could be considered examples of studies within a conversational framework

Figure 1C: Skills gained during the two case studies presented in terms of Gardner's (1993) theory of multiple intelligences

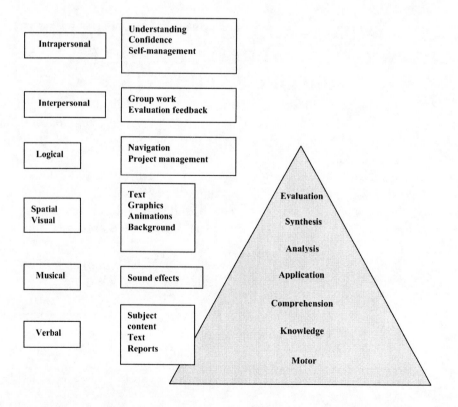

(Laurillard, 1993). Feedback comes in multiple forms: from the tutor, directly from the authoring tools, and from colleagues evaluating the materials. Meta-cognitive skills, the highest orders in Bloom's taxonomy, are developed. However, the range of skills and intelligences demonstrated during this LT project is considerably greater than those described by Bloom (Figure 1C) in that students have used sound, visual, spatial, design, and logical skills during the creation of their LT materials. This wider range of intelligences is better described by Gardner's (1993) multiple intelligences.

Students undertaking these projects were more independent than similar students undertaking laboratory-based projects. They, incidentally, gained transferable programming skills with little help from their supervisor, learning to use Flash, Dreamweaver and Paintshop Pro via their inbuilt tutorials and help files. The project results in a portfolio and product that students could show to future employers. Some students completing these projects have either continued to further training in IT or to immediate employment in the IT industry, despite graduating with biology degrees. A further benefit is the LT materials created can be used as a resource for future students. The projects are inexpensive to organise, as students use their own PC and software.

FUTURE TRENDS

Changes in the computing industry over the last five to ten years have produced a number of programming tools which make it possible for subject specialists, rather than programmers, to create LT materials simply. Use of Web authoring tools such as Flash has been demonstrated in Case Study 2, where biology students built multimedia learning materials. Further progress in the computing industry will make it possible to encourage students to develop their higher-order cognitive skills via these types of projects. Information overload resulting from electronic sources makes it increasingly important that students obtain high-level search and evaluative skills. Most of the submission, discussion, and feedback for these projects were electronic, giving students the opportunity to use email and discussion groups. For example, one student created a Web form to automate collection of evaluation comments from colleagues. Part of the success of these projects may be attributed to providing an environment that, by using the computer as a creative tool, provides a multifaceted learning experience.

CONCLUSION

The aim of this chapter was to relate the learning theories derived from conventional teaching methods to learning technologies. The development and use of LT mirror changes in the computing industry. Early LT materials were simple, generally with linear navigation and limited graphical capability, which supported a didactic behaviourist approach to learning. Multimedia learning materials can offer a rich, student-centred cognitive/constructivist learning environment which utilises multiple intelligences. Text is generally replaced by pictures, diagrams, and animations in multimedia learning materials, helping learners to construct their own interpretation of the information. During the two case studies presented here, LT are used as tools during the development of evaluative skills or to present the learner's view of subject content in learning materials created during their projects. Students' use of sophisticated Web authoring tools is analogous to preparing essays with a word processor or typewriter.

ACKNOWLEDGMENTS

We would like to thank Digby Warren (CAPD, University of North London) for allowing us to use and modify Table 1.

REFERENCES

Biggs, J. B. (1999). *What the student does: Teaching for quality learning in universities*. Buckingham, UK: Society for Research into Higher Education & Open University Press.

Bloom, B. S. (ed.)(1972). *Taxonomy of educational objectives, Book I: Cognitive domain*. London: Longman.

Bloom, B. S., Krathwohl, D. R., & Maisa, J. F. (1979). *Taxonomy of educational objectives, Book II: Affective domain*. London: Longman.

Boyle, T. (1997). *Design for multimedia learning*. Harlow England: Prentice Hall.

Boyle, T. (2001). Towards a theoretical base for educational multimedia design. *Journal of Interactive Media in Education*. Retrieved April 2002 from http://www-jime.open.ac.uk/current.html

Bruner, J. S. (1966). *Towards a theory of instruction*. Cambridge, MA: Harvard University Press.

Cullen, J., Hadjivassiliou, K., Hamilton, E., Kelleher, J., Sommerlad, E., & Stern, E. (2002). *Review of current pedagogic research and practice in the fields of post-compulsory education and lifelong learning*. Retrieved March 2002 from http://www.ex.ac.uk/ESRC-TLRP/pubs.htm

Douglas, D. (1998). Instruction in a postliterate culture: Multimedia in higher education. *Journal of Information Systems Education, 4*. Retrieved April 2002 from http://www.gise.org/JISE/Vol1-5/INSTRUCT.htm

Ellington, H., Percival, F., & Race, P. (1995). *Handbook of educational technology* (3rd ed.). East Brunswick, NJ: Kogan Page.

Friere, P., & Shor, I. (1987). *A pedagogy for liberation*. London: Macmillan.

Gagné, R. M. (1977). *The conditions of learning* (3rd ed.). Hillside, NJ: Holt, Rinehart and Winston.

Gagné, R. M., & Briggs, L. J. (1979). *Principles of instructional design.* Hillside, NJ: Holt Rinehart and Winston.

Gardner, H. (1985). *Frames of mind: The theory of multiple intelligences.* London: Paladin.

Gardner, H. (1993). *Frames of mind: The theory of multiple intelligences* (2nd ed.). London: Paladin.

Grabinger, R. S., & Dunlap, J. C. (1995). Rich environments for active learning: A definition. *ALT-J Association for Learning Technology Journal, 3,* 5-34.

Honey, P. (2000). *Learning styles the key to personalised e-learning?* Retrieved December 2002 from http://www.peterhoney.com/article/66

Honey, P., & Mumford, A. (1992). *The manual of learning styles.* Maidenhead, England. Retrieved December 2002 from http://www.peterhoney.com/Product/23

Jonassen, D. (1998). Designing computer-aided instruction. In W. Wagner & R. Gagné (Eds.), *Instructional Designs for Microcomputer Courseware.* New York: Lawrence Erlbaum Associates.

Jonassen, D., Mayes, T., & McAleese, R. (1993). A manifesto for a constructivist approach to uses of technology in higher education. In T. M. Duffy.

Kolb, D. A. (1984). *Experiential learning: Experience as the source of learning and development.* Englewood Cliffs, NJ: Prentice Hall.

Laurillard, D. (1993). *Rethinking university education: A framework for the effective use of educational technology.* London and New York: Routledge.

Laurillard, D. (1994). Talks given in the period 1994-5 on work on RELL project. Cited in: Draper, S. (1997). *Implementing learning technology.* Learning Technology Dissemination Initiative. Retrieved March 2002 from http://www.icbl.hw.ac.uk/ltdi/

Lave, J., & Wenger, E. (1990). *Situated learning: Legitimate peripheral participation.* Palo Alto, CA: IRL.

Lowyck, J. & Knowles, M. (1984). *Andragogy in action.* Houston, TX: Gulf.

Maier, P. & Warren, A. (2000). *Integrating technology in learning and teaching.* Margate, UK: Kogan Page.

Perkins, D. N. (1991). Technology meets constructivism: Do they make a marriage? *Educational Technology, 31*(5), 18–23.

Perry, W. G. (1970). *Forms of intellectual and ethical development in the college years.* New York: Holt, Rinehart and Winston.

Piaget, J. (1984). The stages of the intellectual development of the child. In P. Mussen (Ed.), *Handbook of Child Psychology, Vol. 1.* New York: John Wiley & Sons.

Rogers, C. (1969). *Freedom to learn.* Columbus, OH: Merrill.

Sieber, V. K. (2001). Web projects for final year students. *CAL-laborate*, 26-28.

Skinner, F. B. (1968). *The technology of teaching*. New York: Appleton Century Crofts.

Vygotsky, L. S. (1978). *Mind in Society: The Development of Higher Psychological Processes*. Cambridge, MA: Harvard University Press.

Chapter XII

Design Cycle Usability Evaluations of an Intercultural Virtual Simulation Game for Collaborative Learning

Elaine M. Raybourn
Sandia National Laboratories, USA

ABSTRACT

The present chapter describes the design cycle employed to create a computer-mediated social-process simulation called the DomeCityMOO. Participants created cultural identities that reflected the power imbalances in society and noted how their power and cultural identity were negotiated though their communication with others. Usability evaluation methodologies employed include design ethnography, contextual inquiry, task analyses, prototyping, and quantitative evaluation. The results indicate that the intercultural problem-solving simulation (DomeCityMOO) designed for a multiuser virtual learning environment may make it easier for educators and learners to explore the essence of cultural identity awareness and intercultural relations skills expressed through one's communication. To date, intercultural real-time simulations are only designed for face-to-face. The DomeCityMOO is the first computer-mediated intercultural, multiuser, real-time simulation designed specifically to address issues of power and identity. The design principles employed in the DomeCityMOO challenge the popular belief that aspects of tacit culture and intercultural awareness can only be taught successfully face-to-face.

INTRODUCTION

Simulation is a relatively new social science research methodology. The field of simulation in the social sciences has been growing at a fast pace in the last 15 years, although simulation was first introduced over three decades ago (Axelrod, 1997). In the social sciences, simulation is defined as an environment used to replicate and teach behavioral models and processes that employ the use of a human in a particular role, actual or simulated (Shubik, 1975). Simulations are used in a variety of professional contexts to model complex systems. The purposes for which a simulation is valuable to social scientists are: prediction, performance, design, training, entertainment, education, proof, discovery, and theory building (Axelrod, 1997; Dawson, 1962).

Social-process simulations are usually designed for and conducted face-to-face. Gredler (1992) argued that the focus of social-process simulations is human interaction, reflection on one's actions, the development of empathy, and the post-simulation discussion. Simulations are often used in education for teaching intercultural communication principles and skills. Intercultural communication describes the exchange, and co-creation, of information and meanings by individuals or groups when at least one party perceives itself to be different from others. Social-process simulations focusing on intercultural relations usually put participants in a frustrating situation in order that they learn to function better in the negative condition. For example, certain early stages of culture shock are often cited as a "negative condition." Unfortunately, placing face-to-face participants in even a *simulated* negative condition (such as culture shock) often produces negative unintended effects (Byrnes & Kiger, 1992; Erickson & Erickson, 1979; Williams & Giles, 1992).

Until recently, designing a social-process simulation for a computer-mediated context did not make design sense. However synchronous computer-mediated contexts such as multiuser dimensions object-oriented (MOOs) and collaborative virtual environments (CVE) can be multiuser settings that provide several new opportunities for social-process simulations (Raybourn, 1997a). MOOs and CVEs are described in greater detail in subsequent sections of the present chapter.

Face-to-face interaction is frequently taken as the benchmark for ideal interaction in a computer-mediated environment (Hollan & Stornetta, 1992). However, instead of striving to make computer-mediated environments more like face-to-face communication by adding video, audio, etc., we should investigate what makes the computer-mediated environment *unique*—the effects of (pseudo) anonymity on education, training, and collaborative learning.

In this chapter I describe the design cycle I employed to create a computer-mediated social-process simulation called the *DomeCity*MOO. The *DomeCity*MOO is a multiuser computer-based simulation in which participants experienced power imbalances that manifested among individuals or groups by building a virtual city together (Raybourn, 1998). Participants created cultural identities that reflected the power imbalances in society and noted how their power and cultural identity were negotiated though their communication with others. The *DomeCity*MOO allowed participants to explore potentially uncomfortable cultural dynamics in a safe, player-controlled, communication-rich environment. I applied lessons learned from prior research conducted on computer game principles, the evaluation of face-to-face simulation design principles, and an ethnographic evaluation of a MOO (Raybourn, 1997a, 1997b, 1998). To complete the usability design life cycle of requirements analysis, prototyping, and user feedback (Mayhew, 1999), I also evaluated the effects of the simulation game participation. Usability evaluation methodologies employed include design ethnography, contextual inquiry, task analyses, prototyping, and quantitative evaluation. A quantitative comparison study of intercultural simulations measured perceptions of threatening topics in both face-to-face and computer-mediated settings. Although not discussed in this chapter, a baseline quantitative analysis of a similar face-to-face simulation, *Ecotonos* (Ecology of Tension), was also performed (Raybourn, 1998).

The combined results of these research efforts indicate that the intercultural problem-solving simulation (*DomeCity*MOO) designed for a multiuser virtual learning environment may make it easier for educators and learners to explore the *essence* of cultural identity awareness and intercultural relations skills expressed through one's communication (Raybourn, 2001). To date, intercultural real-time simulations are only designed for face-to-face. The *DomeCity*MOO is the first computer-mediated intercultural, multiuser, real-time simulation designed specifically to address issues of power and identity. The design principles employed in the *DomeCity*MOO challenge the popular belief that aspects of tacit culture and intercultural awareness can only be taught successfully face-to-face.

In subsequent sections of the present chapter I familiarize the reader with the notion of collaborative virtual environments, specifically with the attributes of MOOs, and provide an outline of some MOOs used as educational settings. Next, I discuss the design cycle of the *DomeCity*MOO—how I first evaluated simulation games in the face-to-face setting in order to discover design principles and then how I evaluated the communication in a MOO through participant observation. I describe different usability methods used in the user requirement and testing phases. Last, I present the user feedback quantitative results and in the conclusions identify the limitations of the study and future directions.

MOOs AS COLLABORATIVE VIRTUAL ENVIRONMENTS

Collaborative virtual environments (CVE) are multiuser environments that often provide a vehicle for friendships, intimate relationships, and learning partnerships that ensue as a result of synchronous pseudo-anonymous computer-mediated communication. A CVE may also be an environment that supports playful exploration of one's online identity. Individuals who communicate in electronic environments such as MOOs and 3D graphical virtual worlds (i.e., Active Worlds) often experiment with gender swapping, disinhibition, and role-playing a romanticized version of the self.

MOOs (multiuser dimension, object-oriented) are real-time, text-based virtual worlds in which inhabitants manipulate their surroundings and communicate with each other in order to create a role-playing environment together. Multiuser dimensions usually fall into two categories: (1) combat or adventure-style role-playing games (MUDs) and (2) social role-playing communities (TinyMUDs or MOOs). MUDs and MOOs are UNIX-type, network-accessible, programmable interactive systems written in the C programming language that are suitable for the construction of text-based games (adventure or social), conferencing systems, and other collaborative software (Blankenship, 1993; Curtis, 1996a). In other words, a MOO is actually a programming language system that is left continuously running on a server. Most MOOs are centralized, that is, the database usually is contained in one computer. In principle, several hundred inhabitants may connect to the MOO server by using Telnet or other client programs. The more inhabitants that are logged on at any given time to the MOO may slow down the response time of the server. This network traffic creates a lag, or lull, in the real-time interactions that may last up to a few minutes depending on the size of the MOO database (Aarseth, 1997).

Pavel Curtis, then at Xerox Palo Alto Research Center (PARC), developed the first large-scale MOO in 1990 from a prototype written by Stephen White at the University of Waterloo (Blankenship, 1993; Curtis, 1992). Curtis was intrigued with the MOO programming language and hacked with it in his spare time while at Xerox PARC. LambdaMOO (named after one of Curtis' MUD characters, Lambda) is known throughout the MOO community as the "mother of all MOOs" (Curtis, 1992). Today there are hundreds of MOOs and over 20,000 MOOers, although the LambdaMOO community is by far the largest and oldest—numbering over 7,000 inhabitants worldwide (Rheingold, 1993; Schiano & White, 1998).

MOO programming code, in particular, mimics the UNIX operating system by using an object-oriented data structure. That is, every person, place, or thing in the MOO is a programmable object, has a corresponding object number, and may be "physically" manipulated. For example, I may be in a room of the *DomeCity*MOO and want to sit in a chair. If the owner of the room has created a "verb" that allows me to interact with the chair, I should be able to witness my character perform this action by typing the command "sit." A verb is a small program assigned to a specific object in a MOO that generates interesting actions when run. By typing the verb "sit" I can generate a subroutine of code that outputs the following message on my screen, "Elaine slips into the sleek, black leather couch and puts her feet up." One of the most distinguishing elements of the MOO is that the coding language is "designed to be written from within the MOO itself. … Users create the objects and write code while inhabiting both; in MOOs users literally build themselves and their surroundings" (Kelley, 1994, p. 3). That is, players contribute to the MOO world by writing subroutines (building rooms, objects, and characters) that create the spatial and social architecture of the MOO.

THE IMPACT OF VIRTUALITY ON HUMAN COMMUNICATION

Human communication is becoming increasingly characterized by the pervasiveness of electronic media. CVEs offer new and somewhat different ways for individuals to communicate. According to Chesebro and Bonsall (1989), computer-mediated communication is a medium of communication that creates new patterns of human relationships. Some of the patterns identified by prior research that provide the foundation for the present chapter are outlined below.

First, MOOers are not required to ever present their real-life (RL) identities. MOOers may therefore perform actions they might not in a face-to-face encounter (Curtis, 1992; Dibbell, 1993; Reid, 1995). Computer-mediated communication is often more intimate, but also more aggressive than real life, as illustrated by Huxor's memory of an accidental encounter with two avatars who were engaged in a private session of cybersex (Huxor, 2001). *Anonymity* produces a lower perceived risk to interlocutors that allows them to express themselves more freely (Raybourn, 2001). As individuals feel more comfortable expressing themselves, they may monitor their communication less and consequently concentrate more on their interactions with others.

Anonymity also supports individual agency. That is, interlocutors decide for themselves the degree to which they wish to reveal facets of their identities and are not limited to enacting their RL roles. MOOers are more aware of the presentation of the self and have more control over whom others perceive them to be. For example, a very shy individual may "clam up" in RL interactions, but may be warm, friendly, and popular in the MOO (Raybourn, 1997b). MOOers can experiment with new modes of being and learn skills that they might use in RL as well. The anonymity of computer-mediated communication in MOOs supports playful experimentation with one's identity and ultimately *mastery* over presenting the self to others in a virtual environment. Thus, computer-mediated communication supports reinvention of the self. According to Csikszentmihalyi (1991), achieving mastery in an activity leads to personal growth and a more in-depth understanding of the self.

Next, community is built on common interests not proximity. Community building in cyberspace reflects the common interests that bring people together, without the stress sometimes associated with the social groups one must belong to because of RL expectations, physical attributes, or geographical locations. The absence of the physical body focuses the interlocutor on striving for communication competence. The disembodied self offers online interlocutors the opportunity to develop new interpersonal communication skills and represent themselves in new ways, including text (Raybourn, 1997b). Text-based communication affords greater control of unintended nonverbal feedback. The potential for contradictory nonverbal messages is thus lessened since online interlocutors have more agency over the kinds of signals they send to others. For example, MOO communication features the potential to edit a message or regulate the kind of feedback given in an exchange. In other words, feedback need not be given immediately. Many MOOs are plagued with a communication "lag" in which messages are delayed for several seconds. This "lag" can offer interlocutors, especially those communicating in a second language, the opportunity to carefully think about the message one is sending.

Last, there is enhanced potential for developing better reading, writing, and imagination. Communicating in a different medium presents the interlocutors with opportunities to develop more sophisticated skills in certain areas. In online interactions conciseness, directness, and imagination are important communication skills. Interlocutors also learn to read and generate messages at the same time. MOOers may print a record of all of their online interactions, creating instances of persistent communication with a traceable history. Some MOOers have kept logs of their intimate relationships that have developed online. Looking over interaction history is like reliving the experience or revisiting memories (Bruckman, 1992; Turkle, 1995).

MOO Educational Spaces: Virtual Universities and Classrooms

The most pervasive adoption of MOO technology has perhaps been by educators who have responded to the need for both physical and virtual collaborative spaces. Educational MOOs primarily serve teachers and groups of students with course-related projects (Galin, 1998). Educational MOOs often provide virtual spaces for teachers to hold lectures or small group discussions; researchers to conduct professional events and conferences; developers to experiment with new interfaces; and programmers to develop new collaborative tools. Educational MOOs fall into several categories: general education, university specific, online writing centers, foreign language, K-12, and experimental or programming (Galin, 1998).

Diversity University (DU) is one of the better-known virtual campuses for teachers to bring classes which offers technical and organizational expertise from the volunteer staff. DU is a nonprofit organization that provides resources and educational services such as the Online Educator's Resource Group (OERG). Lingua

MOO serves the University of Texas at Dallas program in Rhetoric and Writing. Lingua MOO is an online writing community that encourages collaborative research projects on electronic media (Galin, 1998). MediaMOO, developed by Amy Bruckman while at MIT, was designed for research instead of classroom use. MOOSE Crossing is a constructivist learning environment for elementary-age children designed by Amy Bruckman at the Georgia Institute of Technology. Pueblo MOO is a community-based partnership between Longview Elementary School and Phoenix College. Other MOOs, such as JHM (Jay's House MOO), serve the programming community. A more complete discussion of educational MOOs is outside the scope of the present chapter; however, a list and description of active educational MOOs is available in *High Wired: On the Design, Use, and Theory of Educational MOOs*, edited by Cynthia Haynes and Jan Rune Holmevik.

Background Research Informing the Design Cycle of *DomeCity*MOO

The above section introduced educational MOOs and virtual classrooms. Training simulations may also be designed for MOOs and other collaborative virtual environments. For example, Mateas and Lewis (1996) discussed a virtual training simulation in a MOO in which engineers met with "customers" and engaged in structured data gathering activities. According to the authors, this technology was chosen over others because it supported experiential learning. Experiential learning emphasizes interactive, collaborative learning by *doing*. Not only did engineers participating in the virtual training environment learn appropriate communication skills by doing, but also through collaboration and building relationships with other participants in the simulated environment.

Unfortunately, the face-to-face context is largely taken for granted as the optimal setting in which to conduct a *social-process* simulation, especially in intercultural communication training and education. Simulations, role plays, and other learning tools have been developed to explore intercultural communication dynamics *without ever having tested* whether a face-to-face environment is the best medium in which to explore these issues. Therefore, I conducted an evaluation of the design principles of both face-to-face and virtual simulation environments in order to better understand the similarities and differences in simulation design.

In understanding face-to-face simulation game design, I chose to evaluate one of the most well-designed social-process simulations. *Ecotonos* is an intercultural simulation designed for a face-to-face setting that allows participants to personally experience power imbalances in monocultural, mixed, or multicultural groups (Saphiere, 1995). The simulation debriefing addresses participants' emotional response to experiencing the dynamics of the simulation and focuses on the intercultural skills necessary to collaboratively solve problems in multicultural groups. Prior to my usability evaluation (Raybourn, 1998), relatively little was known about the degree of perceived discomfort when discussing cultural dynamics such as identity or power in a face-to-face simulation. I demonstrated that *Ecotonos* participants perceived the face-to-face setting as a threatening one in which to discuss topics related to identity and power, even though the simulation was designed to allow the "safe" exploration of those topics. After evaluating design principles of face-to-face simulations, I conducted an ethnographic evaluation of the communication in MOOs and determined that the MOO environment was an appropriate setting in which to create a social-process simulation that addressed the cultural dynamics of power and identity. This research process is described in greater detail below.

Face-to-Face Simulation Design Principles Evaluation

I studied simulation play over several years by observing others, facilitating simulations, participating in simulations, and taking a university-level course in simulation design. Several design assumptions have come to describe successful social-process simulation design. First, a face-to-face context is widely regarded as the best, if not the only, setting suitable for a multiple-person simulation that supports synchronous communication. Second, instantaneous verbal and nonverbal feedback is preferred. Third, supporting participant anonymity is not usually possible since many social-process simulations hinge on nuances in nonverbal communication. Fourth, these simulations often require involved role descriptions, props, and tasks. Without them, the simulation game simply cannot be played. Fifth, at times, the contrived nature of the simulation play interrupts the experiential learning process. It is not uncommon for participants to ask questions that pull them out of the experience of the simulation game if they do not understand the rules. Last, after a period of time in which participants engage a task, a debriefing is facilitated in which participants explore learning outcomes in a large group; however, the communication is mediated through the facilitator. In other words, the facilitator controls the learning outcomes. There are, on the other hand, many advantages to face-to-face simulation games. For example, face-to-face simulations can be played quickly without very much prior consideration about equipment other than "props." Additionally, some simulations may usually be played easily without having to "train" the participants in basic features such as verbal and nonverbal communication. Later, I discuss how this particular advantage of face-to-face simulations should not be assumed in the computer-mediated context.

I did not evaluate the *Ecotonos* simulation for usability during the design phase as I did for the *DomeCity*MOO, since *Ecotonos* is a published simulation that incorporated extensive usability analyses conducted by the publisher before its release to the public, professionals, trainers, and educators. *Ecotonos* is a widely respected simulation that is used in a variety of professional contexts worldwide (Saphiere, 1995). As a matter of fact, I studied the design principles of *Ecotonos* precisely because it is so well designed for the face-to-face context.

MOO Ethnographic and Design Evaluation

The purpose of the *DomeCity*MOO was to explore the medium of electronic communication as an arena for generating social-process simulation experiences that are engaging, nonthreatening, participant controlled, and authentic. I hypothesized, the simulated reality, albeit in many ways a *real* experience, is a safer arena for some people in which to confront cultural differences. In order for the simulation experience to be as *real* as possible, it was important that the simulation be *engaging*. In order for computer-based games and simulations to actively engage participants, three conditions must exist—curiosity, challenge, and fantasy (Malone, 1980). In evaluating the design of the *DomeCity*MOO I asked the following questions, reflective of the three design principles above: Will the simulation be perceived to be nonthreatening? Is it engaging without the elaborate construction of rules and roles? Can it be played individually and with groups? Can it be played more than once with different learning outcomes and not get boring over time? Does it support different degrees of communication competence? In order to answer these questions and successfully design the *DomeCity*MOO simulation, I exploited characteristics of online synchronous communication identified in my ethnographic study and discussed in a previous section (Raybourn, 1997b, 2001).

MOO Usability Evaluation

MOO usability was tested over several months during the design phase with individuals who did not participate in the study. Evaluations consisted of a task analysis, identifying which communication (appropriate group size and formal versus informal) was best supported by the MOO; the extent to which typing ability influenced an individual's rating of satisfaction communicating in the medium; and learning, or reflecting, about how one was treated by others in the MOO. Additionally, the computer-mediated simulation was prototyped before deployment in the face-to-face environment for playability, comprehension, learning outcome, etc. Information collected during usability analyses informed the design of the *DomeCity*MOO.

Contextual Inquiry in a MOO

To investigate characteristics of MOOs, I conducted pilot tests with 30 undergraduate students at the University of New Mexico. I wanted to explore how users with very little or no experience in a MOO would respond to the real-time, text-based environment. First, I asked students to log on to a MOO and spend some time interacting with others in order to acquaint themselves with the interface. When allowed to interact freely, the students had fun playing with language, communication dynamics, and manipulating the physical world. However, most students expressed frustration with the steepness of the learning curve if their typing skills were inadequate.

On another occasion with another class, I took five small groups, comprised of six students each, into a MOO to accomplish a directed task. Our task was to discuss multiculturalism. Students were given questions on our topic in advance and were to discuss these questions in the MOO. This activity was less successful in that students wanted to stray from the topic and interact more personally with one another. Others were distracted and wanted to interact with the "physical" environment. I concluded that the interactive space of the MOO universe is not used to its potential when asking participants to conduct a focused discussion that does not involve individual exploration and discovery.

After participating in the MOO a number of times, the students were later asked to write how they would improve the interface and whether they preferred synchronous communication over asynchronous. The most important information about users gleaned from these pilot studies came from users' essays. Many suggestions for improving the interface were actually directed at the client (Telnet). For example, users wanted each other's screen text to appear in different colors, and some wanted a longer lag between text prompts. Some users indicated that the text scrolled too rapidly for them to read it. Most users reported that they preferred asynchronous communication (such as email). In fact, I observed that the user's response to the interface was directly related to their typing abilities. Those who could type at least 40 words per minute responded more favorably to the MOO environment than those who could not. In a MOO, participating in a conversation requires adequate typing skills and familiarity with the medium of electronic text.

Important MOO user characteristics were brought out in the contextual inquiry pilot studies. In order to maximize their experiences in the MOO environment, users should (1) have above average typing skills; (2) enjoy communicating in an interactive, electronic text medium; (3) desire to learn to program objects in order to contribute to the architecture of the MOO; (4) develop a quick wit; and (5) enjoy the feeling of mastery that comes from experience and familiarity with the MOO. While possibly not representative of the general mainstream population of computer users, these characteristics are representative of the MOO user subculture—which includes at least several thousand members.

MOOer's Task Analysis

The task of participating in a MOO is twofold: (1) to communicate with other participants in real time and (2) to explore, or interact, with the MOO programming universe. While IRC (inter-relay chat) environments allow participants to communicate with each other in real time, a MOO is much more robust. A participant may enter the MOO world and interact with the objects created by other players for hours before encountering another participant with which to communicate. An IRC does not support these activities. Therefore, it may be said that the MOO exists to support the task of participant communication, exploration, and discovery in a synchronous, programmable, computer-mediated environment (see Figure 1). Note that Figure 1 reflects the participant's ability for complete control and flexibility over the task (inhabiting the MOO). In other words, there is no specific task flow that a participant must follow after s/he has connected to the MOO. Inhabiting the MOO universe is quite organic and is a qualitatively different experience for each participant. For this reason, inhabiting the MOO is fun for many participants—their curiosity is challenged each time they log on to the MOO because the experience is never the same.

Testing and Prototyping

The *DomeCity*MOO was prototyped in a face-to-face environment with approximately 16 people so I could quickly visualize how participants interacted, how they moved about the physical space, and how they collaborated with other roles in the game environment. Participants were told a brief description of the game's objectives, given titles, asked to create an identity, and then given an opportunity to explore the space together. Anonymity was simulated through the use of makeshift masks. The prototyped session was videotaped, and following the game play, a focus group soliciting feedback on the simulation game design was conducted. Participants

Figure 1:   Diagram of participant task flow in a MOO

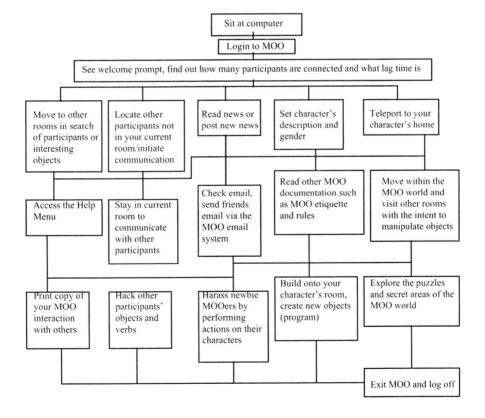

provided valuable suggestions to improve the "usability" of the game design, by focusing on what aspects of the game were confusing to them (i.e., rules, titles, etc.) and what could be improved. The result was the design of the *DomeCity*MOO.

THE DESIGN OF THE VIRTUAL SIMULATION GAME

The simulation game was named *DomeCity*MOO because a domed city is theoretically a closed system that has limited resources and therefore inherent problems that may be logically built into the simulation game. Participants entering the *DomeCity*MOO dystopian environment were given a predetermined, albeit loosely defined, role and asked to create an identity that reflected a racial/ethnic or religious background, age, gender, or sexual orientation.

Every attempt was made to design a simulation game that, like *Ecotonos*, allowed participants to personally experience power imbalances. Additionally, like *Ecotonos*, the simulation provided an opportunity for participants to examine their emotional responses to experiencing the dynamics of the simulation and to focus on the skills necessary to collaboratively solve problems and negotiate outcomes in groups (Raybourn, 2001).

Since the participants' objective was to improve the domed city, the initial environment was designed to reflect a rather depressed city, rife with problems. For example, the sterile environment clearly delineated an affluent and an impoverished area of the MOO. Descriptions of the different areas of the MOO were written to evoke memories and sensations and play on emotions (Raybourn, 2001). The combination of the role interdependencies, environmental power imbalances of the *DomeCity*MOO design, culturally laden titles, and the objective of the game contributed to conflict that encouraged each participant to explore solutions collaboratively. As participants rebuilt their environment, they negotiated expressions of power and powerlessness through their communication with others.

METHODS AND PROCEDURES OF THE QUANTITATIVE EVALUATION

Since identity and power are among the themes explored by users of virtual environments, it is beneficial to determine the effect of designing simulations around these concepts in multiuser collaborative virtual environments. I tested three hypotheses, described below, by mean differences of independent sample t-tests calculated on the posttest scores of questionnaires completed by participants in *DomeCity*MOO and *Ecotonos* simulations. Only the results from the comparison study are discussed in the present paper. Expanded findings for the effects of simulation participation on the perception of threat in a face-to-face setting are available in Raybourn (1998).

The comparison study of the two simulations was very carefully considered since the two environments are arguably very different. The comparison study consisted of measuring the subsequent change (if any) in all respondents' perceptions of threat as a result of having participated in their respective simulations and then comparing the degree of change among the subgroup of respondents who experienced a change from pretest to posttest measure. Every effort was taken to ensure the respondents in each group were treated the same. Both groups received identical questionnaires. Similar pretest and posttest schedules were maintained, and the researcher was not involved in the data collection nor the facilitation of the simulations.

The following research question was explored: To what extent, if any, do participants in the anonymous, computer-based, multiuser *DomeCity*MOO simulation perceive this environment as less threatening concerning the subjects of identity and power compared to participants in the face-to-face *Ecotonos* simulation, following participation in their respective simulations?

For the purposes of the study, the term "nonthreatening" meant *not* a source of immanent stress or harm to an individual. Evidence of the extent to which participants perceived a collaborative virtual simulation or face-to-face simulation as a threatening environment concerning identity and power was operationalized as the mean difference as calculated on the posttest scores by an independent t-test. That is, independent sample t-tests were calculated on the posttest scores of the *DomeCity*MOO and *Ecotonos* groups in order to measure differences following participation in the respective simulations between the *DomeCity*MOO group (who had received the computer-based experimental manipulation) and the *Ecotonos* group (who had received a face-to-face experimental manipulation). The results of the present study were obtained by comparing the effects of the multiuser, anonymous *DomeCity*MOO simulation on respondents' perceptions of threatening topics in a collaborative virtual environment with the effects of the *Ecotonos* simulation on respondents' perceptions of threatening topics in the face-to-face environment.

Simulation Game Study Design and Participants

Respondents participated in the computer-based multiuser simulation by logging in to the *DomeCity*MOO that was run from the Department of Computer Science at the University of New Mexico. Seventeen individuals responded to listserv solicitations for participation in one hour and 30 minute sessions in which they would log into the *DomeCity*MOO simulation. Simulation characters (roles) and passwords, Web-based instructions on how to log in to the *DomeCity*MOO, and pretests (5-point Likert-type scale and open response questions) were emailed to respondents who volunteered to participate in the present study. One day after the respondents had participated in the *DomeCity*MOO simulation, posttests (identical to the pretest) were emailed, completed by respondents in usually one day or two, and returned to the researcher.

The median age of the respondents was 27, the mean 29. Eighty-six percent were male, 14 percent female. None of the respondents had previously participated in the *DomeCity*MOO. Before the sessions, they completed pretests (5-point Likert-type scale). One or two days after participating, respondents completed and returned by email posttests identical to the pretest.

Face-to-Face Study Design and Participants

Students in the *Ecotonos* group attended their class meetings as usual. Pretests were administered at the beginning of the first class period of the fourth week of classes, and posttests were completed at the second class meeting that week. The simulation was conducted over two class periods. A pretest (identical to the 5-point Likert-type scale used in the *DomeCity*MOO study) was administered on the first day, before the simulation. One day elapsed between the two class periods. At the second class period of the week, a debriefing of the simulation was conducted and the posttest (identical to the pretest) was administered after the debriefing was completed.

Participants in the *Ecotonos* simulation consisted of 77 University of New Mexico students. The median age was 22, the mean 23. Sixty-five percent were female, 35 percent were male. Ninety-two percent of the respondents had previously experienced educational simulations at least once, but none had previously participated in the *Ecotonos* nor the *DomeCity*MOO simulations.

RESULTS

Hypothesis 1 stated that *respondents who participate in a computer-based, multiuser simulation will perceive its environment as less threatening, concerning the subject of identity, than respondents who participate in a face-to-face simulation will perceive its environment, following participation in their respective simulations.* Posttest means and t-values of the posttest independent t-tests for the two simulations are found in Tables 1 and 2, respectively. These findings do not support Hypothesis 1.

However, a matched-sample t-test calculated on the pre- and posttest scores revealed that *DomeCity*MOO respondents did not perceive identity to be a threatening topic to discuss in a virtual setting at the time of the pretest, and they believed the *DomeCity*MOO simulation met its goal of creating an environment in which they could explore identity (t= -2.7, [df=16], p<.01). Additionally, a high correlation (r=.74, [N=17], p>.0001) was found between the following questionnaire items: *The anonymity provided by the computer made me feel less threatened in*

Table 1:   Means and standard deviations for posttest scores for the
DomeCity*MOO and* Ecotonos *groups*

Source	N	Posttest Mean	s.d.
Identity			
DomeCity*MOO*	17	3.65	1.11
Ecotonos	77	3.22	1.07
Power			
*DomeCity*MOO	17	3.82	.73
Ecotonos	77	3.38	1.07
MOO Sim Better			
*DomeCity*MOO	17	3.53	.87
Ecotonos	77	2.83	1.07

general, and *I believe the DomeCityMOO simulation allowed me to experience how identity (the role of my character and my perceived power) shaped how others treated me in the MOO.* A moderate correlation (r=.544, [N=17], p<.01) was found between the items *The DomeCityMOO met its goal of creating an environment in which I could explore identity,* and *I believe the DomeCityMOO simulation allowed me to experience how identity (the role of my character and my perceived power) shaped how others treated me in the MOO.*

Hypothesis 2 stated that *respondents who participate in a computer-based, multiuser simulation will perceive its environment as less threatening, concerning the subject of power, than respondents who participate in a face-to-face simulation will perceive its environment, following participation in their respective simulations.* An independent sample t-test was calculated on the post-test scores of the *DomeCity*MOO and *Ecotonos* groups (see Table 2). These findings support Hypothesis 2.

Additionally, a post hoc matched-sample t-test calculated on the pre- and posttest scores revealed that not only did *DomeCity*MOO respondents perceive power to be a nonthreatening topic to discuss in a virtual setting at the time of the pretest, but they also believed the *DomeCity*MOO simulation met its goal of creating an environment in which they could explore power (t=-1.98, [df=16], p<.05). Moderate negative correlations were found between the following questionnaire items: (1) *I felt powerful in the DomeCityMOO simulation,* and *feeling powerless in the simulation was a threatening feeling for me* (r=-.57, [N=16], p<.01); (2) *I felt powerless in the DomeCityMOO simulation,* and *I learned more about myself by participating in the simulation than I would have if I did not participate* (r=-.43, [N=16], p<.05); and (3) *feeling powerless in the simulation was a threatening feeling for me,* and *I learned more about myself by partici-*

Table 2:   Independent sample t-test values on posttest mean difference for DomeCity*MOO and* Ecotonos *groups (equal variances not assumed) *significance at the 5% level*

Post-test Source	df	Mean Difference	t	p (2-tailed)
Identity	23	.43	1.44	.16
Power	32	.45	2.10	.04*
MOO Sim Better	28	.70	2.86	.00*

pating in the simulation than I would have if I did not participate (r=-.49, [N=16], p<.03).

Hypothesis 3 stated that *respondents who participate in a computer-based, multiuser simulation which provides an opportunity for anonymity will perceive its environment as better for learning about prejudice reduction and power differences than respondents who participate in a face-to-face simulation will perceive its environment, following participation in their respective simulations.* An independent sample t-test was calculated for the mean posttest scores of the *DomeCity*MOO and *Ecotonos* groups (see Table 2). These findings support Hypothesis 3.

Post hoc tests of correlation on posttest questionnaire items help describe why respondents who participated in the *DomeCity*MOO simulation perceived its environment as better for learning about power differences than respondents who participated in the *Ecotonos* simulation. Moderate correlations were found on the following items: (1) *A simulation is a realistic representation of reality*, and *the simulation's outcomes were applicable to my real life* (r=.622, [N=17], p<.02); (2) *A simulation is a realistic representation of reality*, and *The DomeCityMOO simulation met its goal of creating an environment in which I could explore identity* (r=.60, [N=17], p<.01); (3) *I was actively engaged by the simulation*, and *I believe the DomeCityMOO simulation allowed me to experience how different people in real life might feel powerless* (r=.58, [N=17], p<.01); and (4) *A simulation is a realistic representation of reality*, and *I believe the anonymity provided by the virtual environment enhanced my ability to communicate candidly and honestly with others* (r=.55, [N=17], p<.01). Additionally, post hoc independent t-tests calculated on the posttest scores indicated that participants of the *DomeCity*MOO simulation reported being actively engaged by the simulation (t=3.77, [df=35], p<.01) and thought they had learned more about themselves by participating in the simulation than they would have learned if they had not participated in the *DomeCity*MOO simulation (t=4.92, [df=28], p<.0001).

DISCUSSION OF QUANTITATIVE RESULTS

The results indicate that, following simulation participation, on the subject of power, participants in *DomeCity*MOO perceived its environment to be less threatening as compared to respondents who participated in the *Ecotonos*. Moreover, the *DomeCity*MOO participants indicated that the *DomeCity*MOO simulation had met its goal of creating an environment in which they could explore power. Additionally, it should be noted that respondents who participated in the *DomeCity*MOO simulation indicated that they did not perceive the virtual environment to be a threatening setting in which to address the subject of identity. In fact, they believed the simulation had met its goal of creating an environment in which to explore identity. Perhaps the anonymity of the computer-based *DomeCity*MOO simulation helped create an environment in which participants felt less threatened by communication in general.

CONCLUSIONS

The objective of the present study was to design a computer-mediated social-process simulation that allowed participants to explore potentially threatening dynamics and evaluate its effects. Evaluation methodologies employed include design ethnography, task analyses, usability studies, prototyping, and quantitative evaluation. A quantitative comparison study of intercultural simulations measured perceptions of threatening topics in both face-to-face and computer-mediated settings. The trials of *DomeCity*MOO, which is the first computer-mediated intercultural, multiuser, real-time simulation designed specifically to address issues of power and identity, have shown encouraging results. The design principles of the *DomeCity*MOO challenge the popular belief that aspects of intercultural awareness as experienced through real-time simulations can only be taught successfully face-to-face.

Participants were able to articulate their experiences with power imbalances in the simulation. These comments are examples of how personal the relationship between identity and power is for each individual. Respondents experienced power and/or powerlessness for a variety of reasons. The variability embedded into the MOO experience enhances the intimate exploration of the relationship among identity and power dynamics. Whether respondents react to the imbalances in power created by the social hierarchy, system constraints, or quality of communication, the corresponding quantitative results indicate that they still learned in what they perceived to be a safe environment.

The *DomeCity*MOO simulation game design supported the goals of taking participants on a personal journey to self-awareness through the vicarious exploration of identity, or self-concept, and power. In order for the experience to be as *real* as possible, it was important that the simulation be *engaging* as well. In order for computer-based games and simulations to actively engage players, three conditions must exist—curiosity, challenge, and fantasy (Malone, 1980). These conditions were built into the MOO environment and the simulation design.

There are several limitations to the present study that should be noted. First, regarding the face-to-face simulation, it is difficult to parse the specific factors that might explain an observed communication event. For example, although every effort was made to achieve standardization in the facilitation and play of the *Ecotonos* simulation, the impact of the group dynamics on individual performance (especially in a simulation) cannot be ignored. A limitation of the comparison study was the relatively small number of respondents that participated in the *DomeCity*MOO simulation. Interaction effects including participants' gender, etc. could not be measured effectively. Future research should attempt not only to replicate the present study, but also to increase the number of participants and investigate interaction effects. Additionally, given the specificity of the study, the results may not generalize to social-process simulations that are significantly different in design, execution, or learning outcome, etc.

Both simulation games (*Ecotonos* and *DomeCity*MOO) offer advantages and disadvantages that should be considered for future research and simulation design. For instance, an advantage to the face-to-face *Ecotonos* simulation is that it provides an opportunity to explore potential consequences of nonverbal communication. Another advantage to *Ecotonos* is that access to a computer, typing skills, or computer literacy is not required. An advantage to the *DomeCity*MOO simulation is that some topics may be perceived by some respondents to be less threatening to address in a virtual setting than in a face-to-face setting. Additionally, *DomeCity*MOO provides a more reflective activity—promoting increased participant awareness of cultural identity and power imbalances/negotiation through one's communication. A disadvantage to an anonymous computer-based simulation is that anonymity may enhance disinhibition and irresponsibility. Another disadvantage is that text-based multiuser simulations may require some training (perhaps one to two hours for basic interaction skills, not including typing skills) and may not be generally valuable learning tools for individuals who are not comfortable using computers. Last, having access to sufficient computers may indeed propose a limitation to the successful use of a virtual simulation in the classroom. In both the face-to-face and computer-mediated contexts the logistics of setting up and running the simulation should be balanced with the intended learning outcomes and discovery opportunities for the students.

A MOO environment can be a particularly rich context in which to explore learning goals of simulations as non-scripted interactions are co-constructed by the participants, outcomes are left open-ended, and the rules of play are very subtle. This type of virtual environment may provide simulation and game designers with the opportunity to develop simulations with less explicit rules and more explicit character or role descriptions. Additionally, anonymity is an important aspect of creating a safe environment for exploring issues of identity, power, and cultural prejudice. A text-based interface exploits the anonymity offered by this kind of computer-mediated communication. For some, inhabiting a MOO can be a very *real* experience—in the sense that participants communicate in real time with others and often have meaningful communication transactions.

Future research should address sophisticated notions of cultural identity as we all become more aware of how electronic media help create more fragmented selves. We can already witness the shift from the general perception that identities are mostly comprised of face-to-face group affiliations, such as national cultures and ethnicity, to a more flexible interpretation of multiple identities created from the absence of physical markers or biological attributes in certain mediated environments. Intercultural theory and research could account for these coexisting identity construction processes in diverse communication environments. Finally, I believe that a computer-simulated environment is a richer medium in certain specific cases for facilitating communication regarding issues of identity and power than is face-to-face communication. We should more fully explore the ways anonymity impacts learning and interpersonal communication as we move toward models of distance learning or computer-supported cooperative learning (CSCL). The benefit of exploring whether a computer-based social-process simulation can be effectively designed to provide the context for cooperative learning and self-discovery can have profound consequences on training, education, and human-computer interaction theory and research.

ACKNOWLEDGMENTS

I thank the reviewers and the study respondents who participated in various stages of this research. I also thank Everett Rogers, Ken Frandsen, Jack Condon, and Ben Bederson. *Sandia is a multiprogram laboratory operated by Sandia Corporation, a Lockheed Martin Company, for the United States Department of Energy under Contract DE-AC04-94AL85000.

REFERENCES

Axelrod, R. (1997). Advancing the art of simulation in the social sciences. *International Conference on Computer Simulation and the Social Sciences.*
Blankenship, L. (1993). *The cow ate my brain or a novice's guide to MOO*

programming, Part I. Retrieved from http://lucien.berkeley.edu/MOO/mootutor1.txt

Bruckman, A. (1992). *Identity workshop: Emergent social and psychological phenomena in text-based virtual reality.* Retrieved from ftp://ftp.parc.xerox.com/pub/MOO/papers/identity-workshop

Byrnes, D. A., & Kiger, G. (1992). Prejudice-reduction simulations: Notes on their use and abuse—A reply to Williams and Giles. *Simulation & Gaming, 23*(4), 485-489.

Chesebro, J. W., & Bonsall, D. G. (1989). *Computer-mediated communication: Human relationships in a computerized world.* Tuscaloosa, AL: University of Alabama Press.

Csikszentmihalyi, M. (1991). *Flow: The psychology of optimal experience.* New York: HarperPerennial.

Curtis, P. (1992). Mudding: Social phenomena in text-based virtual realities. Available via anonymous file://parcftp.xerox.com/pub/MOO/papers/DIA'92.txt

Dawson, R. E. (1962). Simulation in the social sciences. In H. Guetzkow (Ed.), *Simulation in social science: Readings.* Englewood Cliffs, NJ: Prentice Hall.

Dibbell, J. (1993). A rape in cyberspace or how an evil clown, a Haitian trickster spirit, two wizards, and a cast of dozens turned a database into a society. *Village Voice,* 36-42. Also available via anonymous ftp://ftp.parc.xerox.com/pub/MOO/papers/VillageVoice.txt

Erickson, K. V., & Erickson, M. T. (1979). Simulation and game exercises in large lecture classes. *Communication Education, 28*(4), 224-229.

Galin, J. R. (1998). MOO central: Educational, professional, and experimental MOOs on the Internet. In C. Haynes & J. R. Holmevik (Eds.), *High wired: On the design, use, and theory of educational MOOs* (pp. 325-328). Ann Arbor, MI: University of Michigan Press.

Gredler, M. (1992). *Designing and evaluating games and simulations: A process approach.* Houston, TX: Gulf.

Hollan, J., & Stornetta, Y. (1992). Beyond being there. In *Human Factors in Computing Systems CHI '92* (pp. 119-125). ACM Press.

Huxor, A. (2001). The role of the personal in social workspaces: Reflections on working in AlphaWorld. In E. Churchill, D. Snowden, & A. Munro (Eds.), *Collaborative virtual environments: Digital places and spaces for interaction* (pp. 282-296). London: Springer.

Kelley, H. J. (1994). *On-line help: Considering the possibilities for facilitating social services through textual worlds.* Retrieved from http://www.actlab.utexas.edu/~moboid/border/ socMOOs.html

Malone, T. W. (1980). *What makes things fun to learn? A study of intrinsically motivating computer games.* Unpublished doctoral dissertation, Stanford University, Stanford, CA.

Mateas, M. & Lewis, S. (1996). A MOO-based virtual training environment. *Journal of Computer-Mediated Communication, 2*(3). Retrieved from http://www.ascusc.org/jcmc/

Mayhew, D. J. (1999). *The usability engineering lifecycle: A practitioner's handbook for user interface design.* San Francisco, CA: Morgan Kaufmann.

Raybourn, E. M. (1997a). Computer game design: New directions for intercultural simulation game designers. *Developments in Business Simulation and Experiential Learning, 24,* 144-145.

Raybourn, E. M. (1997b). *The quest for power, popularity, and privilege: Identity construction in a text-based multi-user virtual reality.* Paper presented at the Western Communication Association, Denver, CO.

Raybourn, E. M. (1998). *An intercultural computer-based simulation supporting participant exploration of identity and power in a text-based networked virtual reality: DomeCityMOO.* Unpublished doctoral dissertation, University of New Mexico, Albuquerque.

Raybourn, E. M. (2001). Designing an emergent culture of negotiation in collaborative virtual communities: The DomeCityMOO simulation. In E. Churchill, D. Snowden, & A. Munro (Eds.), *Collaborative virtual environments: Digital places and spaces for interaction* (pp. 247-264). London: Springer.

Reid, E. (1995). Virtual worlds: Culture and imagination. In S. G. Jones (Ed.), *Cybersociety: Computer-Mediated Communication and Community.* Newbury Park, CA: Sage, pp. 164-183.

Rheingold, H. (1993). *The virtual community: Homesteading on the electronic frontier.* Reading, MA: Addison-Wesley.

Saphiere, D. M. H. (1995). Ecotonos: A multi-cultural problem-solving simulation. In S. Fowler & M. Mumford (Eds.), *Intercultural sourcebook: Cross-cultural training methods* (Vol. 1, pp. 117-125). Yarmouth, ME: Intercultural Press.

Schiano, D. J., & White, S. (1998). The first noble truth of cyberspace: People are people (even when they MOO). In *CHI '98 Proceedings* (pp. 352-359). Los Angeles, CA: ACM Press.

Shubik, M. (1975). *Games for society, business, and war: Towards a theory of gaming.* Amsterdam: Elsevier.

Turkle, S. (1995). *Life on the screen: Identity in the age of the Internet.* New York: Simon & Schuster.

Williams, A., & Giles, H. (1992, December). Prejudice-reduction simulations: Social cognition, intergroup theory, and ethics. *Simulation & Gaming, 23*(4), 472-484.

Chapter XIII

Computer-Supported Network-Based Learning Environment for the Workplace

Joze Rugelj
University of Ljubljana and the J. Stefan Institute, Slovenia

ABSTRACT

In this chapter we present our experiences in the field of computer-supported network-based learning over the last 10 years. We began our activities in this field with investigation of group communications and of generic models for online learning. Later we extended our interests to implementation of computer-supported network-based learning environments for different user groups and to measures that have to accompany introduction of new learning technologies to schools or workplaces.

INTRODUCTION

In the new economy, companies require employees who are willing and able to continue learning. Workplace learning is the key factor and an essential element in the personal and professional development of employees. It is the main means by which they improve their work and it is a key strategic element in achieving organizational objectives and goals, leading directly to enhanced competitive advantage.

Workplace learning takes place on the job and on the Web; it takes place at home, at conferences, in training facilities and through virtual corporate universities, to name a few. It is a process that can be as individual or as collaborative as the situation requires. Outcomes should be the development of the employee's knowledge, skills, values, attitudes, and actions in relation to the workplace environment.

Learning technology solutions have the power to integrate the process of work and learning to improve knowledge and hence job competence and performance. Learning technologies are not only about delivering education, learning or training electronically. The field of learning technologies is a multidisciplinary one that includes learning theory and instructional design, training, distance education, information communication, performance improvement, knowledge management and human resources.

Learning and training delivery solutions combine a variety of appropriate low- to high-end technologies with an assortment of suitable instructional designs and theories. The objective is to aid, improve or complement a person's learning experience. Learning technologies have been and still are anything from a video, to a drill and practice computer tutorial, to a sophisticated business simulation or knowledge management tool. In the past, learning technology solutions included laser discs, audio, computer projection, and videoconferencing. Today they include these devices but also extend to highly interactive networked learning modules that are available to the desktop. Learning technologies include information retrieval systems, productivity and communication tools, and cognitive tools for just-in-time learning such as electronic performance support.

Today's networking technologies help to turn work environments into open systems where the sharing and accessing of expertise and knowledge is commonplace (Osgoode, 2000). Under these circumstances, individual employees are responsible for driving their own learning and do not have to wait until the next time a course they require becomes available. The course is available anytime they need it, as many times as they need it. If this system works, individuals can learn faster, allowing organizations to learn more quickly.

ONLINE LEARNING ENVIRONMENT

Traditional arguments for in-class training versus technology-based (online) learning have included the immediate availability of an instructor for the students and the higher status that formal certificates have when delivered through classroom training. Until recently, these pros on the classroom side have addressed weaknesses on the technology side. With improvements in technology, these weaknesses are rapidly disappearing. Computer-based training weaknesses often include the fact that there is no expert on hand and that it is difficult to design a product that can handle all questions well. With the emergence of Web-based synchronous and asynchronous learning tools, facilitation of learning content delivered through a computer is improving tremendously. Research indicates that the instructional format itself has little effect on students' achievement as long as the delivery technology is appropriate to the content being offered (Souder, 1993). Good online technology-based learning practices are fundamentally identical to good traditional practices and the factors which influence good instruction may be generally universal across different environments and populations (Naidu, 1994; Wilkes & Burnham, 1991)

A generic model for an online learning environment consists of two basic building blocks: a virtual textbook (learning resources) and a virtual classroom, which consists of virtual community and management tools. These three components are bound together with open learning theory (Rosbottom, Crellin, & Fysh, 2000; Rugelj, 1999).

Virtual Textbook

Virtual multimedia textbooks are a collection of learning materials with some additional functionalities, such as interactive computer-supported examination and access to dynamically changing information resources.

Special attention needs to be paid to preparation of courseware. It can be supported to a great extent by different tools that can help in appropriate organization and structuring of course materials and can simplify graphical design of courseware. Course materials are available on the Internet for online access or on CD-ROMs for those who do not have permanent access to the Internet. Learning materials are thus gathered in more or less virtual multimedia textbooks. They can be a high-quality supplement to existing learning materials or in some cases an adequate substitute for ordinary textbooks (Rugelj, 1997).

To take advantage of the popularity of WWW and its browsers as well as other helper applications (e.g., plug-ins, viewers, players, etc.), we designed our learning environment based on the WWW technology. This approach provides a single unified interface for all system components and their operations. Learners use a WWW browser as a front-end interface to access learning materials. Course materials include not only static components such as text and images, but also active components such as URL links and Java applets.

In many cases virtual multimedia textbooks can, due to their flexibility and interactivity, offer some innovative solutions. One of the important extensions of the virtual textbook is software for computerizing tests and exams. Using such a tool, the lecturer or author of course learning materials enters questions on the study topic into the computer, and people take the test sitting in front of their personal computer. Examinations can be taken after the course is finished to verify the results of education or during the course as a self-assessment tool that can be used to improve the efficiency of the educational process. The computer then marks the answers, can give instant feedback, and stores the answers for the lecturer's analysis.

Virtual Classroom

According to some recent findings, the emphasis in technology-based education should change from information transmission to knowledge construction, from individual to collaborative learning, from separate, nonreusable teaching tools to integrated and adaptable technologies, and from distance as an obstacle to distance as an asset, favouring lifelong learning.

Due to the above mentioned needs for collaboration, a network-based learning environment requires some tools for computer-supported communication that allow students and lecturers to interact asynchronously and synchronously. A virtual classroom is a set of tools for collaboration and communication support that allows collaboration between all participants in the educational process (i.e., lecturers, tutors, learners) and gives them an impression of learning in a community. Asynchronous forms include more traditional tools like email and newsgroups, while synchronous communication tools comprise video and audio desktop conferencing systems, shared whiteboards, and synchronous text-based conferencing tools. Several WWW-based tools for cooperative information sharing have been developed. In some cases, a plain old telephone can be used to support interaction in the learning environment.

Interaction between learners and lecturer is of great importance for effective learning. The lecturer can detect eventual problems and misunderstandings and can give a student additional explanations or instructions for further studying. At the same time, a lecturer can assess students' progress and can encourage them. Interaction between learners can be very useful and stimulating, especially when it is adequately animated by suggested discussion. The selection of a particular communication tool, and consequently the corresponding information throughput, depends heavily on the requirements of the task in the learning process to be carried out and on the availability of resources (McGrath & Hollingshead, 1994). Low-level communication support tools, such as electronic mail and newsgroup systems, primarily support information exchange and can, at the best, produce shared opinion of the group members.

More advanced forms of collaborative learning, where shared understanding of the problem being studied is expected, require high-level collaborative support with communication channels of high capacity and advanced tools for manipulation of shared information (Hansen, Dirckinck-Homfeld, Lewis, & Rugelj, 1999).

The support for communication and collaboration between participants in the educational process is especially important for distance education and for different informal types of education, since participants are distributed in space and time. Usually, most workplace education activities fit precisely into those categories. Virtual presence in a virtual classroom can give participants the impression of a membership in a community (Maly et al., 1997).

The management tools include the provision of an explicit learning structure. Our management tools also include a report generator able to provide a number of useful reports. We have achieved this by utilising the reporting software provided by

WebCT. WebCT is sufficiently flexible that all the default formats can be ignored and pages can be set up to our requirements and preferences, but we can still benefit from the reporting facilities of WebCT and other software elements such as the facility to set simple online tests.

Supplementary Applications of the Learning Environment

The above described computer-supported learning environment can support many other activities at the workplace.

The appropriately adapted virtual textbook can serve as an internal information system for the company. It can also be used to distribute communications concerning organizational matters as well as information about new technologies or new products which are not necessarily integrated into formal educational programs.

Computerized examination tools that are usually part of a textbook can also be used to regularly check employees' competence and to perform recruitment skill tests.

Most of the tools that together form a virtual classroom can support different forms of communication and collaboration between the employees that are not necessarily connected with the educational process. Email, newsgroup systems and conferencing systems can substantially improve collaboration, especially in cases where the company is geographically dispersed or in cases when employees cannot meet face-to-face due to the organization of work in shifts. Employees can use some of these tools to communicate different suggestions to the management.

It is desirable that particular tools are used to support more than one task. Thus users are more familiar with the tools and they do not lose time learning how to use new products and to change their working environment during their work. Lower cost of software and cheaper maintenance are additional advantages of this approach.

ORGANIZATIONAL ASPECTS OF DELIVERING ONLINE COURSES

The first step in introducing an online learning program for the workplace should be to look at the characteristics of the students and tutors, the available resources and all other factors that will influence the learning process.

Running an online course implies most of the organizational aspects of a traditional course. Apart from that, some extra implications come from the fact that the course is supported through computer communication and that there are no traditional lectures and no face-to-face communication between lecturer and students and between students.

In the following sections we are going to survey elements that are indispensable for implementing the environment where online courses run. As is usual for services in computer networks, the virtual classroom and virtual textbook are implemented as a client-server architecture. In a client-server architecture the collection of programs is divided into two groups: those of clients that can issue service requests and servers that service those requests. Clients and servers are connected by means of the communication network.

Client

Each participant in the course has to have the appropriate hardware and client software. The participants taking the course do not always have access to the newest and fastest equipment, but most workplaces are equipped with personal computers or workstations that are adequate to requirements. Participants who do not have a personal computer at their workplace usually need access to 'Web-based class-rooms,' which can be located in the company or at the location of the external course provider. As most widely used systems for online education are now based on the World Wide Web, no specialized client software is needed. It is highly desirable that the computer-supported learning environment is largely similar or identical to the software environment used for daily work. Thus participants in the course need not make additional efforts to learn how to use the system for communication in the virtual classroom and for access to learning materials.

Most personal computers and workstations in companies and other organizations are connected into local area networks and have high-speed connections to the Internet.

More and more participants want access to online courses from their home (Massey, 2000). More than 60% of households in Slovenia have a personal computer and most of them are connected to the Internet. In these cases we have to take into account the limited bandwidth of the communication channel and consequently limitations for information download (e.g., distribution of multimedia learning materials) and limitations for synchronous multimedia communications (e.g., desktop audio-videoconferencing).

Server

Online courses are located on servers, which can be common WWW servers or specialized dedicated servers. Common WWW servers represent a simple and cheap solution for distributing learning materials but as such do not provide additional support facilities for implementing the virtual classroom. Specialized dedicated servers integrate tools for group communication in the virtual classroom, for different course management facilities that allow tutors to supervise the virtual classroom, and for keeping track of student activities. All significant events are logged and reports are generated automatically on request.

Collected data serve multiple purposes. They represent a kind of indirect feedback from students to course authors and tutors. From the frequency of visits to particular pages in the course material, the time spent on them, questions 'asked' in the virtual classroom and eventually also from the correctness of answers in the tests, they can find potential "weak sections" in learning material. This is important for online courses due to lack of the immediate feedback characteristic of traditional courses.

Tutors can detect inactivity of individual participants in the course from the collected data and react in appropriate ways. The usual reaction consists of stimulating discussion and offering help in eventual problems.

Last, but not least, collected data represent an important source of information for assessment of learning. Assessment can have any of three major goals (Rowntree, 1977): to assign a rating or a grade (summative assessment), to give feedback to guide or improve behavior or practice (formative assessment), and to compare alternative elements of a course (comparative assessment). Summative assessment provides educators with means for deciding whether the student has acquired the minimum level of knowledge and has earned a formal certificate. Formative assessment is mainly intended for helping students to learn and for educators to develop an understanding of students' needs. The results of comparative assessment are mainly used by the authors of online courses for course improvements.

An important component of a virtual classroom that can be integrated in the learning environment on a dedicated server is support for group communications. It is usually implemented as an asynchronous conferencing system (e.g., electronic bulletin board). An asynchronous conferencing system is an electronic storage environment for messages which supports its users in discussion of issues over a period of time by enabling them to post and read messages. Its main deficiency is low communication throughput (information exchange is based on a typed text) and relatively long response times, on average, one day. Thus discussion cannot be very intensive and participants lose context between sessions. In spite of these imperfections, asynchronous conferencing systems were used as a primary tool for group communication support in virtual classrooms in the past, as there was no more convenient tool widely available (Herasim, Hiltz, Teles, & Turoff, 1995; Hiltz & Wellman, 1997).

Desktop audio/video synchronous conferencing systems are getting more and more popular, but for the time being their technical characteristics are still a serious limitation. They can, to some extent, support point-to-point connections (with two communicating partners), but they are not an adequate solution for group communications. More intensive information exchange, which is possible with synchronous communications and with video and audio (instead of typed text), can only be used in preplanned meetings in the virtual classroom.

Servers can be located at the company or organization where the participants are employed or with the external provider of the course. The decision for one of these options depends on the size of the company, on its sphere of activity, on the intensity and frequency of workplace learning activities and on internal organizational structure. We found that for many big companies the intermediate solution is adequate, where the courses are developed, designed, implemented, and tested by an external course provider. After the initial phases, when it is ready for exploitation, it is adopted by the company (or more companies) where potential course participants work. As we have already mentioned, experts from the company take an active part in the design of the course, especially for custom-designed courses.

Communication Infrastructure

Communication infrastructure represents a glue that links geographically dispersed clients and server together and gives participants the impression of being in the shared workspace of the virtual classroom.

A local area network connected to the Internet is a typical communication channel in companies and other organizations, while individuals at home connect to Internet providers via dial-up analog or digital connections. The advantage of the former solution is substantially higher throughput and no additional communication costs. But as participants in the courses often want to study out of office hours (especially in the evening or during weekend), they are ready to pay communication costs. It is important that courses are prepared having this fact in mind so that participants can select a less pretentious version of the learning material (i.e., smaller images, less graphic elements, without video or audio clips) for the download and an appropriate communication tool (e.g., IRC chat tool, conferencing system and email).

Important Factors Influencing Course Design and Realization

There are many factors that influence the design of the course and organization of activities when the course is running. The most important are:

- number of participants,
- geographical spread of participants, and
- intensity of learning and deadlines.

Number of participants in an online course depends on the size of the company and on the number of employees interested in the course and has a great influence on the communication patterns and medium used in the course, as well as on the organization of the course. Here we have in mind human resources that are needed as tutors and administrators to run the course and to offer appropriate support for students.

Geographical spread of participants influences the selection of communication media. When running a course in an organization or company located on a single site, it is often the best solution to organize a face-to-face start-up meeting, where principal guidelines for the course are presented and participants and tutors have the opportunity to meet and know each other. This is very important as the need for communication is very strong at the beginning of the course when participants recognize rules as well as tutors and 'classmates' in the virtual classroom. The need for such collaboration can also appear later if the course is based on certain pedagogical methods like problem-based learning.

When the participants are geographically spread across the region or even the country or the continent, desktop videoconferencing is a reasonable solution, in spite of more complex technical and organizational difficulties. The number of participants is limited in such a case (up to 10 or maximum 15 participants), especially when intensity of work and interactivity are high.

Intensity of learning is a parameter of the course which tells us how course activities are organized in the period of time dedicated for the course. When the intensity is high, a lot of activities happen in relatively short periods and students are supposed to learn and participate in interactive events daily. Communication in a virtual classroom has to be synchronous or asynchronous with minimized response times. The number of participants is limited. The results of such an approach are good, since students keep in touch with the subject and do not lose context due to interruptions and gaps between lessons.

Unfortunately, employees taking courses at their workplace can rarely afford such intensive studying. Exceptionally, short courses before radical changes in their work can be run in this way.

We found that less intensive courses are much more convenient. They are supposed to be available for a longer period of time (some weeks or even months) and participants in the course study when they are not very busy with their work or in the evening and during the weekend from their homes.

Although the courses are not running at a great pace, it is recommended to fix some deadlines for carrying out certain tasks or to complete the course. Deadlines encourage participants to keep pace with other participants and as such are stimulative.

Synchronisation of activities achieved by means of deadlines also has an impact on more intensive interaction and collaboration, as participants in the course are likely to face similar problems at approximately the same time.

PREREQUISITES FOR PARTICIPATION IN ONLINE COURSES

There are certain requirements that have to be met by all those engaged in online courses, i.e., course participants or students as well as tutors and other support staff.

Students

As for most educational activities, we expect from students the ability to read and write, and some basic computer literacy is expected from participants in online courses. It consists of basic skills such as starting computer and application software, simple input-output operations (typing, using mouse, printing), and using basic applications like word processors or text editors, Web browsers and other communication software (e.g., email and news clients, dial-up connection, etc.).

It can be very difficult for novices to learn these basic skills in online courses as they do not know how to start, so we usually advise them to take a traditional introductory course. Fortunately, most participants in workplace learning courses have at least the above mentioned basic skills and can start using a virtual textbook and virtual classroom. In more pretentious online courses students can be expected to master some more complex software applications (e.g., viewers for multimedia, simulators, etc.), but once they master basic skills it should not be too difficult for them to get to know these applications by means of quick introductory courses or helper facilities integrated into the virtual classroom.

In the same way students can learn how to install and set up required additional applications on their personal computer.

While the development of technology literacy is a major skill requirement for distance learners, a technology-mediated environment also places a few more demands upon learners in terms of skill development. Students mentioned difficulties in the area of communication skills, navigation skills, time management skills, and research and presentation skills.

For students taking part in an online course, communication with tutors as well as with other students in the course is very important. It is in no way only technical problem. It requires the ability to express ideas in a written form.

Since intonation, facial expression and other types of body language are not available it can be difficult to determine the intent of a message unless the writer takes pains to be clear.

Text-based interaction in the virtual classroom makes extensive demands on learners' time. Students can hardly read all the messages exchanged in the classroom. This is especially a problem before they are comfortable with the technology.

Tutors

Tutors in online courses should be prepared to develop an understanding of distant students' needs and to help with the problems they might encounter. Their teaching style should be adapted to expectations of multiple and often diverse audiences.

Tutors are supposed to develop a working understanding of delivery technology and to have a solid understanding of its strengths and weaknesses, while remaining focused on their teaching role.

Using effective interaction and feedback strategies will enable the instructor to identify and meet individual student needs while providing a forum for suggesting course improvement. To improve interaction and feedback, tutors use pre-class study questions to encourage critical thinking and informed participation of all learners. Early in the course, students should be required to interact among themselves and with the tutor via a conferencing system or electronic mail to get familiar with computer-supported communications. In early phases, telephone and fax can also be used as a medium for communication.

Tutors should contact less active online students to encourage active participation and at the same time politely discourage individual students from monopolizing shared resources in the course.

Detailed comments on written assignments or on online discussion in the virtual classroom are an important supplement to online learning materials and can be used to refer to additional sources for further studies.

Tutors sometimes participate in the course development process as authors or coauthors, especially in custom-designed online courses.

Administrator

The role of the administrator of the online course is to carry out clerical and administrative tasks for virtual classroom functioning and to provide technical support.

Typical administrative tasks in the virtual classroom are student registration, processing statistical data on use of resources and student activity in the virtual classroom, and preparing reports, scheduling different activities in the virtual classroom and granting certificates of qualification. Technical support consists of maintenance of server hardware, software and communication infrastructure, responding to technical problems and questions, archiving collected data, and sometimes also in providing training in the use of technology.

In smaller companies and organizations, the administrator often takes responsibility for technical aspects in the production of online courses.

COMPUTER-SUPPORTED WORKPLACE LEARNING IN SLOVENIA

Market investigation, carried out for J. Stefan Institute in 2001, showed high interest in computer-supported workplace learning by many Slovene companies, especially by high-tech enterprises in the fields of electronics, telecommunications and pharmaceutics, which dominate among the first hundred companies with maximal profit.

The main interest, detected in practically all firms, was in PC-operating competence. So-called computer literacy is another word for skills for using personal computers required by leading multinationals and educational institutes. There is a set of standardised modules such as basic concepts of information technology (IT), using the computer and managing files, word processing, spreadsheets, database, presentation, and information and communication.

Another highly demanded area, where workplace learning is topical, was international quality standards, such as ISO 9000 and ISO 14000.

ISO 9000 is a series of international quality standards, the guiding principle of which is the prevention of defects through the planning and application of best practices at every stage of business—from design through to installation and servicing. These standards focus on identifying the basic disciplines and specifying the general criteria by which any organization, regardless of whether it is manufacturing- or service-oriented, can ensure that a product leaving its facility meets the requirements of its customers. These standards ask a company to first document and implement its systems for quality management and then to verify, by means of an audit conducted by an independent accredited third party, the compliance of those systems to the requirements of the standards.

Similarly to the ISO 9000 quality management system standards, ISO 14001 for environmental management systems provides a highly effective, globally accepted framework for establishing and continually improving applicable management system processes.

The advantage of the above mentioned courses is their general applicability. Once developed, they can be offered to a large number of customers from different companies and organizations with minor changes or even without them. A practical consequence is the lower price per participant on the course and thus a better starting point in the educational market competition.

According to current prices on the market, our calculations show that it pays a course provider to develop an online course for at least 100 to 200 course participants, supposing that a course design already exists in a traditional form. The estimated number holds true for courses with an average complexity and with a limited amount of multimedia materials. Otherwise the numbers can be substantially higher.

Custom-designed courses for different professional groups or for employees in companies are a special challenge for developers. The selected topics are highly specific and the courses are usually designed in collaboration with experts from professional groups or from companies. We designed short training courses for particular working procedures in industry (e.g., assembling of telecommunication devices, maintenance), training and verifications for croupiers in casinos as well as courses on highly theoretical subjects of pharmaceutics.

As the courses cannot or are not permitted to be offered to a wider audience, the number of potential users is limited and the price per course participant is higher. Therefore only limited numbers of customers can afford such courses. Military and governmental services, as well as companies with highly profitable activities where well-trained personnel are required and where there are different obstacles for realization of education, expressed interest in custom-designed courses. In the private sector, telecommunication equipment producers, pharmaceutical companies and gambling houses were interested in such courses.

Implementation Details

We implemented the Web-based virtual classroom for workplace learning in several companies in Slovenia and carried out courses for several hundred participants. In the first phase we focused on the above mentioned computer literacy modules, among which basic concepts of information technology, using the computer and managing files, word processing and communication (Internet) basics were most frequently requested.

Traditional learning materials were used as a basis for preparing virtual textbooks. They were not just simply copied into selected formats, but were rather carefully structured and upgraded with multimedia elements (i.e., figures, animations, and audio clips) which are crucial for successful individual study.

Virtual textbooks were placed in virtual classrooms. Students registered for courses by means of an automated check-in procedure, where they were assigned a user name and password. Courses started on previously announced dates and their duration was limited to three or four weeks. Limited duration of the course stimulated intensive and timely studying. Communication between students in the virtual classroom and between students and tutors is mainly based on an integrated conferencing system or email and is thus asynchronous, with response time less than 24 hours. A conferencing system stimulates different forms of group work and collaboration in the virtual classroom.

Each lesson in the virtual textbook is supplemented with learning targets and with a short test for verifying understanding of learning material studied. During the last two days of the course, participants were invited to online exams. Students who successfully passed the exam received a certificate.

Tutors can, by means of the previously mentioned management tools, at any time track data, which are automatically logged and archived, about student activities in the system. Total time spent in the system, time spent on a particular page, date and time of last access, activities in the conferencing system and the results of online examination can help tutors to follow students, to stimulate their learning and to "push" them if they lose their pace.

The most significant advantages of the virtual classroom over traditional learning in courses are, according to our participants, flexibility about selection of topics, place, time and individually determined pace of studying.

Around 80% of candidates who checked in for the courses 'participated' actively in the online courses. Non-active candidates excused their inactivity with overwork or unexpected absence from the workplace. Most of the participants who attended the course (95%) successfully passed the final exams.

The intensity of collaboration with tutors was relatively high. The conferencing system and email were usually used as a communication medium, but occasionally telephone was used, too. Collaboration between students in the virtual classroom was less intense than we had expected. We assume that there were two reasons for that. First, participants in the course had a possibility to discuss the problems face-to-face (they worked in the same department). The other reason was probably the fact that the courses were not sufficiently problem oriented.

Motivation for Participation in Online Courses

Basically, most learners on online courses are intrinsically motivated. At the present time, more and more knowledge and skills are needed at most workplaces for carrying out work efficiently. Adequate qualifications also provide a certain degree of economic and social security.

We were highly interested in students' opinions about main motivational factors for workplace learning. Several hundred participants in our courses took part in an opinion poll, implemented online in the virtual classroom. According to the results of the poll (Figure 1), the following were the main reasons for participation:

- to be more competent in the workplace,
- to acquire new knowledge,
- out of curiosity,
- on request from superior in rank.

The challenge of each course designer is to create a course that increases or at least maintains intrinsic motivation. Professionally prepared, comprehensible learning material is crucial. This assertion is confirmed by the results of our opinion poll (Figure 2), where this factor was selected as the most important by more than 35% of participants. Numerous images, animations and other multimedia materials represent the most important factor for 23%.

It was somewhat astonishing that socializing with others participants in the virtual classroom was not a very important aspect of the course according to the participants. As can be seen in Figure 3, most of them were not interested in collaboration at all.

Figure 1: The main reasons for participation in the course

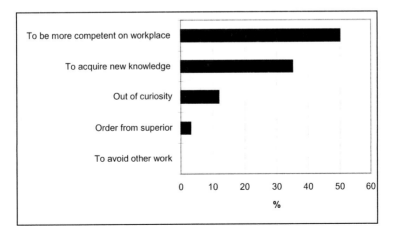

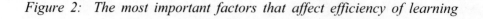

Figure 2:   The most important factors that affect efficiency of learning

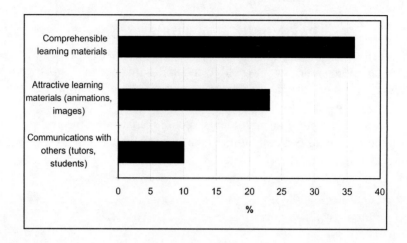

Keeping pace with others on the course is a challenge which stimulates and motivates participants. The importance of this motivational factor depends heavily on the pedagogical approach and consequently on intensity of interaction. Problem-based learning is typically representative of such a highly interactive approach (Rugelj, 2000).

Tutors are supposed to help create an environment where learners feel that they are accepted and respected group members (Stelzer & Vogelzangs, 1994). The tutor and participants should introduce themselves at the beginning of the course. Participants have to feel safe and tutors can support them by means of informal discussions with the entire group after lessons (using videoconferencing, chat or conferencing) and as circumstances require also with individuals (Kinzie, 1990).

To avoid a gradual loss of motivation, a tutor can stimulate participants with variation in the presentation and style of work and can challenge them with different tasks that activate them.

A formal certificate of qualification that is granted the participant who passes the final examination can be an important motivational factor; it might be another step towards promotion or can mean just more security as regards employment.

Practical Problems Identified in Introducing Workplace Learning Environments

After setting up several online educational environments for the workplace in Slovenia, we identified some obstacles that appeared in most settings and can be expected in the future. These obstacles to a great extent impede more extensive use of online education at the workplace for the time being.

If we compare an online course with a traditional one, we easily come to the conclusion that the initial investment is much higher. It pays well only after several

Figure 3:   The impact of communication in the virtual classroom on the efficiency of learning

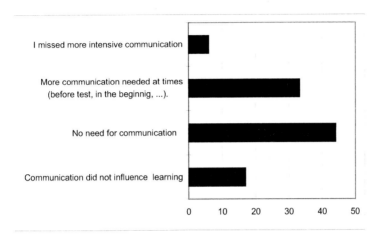

course runs or, in other words, after some critical number of participants is reached. After that moment it is profitable.

For many companies it can be a big problem to invest a lot of money for this purpose and they would rather take ready-made courses from external providers. At the time being, there is still a lack of courses on the market. This holds true even for very common courses, such as computer literacy.

Online student assessment is an important and problematic aspect of every course. It is not so much a problem how to demonstrate to the students how much progress they made. It is a problem how to formally examine their qualification before granting certificate.

It is very difficult or impossible to authenticate the presence of an individual participant in an online examination. Our experience shows that at the moment no technical means can completely prevent frauds. The seriousness of this problem is proportional to the significance of the certificate earned. In cases where we expect that credibility of certificates could be questionable, we have to organize traditional face-to-face classroom examinations or at least an online examination under surveillance. It can be very inconvenient sometimes, but we have not yet found anything better.

CONCLUSIONS

The primary aim of this chapter has been to present a model of a computer-supported collaborative learning environment that is well suited to support workplace learning and is becoming widely recognized as the key to meeting the challenge of delivering appropriate learning and training to employees. It can connect learners, in spite of the barriers of distance and time, with the information and expertise that they want and need. In addition, it can provide users with supplementary functionalities to support the distribution of local information and collaboration.

The learning environment consists of two basic building blocks: virtual multimedia textbook and virtual classroom. While virtual multimedia textbooks contain courseware or other related information, the virtual classroom contains facilities that support communication and collaboration between users as well as tools for the provision of an explicit learning structure and for generation of reports.

Our experiences with practical implementation of the learning environments described above in Slovene companies show a high degree of efficiency of learning and satisfaction of course participants.

REFERENCES

Hansen, T., Dirckinck-Holmfeld, L., Lewis, R., & Rugelj, J. (1999). Using telematics to support collaborative knowledge construction. In P. Dilenbourg (Ed.), *Collaborative learning: Cognitive and computational approaches* (Advances in learning and instruction series; pp. 169-196). Amsterdam: Pergamon Press.

Herasim, L., Hiltz, R., Teles, L., & Turoff, M. (1995). *Learning networks—A field guide to teaching and learning online.* Cambridge, MA: MIT Press.

Hiltz, S. R., & Wellman, B. (1997). Asynchronous learning networks as a virtual classroom. *Communications of the ACM, 40*(9), 44-49.

Kinzie, M. B. (1990). Requirements and benefits of effective interactive instruction: Learner control, self regulation, and continuing motivation. *Educational Technology Research and Development, 38*(1), 1-21.

Maly, K., Abdel-Wahab, H., Overstreet, C.M., Wild, J.C., Gupta, A.K., Youssef, A., et al. (1997). Interactive distance learning over intranets. *IEEE Internet Computing 1*(1), 60-71.

Massey, C. (2000). *Market research report: Professional development markets for online learning.* Vancouver, British Columbia, Canada: TeleLearning Network.

McGrath, J. E., & Hollingshead, A. B. (1994). *Groups interacting with technology.* Thousand Oaks, CA: Sage.

Naidu, S. (1994). Applying learning and instructional strategies in open and distance learning. *Distance Education, 15*(1), 23-41.

Osgoode, K. (2000) *Key success factors and lessons learned in workplace learning technologies* (Tech. Rep.). Sackville, Canada: Mount Allison University, Centre for Learning Technologies.

Rosbottom, J., Crellin, J., & Fysh, D. (2000). A generic model for on-line learning. *ACM SIGCSE Bulletin, 32*(3), 108-111.

Rowntree, D. (1977). *Assessing students.* London: Harper & Row.

Rugelj, J. (1997). Computer supported network based learning environment for the workplace. In *Proceedings 3rd International Conference on Network Entities* (pp. TT3.1-3.4). Ancona, Italy: University of Ancona, European Association for Telematic Application (EATA).

Rugelj, J. (1999). Virtual classroom for tele-education. In *Proceedings International Conference New Horizons in Industry and Education*. Heraklion, Greece: Technological Educational Institute of Crete.

Rugelj, J. (2000). Collaborative virtual environmental for problem based learning. In G. Orange & D. Hobbs (Eds.), *International perspectives on tele-education and virtual learning environments* (pp. 40-155). Aldershot, Burlington, USA, Singapore, Sydney: Ashgate.

Souder, W. E. (1993). The effectiveness of traditional vs. satellite delivery in three management in technology master's degree programs. *American Journal of Distance Education, 7*(1), 37-53.

Stelzer, M., & Vogelzangs, I. (1994, Spring). *Isolation and motivation in on-line and distance learning courses*. Retrieved from http://www.to.utwente.nl/ ism/online95/campus/library/online94/ chap8/chap8.htm

Wilkes, C. W., & Burnham B. R. (1991). Adult learner motivation and electronics distance education. *American Journal of Distance Education, 5*(1), 43-50.

Section III:

Managerial and Social Issues

Chapter XIV

Professional to Manufacturing Mode Due to Online University Education

Roy Rada
University of Maryland, Baltimore County, USA

ABSTRACT

The usability of online education relates to the culture of the profession that is expected to create and deliver online education. This profession is threatened by the manufacturing mode that certain online education entails. Case studies at Washington State University, Pace University, and University of Maryland, Baltimore County, support the hypothesis that successful online degree programs introduce manufacturing characteristics into the academy. Furthermore, the case studies support the claim that university administrations rely on boundary manipulation to move the faculty into positions that the faculty would otherwise refuse to accept. An analogy to health care reinforces the conclusions about the impact of mechanization on the professions.

INTRODUCTION

Usability means "capable of being used." Much has been published about particular technical or methodological features, such as synchronous versus asynchronous communication or student-student feedback versus student-teacher feedback. However, studies have shown that usability is more a function of the environment in which an online program is introduced than it is of any particular technical features of the online program itself. This concern for the environment must include a concern for the organization in which the online program is housed. This paper addresses online educational programs as regards the university profession. Sociological and administrative issues are addressed as they relate to the adoption of online education and the impact on the culture of the academy.

Attention is increasingly being drawn to organization-wide issues as regards the success or failure of online education (Rada, 2001). The Sloan Foundation in the United States has moved from funding asynchronous learning experiments that demonstrate some new tool used in a few classrooms to requiring that funded projects demonstrate widespread organizational change. A special issue of *Interactive Learning Environments* focuses on organizational change. The guest editor Betty Collis emphasized that sociological factors are more important than technical factors in the adoption of online education (Collis & Ring, 1999).

Two of the prominent organizational forms in modern society are the professional and the manufacturing. Universities are one example of the professional form. Automobile factories are one example of the manufacturing organization.

The hypothesis is advanced that online education is facilitating the move of teaching at universities from the professional mode to the manufacturing mode. A derivative hypothesis is that the way that administrators effect change is through manipulation of the boundaries in the organization. The cultural turmoil for faculty is significant whether they win the local battles to keep the old boundaries or not.

PROFESSIONAL VERSUS MACHINE MODE

Various taxonomies of organizational types have been espoused (Mintzberg, 1979). Two notable types are the "professional organization" and the "manufacturing organization."

The manufacturing organization generates its own standards. Its technical staff designs the work standards for its operators, and its line managers enforce them. The machine organization has highly specialized, routine operating tasks; formalized procedures in the operating core; and a proliferation of rules, regulations, and formalized communication throughout the organization.

While the university is a professional organization, introducing online education creates occasions for specialization and mechanization that introduce manufacturing features to the university. How is this change introduced?

Like the manufacturing organization, the professional organization is an inflexible structure. Change in the professional bureaucracy does not come from new administrators taking office with major reforms. Instead, change arrives by the slow process of changing the professionals—changing who can enter the profession, what they learn in its professional schools (norms as well as skills and knowledge), and thereafter how willing they are to upgrade their skills. The professional administration

Table 1: Form and coordination

Organization	Coordination Mechanism
Manufacturing	• Standardize procedures and outputs • Technocrats standardize procedures and outputs
Professional	• Standardize professional skills and norms • Professionals in the operating core (e.g. doctors, professors) rely on roles and skills learned from years of schooling and indoctrination to coordinate their work

lacks power relative to manufacturing organizations and is decentralized. The administrators typically spend their time handling disruptions and negotiations. Nevertheless, administrative structures serve a key role in creating and modifying the boundaries of the organization. Often through this boundary manipulation, the administration implements its will (Wetzel, 2001).

UNIVERSITIES

The modern American research university is a complex, international conglomerate of highly diverse businesses. The University of Michigan, for example, has an annual budget of more than $2.5 billion. If it was a private company, then the University of Michigan would rank roughly 200th on the Fortune 500 list of largest companies in the USA (Duderstadt, 2000). The large research university operates as a holding company for thousands of faculty entrepreneurs. The faculty have teaching duties, but performance in these teaching duties is only modestly linked to salary.

The revenue theory of cost is appropriate for describing American universities (Bowen, 1980). Namely, a university gets as much money each year as it can, spends all that money that year, and next year operates in the same way. From one like university to another like university in the United States, the amount of money spent to educate a student can differ by a factor of two and still the quality of education tends to be the same.

The preceding model of universities does not apply to community colleges. (This terminology is a decidedly parochial American one. However, in numerous countries an analogy exists between the divide in the American system to the divide in the higher education system of the other country.) As one goes from Ph.D.-granting universities to community colleges, one sees something closer to an accounting model in which revenue is related to costs (Bibby, 1983). At a research university a professor may typically teach one course a semester, whereas at a community college the professor teaches 10 times that much (Adams, 1976). The community college is closer to a manufacturing organization than is a research university.

Courses in which all interactions between staff and students are documented and archived facilitate manufacturing-type control. In the early 20th century, correspondence courses were popular and used paper mail. In 1928 R. E. Crump published "Correspondence and Class Extension Work in Oklahoma" to show the utility of these correspondence courses. With the advent of radio and television, countries increased their interests in distance education. Places such as the Open University in England and National Radio Institute in the United States were created in the mid 20th century. These institutions help students access university education despite being somewhere distant from the teacher. They are not research universities but focus on teaching in a systematic (manufacturing-type) way.

A national sample of U.S. households was surveyed by telephone in the spring of 1995 (Dillman, Christenson, Salant, & Warner, 1995). The findings include:

- Teaching only in the traditional classroom will not meet the public's demand for educational services.
- No single educational approach or technique will make lifelong learning accessible to everyone, because different people face different obstacles.
- Distance education strategies have the potential to overcome significant barriers to lifelong learning.

These are the views of the public. University faculty might not agree. Pressures to add machine features to the academy may work against the stakes of the faculty.

CASE STUDIES

Three case studies are presented that illustrate various efforts to introduce online education in American universities.

WSU

Washington State University (WSU) is a research-oriented, traditional, state land-grant university with 19,000 students, 4,800 faculty-staff, and multiple campuses. Its annual budget is about $500 million.

Using technology in education at WSU is highlighted by the development of the Washington Higher Education Telecommunications System (WHETS). WHETS is used to broadcast lectures in real time from one campus of WSU to another campus. WHETS came online in 1985 and exposes place-bound students to degree programs where once it was not practical to have such programs (WHETS, 2001). The WHETS faculty are still masters of their own course that is delivered largely as previously.

In 1995, Washington State University attempted to create a virtual university component. A virtual university academic officer was appointed and a large multicampus effort initiated to define the vision and strategy for the virtual university component. This was closely linked to substantial funding that was expected to come from Microsoft Corporation and the Paul Allen Foundation.

The university task force wanted slow change that honored traditional values of academic freedom. The commercial sponsors wanted dramatic, university-wide change. The faculty refused to cooperate. The commercial sponsors refused to lavishly fund the university. The provost and virtual university academic officer left the university shortly thereafter.

WSU does not have a large virtual university component. The WHETS program has been augmented with an email list server and Web access to a database that provides administrative information about courses. Students print and send by surface mail their submissions to WSU. The augmented WHETS operation has several dozen support staff who route incoming paper mail, recruit teachers to courses, answer phone queries, and maintain the databases of information. The system in place is modest compared to what was touted as the virtual university in 1995 and leaves the vast majority of faculty operating in the time-honored way.

Pace

Pace University is a multicampus private university based in New York City with 15,000 students and an annual budget of approximately $100 million (www.pace.edu). It offers associate, bachelor's, master's, and professional degrees but not Ph.D.s.— the focus is more on teaching than on research. Pace has had negligible involvement in distance education prior to starting in 1998 an online associate of arts degree for employees of the telecommunications industry.

The program developed very quickly under the adroit leadership of the person responsible for continuing education programs, not academic programs. He runs his programs more in the community college mode than in the research university mode. All courses follow a strict pattern. Here is an extract from the Web site describing the program (Pace, 2001): "Lectures and assignments for each week are posted each Thursday morning, and all assignments should be completed by midnight (Eastern Time) the following Wednesday."

Numerous specialists support various operations of the program. In the delivery of courses far more specialization occurs than is the norm in face-to-face teaching, as indicated by the following:

- One role administers quality control surveys on a regular basis, at times weekly, to students in a class.
- Another role phones students whose survey responses suggest a problem.
- Another role answers academic queries about the degree program for students.
- Yet, another role is a mentor from a telecommunications company.

The teacher of the course is not necessarily the person who developed the course content, schedule, examinations, or anything else about the structure or function of the course. Furthermore, the teacher no longer does the quality control or social support expected of a traditional teacher.

The development of course content is also specialized:

- The requirements for the courses have come from industry.
- The template for all courses is fixed in advance.
- Technical staff help place content in courses.

Someone designs the course, but other people teach it. Those who deliver the course are obligated to follow the curriculum developed by the designer.

Faculty get a few thousand dollars to design an online course, and the university owns the copyright on the course. The director has managed the rapid development of a full complement of online courses for an associate of arts degree and staffed the program for successful delivery.

Further evidence of the nontraditional, manufacturing mode of the program is the schedule. Courses each last a traditional 15 weeks. However, rather than starting only in the traditional fall and spring semester, a new semester starts every other month so that students can start whenever they want. The schedule is designed to suit telecommunications workers whose sense of timing is not tied into the academic fall and spring semester schedule.

Although the program only started development in 1998, by 2001 a dozen students had already graduated from the program with associate's degrees earned entirely in the program. The program is a wonderful success in terms of rapid development and successful marketing and delivery.

Not all this change has been desired by the average faculty member at Pace University. However, the administration has introduced the program by modifying the boundaries of Pace. First, the program is not officially offered by Pace but by a coalition called NACTEL that is completely independent of Pace University. The tuition for employees of telecommunications firms is much lower than the tuition for other Pace University courses but this information is hidden from the public or university faculty. The tuition fees for employees of telecommunications companies are only learned after one demonstrates that one is an employee and makes a private communication with the NACTEL program. The telecommunications companies would not have been willing to contract with Pace for this program had Pace charged its normal tuition fees. Faculty who teach on the program do it as an extra teaching obligation for extra pay.

UMBC

UMBC is a one-campus state university with 10,000 students and 500 faculty with Ph.D.s offered in 20 disciplines. The annual budget is about $170 million per year.

UMBC has no history of delivering online education prior to a program first offered in the year 2000. Then, in response to the desires to compete aggressively with other institutions for online students in information systems, a special program was initiated that the Department of Information Systems faculty were promised would be completely separate from the traditional program.

Collaboration was arranged with the United States Open University (a part of the larger organization typically called the British Open University). The British Open University has a long history of operating in manufacturing mode. It has over 100,000 students enrolled at any one time. Fewer than 1,000 staff are academics per se. About 8,000 people are tutorial staff or teaching assistants (Open, 1997). The university has annual revenue of about $300 million dollars. The expenditures include 30% to academic costs, 25% to support for tutoring, and 20% for courseware production. These courseware production costs would not be seen in typical universities where teachers use existing textbooks.

UMBC's program follows the model of the Open University. An author develops a course following a general template. The course is taught by "teaching assistants" or "tutors." The tutors are supported by a sophisticated delivery network that includes supervisors of the tutors and staff that monitor student satisfaction.

The UMBC faculty has been at odds with the new program in many ways. The faculty are comfortable with teaching face-to-face and having substantial autonomy in what they teach and how they teach it. They naturally want to increase faculty numbers as the student population grows as much as possible, which works best with the traditional model of "one section of students corresponds with one faculty member" rather than "one section of students corresponds with one teaching assistant." However, the university administration has seen this program as a source of significant advantage to the university and manipulates boundaries frequently to achieve its ends. For instance, in recent debates the administration said that it would move the authority for the program to the Continuing Education Department if the Department of Information Systems did not want to run the program in the way that the upper administration wanted it to run.

The university has invested substantial funding in marketing its online master's degree—more than in all other activities supporting the master's degree combined. This is another sign of something different from the traditional research university model. The program has succeeded in enrolling over 100 students in its second semester of full-time operation.

HEALTH-CARE ANALOGY

What can be learned from another profession? The health-care industry is considered to operate in professional mode. The physician is traditionally the leader of the health-care team. A physician is qualified by formal education and legal authority to practice medicine and wants great independence.

However, a change has been in the making. Before 1850, health care in the United States was a loose collection of individual services functioning independently without much relation to each other or to anything else. The modern American health system can be depicted in three stages (Torrens, 1993):

- 1900-1940: science and technology introduced,
- 1940-1980: some manufacturing organization characteristics introduced, and
- 1980-now: quality control introduced.

The increasing role division in health care also demonstrates the move from a professional organization to a manufacturing organization. Physicians constituted 30% of all health personnel in 1910 but 10% in 1990. Allied health technicians, technologists, aides, and assistants constituted 1% in 1910 and over half the health workforce in 1990 (Mick & Moscovice, 1993). The move is gradual but relentless from a purely professional organization to an organization with numerous manufacturing characteristics.

In the meantime, physicians resist this change. The U.S. President's Advisory Commission on Consumer Protection and Quality in the Health Care Industry (President's Advisory Commission, 1998) elaborates how information systems are critical to quality health care and identifies clinician resistance as a key barrier to diffusion.

Supporters of automation see great potential in using computer-generated "reminders" to prompt clinicians to ask patients certain questions or run particular tests. Clinicians, however, may see this as cookbook medicine that limits their professional autonomy (Dowling, 1987). Supporters of computerized patient records see great opportunity to automate quality control. If, however, this information is primarily used to identify "poor performers" rather than to guide improvement efforts, health professionals may come to view the system with suspicion. The lesson to be learned for the university is that initial implementation of online programs with semiautomatic quality control procedures for their teaching should be run in a "blame-free" environment.

Whoever is involved in new systems in health care has to nurture collective participation (Wetzel, 2001). Decisions cannot be made

- solely by a centralized administration nor
- based upon detailed in-house knowledge provided by technical staff.

Neither the administration nor the technical staff possesses the required power, work resources, or available knowledge of organizational processes. The low motivation among professionals to participate in collective efforts may also aggravate the situation. System changes are often perceived not to be in the interest of the professional. In some cases the benefits that new systems may bring the entire organization may reduce resources to certain individual units that will then resist the implementation. The recognition of subtle power plays and existing alliances between various units assumes a greater role in health-care systems than in manufacturing organizations, where well-defined teams have strong authority over new systems' implementations. What has been said for the challenges of implementing new systems in health care applies equally to universities.

CONCLUSION

The data in the case studies and the analogy to health care support the hypotheses. The introduction of online degrees corresponds with the introduction of further manufacturing characteristics into the professional environment. Administration accomplishes this change—otherwise opposed by faculty—by modifying the boundaries. One prominent way to modify the boundaries is to involve a partnership with another organization and say the program is an experiment separate from the normal academy operation.

Based on the admittedly limited data from the three cases, one might also speculate whether universities with a smaller budget per student are more likely to effectively put entire degrees online that reach to new markets of students and substantially increase enrollment. Conversely, the richer the university in terms of budget per student the less likely the university is to accept a manufacturing approach.

The influential book *Dancing with the Devil: Information Technology and the New Competition in Higher Education* (Katz, 1998) talks about the formidable challenges facing campuses. The authors realize that online education threatens to change the character of the university from a professional one to a manufacturing one. Yet, certain forces make online education likely to grow in importance rather than decrease in importance. Given that some activities of the academy, such as pure research, are intrinsically suited to a professional rather than a manufacturing organization, universities might further specialize to adapt.

REFERENCES

Adams, W. (1976). Faculty load. *Improving College and University Teaching, 24*(4), 215-218.

Beshears, F. (2001). *Mintzberg's classification of organizational forms.* Retrieved July 2001 from http://ist-socrates.berkeley.edu/~fmb/articles/mintzberg/

Bibby, P. (1983). *An academic accounting model for community colleges.* Unpublished doctoral dissertation, University of Florida.

Bowen, H. (1980). *The costs of higher education: How much do colleges and universities spend per student and how much should they spend?* San Francisco, CA: Jossey-Bass.

Collis, B. & Ring, J. (1999). Scaling up: Faculty change and the WWW. *Interactive Learning Environments, 7*(2/3), 87-92.

Dillman, D., Christenson, J., Salant, P., & Warner, P. (1995). *What the public wants from higher education: Work force implications from a 1995 national survey.* Pullman, WA: Washington State University, Social & Economic Sciences Research Center.

Dowling, A. (1987). Do hospital staff interfere with computer system implementation? In J. Anderson & S. Jay (Eds.), *Use and impact of computers in clinical medicine.* (pp. 302-317) New York: Springer-Verlag.

Duderstadt, J. (2000). *A University for the 21st Century*. Ann Arbor, MI: University of Michigan Press.

Katz, R. (1998). *Dancing with the devil: Information technology and the new competition in higher education*. San Francisco, CA: Jossey-Bass.

Mick, S. & Moscovice, I. (1993). Health care professionals. In S. Williams & P. Torrens (Eds.), *Introduction to health services* (pp. 269-296). New York: Delmar.

Mintzberg, H. (1979). *The structuring of organizations*. Reading, NJ: Prentice Hall.

Open University. (1997). *Facts and figures*. Retrieved July 1997 from: http://www.open.ac.uk/

Pace University. (2001). *Pace University/NACTEL program*. Retrieved September 2001 from Pace University, School of Computer Science and Information Systems Web site: http://support.csis.pace.edu/nactel/program/index.cfm

President's Advisory Commission. (1998). Investing in information systems. In President's Advisory Commission on Consumer Protection and Quality in the Health Care Industry, *Quality first: Better health care for all Americans* (Chap. 14). Retrieved September 2000 from http://www.hcqualitycommission.gov/final/chap14.html (pp. 138-147).

Rada, R. (2001). *Understanding virtual universities*. Oxford, England: Intellect Books. Torrens, P. (1993). Historical evolution and overview of health care systems in the United States. In S. Williams & P. Torrens (Eds.), *Introduction to health services* (pp. 1-28). New York: Delmar.

Washington Higher Education Telecommunication System. (2001). Retrieved November 2001 from http://www.tricity.wsu.edu/mediaservices/whetsh.htm

Wetzel, I. (2001). Information systems development with anticipation of change: Focusing on professional bureaucracies. In *Proceedings of Hawaii International Conference on System Sciences, HICCS-34*. IEEE Computer Society, (January, pp. 1-12).

Chapter XV

Changing Roles and Processes in Online Tuition for Higher Education: A Case Study from the UK Open University

Gordon Dyer
Open University in the East of England, Cambridge, UK

ABSTRACT

The case study examines a Level 1 undergraduate course delivered totally online to 8,500 students of the UK Open University (OU). Context, philosophy, design and learning outcomes are described. The author compares personal experience of tutoring the course to normal OU distance teaching methods and argues that computer-mediated conferencing (CMC) has a major impact on student learning styles and in changing roles within the teaching team; a learning community develops, triggering co-learning, co-tuition and co-counseling. The CMC also enables efficient academic and administrative information flow, and fast feedback for informal evaluation. The evaluation cycle is completed by reference to student feedback via a Web-site questionnaire and institutional change action. The study shows that technology to support global delivery is adequately robust, and success rates on the programme are similar to other OU courses. Pre-entry and online educational guidance is identified as an area needing further consideration.

INTRODUCTION

This chapter is written from the perspective of a tutor on the UK Open University (OU) course T171, which was first presented in February 2000. The course, called You, Your Computer, and the Net, is a 200-hour, 30 CATS points, Level 1 (1st year undergraduate) course which is delivered entirely online to mass numbers of students who can be based anywhere, assuming they have access to the Internet. Over 8,500 students initially registered for the February 2000 course; another 3,100 initially registered for a May intake. The intakes for 2001 were similar.

The move to mass online tuition and support represents a major step for the OU. Its first experiments with computer-assisted distance learning were in 1988, when computer-mediated conferencing (CMC) was introduced as part of the support arrangements for one of its social science courses. This was 17 years after the OU started its distance teaching programmes. In 1988 CMC via a home-based PC was viewed simply as one component of a multimedia package for course delivery and support. It supplemented the support from the tutor normally given through face-face contact and telephone. The course materials, in the form of high quality workbooks, came through the post as is normal for other OU courses; student assessment was via the normal form of written or typed assignments sent from student to tutor, also via post. All this has changed with the T171 online model of delivery, as has the relationship between student and tutor, along with many educational and administrative processes, including evaluation.

Hence this chapter will:

- provide some background to the OU and its development over the last 30 years of supported open-learning programmes using multimedia methods, and how this classical form of delivery is being augmented and challenged by experiments using Internet delivery;
- describe the underpinning philosophy and intended learning outcomes for T171, key to which are working collaboratively with other students using CMC and developing the necessarily skills of evaluating the information found on the Internet when undertaking research;
- describe the impact that CMC and Internet delivery is having on the relationships between tutor and student, which will be characterised by the terms co-learning, co-tuition and co-counseling, as well as the impact on the administration and evaluation of the course; and
- demonstrate the robustness of online delivery in terms of server and support systems and in terms of overall student success rate.

While the focus of the chapter is evaluation from a tutor perspective, to complete the evaluation cycle a reference to student feedback mechanisms will be provided to explain the institutional response in making changes to the programme in 2001 and 2002.

FOUR DECADES OF OU ACTIVITY

The OU received its Royal Charter in 1969 and grew rapidly to become the largest university in the UK, with 140,000 undergraduate students and 40,000 postgraduate students following its courses in 2000 (OU Planning Office, 2001). It ranks 10th in the league table of UK universities for its teaching quality as measured by the independent assessment carried out by the Quality Assurance Agency. It also has a strong international reputation and following, with some 25,000 students enrolled on its courses overseas: throughout the EU and most of Eastern Europe including Russia, in East Africa (Ethiopia), and in the Far East (Hong Kong and Singapore).

The role of an OU tutor is different to that of a conventional university academic; there is no responsibility for course content, which is defined by a course team. The tutor role is to act as a learning facilitator in assisting and supporting their students to meet the course objectives. This they do normally by a combination of face-to-face group tutorials, which serve as an opportunity to clarify course concepts and deal with any specific issues that anyone in the group may be having, and by their feedback and teaching comments on assignments. Any other specific problems for individuals are met through a combination of communications methods: letter, phone, and, from 1988, email and CMC. This classical OU model of supported open-learning, is summarised in Figure 1.

The four decades of OU delivery may be characterised as follows. The first decade, the 1970s, confirmed through rigorous external assessment that the model of part-time supported open-learning met all the requirements for successful

Figure 1:   The classical OU model of supported open-learning

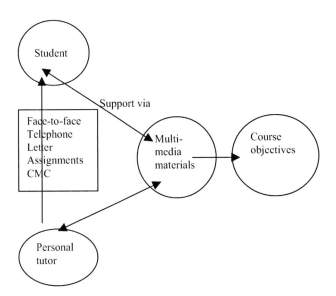

teaching, assessment and accreditation at higher education level. During the 1980s, the OU delivery model was extended to post-experience and postgraduate programmes for managers in business, commerce and industry and to Europe. The 1990s led to major expansion overseas and further diversification in professional areas of teacher training, social work training, law and foreign languages.

The inclusion of CMC in the support arrangements for the OU course DT200 Information Technology and Society in 1988 was something of a watershed. The opportunity for students to communicate electronically both by email (one-to-one and one-to-many) and through conferencing (many-to-many) provided the first indications that the potential impact of CMC on learning-at-a-distance would be far-reaching. Mason (1989) provides an evaluation of the impact of this first experiment in the book *Mindweave*. Being able to communicate electronically opened up new possibilities for students who faced great problems with accessing learning, e.g., the housebound disabled or otherwise isolated through geography, work demands, family or other difficulties and who could not attend normal OU tutorials. This author conducted a follow-up experiment with a group of 12 housebound and isolated students in the East Anglian region in 1990 which confirmed the value of CMC as a support tool (Dyer, 1991).

The conclusions to be drawn from all this earlier work was that CMC had stimulated:

- *Co-learning*—in that students learned from and collaborated with each other in new and potentially effective ways; for example, in group projects where drafts could quickly be transferred between remote team members. Also tutors could learn from and share ideas with each other.
- Students to play a more active role in learning than is possible with most face-to-face interactions, for example, everyone has the chance to "speak."
- *Co-counseling*—via the student peer-group, where students who have appropriate experience can give help and advice to others.
- *Co-tuition*—central academics and other course production team members can interact directly with students. This is normally unavailable to them in classical OU course structures where teaching is carried out by regionally based part-time staff.
- Part-time tutors to contribute at a regional or national level rather than with just their own local group.

In addition to these general changes to educational processes, CMC had allowed:

- students to evaluate the performance of their own tutor by comparing notes electronically, and
- a very open appraisal system of tutors, central academics and course team members through their contributions to national and regional electronic conferences.

Other OU faculties were keen to exploit the new possibilities. Various initiatives contributed to the development of key systems and procedures for online support and delivery, e.g., central server arrangements and systems for handling student assignments sent and returned electronically, following comments and grading by tutors. The Institute of Educational Technology developed a master's in open and distance education in 1997. This was offered on a worldwide basis but presented from Milton Keynes using OU experts. The course materials were in the form of printed text and sent to students overseas, but it was clear that student support could only be provided using CMC. For an evaluation of this programme, see Mason (1999).

The software package FirstClass, from SoftArc, emerged as the preferred CMC facility. A major advantage was that it could handle the very large number of user accounts (100,000 plus) that the OU required. Another major breakthrough was when FirstClass servers became accessible with a Web browser, albeit with some reduced facilities. Browser access opened up the possibility for people who had a very mobile lifestyle to continue to get support and participate in their course. By 1999 a variety of courses had emerged where some online features of course support and delivery had been included. Some simply use CMC to supplement their support arrangements, and at the current time about 100,000 OU students benefit from this. Others provide the course materials on a server and invite electronic submission of assignments but still insist on the student being examined under controlled conditions in an exam centre. However, T171 is the first course where **all** key aspects of the course—materials, support, continuous and final assessment—are handled online, along with the collection of evaluation data. This major development in providing total course delivery online was possible through availability of: cheaper, more effective and reliable hardware and software, new pressures from the higher education environment to expand students' numbers, and a course team vision that this was now philosophically appropriate. Let us now move to T171 itself.

T171—PHILOSOPHY AND DESIGN

The T171 course proposal was ambitious as it needed to cater for many OU entry students who perhaps had not studied for many years, who typically are unclear of the requirements of study at HE level, and who may lack confidence. However, it was to be expected that in the subject area of computing there would be a wide variety of experience of basic skills and experience. The T171 course team needed to design an intake process that could cater for this. The team was very clear on the underpinning philosophy to drive the project:

- The Internet was a key 21st-century technology—it was essential to place this at the centre of the approach for the technology faculty's new foundation course.

- The focus should be to make computing and the Internet accessible to all — the approach would be to humanise the topic by teaching the story of the development of the new technology.
- To exploit the evidence that email and computer conferencing provide the opportunity for more dialogue than in a conventional OU learning situation. This derives from the analysis that, for example, not all students can attend OU face-to-face tutorials, as the dates may be inconvenient due to work or other demands. CMC takes place in an asynchronous mode so students can always catch up with a discussion.

The learning outcomes for the course follow from this underpinning philosophy, i.e.:

- be comfortable and skilled in using a PC for standard applications
- be experienced in using electronic conferencing for effective communication
- possess confidence and ability to use the Internet for information retrieval and dissemination:
  - use search engines and evaluate the reliability and quality of material found
  - write and publish Web pages and manage a small Website
- work effectively in a team on a collaborative project
- have a good knowledge/understanding of the growth and development of the PC and WWW
- have an understanding of how a PC and the Internet work
- appreciate the impact of computers and Internet on society

as did the skills to be developed, i.e.:

- clear thinking (or sense of academic criticism)
- communication
- handling information and using IT
- working with others
- reflective learning
- generic study skills

A course structure emerged based around a preparatory period and three taught modules. The summary description that follows highlights the key points of interest and novelty in design. Fuller descriptions are available (Weller, 1999, 2000a).

A 14-week preparatory period before course start is optional and caters for the variety of skill and experience of the student intake. It is intended to bring students to a common basic standard by the start of Module 1. It is activity based, around the only material sent through the post. It includes course and preparatory guides, plus T171 and FirstClass CD-ROMs. The first carries diagnostic exercises on Windows;

other items of software (freeware) that the students will use on the course, including a basic HTML editor; and a browser tutorial, including connecting to the Web and finding the T171 course Website, where all the course materials are based. The preparatory work also includes written study skills exercises. Most important of these, in terms of a precursor to their future activity in retrieving and evaluating information from the Internet, are exercises on clear thinking. This introduces the concept of academic criticism and the need to be alert to the perspective and bias in any writing.

Module 1, called Computing With Confidence, is aimed at developing individual skills. It lasts 10 weeks and is focussed on learning in cyberspace, group learning in cyberspace, computing, and developing Web skills. This involves activity using the course Website and using CMC. Crucial at this stage is the introduction and discussion of Netiquette to ensure that group cohesion and effectiveness is maintained during collaborative work. The students are provided with weekly online study guides, a sample of which may be accessed (see Weller, 2000b).

Assessment in the OU is based on tutor-marked assignments (TMAs). There are two TMAs in the module; both require participation in online practical group work using CMC. The first typically requires a review of a number of papers on group work taken from a variety of sources and written from different perspectives. Most of these papers assume a context of face-to-face collaboration. The challenge for students is to discuss through CMC a set of protocols that the group might adopt for its work in the coming year. They present their own views as part of the TMA. The achievement of learning outcomes is confirmed through the second assignment, where they need to work collaboratively in small groups (six or seven) to jointly develop a Web channel with a group home page that then links to individual Websites of team members. The team members are expected to discuss and agree some common aspects of the overall Web-site design. Their personal evaluation of performance is a strong focus in the TMA, both on how the group itself worked and of any information for their topic obtained from Websites. They are expected to evaluate that evidence by commenting on the perspective and possible bias of the site author.

Module 2, called Your Computer: The Story of the PC, explores the development of the personal computer. Over nine weeks the students examine the key people, organisations and technologies that played a significant part in the development of the hardware and software involved. They are expected to appreciate the cultural context in which the developments took place and the key business concepts particular to the PC industry. Though this is contemporary history, as history it has plenty of controversy and offers good opportunity to test students' achievement of learning outcomes. The Web-site material is linked to one particular account of this history, as given in the book *Accidental Empires* (Cringley, 1996). But students will be expected to search for alternative accounts of the history from the Web and evaluate the various accounts. The following TMA, which required a 1,500-word

Web-based report, illustrates the opportunity for Web search, analysis and evaluation:

> *Examine the importance of the operating system in the development of the PC. Your answer should make reference to the function of an operating system, the significant operating systems in the development of the PC, what these have meant for the computer industry, and the possible future directions of operating systems.*

Module 3, or The Net: Where It Came From, How It works, also lasts nine weeks and covers the evolution of the Internet from its origins to its explosive growth in the 1990s. It covers the key technologies and the people and institutions involved in its development. As in Module 2, the Website material links to a set book which presents one account of the history, but again a large amount of additional material is presented on the Website. The TMA similarly gives opportunity to provoke search activity and need to evaluate information on the Web.

This module includes the end-of-course assessment (ECA), which serves as an alternative to a final written exam. For the ECA, students produce an electronic portfolio of their work over the year in the form of a Website. They have to produce examples of work from each of the modules, including their contributions to CMC discussions. They need to demonstrate their ability as a reflective learner, for example, how they set out learning plans and how these were revised, perhaps following feedback from their tutor on an assignment. An independent examiner assesses the ECA.

T171—ONLINE TUITION AND SUPPORT

The intake for the first presentation of T171 in February 2000 was closed when 8,575 had initially registered. This intake required a tutor cohort of some 519 staff, at the planning staff:student ratio of ~ 15:1. Of these, 47 were recruited in the East of England region, including the author. As a tutor on the previous technology foundation course I valued providing face-to-face tutorial support to students. The prospect of operating only in an online tutor mode seemed both limiting and daunting. After the experience of teaching the course in 2000 my attitude changed. A first key point was that dealing with the possible problems that students might have with course software and logging into FirstClass is dealt with centrally through a telephone Student Help Desk, which is open till 10 p.m. and also operates at weekend. The course preparatory period is very important in allowing tutors to do the necessary online training for acting as a moderator for FirstClass conferencing and for handling and marking electronic TMAs (eTMAs). The moderator function enables control of a conference and carries with it the necessary permissions to establish a tutor-group conference and sub-conferences and to set permission levels, i.e., who can access the conference and what they can do. For a particular tutor, those with permission to access the group conference would only be the student members of that group. However, for monitoring purposes, permission is usually set for line managers to access group conferences. As matter of courtesy, a staff tutor would always ask permission before entering a conference and would normally only be permitted to "read" rather than "contribute." Welcome messages were posted into the group conference before course start. Such facility complemented the normal tutor-to-group postal mailing that would take place at this time of year. Once CMC was fully operational in the group, the ability to post messages to some or all via email was a great saving in time and postage, both for individual tutors and the course team.

The moderator role is a crucial function of the T171 tutor; see, for example, Salmon's (2000) description of what she calls e-moderating. Once the course starts, the tutor is expected to facilitate regular electronic-based discussions around a key aspect of the course materials. This requires setting discussions up, running them and then summarising. This happens every two or three weeks. The quality of this process is much helped by a central emailing from the course team that reminds tutors of the aims and offers suggested texts for use in setting up the time-tabled discussion. It was easy to arrange for the conferencing to take place as a single group or in subgroups, as relevant to the needs of the exercise.

A snapshot (screen dump) of my FirstClass desktop at the transition from study of Module 2 to Module 3 is shown in Figure 2. This shows the three levels of conferences, e.g., a National Café, a regional conference for R06 T171 tutors, and some nine conferences, labelled T171 gcd2 ***, which I set up for electronic discussions within my own group on course topics.

Figure 2:   Snapshot of FirstClass desktop

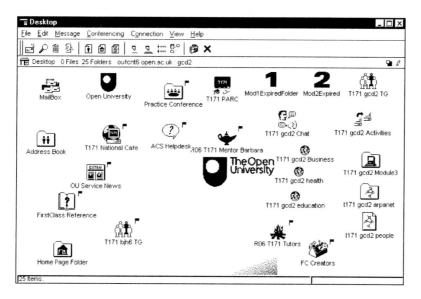

The course material for T171 is on a separate Web server. The material is made available on a "publisher model" basis, i.e., about two weeks before it is due to be studied. This model means that the latest information can be included very quickly into the course. The T171 Office emails student study guides and tutor guides every two weeks. These are extremely valuable in maintaining the pace of the course throughout the year, as they detail clearly which sections of the Web site need to be studied each week in the period and carry useful reminders to both groups of other key points, e.g., that an assignment is due. The first module includes an extremely important mechanism to indicate student progress. The end of each section of the module carries an email link which is automatically set to send to the tutor's mailbox a message saying the student has completed that section of work.

Two other servers need to be accessed to complete the tutor role. One is the server used for eTMAs. Students upload their assignments to the server by the due date; the tutor accesses the server and downloads the assignment for marking and commenting using the marking tool. When the assignment is returned, the system completes the necessary processes to record the marks on the student record and to trigger a payment to the tutor. The eTMA server provides a very useful control system for line managers, who need to check that tutors are returning the eTMAs within the laid-down 10 working days. The server provides a list of when assignments were submitted, when collected by the tutor and when they were returned. Knowing that this record is so transparent, it is an incentive to tutors to achieve the turn-round time performance indicator. As is normal with OU assignments, a sample of marked work from each tutor is monitored to ensure the sufficiency and adequacy of teaching comments to students and consistency of marking. The tutors also have access to another server that provides a record of their students' details and academic history.

CO-LEARNING, CO-TUITION, AND CO-COUNSELING

The T171 FirstClass conferencing structure makes fundamental changes to the relationships between a tutor and the members of their group. These changes are generally very beneficial and can be characterised by the terms co-learning, co-tuition, and co-counseling. A general description of these concepts and then some specific examples follow. In distinct contrast to the conventional learning situation—in the OU or a conventional university—there is a general understanding that a particular group of students "belong" to a particular tutor. A student with a problem will talk firstly to his or her own tutor. There are many reasons for this, but the practice presents obvious obstacles to learning. In the CMC environment this formal convention evaporates, and a truly overall learning community—students, tutors and course team—is established. Students can share ideas with and learn from other students, tutors from other tutors, tutors from students, etc. This is firstly achieved through a structure of national or pan-regional conferences that act as an umbrella for all the individual tutor group conferences. These national conferences deal with issues and problems that may be of interest to all or many in the community. For example, they can be very useful for the specific issue of future course choice, when both tutors and students who have already done particular courses can input comments and advice on questions asked by prospective students for those courses. Thus the regional and national conferences represent a huge source of informal counselling advice and support; they also provide feedback to aid personal and institutional evaluation.

For the learning community to be effective everyone needs to be clear about the possibilities that the new environment offers. Students need to understand that they have access to the community as a source of advice. Similarly, tutors have to adjust to feeling happy about "letting go" of responsibility for all problems that individuals in their group may have. They need to be open to co-tuition as a principle. Given below is the text of a message that I posted to my group conference on February 24, 2000, to encourage them to exploit the potential of the learning community:

> *I have had a number of technical queries about FC and FCemail since the course began, of the form "I haven't been able to do this" or "I get this problem." Though I have had some ideas in some cases, because your computer hardware and software setup is likely to be different to mine, others can stump me and then I have to refer them on to someone else. It would be much better in future if you would post queries in the national student conferences, as there are people eager to answer them. These conferences are behind the main T171 icon on your desktop. There is a sub-conference called T171FCEmail and another called FC/FCEmail FAQs. I suggest that you look there and in the other sub-conferences when you come up against a problem. It is possible that it has already been answered. The huge advantage to a course like T171 is that instead of just one person (i.e., your own tutor) being a source of support, you have the potential support from several thousands of students, many hundreds of tutors, plus members of the course team who are drifting around the conferences to see if they can help with problems.*

The same principles of co-learning and co-tuition and new roles for students will emerge in the online tutorials for course work. Take the example of the stage in the course where the students are developing their skills in evaluating Websites prior to designing their own. Given that my aim is to encourage collaborative learning, I might begin by splitting the students into two subgroups of six to seven. I might then invite each subgroup to take a topic—e.g., an idea, a technology, an individual or a company/organisation—and then compare and contrast two Websites related to this topic in terms of a number of relevant criteria, e.g., content and coverage;

perspective and reliability; intended audience; and navigation. They are expected to work collaboratively over a period, sharing out tasks and deciding who in the subgroup would collate and then upload their joint efforts to a personal home page. After the reports are posted, students might then be invited to individually visit the Web page made by the other group and then to post a message in the group and subgroup conferences stating one aspect of the page they think is really good and one aspect of the page they think might be improved. I would then provide my own feedback on the work, supporting or moderating student comment as necessary. In this way the expertise in the group is shared and learning is enhanced.

The experience showed that many students are enthusiastic to share and collaborate in this way, in effect to take on a new role within the learning community. This is illustrated by the following quote from a student contribution to the end-of-course evaluation provided by T171 Office (Personal Communication, February 9, 2001):

> I have thoroughly enjoyed this course—it wasn't easy but I have learned a lot, some of it unexpected, e.g., "people" skills. The social side of the course, e.g., T171 National Café, should be emphasised. Distance learning can be tough at times and having peer group advice and having a laugh can make a big difference. Many of the students in the café have provided an unofficial support system and have, I believe, stopped many others from giving up. I feel the OU should consider using some of these people as moderators for future courses to "kick start" the communication process that has turned out to be such a vital part of the course.

The above discussion has concentrated on student co-learning. But there is also a cluster of pan-regional and regional conferences set up specifically for tutors, so that their co-learning can take place. These include FAQs from tutors. Others allow the sharing of good practice, for example, on how to deal with a particular aspect of a group discussion or interpreting the marking guide for an assignment provided by the course team. They often carry tips or postings on good Websites that individual tutors may have discovered or which have been passed to them by one of their students. This is an invaluable resource and I am indebted to a colleague T171 tutor, Lynne Dixon, for the approach to the tutorial exercise comparing Websites described above. I am also pleased to be able to contribute my own ideas to the conference for others to consider using.

PERSONAL EVALUATION

By the end of the year my initial apprehensions about teaching the course had largely evaporated. The regularity of the electronic tutorials via CMC activity confirmed the view that opportunity for tutor-student and student-student dialogue was greater than in the conventional (classical OU) learning situation. The FirstClass *history* function enables a check to be made on who has read any particular message. This, combined with individuals' input to CMC activity and section completed emails, enables very positive checks on student progress to be made. The fact that FirstClass can be read via a browser, albeit with some restrictions on facilities compared to using the client software, also had benefits when I was abroad during 2000. This happened on two occasions, when I spent a week in Austria in May and a week in the USA later in the year. In May I attended a conference based in a hotel. Colleagues from the University of Linz arranged an Internet connection from the hotel and I was able to catch up with the group's work with no difficulty. The connection from the USA was equally easy and robust.

Along with all other tutors, I faced one major difficulty during the first three months of the course. The initial marking tool which was provided turned out to be very unstable and randomly caused PCs to hang up or crash during the marking process. This was particularly galling if one had spent time assessing assignments to find that the work had been lost. The bugs in the marking tool were not fully fixed until the third assignment. The OU recognised the problem that tutors faced in marking the first two assignments by giving them an additional payment.

Teaching T171 was enjoyable and represented a considerable personal development programme for me. The features of T171 described above are largely seen as advantages, but they need to be balanced against a few disadvantages. While there is plenty of CMC dialogue, without face-to-face contact at a study centre it is more difficult to sense the need to provide an individual with educational guidance via an extended conversation. Giving educational guidance remains a problematic area from student enrolment onwards, especially as the enrolment process can itself take place online. It is clearly important to encourage students to take the initiative when they feel that they need educational guidance.

COURSE TEAM AND INSTITUTIONAL EVALUATION

To complete the evaluation cycle I will end this chapter with brief comment on feedback mechanisms on the programme and institutional response. Programme evaluation by the course team was possible at both the informal level and by online questionnaires. It is a unique benefit of this type of CMC-supported programme that the course team can also observe or contribute to the discussions that are taking place in the national and pan-regional conferences (PARC). The discussions represent a major source of lag-free feedback on how students and tutors are finding the course and where changes might be considered for the next presentation.

A full evaluation of a 1999 pilot course was undertaken by the OU's Institute of Educational Technology. A commentary on one area of results is available in the form of a dialogue between the evaluator and course team chair (Mason & Weller, 2000). They discuss the findings as they relate to students' satisfaction with the course. Seven key issues are raised: skills versus academic content, students' previous computing experience, interaction through CMC, online group work, online tutoring, students' lack of time, and revising the course in the light of evaluation. The data was gathered by Web-site questionnaires for students to complete at the end of each of the three modules. Electronic collection leads to fast analysis and has allowed ongoing student and tutor evaluation of each module of the 2000 and 2001 presentations of the course, with quick dissemination of results. For example, to indicate the volume of student evaluation data continuing to be available to the course team in 2001, 4,161 (~60%) students completed the online evaluation for Module 1 after it ended on April 28, 2001. The analysed data was placed in the tutor conference on June 9, 2001, thus enabling all tutors to be promptly updated on key course issues as they emerged. The analysis included the usability of the Web material, as assessed by how much students were printing out materials and why it was printed out, and how and for what reason individuals are using the tutor group conferences.

Another source of evaluation data is usage of the T171 Website; see Table 1, which is based on data from the T171 Office to the tutor team (Personal Communication, July 20, 2001).

The maximum hit rate data in March is most likely explained by the fact that an assignment was due at the end of the month. The student population of ~ 7,000 in the period gives a hit rate of ~ nine per user per day in March and approximately three to four per user per day in other months. These data reflect the interactive nature of activity in the course, which is typically to study some T171 text, use a link to another site to seek information and then return to the course Website for directions on the next task. For the volume of hits, the relatively low percentage of failures, > 1.0 and < 3.0, illustrates an acceptable robustness of the server.

In terms of overall success rates, of the 7,385 students who finally enrolled on the February course in 2000, 52.5% proceeded to final assessment and, of these, 95.5% passed (OU Planning Office, 2001). The final registration percentage and overall success rate were similar to that for T172 (another component in the Technology Level 1 suite) and that for MU120 (a course in the Maths Level 1 suite), but these courses are taught by the classical OU model. Withdrawals were a

Table 1: T171 Website usage, March-June 2001

Measure	Period		
	March	April	June
Total hits	1934981	627316	793834
Mean hits/day	60953	20322	26181
Mean session time, min,	19	16	18
% Failed hits	2.34	2.81	1.05

concern, and a bimodal distribution of difficulty was identified. Some initially registered students lacked basic computer literacy and found the pace and range of the course too great. Others, often highly computer literate, had assumed that the course would teach them more about Web-site design. They tended to find the collaborative work and the academic focus in Module 2 and 3 difficult. The course review led to a major change and decision to split T171 into two separate courses. Module 1 was repackaged to become a separate 10 CATS points course (TU170) aimed at improving computing skills, including basic Web page design, and give an introduction to collaborative learning via CMC. This was first presented in May 2001. To cater for the needs of the more experienced, a revised version of T171 was presented in February 2002, consisting of Modules 2 and 3 from the current course with a new module on e-commerce.

CONCLUSION

The T171 example of mass online tuition by the OU has been successful in several dimensions. The extensive use of CMC for discussions, particularly in collaborative projects, fundamentally changes the traditional roles and relationships between tutors, students and course team. There is no longer a single tight link between a personal tutor and his/her students. A vibrant learning community emerges which encourages students, tutors and course team to share ideas with and learn from each other and thus enhances the evaluation of the programme. Co-learning, co-tuition and co-counseling are emergent characteristics of online programmes supported by CMC. Once an initial bug with the electronic marking tool had been fixed, teaching on the course was a rewarding experience.

The CMC arrangements also enable efficient administrative and academic information flow between the course team or T171 Office, and students and tutors. It also enables fast feedback and represents an effective source of informal evaluation. Web-site collection of student questionnaire data leads to fast analysis and has allowed evaluation of each module of the 2000 and 2001 presentations of the course, with quick dissemination of results to teaching staff. Without this, full evaluation of a course with 8,500 students would be impracticable.

The university has an online foundation course which is deliverable via robust server and system arrangements to students anywhere in the world. Given careful design of systems and materials, the absence of face-to-face tutorial contact can be largely offset. Indeed, monitoring of student progress is more effective than with the conventional OU model. Without regular face-to-face contact, there is more likelihood that the need for an individual student to have on-course education guidance is missed. Also, the case study shows that educational guidance for an open-entry programme of this type, especially by online registration, is highly important. Problems arise if students are not adequately prepared to begin the course or if it does not match their expectations. The OU should review pre-entry and on-course educational guidance arrangements as part of the evaluation of the impact of the decision to split T171 into two courses from 2002.

REFERENCES

Cringely, R. X. (1996). *Accidental empires*. London: Penguin.

Dyer, G. C. (1991). Empowerment and reduction of isolation of housebound disabled students: A computer-mediated communications project at the UK Open University. *Electronic Networking*, *1*(2), 23-28.

Mason, R. (1989). An evaluation of CoSy on an Open University course. In R. Mason & A. Kaye (Eds.), *Mindweave: Communication, computers and distance education* (pp. 115-145). Oxford, England: Pergamon Press.

Mason, R. (1999). *IET's masters in open and distance education: What have we learned?* Retrieved March 12, 2002, from Open University, Institute of Educational Technology Web site: http://iet.open.ac.uk/pp/r.d.mason/down-loads/MAEval.PDF

Mason, R., & Weller, M. (2000). Factors affecting students' satisfaction on a Web course. *Australian Journal of Educational Technology*, *16*(2), 173-200. Retrieved March 12, 2002, from http://cleo.murdoch.edu.au/ajet/ajet16/mason.HTML

Open University Planning Office (2001) (published in OU Staff Diary 2001 and various other internal open sources).

Salmon, G. (2000). *E-moderating: The key to teaching and learning online* London: Kogan Page.

Weller, M. (1999). A large scale Internet based course for computer beginners. In B. Collis & R. Oliver (Eds.), *Proceedings EdMedia 99*. Seattle, WA: Association for the Advancement of Computing in Education (AACE), Vancouver.

Weller, M. (2000a). Creating a large-scale third-generation distance education course. *Open Learning*, *15*(3), 243-252.

Weller, M. (2000b). The use of narrative to provide a cohesive structure for a Web based computing course. *Journal of Interactive Media in Education*, *2000*(1). Retrieved March 13, 2002, from http://www-jime.open.ac.uk/00/1

Chapter XVI

Learnability

Philip Duchastel
Information Design Atelier, USA

ABSTRACT

This chapter discusses usability in terms of the concept of learnability, that is, what makes the content of an online learning site learnable? It considers three core issues underlying learnability: learning theory, instructional design, and curriculum choices. For learning, it proposes a model integrating comprehension, interest, and memorizing. For design, it distinguishes between representational models, illustrative cases, and simple facts. For curriculum content, it suggests focusing on structural issues and contrasts content design with process design. In looking to the future, it emphasizes information design as the true basis for learnability and places online instruction within the larger context of all instructional design.

NATURE OF LEARNABILITY

The usability of online learning programs can be broken down into two distinct issues: the usability of an online university site and the learnability of the course contents.

The first issue concerns the more usual Web site usability questions, such as how easy it is for new visitors to orient themselves and get a good overview of what the online university offers and what is involved for themselves in e-learning. Or again, we might consider how easy it is for the actual students to interact with the course materials while engaged in learning. These are the traditional issues of usability, important to consider but hardly the most interesting.

It is the second issue, that of learnability, that is the more pressing for designers and educators. The basic question is this: What makes the content of a site (or of some resource) learnable? Take any one of the many thousands of online learning courses currently available on the Web and ask yourself: Does this course seem difficult to learn (assuming you have the proper background for it)? What would improve it? What would the ideal online course in this area look like? These questions all underlie the learnability of the course.

What then is learnability? Could we say that it is defined by successful learning? That would mean that students who study the course thoroughly learn its content, as evidenced on a good test, for instance. Or could we say that a main criterion is ease of learning? That would mean that students experience good intellectual flow and enjoy the course.

Both of these factors, success in learning and enjoyment of learning, can be considered criteria of learnability. Are there others? That is the issue of learnability and that is what is explored in this chapter.

The Locus of Learnability

The skeptic will immediately insist that learning takes place within a learner and that it is that locus that mainly determines learnability—that is, the curiosity, intelligence, motivation and persistence of the learner. These are what make or break learning. The teaching materials can only go so far; the learner has to make a go of it, make it succeed.

While there is some truth to that view, it is certainly not the full picture nor the most useful picture. Consider traditional usability in Web sites or software products. There too, the user plays a role. If he is very dull-witted, or perhaps too pressed for time (showing a lack of interest), or just resistant to learning the basics (you know, jumping in and thrashing around—as often happens), well, there is little scope for success no matter how usable the site or program may have been made.

But we don't give up on usability because of that. We acknowledge the limitations and make assumptions about both the state of the user and the context of usage, then proceed to design to those assumptions. It may not be comprehensive, but it is practical and that is a useful value.

The point is we do not blame the user for incompetence, for ill will or for the lack of success of our site or program. We maximize usability, realizing well enough that usability is certainly contextual. The same applies, as it should, to learnability: success in learning can be maximized through the product, over and beyond context issues (or in spite of them).

The product view of instruction is an important one, one that is emphasized in the discussion below. An alternate view is a process one: learning is a process and so is instruction, in the sense of manipulating the situation so as to facilitate learning. The process view is not to be denigrated, but a product view can incorporate processes and has definite design advantages. Leanability, it is argued, is best considered in this light.

Learnability of course materials starts then in an attitude, one of ascribing merit to the design of the materials. We may not be able to do much about the state of the learners or about the context of learning (those being educational issues in the institutional sense), but we can maximize learnability via the design of the materials.

Just consider this basic notion: We can all usually identify poor learning materials, even though we will have trouble in the borderland between good and bad and additional trouble in explicating clearly what the features of excellent learning materials might be. In sum, therefore, learnability is a very real issue.

LEADING QUESTIONS

The challenge before us is to identify those features of excellent learning materials. What makes something learnable? Very learnable, most learnable?

But first, why is it so difficult to pinpoint these features? What are the deep issues underlying learnability? There are three of them I want to raise and discuss in this chapter. They are learning, design, and curriculum. Each is difficult in its own right and learnability involves considering them jointly—you can see the magnitude of the challenge.

The first deep question is what is learning? The field of learning has long been a core issue in psychology, and numerous theories of learning have been put forth in answer. The issue is far from settled, as practitioners such as educators well know (Cotton, 1996). There is acknowledgment of different kinds of learning, with different factors at play, but no large agreement on these or on the overall picture (Catania, 1998).

The second deep question concerns teaching. How do you design for learning? There are general principles that have evolved over time, codified broadly in what is known as the field of instructional design (Reigeluth, 1999b). But here too, there is hardly agreement. All of course will subscribe to general systems principles like those found in software design or in HCI. All subscribe to the value of usability testing, the trying out of the materials designed with sample students in order to verify the strength of the design and capture any ways of improvement. But given divergences in views of learning, it is natural that hard disagreements will occur here too, in how to design for learning.

The third deep question concerns what to teach, the content. At first, you might think that this is an outside issue: that you first decide what to teach, then only after that, how to teach it, how to design it. Or you might think that teachers and curriculum specialists or professors and institutions determine the content "to be covered." Or you might even think that learnability applies to any content, whatever it is determined it should be. But that overlooks the crucial notion that the what and the how of learning are inextricably linked, just as in communication more generally. An instructional designer must fashion the content as much as the process, in the same way an information designer fashions information well beyond the graphic design aspect.

Both are information architects, but that is not yet widely recognized, which creates great difficulties for learnability.

We need to consider each of these three issues in turn in addressing learnability. Given the theoretical divergences that enrich the debate, it is impossible to be impartial or to be too firm in one's perspective. Any representation of learnability will thus be one among many possible.

LEARNING—THE CIM MODEL

At its most general, learning is the process of internalizing information in memory, making that information available later on, when needed. But learning the names of the bones in the body and learning the principles of acoustics are rather different forms of learning. We learn them in different ways. What are the commonalities? What are the differences?

There are three types of learning, conveniently contrasted in what we can call the CIM model. CIM stands for comprehension, interest, and memorizing, these being the three factors involved in the learning process.

Comprehension is based on our ability to reason, to fit things together, to see how they all work together. Comprehension is the process of generating internal models of the world in all its workings, large and small. We comprehend when we see how things fit together, how it all makes sense. Learning how the ear processes sound, for instance, involves building a cognitive model of how the ear's structures handle the acoustic vibrations that fall on them. Understanding is a process of rational model building.

Interest, the second element in CIM, is the attentional factor in learning. If something stands out from its context, it will be more easily remembered, as will things that are extremely vivid or of great personal importance. More usually, we try to learn things that are only of mild interest and then, if attention wanders, learning suffers. Interest has the function of keeping us on task.

The third element, memorizing, handles things that do not fit well together, that have no basis in rationality. The name "cochlea," used to represent one of the components of the ear, is quite arbitrary to us—there is no reason for it (no reason that we know). To us, it is simply formally stated and no amount of reasoning will assist in "understanding" it. We just have to mentally associate the name and the component.

These then are the elements of learning, each contributing in its own way to capture information and internalize it in memory. Each has certain ways to run smoothly as a process. Comprehension can be enhanced by varying perspective, by seeing something from a different angle. Interest can be engaged strongly through interactivity, a technique much used in many different forms of instruction. And memory of arbitrary elements can be solidified through repeated practice. At a general level, these PIP strategies (perspective, interactivity, and practice) are the processes engaged in to provoke learning. We can do it ourselves if we have the initiative, or we can let educators create the learning environment that will do it for us through various forms of instruction.

Validity of the Model

What of the validity of the CIM model? There is a very general and traditional description of learning as simply the acquisition of knowledge and skills (a unitary definition of learning), but we quickly realize it is too general when we consider processes. Learning the multiplication table and learning to solve mathematical equations involve different, incompatible learning processes.

While there are different types of learning, there is no agreement on exactly what these types are (Duchastel, 1998). The view of comprehension and memorizing as two important types has been long accepted in educational psychology, often called meaningful versus rote learning, or cognitive versus associative learning. But what about interest as a type of learning?

We often consider interest as a condition of learning, or as a factor of learning, or even as a secondary result of learning. But one could say the same about meaningfulness (in the case of comprehension) and of explicitness (in the case of memorizing). Describing learning is indeed tricky.

While interest may not be a type of learning as such, the case for interest as a type of motivation is more appealing, for it corresponds to a psychological process distinct from the other two types. Comprehending and memorizing are two processes, as is also becoming and remaining interested in something. Considering learning to involve three distinct processes directs our thinking in considering how to design for learning, and hence learnability.

DESIGN—THE MOCAF MODEL

Based on the CIM model, we can see that there will be three types of elements that are needed within an instructional product: models, cases, and facts. Combining these (and any product would have all three) leads to the acronym MoCaF for the design model appropriate for the creation of highly learnable instructional products.

Models are the tools of understanding; they are what lead to comprehension. Cases are the illustrative materials that instantiate the models in particular settings. They are the main means of grabbing and holding attention. As for facts, they are just the basics that need to be brutely memorized.

Let us look at each of these three components in turn. I will illustrate them with a discussion of what might be involved in a medical instructional product dealing with hearing and the ear.

Models

Models are what drive comprehension. The aim of design in this area is to create models that embody the disparate elements of content while synthesizing them in an artifact (the model) that clearly communicates and is easily learned. Models show how elements relate to one another; they capture relationships and interactions.

The craft of developing models is one of establishing the underlying structures in a field (content expertise is essential here) and of then representing those structures in synthetic form that facilitates communication and understanding (Wurman, 2000).

Graphic design is a field that has very similar goals when it deals with explanatory designs. A well-known case, not dealing with instruction but with navigation, is the design of the London underground (subway) map, as are subway maps generally speaking. All these are models in that they structure the appropriate information in abstract designs that simplify in order to better communicate and be understood.

In a medical course about the ear, a number of such models are needed to cover the student's needs. The following models can be seen as appropriate:
1.   Structure of the ear
2.   Functioning of the ear
3.   Abnormalities of structure
4.   Ill-functioning
5.   Diagnostic process
6.   Therapy

These six models are interesting in more ways than one. First, notice the parallels between the first two and the next two—models of normalcy and abnormalcy, respectively. Then, consider the last two: models of action to redress a situation (that being the aim of medicine)—the first four models representing what is, rather than what to do. In that category, we also have an internal distinction (one versus two and three versus four) between structure and function.

These relationships can all be fitted into a table that models the structure of the knowledge in this field (see Table 1).

Now, a further interesting point here is that this knowledge model fits not only the ear, but other body parts as well. It pretty well covers all of individual medicine and can become a framework for medical information and medical education as a whole. Generalizing even more, it can be seen as a structure that can be useful in

Table 1:   Knowledge model relationships

	Normalcy	**Abnormalcy**	**Correction**
Situation	Structure	Abnormalities	
	Function	Ill-functioning	
Action		Diagnosis	Therapy

modeling many fields, perhaps most. In particular professional fields, emphasis may be placed in one model or another, but all models are active in their own way.

Cases

Cases are the illustrative material in instructional content. They embody the living problems and the living application of the models. They range from simple examples to complex case studies. Of particular interest are those relatively complex cases that mirror difficult real-life settings, such as those used in problem-based medical education or in business education.

Cases are multifunctional in an instructional application. At least three functions can be served:

1. To illustrate the content of a model, instantiating it and situating it in real life.
2. To provide practice to the student in applying knowledge.
3. To test the student's knowledge (either self-testing for monitoring purposes or formal testing for assessment and validation purposes).

So, for instance, medical students studying the ear would be shown actual cases of structural malformations so that these might be recognized later on when patients are examined. Cases depicting patients arriving at the clinic with various symptoms could be posed as problems for the student to solve, either to practice applying the models or to assess the student's level of mastery.

Developing cases is generally a labor-intensive process, whose value is also often under-rated. If we consider our knowledge as being dimensionalized in terms of abstraction, cases are the concrete instances of what is encountered in the world, whereas models are the abstract, simplified representations of those structures and events. A full knowledge of a field involves comfortably sliding along back and forth on the full range of this dimension.

Facts

Facts are those ill-fitting elements of knowledge that are considered important to know and that hang out there on their own, only incidentally attached to some model or other.

In the domain of the ear, for instance, terminology is factual, as are various side effects of drugs used in therapy, as is also the incidence of various types of ear infection. None of these cohere naturally in a model, but yet they are essential to know and must be learned.

Facts are simple to state, for instance, in a textbook or in a presentation. But that does not ensure they will be learned. While simple to state, facts are hard to enrobe in a context that will make them easily learnable. As indicated in the section on learning, practice or an eventful context is needed. There are means to accomplish this in instructional terms, such as through games, problems, contests, high-impact media, etc. Often, though, when these are not developed, the student is left pretty much to his or her own devices for rehearsing the facts to be learned. This is not an optimal situation.

Much more can be said about models, cases, and facts and about how to design instructional applications to enhance their learnability. More will be said in the next section in dealing with content, but only so much, as this is a broad topic in itself and needs separate and more elaborate treatment on its own.

CONTENT

Learning involves interacting with information. And so it is the design of that information that is crucial to learnability. We are dealing here with the content of the instructional product, that content being modeled through design into a certain form that makes it understandable, interesting, and memorizable.

Dealing With Content

It is often thought that the content of an instructional product is given, that it is an entity that preexists, and therefore that instructional design is the craft of designing the presentation and surrounding the content with activities that will help the student acquire the content.

This is an unhealthy view of instructional design because that initial assumption about content is wrong. The content is not simply there, to be communicated. Each actual representation of the content is already an expression of it, a way of putting it. There can be no content without expression.

Every depiction of instructional content, whether in formal fields like the scientific ones or more interpretive ones like the humanities, is a model. Each is a statement of the content at a certain level of complexity. Every model is a simplification, an overlay on reality to help bring out its structure or functioning.

The design of those models is crucial to learnability. It is what will make the content learnable—easy, or difficult, or impossible to learn. The models are what anchor the entire content of a particular field in an overall coherent structure that the student can assimilate and then use beneficially in building his or her own cognitive structures to represent the field internally. It is also those coherent cognitive structures that will help the student overcome any preconceptions that he or she may have brought to the learning situation.

Models essentially provide structure to hang particulars on, and so the main issue with models will be that of levels. Broad models encompass many more specific models, which contain still more detailed models, which in turn relate the particular facts to one another. A definite hierarchy is involved, from the broad, simplified models at the top to the detailed, complex information at the bottom.

In the medical information of the ear discussed in the previous section, a broad model of medical knowledge is involved at the top level: It relates normal structure and functioning to abnormal forms of them and then to medical action (diagnosis and treatment). Then, each of these six components forms its own model, for instance, a model of the structure of the ear. And each is broken down into further, more detailed models describing more particular and complex elements. Learning about the ear involves principally learning these models.

As mentioned above, instructional design has not traditionally paid great attention to this structural issue, focusing instead on process aspects of the situation. There are, however, two instructional theories that stand out in their attention to the structural modeling issue and the need to consider hierarchy in learning: Ausubel's (1968) advance organizer theory and Reigeluth's (1999a) elaboration theory. Both call for a progression from broad, organizing models to more specific, elaborate ones as a basis for sequencing the learning experience. Both deal directly with models even if they do not use that descriptor.

The detailed content complement to models, which abstract from reality and simplify, are the cases, which provide the flesh of reality in all its complexity. As for the facts, they just hang loose, without rime or reason, but still have to be learned.

Instructional theory has recently focused on cases in a major way through approaches known as problem-based teaching, simulations, and instructional design based on constructivism (Jonassen, 1999). These varied approaches encourage the learners to approach complex issues from their own perspective and figure things out while pulling them together. The main value of cases (problems) is seen in the interest factor, accentuated by the complexity and the challenge of the situation requiring personal investment and deep problem-solving.

While cases are necessarily particularistic, their complexity can vary and this type of content therefore requires design. The case has to be simple enough to be tackled and yet complex enough to challenge, those factors being dependent of course on the assumed sophistication of the learner.

Context Design and Process Design

Models, cases, and facts are all basically information content of particular sorts, information with which the learner will interact during learning. To a very large extent, then, instructional design is mostly a matter of information design, a notion that needs to become widely recognized. Even the more recent notion of interaction design (often applied to Web site design or to exhibition design) is largely a matter of information design involving models (structures), cases (events), and facts (impressions). In sum, learnability must focus primarily on the content to be included in an instructional product, i.e., on information design.

Now, we might ask whether a product or a process view of design is the better one? Instruction can be viewed both ways and instructional design theory needs to consider both (Duchastel, 1998). As mentioned there, learning is an interaction with information products and occurs over time in an organized sequence fashioned as an event. All products unfold events, just as all events involve products.

The product view, however, is better for the designer and for the learnability analyst. The product is the artifact that directs the interaction and that is fully examinable as a designed artifact. It is public, while interactions involve private cognitive processes that are harder to capture and more ephemeral and hence difficult to deal with.

The product embodies the learning event and hence is the locus of learnability. It is what we can most easily point to, comment on, and improve; it is that part of an instructional situation that is touchable. It is basically what instructional designers design.

This is not to say that we focus only on content and not on interaction, on feedback, on level of directivity, learner adaptability, etc.—those being essential elements of consideration in the traditional design of instruction. What the product focus means is that all these traditional criteria of educational soundness must be considered as they are incorporated and embodied in the instructional product. The product shapes all these processes (or not, depending on the case).

But the focus on information design is more crucial in another respect. At its core, information design is an abstraction process, one of determining what to include and what to leave out, in effect, determining at what level and how to present specific content. The subway map mentioned earlier is prototypical of all information design in this respect. It simplifies, it codes (color-coding) and it eliminates the unnecessary detail.

The same abstraction process must be engaged by the instructional designer, who, before deciding how to present information, must first decide what to present (and what to leave out), i.e., what level of abstraction is warranted in any given model, case, or list of facts. All the details that are mandated by those who control the curriculum may eventually be presented (in further sub-models, etc.), but how the models are designed is an information design issue, a learnability issue. Learning the subway map of your city might be pretty easy by contrast to learning how to deal with the ear and its problems, but both tasks follow similar routes and are made easier by similar processes of information design. There is full scalability of process.

FUTURE

Perhaps the strongest thrust of the argument in this chapter is that to take learnability seriously, one must go beyond superficial design issues and tackle deep concerns in still murky theoretical fields. Not an easy process, to be sure, particularly since it goes up against established traditions—ones that we must rethink if we want to advance the study and practice of learnability.

What are these many traditions? The foremost to overcome is the practice mentioned earlier of assuming that learning success is mostly due to the learner rather than to the learning materials. It is never all one or the other of course, but the balance of responsibility is traditionally skewed. The implication underlying the assumption is that since the learning materials are prepared by someone in the know (the teacher, author, professor; in sum, the expert), they must be fine. The confusion of content expertise with expertise in learning and design is very evident, but yet the tradition persists in a widespread manner. Accepting learnability as a factor in learning is a first step in removing the confusion.

A second tradition to tackle is the one prevalent in some software circles, that the interface designer can add bells and whistles and otherwise enhance appeal and ease of use, but heaven forbid any transgressions into the actual design of the software. By extension, the instructional designer can come up with novel twists to interest the learner, but heaven forbid any thoughts of restructuring the content. Information architecture teams comprising expertise in varied areas must design from the ground up, in an open fashion, through deep respect for the value of collaboration. Any nostalgia for the Frank Lloyd Wright stance of illustrious creator must be done away with.

A third tradition to overcome is a paradoxical one: that more is better and yet we offer less than needed. This should be read as follows: that more verbose content (explanations, extrapolations, etc.) is naturally helpful, but that illustrations and cases are too expensive to include and are thus left out. This is the ease-of-preparation tradition that assumes wrongly that learnability can be had at cheap cost (the professor will simply put together the course). Professors may not have the time to do good case studies, but they are often at ease in being verbose.

Three traditions that come in the way of learnability, not because of ill intent, but simply because any novel scheme to do things differently is ... well, different. That after all is what a tradition is. We are on grounds very familiar to usability experts here.

Information Design

Perhaps the greatest trend emerging in the future with respect to learnability will be the continuing merging of instructional design into information design. As access to information becomes more ready, we will likely see a reduction of our need to memorize arbitrary information beyond the frequently used or crucial to know kind. Our external memory supports will fill the need for the less-needed information.

This merging of the two traditionally distinct design worlds (information and instruction) is particularly informative for the learner-control issue in education. Adult learners like to have more control (or like to think they do) over what they learn, how they learn it and when they learn. They operate more in an access mode than in a traditionally receptive educational mode.

Well-designed information/instruction products will facilitate this approach, being used at times for informational purposes and at other times for instructional purposes. Informal learning (outside of academic structures) and formal instruction both involve learning, both involve interacting with information, both profit from good information design.

The issue of learner control is not an easy one, for it touches on the very nature of instruction as a deliberate attempt to organize learning in a focused way and, at its core, an intentional, albeit benevolent, effort to influence a person's thinking (Duchastel, 1998). Irrespective of philosophical views, though, it remains that learning will be impacted by this merging of information design and instructional design.

Learnability for Online Learning

Finally, the issue of generality must be considered. Learnability as discussed here applies to all pedagogical contexts. But does each specific one have perhaps additional learnability constraints or requirements? In particular, does online learning have specific requirements all its own?

My answer is generally negative. Any specific situation will have constraints and needs that are particular to it—a specific anticipated audience, with certain prerequisites and not others, a controlled time frame, perhaps pre-dictated media usage or other conditions, and so on. And a designer will naturally adapt the design accordingly.

Concern may be voiced over the lack of attention in this respect to cultural factors and the communicability of the information (its linguistic and more general cultural grounding). These are important context factors, but we must not overestimate their role in learning. The plasticity of cognition and the general processes of learning are yet more important and give a certain universality to learnability.

While still important, these context issues are all nevertheless secondary to the learnability issues discussed above. So while there are additional features to specific instructional situations, it remains the general learnability factors that must be primarily considered in establishing the usability of an instructional product.

This applies to online instruction as well as to more traditional forms. There are technical limitations that flavor the tone of current online instruction, such as information transfer rates, limits to the forms of communication, etc., but all these are but temporary constraints that will be overcome in time. The design constraints will likewise change with time. What will remain are the general learnability factors.

The design of e-learning materials also might offer more means of controlling interaction than does, for instance, the design of a textbook or of other printed materials. This may or may not be an advantage, depending on a whole host of factors, such as maturity of the learners, prior knowledge of the learners, and other context factors. But it does raise once again the general issue of content versus process.

This philosophical issue remains a challenging one, as well as a thorn in any attempt to devise an overarching theory of learning and instruction. One facet of this issue, and I will conclude with it, is why we speak of the learnability of instructional products. After all, we learn also a great deal from interacting with the world at large, not just with artifacts.

The way to come to grips with this issue is to adopt a wide conception of information, as does the field of semiotics. Information goes far beyond the written word and beyond the world of illustration too. Information is structure that lies within the world around us, both in its structural elements and in its processes. Some of these are found elements; others are designed artifacts and therefore ones the design of which we can control. This is where we can affect the learnability of a product or of a structured process.

CONCLUSION

This chapter discussed usability in terms of the concept of learnability, that is, what makes the content of an online learning site learnable? While this is not the only question relevant to the usability of an online learning site, it is certainly the most important, for learning is the whole purpose of the site.

We considered three core issues underlying learnability: learning theory, instructional design, and curriculum choices. For learning, we considered a model integrating comprehension, interest, and memorizing (the CIM model). For design, we distinguished between representational models, illustrative cases, and simple facts (the MoCaF model). For curriculum content, we suggested focusing on structural issues and we found it useful to contrast content design with process design.

In looking to the future, information design was stressed as the true basis for learnability. This becomes particularly evident as informal learning from online resources gains in importance and as online learning resources that accompany formal educational programs continue to multiply. These trends serve to place online instruction within the larger context of all instructional design. They emphasize the similarities between online and traditional instruction, rather than their gradually disappearing differences.

I hope to have convinced you in this chapter that the usability of learning materials in terms of learnability is of tremendous value to pursue. Imagine not only how performance can be improved through learnability design, but also how much anguish in learning might be eliminated, or at any rate lessened, and what that could do for the practical nature of education. Bringing learnability to this massive enterprise is indeed a worthy cause.

ACKNOWLEDGMENTS

I am grateful for comments from colleagues, particularly from Reinhard Oppermann (Fraunhofer Institute for Applied Information Technology, Germany) and Markus Molz (Universität Koblenz-Landau).

REFERENCES

Ausubel, D. (1968). *Educational psychology: A cognitive view.* New York: Holt, Rinehart and Winston.

Catania, C. (1998). *Learning* (4th ed.). New York: Prentice Hall.

Cotton, J. (1996). *The theory of Learning*. London: Kogan Page.

Duchastel, P. (1998). *Prolegomena to a theory of instructional design*. ITFORUM, Article 27. Retrieved on November 26, 2002, from http://itech1.coe.uga.edu/itforum/paper27/paper27.html

Jonassen, D. (1999). Designing constructivist, case-based learning environments. In C. Reigeluth (Ed.), *Instructional design theories and models: A new paradigm of instructional theory* (Vol. 2, pp. 185-203). Mahwah, NJ: Erlbaum.

Reigeluth, C. (1999a). The elaboration theory: Guidance for scope and sequence decisions. In C. Reigeluth (Ed.), *Instructional design theories and models: A new paradigm of instructional theory* (Vol. 2, pp. 374-389). Mahwah, NJ: Erlbaum.

Reigeluth, C. (1999b). (Ed.). *Instructional design theories and models: A new paradigm of instructional theory* (Vol. 2). Mahwah, NJ: Erlbaum.

Wurman, R. S. (2000). *Information anxiety 2*. Indianapolis, IN: Que.

Chapter XVII

Usability Evaluation of Online Learning Programs: A Sociological Standpoint

Bernard Blandin
CESI-Online, France

ABSTRACT

"Usability" addresses the relationship between tools and their users. Such a relationship is generally considered as independent of any contextual, social or cultural aspects: Usability criteria relate to "human factors" taken as universal. But users do not live or act in an abstract world in which they are alone with the tool they are using. Users, as human beings, live and act in a world which is at the same time social and material. This paper provides some clues on how teacher's or trainer's epistemological stance, learner's motivation, organisational learning culture and environmental factors interact to produce conditions determining the use of online learning programs. As a consequence, usability has to take into account the user's social and material environment. This is why, according to the author, usability has to be "situated."

INTRODUCTION

In its broad sense, "usability" addresses the relationship between tools and their users. Usability depends on a number of factors measuring how well the functionality of the tool fits user needs. For software, this may include how well the flow through the application fits user tasks, how well the response of the application fits user expectations, etc. Generally, this relationship between a human being and an artifact or an object is considered as independent of any contextual, social or cultural aspects: Usability criteria relate to "human factors" considered as universal.

From a designer's viewpoint, usability is seen as a relationship between a human being and an artifact which measures the productivity of a user using the artifact (Nielsen, 1994). This global approach may appear confusing, since it does not distinguish between two usability-related concepts, "ease of use" and "usefulness." Therefore, I prefer to use the extended notion of usability proposed by Notess (2001), following Norman and the "user-centred design" school of the University of California, which distinguishes clearly between this two usability-related concepts but takes them both into account into its notion of "usability." This also responds to the questions crossing "utility" and "usability" raised by authors like Grudin (1992) or more recently Tricot and Tricot (2000) and Tricot and Lafontaine (2002).

I will make the case for a strong dependence of "usability" on social and cultural aspects, because the use of any object is a social activity, implicitly implying social relations belonging to different registers (Blandin, 2002). I will demonstrate that there are no universal "human factors" on which to build usability criteria and that, for this reason, we have to take into account contingency factors, for which we need appropriate conceptualisation.

The discussion in this chapter will focus on usability of online learning programs, but I do think that the thesis in this chapter applies more generally and there is a general issue at stake here: Usability evaluation should not be limited to consider "simply ease of use of a tool" criteria, but should also take into account all the conditions which lead a user to actually use a tool. Technology museums are full of products that people found easy to use, but which have never been used (Jennings, 2001), and many current e-learning programs seem to be good examples of such products, if we follow Quinn (2001)!

This chapter is rather theoretical and therefore targets first those who are not only looking for practical guidelines to develop usable online learning programs, but are also looking for thought-provoking discussions of the notion of usability. I will present and discuss both the narrow and extended notion of "usability" used in software design and engineering, in order to show that "usefulness" is a social issue and that evaluation of usability has to take this fact into account. I will then propose enhanced usability heuristics, illustrated by case studies. Then, I will put forward some hypothesis on social factors which impact usability of online learning programs. And finally, I will propose to develop a sociological standpoint on usability and on "user experience," as named by Norman (1988). At the end of this chapter, the reader will understand:

- why usability should take into account social and cultural factors,
- which factors impact on usability of e-learning, besides the interface-design-related factors which are the more commonly cited,

- why new learning cultures have often to be implemented to make online learning programs usable, and
- why implementation of self-directed learning situations is necessary to fully develop online learning programs' usability.

Background

Usability, in its primary sense in the field of software design and engineering, is synonymous of "ergonomical issues." It intends to define rules to design the application in order to match users' habits—whatever they are—various types of equipments, various languages, etc. One of the fathers of the discipline, in his latest books on Web usability, focuses on page, content, site and intranet design, addressing issues such as viewing pages on various monitor sizes, which has to be disconnected to writing concise texts for "scanability," or paying attention to users with disabilities or international users (Nielsen, 1999).

The basic principles of a good design for usability are described in Norman (1988):

1. Provide a good conceptual model,
2. Make things visible,
3. Map the controls, their movements and their results in the real world,
4. Provide feedback for any actions.

In the field of e-learning, an illustration of how these principles apply to online learning programs' design can be found in Quinn's findings concerning widespread usability problems of e-learning products (Quinn, 2001, p. 3):

- "counter-intuitive reading order of on-screen material" (breaking Rule 1),
- "failure to relate to the real-world experience of the user" (breaking Rule 3),
- "poor presentation of key information" (breaking Rule 2),
- "lack of accessibility, even in the most basic sense" (breaking simultaneously all the rules, as shown in the examples given in the following pages of Quinn's paper).

No doubt that Norman's rules and user-centred design principles, also called "usability engineering" (Notess, 2001), apply to online learning programs and that their application may, in some sense, facilitate their use. Elaboration on these rules led Nielsen to propose his "ten usability heuristics" (Nielsen, n.d.), in which we find the same principles. I would argue that to apply these types of rules to designing e-learning programs will never guarantee that they will be "usable." My discussion will be twofold: I will first discuss these rules from cognitive standpoints, then from sociological ones.

I will start by questioning the first rule: Is it possible to find a "good conceptual model"? What is a "conceptual model"? According to researchers in the field of cognitive sciences, such as M. Johnson and G. Lakoff, "conceptual models" are based on "image schemata" and their metaphorical projections onto languages (Johnson, 1987) and linguistic categories (Lakoff, 1987). These schemata and these categories literally *format* meaning and reasoning within a particular human group (Johnson, 1987; Lakoff, 1987; Lakoff & Johnson, 1999).

Without looking too much in depth into this topic, since I have already done it in previous writings (see References), I will just highlight the conclusion that we must draw from this: *There is no universal "good conceptual model."* All conceptual models are formatted by language and categories and are specific to a particular population. Evidence is given by Lakoff's numerous examples, among which are the Dyirbal (an Australian aboriginal tribe) classification of the universe into four categories, which disappear when the young generations start to learn English, or the Japanese "Hon" category, regrouping long objects (hairs as well as sticks or pencils, candles, etc.), which has no equivalent in any other language (Lakoff, 1987). Even what could appear to us as a basic human category, based on human physiology, such as colour categories, is a cultural production, and the ability to distinguish between two colours, like blue and green, appears to be related to the fact that these categories can be named in a given language, as shown by the Kay-Kempton experiment comparing English-speaking subjects and Dani-only-speaking subjects—a New Guinea tribe which only distinguishes two categories of colours and for whom blue and green belong to the same category (Kay & Kempton, 1984). The epistemological consequences of such an experiment are analysed in Varela, Thompson, and Rosch (1993).

This leads to an evidence: Usability of a software tool, even in its restricted sense, has to be related to the cultural context in which the tool has to be used. Just think that the "intuitive reading order" rule proposed by Quinn (2001) cannot produce the same screen layout in Western countries, in Japan, or in Arabic countries, because reading order in these cultures is different. What is true for any software tool should be true for online learning programs, since learning is a process deeply rooted in a particular culture and even diversified within a given culture into several "learning styles" addressed by different "learning cultures."

Secondly, I will question the concept of "real world," which appears to be the ultimate reference for the user to be taken into account by designers from the "social constructivism" standpoint (Berger & Luckmann, 1966). Is this "real world"—which also appears as the second of Nielsen's (n.d.) usability heuristics—unique? From the social constructivism viewpoint, the answer is, definitely, "No!" The "real world" is a social construction which arises from situations which the subject is confronted with. The "situated cognition" approach is rooted on similar considerations. As far as tools are concerned, this means, as expressed by Brown, Collins, and Duguid (1989, p.33), that

> *"the occasions and conditions for use arise directly out of the context of activities of each community that uses the tool, framed by the way members of that community see the world. The community and its viewpoint, quite as much as the tool itself, determine how a tool is used. Thus, carpenters and cabinet makers use chisels differently."*

Again, this leads us to the conclusion that social and cultural context has to be taken into account to evaluate usability.

Thirdly, I will point out another evidence, stemming from sociology of uses. Punie's (1997) findings, in his survey on "non uses" of several ICT applications in Flemish households, reveal that there is a precondition to use a tool: The tool must be part of the response to a particular need. "No need" is the main argument for people to explain why they do not use a device like a videotape recorder, a microcomputer or pay-TV.

So, "usefulness" appears as the primary necessary step to use a tool. "No need" does not mean no relation at all with the object: There could be some cognitive or emotional relation with it; the object can be considered as an indicator of a social status, etc. (Dagognet, 1996; Ling, 1999). If we admit that *"usability addresses the relationship between tools and their users"* (Usability First, n.d.), "usefulness" has to be considered as a component of "usability" in its broader sense. This is also true for online learning programs, as asserted by several recent papers on e-learning usability (Notess, 2001; Quinn, 2001): E-learning programs are not used because of users' lack of motivation to use them, and this has to be taken into account to assess usability, as explicitly stated by Notess. That e-learning programs are not used is also one of the findings of Masie (2001), which goes beyond simply establishing the fact: This survey, conducted in American companies, clearly shows that key factors to successfully implement corporate e-learning programs, i.e., to have them *used* by employees, are mainly determined by the organisation in which the programs are implemented *and not or very little* by the intrinsic characteristics of the programs themselves.

In this survey, e-learning motivators determining acceptance level appear to be the following:

- good advertisement within the company and championship fostering,
- completion time and support provided during working hours,
- creation of an e-learning culture within the company, and
- provision of incentives such as peer recognition and career advance.

Similar findings appear in Sheila Paxton's (2000) white paper on "how to make e-learning work." This clearly means that to successfully implement e-learning programs, organisational support to users' motivation plays the main part. To such an extent, successfully implementing e-learning does not appear to be very different from successfully implementing "organisational learning" within a company. Thus, from the sociology of organisation viewpoint as well, social and cultural context is to be taken into account to set up criteria for usefulness, and therefore for usability criteria.

To conclude, a convergence appears between cognitive approaches and sociological approaches which advocates the importance of cultural and sociological context for determining "usability" of tools, in both its restricted and broad acceptances.

A NEW SET OF USABILITY HEURISTICS TO ACCOUNT FOR CONTEXTUAL DEPENDENCY OF USES

In the previous section, I have given three arguments which show the necessity to take into account the environment in which a tool is used to assess its usability. As for any tool, the use of online learning programs is, to me, heavily dependent on what I call "social schemata of uses" (Blandin, 2002). These social schemata of uses determine and format conditions for using a tool as well as the way the tool is used. These social schemata of uses are literally "embodied" within the users; they "frame" their mind and the way they think about a tool and its uses as well as they determine the ability and the gestures to handle and physically use the tool. These schemata of uses are "social" in the sense that they result from accumulated prior learning in a given culture, from prior acquisition of gestures, postures, image schemata (Johnson, 1987) and therefore ways of thinking, which are themselves productions that human beings build up from their social environment since their birth.

Let's illustrate this point: I always have "usability" problems when I go to North America, where domestic electric appliances, like a hair dryer or a boiler, implementing "user-centred design" recommendations (Norman, 1988) have a "on" button and an "off" button instead of an "on-off" switch as we have in Europe. I know this fact, but my fingers simply *refuse* to use a second button to switch off the device, and my reflex action, always repeated, is always unsuccessful when trying to press again the "on" button. Other similar cases can be provided from daily life casual actions, like sitting on a chair or using a fork, which both appeared to be quite uncommon in Japan, or starting a car engine by turning the key while pressing the brake pedal in the United States for security reasons, which is far from being the normal way to start a car engine in Europe! This also applies to online learning programs or learning software tools, as shown by the following case studies.

Social Schemata of Uses and Learning Software: Two Case Studies

The first case study has for long remained unexplainable to me, before discovering the concept of social schemata of uses and its application. I was pilot-testing one of the first multimedia learning software developed in my department. This software was devised to help adults to learn the fundamentals of mathematical functions and provided lots of exercises on the "linear function" ($Y = aX$). One of these exercises intended to facilitate the understanding of the notion of "variable" and presented in column a series of very simple equations to resolve, like the following, where the value of a and X were selected at random by the system, each screen page corresponding to an exercise with the same value of a:

$X = 2$; $Y = 3X = ?$
$X = 5$; $Y = 3X = ?$

One of our learners succeeded in resolving all the exercises, except the one which was at the bottom of the screen page. She did the exercises several times for different values of a, and every time she did an exercise, the results were correct except the bottom-line answer. I interviewed her in order to understand what was wrong, and it appeared that she understood the exercise and what was expected, that she knew how to do a multiplication etc. Upon insisting on the reason why the last line was incorrect, she simply said: "It is not incorrect, the last line should be the sum of the numbers in the column." "Why?" "I am an accountant, and this is what I was told and what I am used to doing every day in bookkeeping!"

To put the total of all figures in the column on the last line of the page had become for her a habit, which prevailed over any other type of operation! Or, to put it in other terms, *adding the numbers at the end of a page had become an unconscious operative schema which automatically applied to any situations in which figures were presented in columns.* To confirm this hypothesis, we changed the layout in order to leave only a single equation on each screen page, and then she did all the exercises without errors.

A second case study, more dramatic, is reported by Pugibet and Viselthier (2002): They experimented the use of an off-the-shelf electronic dictionary in two primary schools in Paris, one being located in a wealthy part of the French capital city and the other in a less favoured array. This experiment took place in the first year of schooling and was twofold: a first part, in the beginning of the school year (October), did not show much difference between the pupils which were quite unable to use the dictionary in both schools. But at the end of the school year (May/June), the reading skills were much more developed in the school located in the wealthy part of the city, and it proved to have an influence on the pupils' abilities to navigate within the CD-ROM. The authors said that these pupils were even able to conceptualise the functionalities of the dictionary (to search definition or spelling of words), which was not the case in the other school, where "sociability behaviours (shyness overcoming ease, assurance, etc.)" were less developed, together with reading and speaking skills. *As a conclusion of this research, social environment appeared to the authors to be a critical factor influencing both use and usability of the CD-ROM.*

In both of these case studies, professional or social environment, i.e., *cultural factors*, appears to have an influence on the way people use a piece of software.

"Situated Usability" Heuristics

The existence of "social schemata of uses" makes the case for encompassing factors describing the environment of uses in any usability assessment. This is why I incline to propose the notion of "**situated usability**" to name a new set of "heuristics" that account for describing how the environment impacts usability factors. These heuristics are the following:

1. **Social Schemata of Uses**: to be used within a given community, a tool should embed common social schemata of uses of this community;

2. **Type of Action**: to be used in a given situation, a tool should correspond to user's need and purposes in this situation and allow him/her to perform a given action;
3. **Culture of the Users**: to be used within a given community, a tool should convey representations and practices which are considered as "commonsense knowledge" by the user;
4. **Culture of the Environment**: to be used within a given community, a tool should convey representations and practices which are considered as "commonsense knowledge" by the community;
5. **Tool Efficiency in a Given Situation**: to be used in a given situation, a tool should have proved efficiency in such a situation;
6. **Ability of the User to Use the Tool**: to be used in a given situation, a tool must be mastered, to some extent, by the user; which also means that an object does not become a tool at hand;
7. **Motivation of the User to Use the Tool**: to be used in a given situation, a tool should interest enough the user to perform his/her action using this tool rather than in any other manner.

These heuristics are quite general and may apply to any type of tool. They could be refined in the case of online learning programs, if we are able to identify configurations in which particular conditions apply.

UNDERSTANDING LEARNING CULTURES TO ACCOUNT FOR THE EXISTENCE OF VARIOUS ENVIRONMENTS FOR USE

The Masie (2001) survey and Paxton (2000) white paper provide some clues to a list of organisational factors accountable for usability of e-learning in organisations. But we have to take into consideration various contexts, including academic ones, and to identify factors accountable for the efficiency of a particular process, which consists in using an online learning program to carry out a learning activity in a given context.

Traditional concepts either from sociology of organisations or from sociology of uses appear not to be sufficient here, since they do not account easily for the relationship between the organisation supporting the learning process and theories of learning, which also determine conditions for learning efficiency. To address the usability issue taking into account, at the same time, cognitive and organisational aspects and their articulation to produce learning situations in which learning activity takes place, there is a need for new concepts. These concepts should allow to account for the "*situatedness,*" if I can say so, of a learning activity or to describe its indexicality, to use the ethnomethodology terminology (Garfinkel, 1967).

I will briefly introduce two concepts and how they allow one to describe various environments in which online learning programs are used.

Learning Cultures

Brown et al. (1989) consider the differences between learning process as implemented at school and activity-based learning process as naturally developed by practitioners in their professional life and "just plain folks" in their daily life as a consequence of two different *"cultures of learning."* I will use the "learning culture" concept in a similar way. Brown et al. (1989) describe a difference also sometimes designated by the "formal/informal learning" dichotomy. But there are more learning cultures than the two described by these authors, since man has been very creative in producing "formal learning systems," relying upon various learning theories.

Following principles used by Lakoff and Johnson (1999) to analyse Western philosophy, I consider four families of "learning cultures," based on four different "learning metaphors," or four different "learning paradigms," built upon different learning theories throughout our history. These "learning cultures" correspond to different communities of thinking within the educational world.

The "Learning is Remembering" Metaphor

This is probably the oldest metaphor for learning, attributed to Socrates and unveiled by Plato in his *Phaedrus* and in the "Allegory of the Cave." The realm of ideas is the source of any knowledge, and the soul incarnated into a human body is considered as having known everything before its incarnation. Thus, for human beings, knowing is simply remembering what their soul already knew before their birth. This is why pedagogy takes the form of the "Socratic dialog," which is formatted to facilitate the learner's remembrance. Today, a kind of neo-Platonism appears in some approaches, in which knowledge is supposed to reside within a group of learners, as illustrated by the "learning conversation" theory developed by some of Roger's followers (Harri-Augstein & Thomas, 1991). It has also developed into applications to email-based tutoring, since Socratic discussion is considered as a way to develop critical thinking (Garson, 1999).

The "Learning is Recording" Metaphor

This metaphor is the most commonly used by schooling and academic institutions. It is based on the formula, attributed to Aristotle, according to which *"there is nothing in our mind that has not previously been in our senses."* Modern conception of pedagogy relying on this metaphor first appears in John Comenius's *Great Didactic* and few years later in John Locke's *Essay Concerning Human Understanding*, in which the human mind is an empty box that an empirical pedagogy has to fill from the scratch. Knowledge is considered as *"an integral, self-sufficient substance"* (Brown et al., 1989, p.32) which has to be formatted in order to be recorded. Thus, the related pedagogy is the art to format knowledge so that it facilitates recording: Well-structured exposition of how the world is organised and behaves is supposed to help the learner store representations and associated knowledge in his/her mind. "Knowledge management" theories also rely on such a metaphor, considering knowledge as a stand-alone substance which can be recorded into databases and learned at once by anyone able to retrieve it.

The "Learning is Training" Metaphor

This metaphor results from the behaviourist theory of learning, developed by Pavlov, J. B. Watson, B. F. Skinner and others. Skinner, in particular, extended this approach from behavioural acquisition to knowledge acquisition. Learning results from a "conditioning" process, achieved by repeating sequences of stimulus and responses to the stimulus. In the Skinnerian approach, in order to facilitate learning, knowledge should be decomposed into small chunks, each of which is then assimilated by the learner through a sequence of presentations and tests. Thus, according to this metaphor, pedagogy is the art of organising sequences of "learning units," dedicated to the acquisition of a particular "knowledge chunk." This was called "mastery learning" and gave raise to programmed learning in the 1960s and shortly after, when the number of knowledge chunks was becoming to big to be handled on paper, to the first computer-based training system, the PLATO system, developed by the University of Illinois. It is the ancestor of all online learning programs (Dooijes, n.d.; Garson, 1999). *We must keep in mind that most of today's online learning programs' design is still based on this learning metaphor.*

The "Learning is Building" Metaphor

This is the metaphor on which are based modern constructivist theories, from Wallon and Piaget in France, to Vygotski and Leontiev in Russia, to Bruner, Jonassen and others in the USA. Situated cognition and many approaches considering knowledge and mind as embodied are also based upon such a metaphor, which the researches in cognitive neurosciences consider today to better represent than any other theory how the human brain works. According to these theories, knowledge is a result of the learner's activity and is an incremental process depending on prior learning. Pedagogy, in these perspectives, is the art of creating learning situations in which "*authentic activities*" (Brown et al., 1989) allow the learner to build his/her own representations and mental processes.

Some tools originated in or better fit with a particular learning culture. It is the case of mail and other written communication tools, which better fit with the Socratic discussion, or computer-based training programs originated from the behaviourist approach. This allows one to make a hypothesis: One of the reasons why some tools are not used could be because there is a "trench" (Brown et al., 1989) between the learning culture which they implicitly embed and the learning culture of the learner or of the learning system in which these tools are inserted. This cultural gap generates learning situations either ill-formed—and thus inefficient—or which are rejected by the actors, the teacher or the learner. To develop this issue, we also need to discuss the place where the control of the learning process is located in each of the learning cultures.

Human beings learn all the time, if we consider, with some authors, that "learning" is the name given to any process leading to sustainable transformation of neural connexions in human brain (Varela, 1980). "Formal learning systems" designate situations and environments which are specially *designed* to facilitate this process. This allows one to distinguish these latter from other situations and environments in which informal learning occurs, which cover the biggest part of human lifetime. We can further analyse how formal learning relates to learning cultures.

I have identified so far some categories of what I called "elementary" or "basic" formal learning systems (Blandin, 2000), and these categories are now becoming an accepted way of classifying them (Collectif de Chasseneuil, 2001; Ttnet Dossier n°4, 2001). A formal learning system is associated with (and sometimes rooted in) a particular type of communication technology, in the broad sense including human voice on one side and physical transport at the other. Almost any technology has been used shortly after its invention to support educational aims. Most of them gave raise to a specific formal learning system relying upon it: School is rooted in the invention of writing, as it was the dedicated place where scribes learned how to write according to a specific methodology (Goody, 1977). The history of media shows that wood engraving, printing, and even the magic lantern were technologies used by churches to disseminate the holy words as soon as they have been invented. Telephone, radio and television have found educational application a very short time after becoming fully operational (Perriault, 1989). Isaac Pitman launched the first correspondence course in 1840, the year which saw United Kingdom Royal Mail creating the postage stamp, thus securing postal exchanges by transferring payment to sender. Many formal learning systems disappeared when the technology they were rooted in became obsolete, but others still survive, like the classroom.

Basic formal learning systems *embed the learning culture of whom invented them*, because it is this learning culture which gave form to them. Because of that, a formal learning system is much more than a mere structure shaping learning situations. It really conveys the learning culture of its inventors or promoters, because learning is a social process, which links in a indefectible way the learner, a learning object, and "the other," may he/she be represented only by a "cultural" presence, or the "generalized other" (Mead, 1934). This cultural presence appears through the learning culture. This is why Comenius's theory of knowledge, a type of Aristotelianism on which is grounded the "classroom" learning system, is still there, though totally implicit, carried out by the formal system we continue to use. This might explain the "trench" explored by Brown et al. (1989) and deplored by Garson (1999) between traditional classroom pedagogy and what we now know about the learning process, due to the development of cognitive sciences.

In the same way, the structure of computer-based training programs inherits implicitly from its origin a format which, first, breaks down the content into small chunks (chapters, learning units, "learning granules," "learning objects," etc.) and, second, organises each chunk as a sequence of the following interactions: (1) presentation, (2) question/answer to test acquisition of the content presented, (3) feedback, and (4) branching to another sequence. This is typically a structure coming from programmed instruction, which now appears as good practice for designing commercial e-learning programs as shown, for example, by the "NETg Learning Objects" model (NETg, 2001).

If we map basic formal learning systems onto our four learning cultures (or learning metaphors), we get the following classification: **The "learning is remembering" metaphor** category includes *virtual communities* and *virtual campuses.* **The "learning is recording" metaphor** category includes classroom, correspondence courses, broadcast courses (radio, TV), *information-based learning systems (EPSS, "Electronic Resources," etc.), Webcast courses or Webcast conferences (audio or video streaming),* and *virtual presence (virtual classrooms systems, audio- or videoconferences with or without remote control, etc.).* **The "learning is training" metaphor** includes *interactive learning systems 1 (CBT, WBT, etc.).* **The "learning is building" metaphor** includes workshop, learning resource centre, *interactive learning systems 2 ("virtual labs," simulators, etc.).*

Online learning programs' components appear to be scattered all over the four categories, which means that some combinations of these components into "*blended solutions*" might be impossible. We can make the hypothesis, at this stage, that prominence of different paradigms might generate different practices, and that these practices might influence the way the actors, learners or teachers feel comfortable with the learning systems which are proposed to them and therefore the usability of the resources embedded in these systems.

The Learning Process Control and How It Differs Within the Four Learning Cultures

Process-oriented prominent paradigms like the constructivist one generate "tailored" learning systems, taking into account individual needs, whereas prominent content-oriented paradigms like the Aristotelian or the behaviourist ones generate learning systems in which content prevails and in which content tends to be standardised. If we examine our four learning cultures, at least two of them, those based on the "learning is remembering" metaphor and on the "learning is recording" metaphor, explicitly state that *there is a need for somebody other than the learner* to make learning happen: Remembering or recording knowledge as a *stand-alone substance* requires a facilitator either to question the learner or to present what he/she has to learn in the appropriate way. In that case, I will say that the control of the learning process is in the teacher's hand.

In the behaviourist paradigm—though the "learning is training" metaphor states that learning is a process which is located within the learner's brain—creating an efficient "conditioning" environment nevertheless supposes that the control of the learning process is also external to the learner: It might reside in the learning situation, if not directly in the teacher's hand.

Finally, the only learning culture admitting that the control of the learning process can be in the learner's hand is the constructivist one. Which means that my heuristics numbered (2), (3), (6) and (7) have little chances to be fully implemented in any of the three other learning cultures!

HOW LEARNING CULTURES INFLUENCE THE USE OF ONLINE LEARNING PROGRAMS

Learning institutions do not constitute an homogeneous category: as shown above, there are different learning cultures, in which the use of online learning programs might be differently appreciated, organised, supported, etc.

I will examine different cases of potential mismatches between online learning programs and the environment in which they are used. These types of mismatches can be seen as usability problems which infringe my heuristics and correspond to specific usability criteria.

Why Teachers Generally Recommend to Use Only the Online Learning Programs They Develop Themselves

When surveying use of online learning programs in universities, it appears commonly that "off-the-shelf" online learning programs are likely to be rejected by teachers, unless they are developed by the teacher himself! Why?

Off-the-shelf online learning programs could be CBT programs, structured according to a behaviourist paradigm in a succession of trial and error situations. They could also belong to the simulator or virtual laboratory types and offer learning situations according to a constructivist paradigm. They could also be Aristotelian-style presentations. If we now consider the teacher's learning culture, which can be one of the four identified above, there are many cases in which the teacher's learning culture conflicts with the one a given off-the-shelf online learning program is embedded or rooted in. Here, the potential mismatch appears as a competition or a conflict between different paradigms, thus leading to low evaluation and therefore to *"no-use" recommendations* for the industrialised product from the teacher's side. This case of "not invented here syndrome" applies in particular to online learning programs, as soon as they do not match with the teacher's learning culture. In many cases, it is the explanation of the reluctance with which teachers accept to use "off-the-shelf" learning programs which they have not carefully selected or produced themselves.

Here are some usability-related issues from the teacher's side: adequacy between learning paradigm embedded within the learning program and learning paradigm in use within the organisation; adequacy between content of the learning program and course curriculum; and adequacy between content of the learning program and the way content is taught by the teacher in charge of the course.

Why Online Learning Programs Provided by Online Learning Providers Are Not Used

What online learning providers offer is not consistent in terms of "learning culture": products in use are generally developed according to the behaviourist paradigm, whereas services supporting the use of these products are generally rooted in the Socratic dialog paradigm, to reflect "best practices" of product design on one hand and of distance tutoring on the other. These paradigms are opponent to each other: Behaviourism considers knowledge as embodied and is content-centred, while Socratic dialog considers knowledge as a stand-alone substance and is learning-process-centred. Such a blend is likely to generate a tutoring process out of tune with the online learning program philosophy: On one hand, the learning program encourages trial and error and repetition, with poor explanations, and leaves the learning process control to the learning situation created; on the other hand, the tutor questions the learner about things he/she might not have so far understood and tends to take the learning process control in hand, which is confusing for learners and might be a reason for dropout and low completion rates. This raises the following usability issue: adequacy between learning paradigm embedded within the online learning program and learning paradigm in which tutoring support is rooted.

Another configuration provides only Aristotelian-type presentations together with tutoring support. Such a blend mainly results from the lack of knowledge and experience of start-up companies Learning Software Designers in the field of cognitive sciences or educational sciences. It appears to be a blend quite similar to the "mix model" described by Bang and Dondi (2000), in which there is no major contradiction and no conflict between paradigms in use since the learning process control is supposed in the teacher's hand, but the products generally fail to keep the learner's attention because of their poor interactivity: Who is able to keep attention to a talking head stuttering in a small video window for hours? The result is that completion rates appear to be even lower than in the previous example, thus questioning again usability issues in terms of adequacy between learning paradigm embedded within the online learning program and efficient learning strategies.

Which Conditions Facilitate the Use of Online Learning Programs?

As a conclusion of recent surveys (Masie, 2001; Quinn, 2001), the presence of a trainer/teacher appears as a sine qua non condition in any model. We might assume that configurations that work should be learning process centred and take into account and embed what Malcolm Knowles and others consider as being the main characteristic of adult learning: self-directed learning (Knowles, 1975; Long, 1995). In other words, they should provide favourable conditions to develop self-directed learning, and the motivators determining acceptance of the online learning programs are nothing else than what Philippe Carre (2002) named "the seven pillars of self-directed learning." But "self-directed learning" is a concept which has no place within the Aristotelian and the Socratic dialog learning cultures because these learning cultures simply deny the fact that the learner can acquire knowledge or know-how *without the help of someone else who knows*. At the opposite, constructivism describes a learning process in which the learner's involvement plays a major part and which can be greatly enhanced when the learner's motivation and "self-directed learning readiness" (Guglielmino, 1977) is high.

Self-directed learning appears to be the foundation on which are built the formal learning systems which give a large place to the learner's motivation. To make e-learning effective, support and learning environment must be organised in order either to keep high motivation or to increase the learner's motivation all along the learning process, and this can only be done by implementing the "seven pillars of self-directed learning" (Carre, 2002). Then appear the "e-learning motivators" identified by different researches such as Masie (2001) and Paxton (2000): incentives, supporting corporate learning culture, etc. Therefore, we can assume that there could be a correlation between the use of learning material—in particular, online learning programs—and the learner's motivation and his/her self-directed learning readiness, which means that usability criteria must also take this issue into account. When self-directed learning is implemented in an organisation, then usability of learning software depends on the following criteria: adequacy between the learner's ranking in self-directed learning readiness scale and the kind of support provided and adequacy between learning environment culture and supportiveness and the expected motivation of learners.

CONCLUSION:
TOWARDS "SITUATED" USABILITY

Teacher's or trainer's epistemological stance, learner's motivation, organisational learning culture, and environmental factors strongly interact to produce conditions determining the use of online learning programs. Users do not live or act in an abstract world in which they are alone with the tool they are using. Users, as human beings, live and act in a world which is at the same time social and material. Use of tools is deeply rooted in users' culture, which means that it is rooted in what they learned previously from their social and material environment. As a consequence, usability has to take into account the user's social and material environment. This is why usability has to be "situated." This simply means that usability has to take into account "user experience," in its broad sense, which is certainly one of the best design principles but also probably the most difficult to implement. "User experience" and, in particular, the relationship between the user and an object or an artifact are context-dependent and therefore require a sociological standpoint to be fully understood.

REFERENCES

Bang, J., & Dondi, C. (2000). The challenge of ICT to university education: Networking, virtual mobility and collaborative learning. In A. R. Trindade (Ed.), *New learning* (pp. 380-418). Lisbon, Portugal: Universidade Aberta.

Berger, P., & Luckmann, T. (1966). *The social construction of reality.* New York: Doubleday.

Blandin, B. (2000). Open and distance learning within the world of vocational training and lifelong learning: Part 1. Open and distance learning: An overall survey at the beginning of 2000. In A. R. Trindade (Ed.), *New learning* (pp. 104-141). Lisbon, Portugal: Universidade Aberta.

Blandin, B. (2002). *La construction du social par les objets.* Paris: Presses Universitaires de France.

Brown, J. S., Collins, A., & Duguid, P. (1989). Situated cognition and the culture of learning. *Educational Researcher, 18*(1), 32-42.

Carre, P. (2002). Accompagner l'autoformation en APP. *Actualité de la formation permanente, 176,* 100-106.

Collectif de Chasseneuil. (2001). *Accompagner des formations ouvertes: Une conférence de consensus.* Paris: L'Harmattan.

Dagognet, F. (1996). *Les dieux sont dans la cuisine. Philosophie des objets et objets de la philosophie.* Editions Synthélabo, Le Plessis Robinson (France).

Dooijes, E. H. (n.d.). *The Plato IV system for computer aided instruction.* Retrieved August 25, 2001, from http://www.science.uva.nl/faculteit/museum/PLATO.html

Garfinkel, H. (1967). *Studies in ethnomethodology.* Cambridge, UK: Prentice Hall.

Garson, J. D. (1999). *The role of technology in quality education.* Retrieved August 25, 2001, from http://hcl.chass.ncsu.edu/sscore/garson2.htm

Goody, J. (1977). *The domestication of savage mind.* Cambridge, UK: Cambridge University Press.

Grudin, J. (1992). Utility and usability: Research issues and development context. *Interacting With Computers, 4*(2), 209-217.

Guglielmino, L. (1977). *Development of the self-directed learning readiness scale.* Unpublished doctoral dissertation, University of Georgia, Athens.

Harri-Augstein, S., & Thomas, L. (1991). *Learning conversations.* London: Routledge.

Jennings, T. (2001). *Dead Media Project working notes by categories.* Retrieved August 25, 2001, from http://www.deadmedia.org/notes/index-cat.html

Johnson, M. (1987). *The body in the mind: The bodily basis of meaning, imagination and reason.* Chicago, IL: University of Chicago Press.

Kay, P., & Kempton, W. (1984). What is the Sapir-Whorf hypothesis. *American Anthropologist, 86*(1), 65-79.

Knowles, M. (1975). *Self-directed learning: A guide for learners and teachers.* New York: Association Press.

Lakoff, G. (1987). *Women, fire and dangerous things: What categories reveal about the mind.* Chicago, IL: University of Chicago Press.

Lakoff, G., & Johnson, M. (1999). *Philosophy in the flesh: The embodied mind and its challenge to Western thought.* New York, NY: Basic Books.

Ling, R. (1999). C'est bien d'être joignable! L'usage du téléphone fixe et mobile chez les jeunes norvégiens. *Réseaux, 92/93,* 261-291.

Long, H. (Ed.). (1995). *New dimensions in self-directed learning.* Norman, OK: University of Oklahoma.

Masie, E. (2001). *E-learning: If we build it, will they come?* Alexandria, VA: American Society for Training and Development.

Mead, G. H. (1934). *Mind, self, and society from the standpoint of a social behaviorist.* Chicago, IL: University of Chicago Press.

NETg. (2001). *NETg Learning Object.* Retrieved September 8, 2001, from http://www.netg.com/us/architecture/nlo.asp

Nielsen, J. (n.d.). *Jacob Nielsen online writings on heuristics evaluation.* Retrieved August 25, 2001, from http://www.useit.com/papers/heuristic/

Nielsen, J. (1994). *Usability engineering.* San Francisco, CA: Morgan Kaufmann.

Nielsen, J. (1999). *Designing Web usability: The practice of simplicity.* Indianapolis, IN: New Riders.

Norman, D. (1988). *The psychology of everyday things.* New York, NY: Basic Books.

Notess, M. (2001). Usability, user experience, and learner experience. *E-Learn Magazine In-Depth Tutorials.* Retrieved August 25, 2001 from http://www.elearnmag.org/subpage/sub_page.cfm?section=4&list_item=2&page=1

Paxton, S. L. (2000). *When success matters: How to make e-learning work?* Retrieved August 25, 2001, from http://www.frontline-group.com/e_news_brief/wpaper.pdf

Perriault, J. (1989). *La logique de l'usage. Essai sur les machines à communiquer.* Paris: Flammarion.

Pugibet, V., & Viselthier, B. (2002). De l'image à l'écriture: Appropriation d'un dictionnaire sur CD-ROM en cours préparatoire. In *Apprentissage des langues et technologies: Usages en émergence* (pp. 110-121). Paris: Clé International.

Punie, Y. (1997). Imagining "non uses." Rejection of ICTs in Flemish households. In *Imagining Uses. Proceedings of the 1st International Conference* (pp. 165-176).

Quinn, A. (2001). *Why people can't use e-learning. What the e-learning sector needs to learn about usability*. Retrieved August 25, 2001, from http://infocentre.frontend.com/servlet/Infocentre?access=no&page=article&rows=5&id=163

Tricot, A., & Lafontaine, J. (2002). Evaluer l'utilisation d'un outil multimédia et l'apprentissage. In *Apprentissage des langues et technologies: Usages en émergence* (pp. 45-56). Paris: Clé International.

Tricot, A., & Tricot, M. (2000). Un cadre formel pour interpréter les liens entre utilisabilité et utilité des systèmes d'information. In *Actes du colloque Ergo-IHM* (pp. 195-202).

TTnet Dossier n°4. (2001). *Open and distance learning and the professionalisation of trainers*. Thessaloniki, Greece: CEDEFOP.

Usability First. (n.d.). *Introduction to usability*. Retrieved August 25, 2001 from http://www.usabilityfirst.com/intro/index.txl

Varela, F. (1980). *Principles of biological autonomy*. New York: Elsevier North Holland.

Varela F., Thompson E., & Rosch E. (1993). *L'inscription corporelle de l'esprit. Sciences cognitives et expérience humaine*. Paris: Le Seuil.

Chapter XVIII

Security and Online Learning: To Protect or Prohibit

Anne Adams
Middlesex University, UK

Ann Blandford
UCL Interaction Centre, UK

ABSTRACT

The rapid development of online learning is opening up many new learning opportunities. Yet, with this increased potential come a myriad of risks. Usable security systems are essential as poor usability in security can result in excluding intended users while allowing sensitive data to be released to unacceptable recipients. This chapter presents findings concerned with usability for two security issues: authentication mechanisms and privacy. Usability issues such as memorability, feedback, guidance, context of use and concepts of information ownership are reviewed within various environments. This chapter also reviews the roots of these usability difficulties in the culture clash between the non-user-oriented perspective of security and the information exchange culture of the education domain. Finally an account is provided of how future systems can be developed which maintain security and yet are still usable.

INTRODUCTION

The World Wide Web is facilitating new forms of remote education. These online environments provide a wealth of possibilities for supporting learning throughout the world. Yet, with the many opportunities come a myriad of risks. Risks to the system and its data can dramatically affect users' perceptions of a system's reliability and trustworthiness. Whether these infractions are malicious or accidental, they can have serious repercussions for a system and its administrators. Security is therefore essential to retain users' trust in an online learning program.

Although security is an essential part of any system it should not impede the original objectives of that system. However, security mechanisms and their poor implementation have been found to present serious usability problems. There are two principal security issues, authentication and privacy, where usability is a source of problems for online learning systems (OLS). Initially, users encounter a variety of usability problems with authentication procedures, such as passwords, which incur high user overheads or are simply unworkable. The result is that users either try to circumvent the mechanisms or use other systems to complete their task (Adams & Sasse, 1999c; Adams, Sasse, & Lunt, 1997; Holmström, 1999; Preece, 2000; Whitten & Tygar, 1999). Users seeking to protect their privacy encounter further complex usability problems. These usability issues often relate to concepts of ownership (e.g., intellectual property rights, copyright, privacy rights). Many OLS, however, do not provide adequate feedback or control rights (Adams, 1999a; Bellotti & Sellen, 1993; Preece, 2000). Although some usability issues only relate to specific online settings, others are more universal.

For security mechanisms in OLS to effectively protect our information they must be designed appropriately to the users' needs. Usability, in this sense, would relate to providing users with adequate control to protect their data. In this context, users may be the providers of learning materials, in which case the concern is commonly over authorised access to proprietary learning materials. Alternatively, users may be learners, in which case the concern may be over their answers to questions, their results or even their images (notably in videoconferencing systems, where even matters as apparently trivial as the quality of a video image can affect perceptions enormously). Various OLS, however, do not provide adequate feedback or control rights to allow this control.

This chapter details why we need security in OLS and the factors underpinning how that security is provided within various environments. A review is also provided of the fundamental differences between the culture of security and online learning that produce clashes between the two disciplines. These clashes are often the root cause of usability issues in security mechanisms for OLS. Finally, an account is provided of how future systems can be developed which maintain security and yet are still usable.

Ultimately, this chapter seeks to review three important concerns:

- why current security mechanisms, frequently used in online learning programs, lack usability;
- why the current security discipline, which is not user centred, leads to serious security risks being overlooked;
- how security mechanisms in online education programs can be developed to be both usable and secure.

BACKGROUND

Security issues such as authenticating users, intellectual property rights and privacy are certain to increase in the new millennium with the development of new ubiquitous learning technologies. With the growth of such technologies, security breaches are becoming more frequent and their impact is increasing. Security is, therefore, a vital part of an online learning system (OLS) to ensure that only appropriate people have access to it and the information it contains. Computer security has developed various mechanisms to aid in system and information protection within online environments. However, there are many issues that reduce the effectiveness of these devices.

Despite considerable resources being spent on security mechanisms and their maintenance (e.g., password resetting, encryption techniques), breaches and associated problems are still increasing (DeAlvare, 1990; Hitchings, 1995; Sasse, Brostoff, & Weirich, 2001). Many of these security breaches are directly related to users (e.g., poor password design, security knowledge). The technique of *social engineering* specifically exploits users' lack of security awareness to breach security (i.e., obtaining access to information by deception or persuasion). It appears that, currently, hackers pay more attention to human factors than do security designers. Davis and Price (1987) have argued that, as security is designed, implemented, used and breached by people, human factors should be considered in the design of security mechanisms. However, the security domain relates the problem to user weaknesses rather than usability issues (Adams & Sasse, 1999c; Sasse et al., 2001; Schneier, 2000).

When assessing the level of security required for different information, the security domain again disregards users' perceptions. It has been argued that ethically there are many inalienable privacy rights that should never be disregarded when developing systems (Davies, 1997). Similarly it is also maintained that privacy experts understand potential privacy risks at a greater depth than users (Bennett, 1997). However, privacy is socially determined, being defined by our perceptions of it. To be private, therefore, relies on our perception of ourselves as secluded from a public environment (Goffman, 1969; Wacks, 1989). Taking this into account, therefore, the importance of users' perceptions in designing privacy mechanisms is paramount. It is interesting to note that of all the invasions of privacy identified by

Adams and Sasse (1999a, 1999b, 2001), none was intentional or malicious but all were related to design issues (e.g., poor feedback, inappropriate design, inadequate user control).

The culture of the security discipline thus has a significant effect on how security is developed and administered. Of key importance is that usability, until recently, was not considered an important aspect of security design. We highlight how this oversight relates to the culture of the security discipline. Furthermore we highlight how the culture of security clashes with that of the online learning domain to produce further usability problems.

Culture of Security

Despite the importance of usability of security mechanisms, there is very little research in this field. The handful of publications that exist all argue that previous research is limited, technically biased and for use by professionals (Adams, 2000; Adams & Sasse, 1999c; Adams et al., 1997; Holmström, 1999; Sasse et al., 2001; Whitten & Tygar, 1999). Users' poor security knowledge, behaviours and education are often criticised rather than the usability of security mechanisms. To understand the lack of usability research in this field and the adversarial approach to security implementation we must review the cultural roots of this discipline.

The security discipline has, until recently, regarded the development of security systems as solely a technical issue. Users' work practices, organisational strategies and usability factors are rarely considered during the design and implementation of most security mechanisms today. It could be argued that many of these issues are not reviewed because the off-line roots of security lie in the militia and mathematics. It should therefore be of no surprise then that online solutions should be technically biased, mathematically complex (e.g., cryptography) and dependent on organisational hierarchies. Hitchings (1995) argues that this perspective has produced security mechanisms that are much less effective than they are generally thought to be. This technically biased approach could be the cause of poor usability design in many security systems. However, within the security domain, these problems are further complicated by its military-style culture.

The authoritarian approach of security has led to the security discipline's reluctance to communicate with users. Parker (1992) has noted that a major doctrine of security, adopted from the military, is the *need-to-know* principle. This principle assumes that the more known about a system's security, the easier it is to attack. Informing users about security mechanisms and threats is seen as lowering security by increasing the possibility of information leaks. Part of a system's defence, therefore, is to restrict information only to those who *need-to-know*. Ultimately this approach produces a tendency to inform users as little as possible. This lack of communication results in users being uninformed and thus lacking security awareness. Security departments, conversely, lack knowledge about users and produce security mechanisms and systems which are not usable.

It is important to note that the security discipline's perspective of users is as a risk to be controlled. When users are considered within security, it is often as the *weakest link* in the security chain (Schneier, 2000). Users' insecure work practices and low security motivation have been identified by information security research as a major problem that must be addressed (Davis & Ganesan, 1993; DeAlvare, 1990; Ford, 1994). Security departments' approach to these problems, however, is not to discover the specific causes to address, but to place the blame on users' security knowledge and motivation. The traditional military culture of security assumes that users are not inherently motivated towards these behaviours. It is assumed that users will lack security motivation until they are made aware or forced into completing secure behaviours. However, recent research reveals that users' insecure work practices and low security motivation can be caused by poor user-centred design of security mechanisms and policy. Moreover, forcing users to conform may only produce a *facade* of them having completed secure actions (Adams & Sasse, 1999c, 2001).

The culture of the security domain determines the type of security problems identified and the approach to potential solutions. To date, the security discipline has focused on malicious intruders and technological solutions rather than users' perceptions and usability. These guiding principles have produced technical mechanisms that are both unusable and inappropriate solutions.

Whitten and Tygar (1999) propose that users' understanding of security is impeded by the complexity of security mechanisms (e.g., email encryption mechanisms). Current mechanisms, such as PGP (pretty good privacy), are identified as too difficult and confusing for a conventional computer user. Holmström (1999) and Adams and Sasse (1999c) argue that this is because security features in current software are technology orientated. This impedes the systems' usability, as users are required to have a basic knowledge of the underlying technology to use the systems correctly.

Within the sphere of user authentication, the technical bias of the discipline has produced mechanisms that are restrictive and authoritarian. Security measures have centred on forcing the user towards secure behaviours by enforcing more restrictive authentication regimes, such as:

- increasing change regimes (change password once a month);
- longer and more complex passwords (alphanumeric and required length);
- reduction in allowed input error rates.

Adams et al. (1997) found, however, that the effect of these measures is the opposite of that intended. The more restrictive security mechanisms are, the more likely it is that users will evade them, resulting in behaviours which are even less secure. A dramatic decrease in usability is identified as the cause of this apparent paradox, as more restrictions in authentication mechanisms create more usability problems. Current procedures are circumvented because user costs are too high (e.g., time-consuming) while the benefits (i.e., increased security) are rarely established for users. The causes of these user costs are often security mechanisms and policies that do not take account of users' work practices. Systems are subsequently designed which, in practice, are at best impractical and at worst impossible. Users were also found to be highly security-conscious if they perceived the need for these actions (i.e., obvious external threats).

The field of privacy has concentrated more on policies and mechanisms that increase users' trust in the systems (Preece, 2000). However, experts' rather than users' viewpoints direct the identification of problems and potential solutions. To date, security experts have concentrated on protecting the individual against a malicious invasion of privacy. This perspective reveals the adversarial nature of the security domain. However, as this chapter will identify, many invasions of privacy occur unintentionally through poor interface design.

The technical predisposition of the security discipline has resulted in a focus on the security of data rather than the user (Clarke, 1997). Privacy solutions centre on technical mechanisms (e.g., encryption tools) and policies without understanding how users perceive online systems or the mechanisms in question (Diffie & Landau, 1998; Needham & Schroeder, 1978). These mechanisms are based on the traditional *personal information* assumptions, i.e., that potentially invasive information only relates to data that identifies the individual. This approach leads to the conclusion that to make the data, or the user, anonymous would take away the ability to identify them personally and thus secure their privacy. However, with the development of complex online learning environments, the issues of the future may not be well met by this narrow perspective.

Online Learning Systems Culture Clash With Security

Within the realm of education and learning, an ethos tends to prevail of cooperation and collaboration. A course of study is presented so as to encourage students to assimilate and understand it. Online learning systems (OLS) seek to encourage trust, information sharing and freedom of expression to develop an environment that is appropriate for learning.

With the growth of networked services, more and more people from different backgrounds and cultures with varying skills are using online learning programs. Online services seek, if sometimes inadequately, to support and aid these students in their educational goals. It is important to understand when designing these systems that we are social creatures who relate to each other via social norms for specific situations and surroundings. Online learning systems must facilitate users from vastly different cultures and backgrounds in establishing a joint understanding of the social norms for that system. Furthermore the continual intake of new users at the beginning of courses means that the acquisition of the OLS culture must be quickly and easily assimilated. To facilitate the effective development of these norms requires the communication and adaptability often provided by reputable educational establishments and their online systems. The theme of this book also highlights the importance within the education discipline for the usability principles of communication, feedback and the free flow of information.

It is important to understand how the non-user-orientated perspective of security clashes with the information exchange culture of the education domain. The current focus of the security community on technical mechanisms to enforce and protect desired behaviours does not fit well within a learning environment. The learning arena thrives upon a tradition of trust, information exchange and discussion. The security domain, in contrast, relies on a culture of distrust, restricted information flow and autocratic rules. It should also be noted that students do not respond well to the traditional authoritarian approach of many security departments.

What is of increased importance is how the clash between these two disciplines can be seen as the root of many usability difficulties with security in online learning systems. Within the domain of online learning, users relate to the established norms of feedback and help when they encounter usability problems. However, usability problems encountered with security mechanisms are often not supported by traditional help facilities. Users' isolation encourages contrary perceptions of the system working against, rather than with, them. The segregation of those traditionally placed to help users (e.g., tutors, administrators) form an understanding of security mechanisms further increases potential usability problems.

Ultimately, a new approach is required that promotes the protective aims of security without confronting the users with unusable systems. The beginning of many solutions starts with a reengineering of the security culture to work with, rather than against, the user. The user, as previously noted, is a crucial link in the security chain that must be considered as a valued asset rather than a flawed chink in the armour. A recent move within security research has tried to counteract current security limitations by highlighting the importance of users' conceptual models and their understanding of security mechanisms (Adams & Sasse, 1999c, 2001; Holmström, 1999; Whitten & Tygar, 1999). The need for more research into user-directed security is imperative, however, as the need for security increases and our understanding of trust is diluted in online environments.

ONLINE LEARNING SYSTEM ACCESS: AUTHENTICATION

Security, in general terms, is often taken to mean *protection from danger*. With regard to computer security, that danger relates to malicious or accidental misuse (Neumann, 1995). Computer security, therefore, tends to concentrate on human misuse rather than computer malfunctions. Two important aspects of security are *confidentiality* and *integrity*. Confidentiality is concerned with protection of information from unauthorised access, while integrity refers to maintaining the unimpaired condition of both the system and the data used. Both confidentiality and integrity closely relate to the endeavour of making sure that misuse does not impact on computer reliability. Ultimately, security seeks to ensure that learning resources are available, unimpaired, to all authorised users when they are needed. To maintain the commercial viability of online learning systems (OLS) it is therefore vital to ensure that the people who pay for services have access while other non-authorised users are excluded. To retain this access to unimpaired data it is necessary to deal with issues of authentication and ownership. It is essential that the appropriate people have access to information with the correct data manipulation rights (Preece, 2000).

Security issues, however, are often not directly considered by online learning administrators. Articles that do review security issues for online learning systems tend to concentrate on issues of intellectual property rights and copyright law (Diotalevi, 2000; McAlister, Rivera, & Hallam, 2001). Recent articles, however, are identifying further security issues for OLS, especially with regard to user feedback and assessment (Bateman, 2000; McAlister et al.). McAlister et al. notes that authenticating a user is especially important when assessing students' progress online. However, administering this authentication is troublesome as normal security procedures (e.g., seeing the student complete the assessment unaided) are not applicable in many online scenarios. It is suggested that if identification for assessment purposes is essential then local supervised sessions could be provided.

Authentication Stages and Methods

Authentication is pivotal to the concept of confidentiality but it also relates to integrity. To maintain appropriate access to information and yet protect it from unsanctioned manipulation, it is crucial accurately to authenticate users.

Authentication procedures are usually divided into two stages. The first stage, *user identification* (User ID), identifies the user interacting with the system. As it is merely a means of specifying who the user is, this ID does not have to be secured. Once the user is identified the second stage, *user authentication*, verifies them as the legitimate user of that ID. The means of authentication, therefore, must remain secret.

There are three different ways to authenticate a user by an online learning program (Garfinkel & Spafford, 1996):
1. Knowledge-based authentication: The user *tells* the computer something only they know (e.g., password).
2. Token-based authentication: The user *shows* the computer something only they possess (e.g., a key card).
3. Biometrics: The user themselves is *measured* by the computer (e.g., fingerprint).

Security research has tended to concentrate on technical mechanisms for authentication (e.g., iris scanning, smart cards). However, although these technologies have great potential in future applications, passwords and personal identification numbers (PINs) are currently the most widely used form of authentication. Even where the other forms of authentication (i.e., token-based or biometrics) are used, they are invariably reinforced by the use of a PIN or password. Knowledge-based authentication has the advantage of being both simple and economical. These two factors probably account for its universal appeal and ensure its use for many systems and years to come.

One of the problems with popular knowledge-based authentication mechanisms, such as passwords and PINs, are their poor usability. Current mechanisms rely on users to recall data to be input rather than recognising the correct authorisation information. To counteract these problems there are a wide variety of knowledge-based authentication mechanisms that claim to be more usable and yet secure:

- passphrases (a phrase required instead of a word);
- cognitive passwords (question-and-answer session of personal details);
- associative passwords (a series of words and associations);
- passfaces (user selection of faces).

However, the take-up of these mechanisms has, to date, been limited (Sasse et al., 2001). One-word passwords and PINs are still the easiest and cheapest to apply and thus most often implemented.

Passwords: Security Issues

Passwords are either system- or user-generated, with the former ensuring a more "secure" combination of characters in the password than the latter. However, users find *system-generated* passwords are not usable (i.e., hard to remember correctly) and so have been found to write them down, thus decreasing security. Furthermore, the process of distributing system-generated passwords often led to increased security risks (i.e., unauthorised access to the passwords). Both of these reasons have led to *user-generated passwords* as the most widely used process for password production.

The level of security provided by *user-generated passwords* can vary greatly, depending on the individual user's password design expertise and security awareness. When generating a password its *crackability* is often vastly underrated by users (Davis & Ganesan, 1993). There are, however, several criteria that should be used to ensure a reasonable level of password security (Federal Information Processing Standars, 1985).

Password composition is a vital element in a password's *crackability*. A password composed of characters chosen from a large character set decreases its level of crackability. An alphanumeric password is therefore more secure than one composed of letters only. The *lifetime* of a password (i.e., *change regimes*) relates to the frequency with which the composition of a password is required to be changed. Some systems apply a strict *change regime*, e.g., requiring passwords to be changed every 30 days and not to repeat one of the past 10 chosen. However, it must be understood that *change regimes* do not actually increase security, but decrease the damage that can be done once a breach has occurred. In addition, frequent *change regimes* are only required for highly confidential information. The sensitivity of the information protected should, therefore, be considered before introducing frequent *change regimes*. Finally, the security domain emphasises the importance of individual ownership of passwords because they:

- increase individual accountability;
- reduce illicit usage;
- make it possible to audit system usage;
- reduce frequent password changes due to group membership fluctuations.

Ultimately, the level of security a password affords is tightly interwoven with its design. However, support for users on password design is often very limited.

Passwords: Usability Issues and Solutions

Security systems should be deemed ineffective and unusable if the user costs (mental overhead, time-consuming, etc.) and computer costs (costly implementation, continual system updating) are high and yet the overall security of the systems is low. By these standards, the desired performance of most security mechanisms is unacceptable. The consequences of inadequate usability, however, are high : Poor usability of security mechanisms can result in excluding intended users while allowing sensitive data to be released to unacceptable recipients. There are a wide variety of usability problems within password systems. However, this section will initially review the major issues associated with users' memory limitations and how to counteract those problems by increasing password memorability. Further issues of poor feedback and guidance are presented with potential solutions including guidance in password design. Finally the importance of understanding the *context of use* with regard to password usability is evaluated.

Memorability. As technology infiltrates more aspects of people's lives, the number of PINs and passwords required can become excessive. Most people have a PIN for a bank card, mobile phone, voice mail and even entry door systems. A multitude of passwords is also required in our daily lives; for logging on to networks, specific applications and a multitude of Web sites. Online learning programs are also inclined to use passwords rather than other forms of authentication. The result is a considerable challenge for users, not just in terms of the number of items to recall but the complexity of the information to be memorised.

Authentication mechanisms, often unnecessarily, increase the memory load on users. Most systems allow the user to choose a PIN or password, to increase its memorability. However, the user's choice is often constrained by security parameters, for example, that it has to be of a certain length or format. This is because the security of a password system ultimately relies on the level of security afforded by the password content. With the use of dictionary checkers, a short alphanumeric password affords more security than a longer word (since alphanumeric strings are not listed in such dictionaries). A password's content, though, also affects its level of memorability. As Carroll (1996) observes, the very characteristics that make a password more secure (e.g., long, nonsensical combinations) also make it less memorable. A word can be far more memorable than a nonsensical combination, but the security afforded by the former is far less than the latter. A password system's security and its memorability, therefore, lie in the hands of the user. Users are required to construct a memorable combination within the security constraints provided, often within a short time frame, and are rarely given feedback on how to construct these passwords (Adams & Sasse, 1999c; Adams et al., 1997; Sasse et al., 2001). Many users feel they are forced into circumventing unusable security procedures, which decreases their security motivation. Hackers using *social engineering* techniques rely on the lowered security motivation of users to breach security mechanisms. A simple phone call or email, together with users' poor security awareness, is all that is required.

Another serious constraint on password memorability is the implementation of *change regimes*. Harsh *change regimes* (e.g., password changed once a month, once every 3 months) not only decrease the memorability of a password system but also increase security risks. Adams and Sasse (1999c) found that users who were required to change their passwords frequently produced less secure passwords and disclosed their passwords more frequently. The increased security risks (e.g., writing down passwords, poor security motivation) incurred by introducing frequent *change regimes* should also be considered before introducing these measures.

Finally another interface flaw, which increases the users' memory burden, is a failure to clearly distinguish between the openly disclosed aspects of user identification (ID) and the undisclosed secret aspects of the password section. Adams et al. (1997) found that many users confused user identification (user IDs) and the password sections of the authentication process. Without knowledge of the authentication process, users assumed that these IDs were another form of password to be secured and recalled in the same manner. Recall of the user ID then became an extra memory burden on the user. User confusions were found to be related to authentication mechanisms which automatically allocated user IDs as nonwords without meaning. Even when authentication systems require a user's name, they do not state the format that it is required in. Consequently users returning to one of many systems they use encounter problems remembering which form of their name they need for this system (e.g., A. Adams; A. L. Adams; Anne Adams; anne adams).

Increasing password memorability.   An important aspect of usability is to design user recognition into a system rather than relying on users' abilities to recall information. However, passwords rely on users' long-term memory, with all its limitations and flaws. This has produced efforts to identify mechanisms for generating memorable yet secure passwords which rely on users' recognition rather than recall abilities (Barton & Barton, 1984; DeAlvare, 1990; Sasse et al., 2001). The impact of these recommendations, however, seems to have been limited, in that few developers are aware of them (e.g., passfaces, associative passwords, etc.).

One serious impediment to the recall of passwords is the interference in retrieving the information from memory caused by the increasing numbers of passwords requiring memorisation. A technical solution to this problem has been suggested, in the form of a single sign-on (Adams & Sasse, 1999c). With this method of authentication, systems are interlinked only for authentication purposes and the user can use one password for multiple systems. However, if this approach is technically inappropriate or too expensive, there are non-technical solutions. If the security afforded by a single password is acceptable, users should be advised to use a single password for all systems. It should be noted, though, that from a security perspective there could be some problems with this approach as different systems hold more sensitive information (e.g., exam marks, tutors' course-work comments) than others and require tighter security protocols. What must be emphasised to the users is that linked (e.g., tom1, tom2, tom3) passwords should *not* be used for different systems as they have a lower memorability than unlinked (e.g., to2m, pofad, sa1ly) passwords (Adams et al., 1997), in terms of which password applies to which system. It must also be noted that the memory advantages of single sign-on can be counteracted if frequent change regimes are introduced since interference will still reduce password memorability (i.e., interference between old and new passwords).

Some memory aids are a useful tool in increasing the memorable content of passwords without decreasing its level of security. Initial letters of a sentence or a rhyme can look like a complex secure password combination (e.g., 12Bms34Kotd) and yet be memorable with an appropriate cue (e.g. 1, 2 **Buckle my s**hoe. 3, 4 **K**nock **on the d**oor). If the sentence cue relates to the interaction task then for many users this can increase the password memorability still further. For some users, the pattern of the input keys on the keyboard can greatly aid memorability. However, this aid is a better support for frequently used password or PIN numbers and can cause problems if a frequent change regime is employed.

Finally, as previously mentioned, many user authentication mechanisms incur further memorability problems by not distinguishing between the user ID and the password sections of the authentication procedure. It is important that the interface of a user authentication system clearly highlights the difference between these sections. Currently the only distinction provided between these sections is the standard feedback for the ID data input (e.g., anne adams) and a secret feedback for the password data input (e.g., *****). As the user ID section does not require free recall to increase security it can be prompted. It could increase the usability of these systems if, instead of asking for a user ID, they presented a box asking for the user's first name followed by a box asking for a surname. If the ID section accepted the data in either case (upper or lower), this could further increase the system's usability.

Feedback and guidance. One major problem with all security mechanisms is the distinct lack of user support provided. Adams et al. (1997) found that limited and unsuitable feedback in security systems can produce inappropriate, time-consuming user actions and pointless interactions. Whitten and Tygar (1999) also point out that to prevent dangerous errors, appropriate feedback is essential. An essential aid to system usability, therefore, is the provision of simple, straightforward, accurate documentation for user support and help facilities. However, it is difficult for security mechanisms to provide these facilities because the system needs to aid the user without supporting security breaches (Sasse et al., 2001). There is, therefore, an important balancing act between usability and security. For example, a user having recently returned from a vacation types in their password; the system states it is incorrect; the user is certain that this is their password, so assumes they have typed it in incorrectly and types it again; the system again states that it is incorrect; and the user tries one last time and is shut out of the system. How could the system have supported the user without decreasing security by aiding an unauthorised user? Often to increase usability, prompts are used to guide the user through a task. However, providing prompts or clues about the password to the user would increase security risks. Associative passwords (i.e., a series of words and associations) could be used as a backup, because although they are time-consuming they are cheaper and quicker than password reinstatement procedures. Another prompt that could be provided would be for the user to receive some simple feedback, for example, reminding them that the system is case-sensitive. As noted by Adams et al. (1997), many users have problems with passwords not because they have forgotten the password but simply that they have forgotten that the system is case-sensitive. This feedback would potentially support some users and yet not decrease security since most hackers assume case-sensitivity in their cracking attempts.

Not only do users require support in their use of authentication mechanisms but also in the design or choice of passwords. Users also have to develop rules for using passwords which satisfy the criteria for a secure password and, at the same time, minimise the burden on themselves. As Adams and Sasse (1999c) observe, however, users are rarely given support in these procedures (e.g., how to design effective passwords, manage your security, interact with the system, reinstate forgotten passwords, change passwords). Users' lack of basic knowledge was found to result in them making their own judgements about which practices are secure, and these judgements are often wildly inaccurate. We suggest that the reason behind poor user support and usability of security mechanisms lies in the security culture of reduced communication with users. The solution is to provide open support and guidance in password construction and secure behaviours. The support provided, however, should not take the traditional authoritarian approach (e.g., tell us what you're doing wrong so we can reprimand you). Two-way communication should be established so that users and security designers are encouraged to think of security as a joint responsibility, with security administrators acknowledging users' needs and work practices.

Understanding the context of use. When designing an authentication screen it is important to understand the user's context of use. The mental model that users have of the relationship between the virtual- and real-world library is essential if security procedures rely on them. A recent study we conducted, within an UK academic setting, identified problems with access to a digital library. Users who initially attempted to access digital libraries online were presented with no information about what specific authentication was required (e.g., an *Athens* ID and password), how to obtain these details and who to contact if they had any problems with the system. As with many online learning programs the only information provided in the authentication process was a screen asking for user ID and password. Users became further confused when they found out (via off-line sources) that they had to physically attend their local library to obtain a password in order to remotely access digital libraries. Further research into these usability problems identified that users' understanding of the context is complicated by the inconsistent use of terminology. In this example, users were confused when the name for the online learning system (i.e., OVID) did not correspond with the name of the system required to access it (i.e., *Athens* password and ID).

Further terminology problems can be encountered when technical terms such as *ID* are used without detailing what they relate to or how to enter the required information (e.g., case-sensitive, limited number of characters). The use of these terms between systems is also frequently inconsistent. For example, one popular online system not only asks for an access ID, but also an authentication ID and a password. There is no explanation about the differences between these components and their different security levels. The use of multiple types of IDs also increases the potential for user errors in remembering and entering these items.

Users confused by inconsistencies within and between systems are even more confused by similarities between different digital library authentication mechanisms. In our digital library study, it was found that users would effortlessly jump between digital libraries, but frequently became disorientated about which library they were currently accessing. Users frequently tried to proceed in library A using library B's password. Other users did not realise they had followed a link from one library to another and that further registration was required. Unaware of their errors, users were often locked out of the system altogether. Ultimately, it is important to understand that users consider authentication mechanisms as a part of the learning interaction. When designing online learning programs we must, therefore, consider their usability with regard to their context of use.

PROTECTING PRIVACY IN ONLINE LEARNING SYSTEMS

Data is increasingly being treated as property, and the ownership of that property is fiercely debated. For example, sports organisations have claimed that online service providers misappropriate their proprietary rights to scores. In contrast, governments sell the rights to potentially *personal information* they collect. The World Intellectual Property Organisation is continually debating the protection of databases and expanding copyright protection for digital works (Cranor, 2000). Legislative developments have not untangled this complexity. Over the last 30 years U.S. courts have increasingly ruled that personal records belong to an organisation and access to the information cannot be restricted by the person in question (Kling, 1996).

In security terms, information ownership (i.e., intellectual property rights, copyright, privacy rights) can determine access and manipulation rights. Issues of ownership, therefore, relate to both confidentiality and integrity. However, it is important to note that the users' concept of ownership is closely intertwined with that of privacy. It is vital, therefore, to understand users' perceptions of information ownership, usage and privacy when developing online learning systems. Privacy and intellectual property rights rely on our perception of them. As well as how well we are protected, it is also important that we perceive ourselves and our information to be safe and private. Therefore identifying users' perceptions of privacy and ownership is an important element in identifying what needs to be protected and how best to protect it.

People often feel they own data about themselves and that security should reflect how much they feel misuse of that data could invade their privacy (Adams, 2001; Adams et al., 1997). However, with the increasing availability and use of various data and applications, associated *privacy risks,* out of users' control, are greatly increasing (Bellotti, 1996; Neumann, 1995; Preece, 2000; Smith, 1993). Kling (1996) suggests that over the past 30 years there has been a growing view that computerisation has decreased people's privacy. Computerisation, however, is not the only culprit in people's perceptions of decreased privacy. Slow-to-react organisations have played a key role in this decline: Organisations that develop privacy policies retrospectively, after an external threat, produce policies that have been outgrown by changes in either society or the organisation's activities (Smith, 1993).

Just as there are many inalienable rights that should never be disregarded when developing systems (Davies, 1997) , it is also maintained that security experts understand potential risks at a greater depth than users (Bennett, 1997). Both these arguments have directed security research and the identification of security requirements in system development towards appraisals by security experts. The problem with *only* taking this approach is that any expert may have a distorted perception of a situation that does not reflect the perceptions of the users. Ultimately, to satisfy users' privacy needs, it is necessary to understand their perception of the information being used, how it is used and those manipulating it (Adams, 2001; Adams & Sasse, 2001).

Privacy of Learners' Working Materials

The issue of ownership when dealing with distance education can be very complex and is often not written in stone, making it hard to apply accurately (Diotalevi, 2000). McAlister et al. (2001) suggest that it is important to establish ownership rights and compensations prior to offering Web courses to minimise future misunderstandings. However, problems often occur because of difficulties in distinguishing what information needs to be protected and by whom (Adams, 1999a, 1999b, 2000). These fundamental issues often lead to inappropriate design of security mechanisms that, in turn, provide poor usability for safeguarding what users want protected.

Despite information ownership being a complex issue, students perceive their ownership of the essays and course work they produce as straightforward. It is important that users can rely upon an online learning system to protect their information from misuse (Preece, 2000). Users' control over access rights to this information, however, is sometimes negated by system settings. A particular worry for students is that when working online their documents will be viewed before they feel ready for them to be accessed. A student whose course work or assessment mark is available to others, without their prior knowledge, will be less willing to use the system in the future. Previous research into multimedia educational systems has identified the importance of *freedom of expression* in the learning process. However, our ability to express ourselves free from social inhibitors relies upon a secure context for private expression and autonomy (Schoeman, 1992). Adams (2001) found that students were negative when online learning systems allowed tutors automatic viewing rights to them (e.g., video-conferencing systems) or their work without their control or prior knowledge. Cranor, Reagle, and Ackerman (1999) also found that users have a particular dislike of the automatic transfer of data about themselves and their patterns of use.

Although monitoring learners' progress and participation in learning applications is vital, it must be carefully applied. Users' security needs (e.g., privacy) are occasionally overlooked when developing monitoring mechanisms. Tracking devices used to tailor learning situations for the user can be invasive if information is inappropriately obtained and applied. Intelligent agents that identify information requirements can invade users' privacy, depending on how the information is used. These issues are further complicated within an online environment, where trust in a faceless entity is difficult, technology distorts social interactions, and social norms vary across continents. Poor usability in protecting online users' rights can have serious consequences as users lose trust and reject the technology in question (Adams, 1999a, 1999b, 2000; Adams & Sasse, 2001; Preece, 2000).

Ultimately, the importance of correctly applying security for online learning programs should not be underestimated. A study of United States users found that protecting *personal information* privacy should increase Internet usage 78% amongst those who already use it and 61% for those who currently do not (Harris & Westin, 1998). These figures show the economic importance of these issues for online learning systems. One way to protect sensitive information transmitted over the Internet is through encryption. Electronic cryptography provides a collection of techniques for encoding communications so that only their intended recipients can understand them.

Encryption Techniques—PGP

It is important in any communications that the sender is assured that what they send is what is received, without any unauthorised access and manipulation. Encryption tools are often used to ensure the *integrity* of the data and the authorised nature of the recipient. The potential advantages of these tools for online learning are clear: Course work or sensitive emails can be communicated with the students' confidence that they are private. The usability of these techniques, however, is debateable.

The marketers of PGP (pretty good privacy), a popular document transfer encryption tool, claim that its graphical user interface allows novice computer users to utilise complex mathematical cryptography. Whitten and Tygar (1999), however, have identified problems with the terminology used by PGP. The system designers have tried to steer away from complex cryptographic terminology by using real-world terms, but those terms are used in uncharacteristic ways. For example, in the real world the same key is used to lock and unlock a door. However, in cryptography and in particular PGP, there is a distinction made between public and private keys. PGP presents no online help to explain the important distinction between these two key icons. Users were either left to work out the distinctions based on other key type data, thumb through a 132-page manual or misinterpret the metaphor. Similarly *a signature* is another cryptographic term that would imply, invoking the real-world metaphor, the use of a mechanism to sign a document. However, within PGP the term is used to denote a step in the encryption procedure (along with private keys) rather than simply signing a document. Even once users understand the terms used within PGP, their use is further complicated by system inconsistencies. Throughout the process the terms *encryption* and *signing* are used, but once the system is encrypting, it presents feedback on the process stating that the system is currently *encoding*.

Ultimately, the language and structure of security mechanisms can often decrease system usability. Whitten and Tygar (1999) identified that the poor usability of *PGP* meant that two thirds of their study participants could not encrypt their data within 90 minutes of using the application. Worse than this was that one-quarter of the users in the study accidentally emailed their secret data unencrypted. Redesigning the interface, however, could have solved many of the usability problems. Several usability issues arose from the metaphors used, which encouraged users to develop inappropriate assumptions about the interface (e.g., keys, signatures). A redesign would have to develop the system to comply with real-world metaphor assumptions (e.g., a key opens and locks a door, a signature identifies who sent a communication but does not make it private). The system also used technical jargon inconsistently, which should be avoided.

Group Working in Videoconferencing and Virtual Reality Systems

The primary usability considerations of online security mechanisms varies according to the different types of online learning environments (Preece, 2000). Online learning environments range from one-to-one text communication to videoconferencing and virtual reality many-to-many collaboration. The greatest challenges to security, including privacy, are presented by videoconferencing and virtual reality systems.

Videoconferencing is increasingly being used to support online learning via computer-supported collaborative learning (CSCL). Videoconferencing really began with the transmission of group images from one room to another via a common monitor (Isaacs & Tang, 1997). However, multimedia communications to support online learning came into their own with the advent of desktop videoconferencing. Users sit in front of their computer and communicate in real time via a microphone, camera and, often, a digital workspace. This configuration is often referred to as a *picture-in-a-picture* (PIP) setup.

Virtual reality applications allow human-computer and human-human interactivity through a sensory environment called the *virtual world* which is *dynamically* controlled by the user's actions. Exploration of that world for learning purposes is often achieved via a computer-animated actor (an avatar). An avatar helps the user relate to and collaborate with the world and other users (Granieri & Badler, 1995; Preece, 2000).

Virtual reality (VR) environments rely heavily on the notion of immersion, both physically and cognitively (Preece, 2000). Keyboard and monitor input devices allow a user to be partially immersed, whilst head-mounted displays produce total immersion in the environment. A user is cognitively immersed in the environment when they feel immersed in the action (Fluckiger, 1995; Tromp, 1995). Initially VR was used for entertainment and training purposes. Virtual simulations of complex real-world systems have been used as learning environments for various conditions (Preece, 2000; Smets, Sappers, Overbeeke, & Van Der Mast, 1995). Collaborative VR environments provide remotely located users with the ability to collaborate via real interactions in a shared artificial environment (Brna & Aspin, 1997). It is frequently argued by constructivists[1] that the advantages of VR for collaborative learning relate to the authenticity of the context (Vygotsky, 1978). VR communication environments have been argued to provide a natural, intuitive environment for communication whilst releasing some of the social taboos from social interactions (Kaur, 1997). However, we note that, as the realism of virtual worlds increases, users are more likely to make inaccurate assumptions about the virtual world's capabilities and limitations, decreasing its usability.

Virtual reality provides an anonymous environment which, this chapter will show, can still allow inappropriate and invasive behaviours. The focus of security protection upon the individual may also be inadequate for threats in the future. It could be argued that a social grouping itself has its own identity, which relates to the individual. This would mean that although an individual is anonymous, if the social grouping is identified then the individual is indirectly identified. Individuals could similarly find it invasive if sensitive information is made public about anonymous individuals from their specific school, church or social group. Online groups formed for learning interactions must therefore be managed as a unit, with their own security needs. It could be argued that, as our societies become larger and more multicultural, the smaller social groupings we join which support our beliefs, feelings and biases become more important.

User's VC/VR Representation Projected to Others

As we move into the future of online learning systems, there are interesting challenges for security mechanisms and their usability. The great advantages of video-conferencing (VC) and virtual reality (VR) are already being realised by many students. However, for us wisely to implement these technologies we must understand potential security problems before they arise. This section reviews many of the foreseeable usability problems through reviews of current multimedia applications (i.e., VC and VR). It is important to note that most multimedia invasions of privacy are not intentional or malicious but design related. Designers' failure to anticipate how information could be used, by whom, and how this might affect users is a significant factor in users perceiving their privacy as having been invaded.

One significant multimedia usability issue relates to technology's ability to distort interactions, thus making them invasive. Ensuring that users are protected from disclosing information they would not wish to have disclosed requires an understanding of these issues. For example, interpersonal distance has been found to dictate the intensity of a response: Faces in a close-up are scrutinised more often than those in the background. Reeves and Nass (1996) argue that, because the size of a face is more than just a representation of an individual, it can influence psychological judgements of a person and thus become an invasive piece of information. Similarly, image quality and camera angles might result in a perception of the user that they regard as inaccurate. Many learning environments rely on social interaction with peers and teachers to aid in the learning process (Preece, 2000). However, users can misjudge the sensitivity of these interactions and the potential threats, resulting in them not adopting appropriately secure behaviours. Similarly inaccurate assumptions could also occur because multimedia communication environments often lack the social, physical and context cues required for users to accurately judge the situation and adapt their behaviour accordingly. A student collaborating in a home setting will act differently from one in a public college setting. Videoconferencing systems that mix the two settings can produce misinterpretations of the situation and inappropriate behaviour for a public interaction (Adams, 2001).

Privacy invasions are frequently due to inaccurate interpretation of the data being received within an interaction. If a user's image has been enlarged (without their knowing it) by a recipient, this can produce the misconception that no one is staring directly at them. In turn the user does not adjust their behaviour accordingly, as they would if someone were staring directly at them in the real world. However, the person receiving the data often does not realise how their actions or potential actions with the user's data may invade the user's privacy. A lack of the facial and body cues that we take for granted in real-world situations can produce an isolating and inhibiting situation for a user. Many virtual reality environments have usability problems with relaying proximity to the users (Preece, 2000). One result of this, which was identified in a virtual reality learning environment, left a user feeling she was being stalked (i.e., followed throughout the environment, stared at). However, the *stalker* had no knowledge of their actions except that they had encountered usability problems (e.g., judging their location within the environment and proximity to other users) with their avatar.

Ultimately, technology can be used, intentionally or unintentionally, to distort assumptions made by those using it. Multimedia environments, in particular, can incur varied and complex privacy problems. The more realistic an environment appears, the more assumptions a user unconsciously accepts. Video-conferencing users will typically assume that the audio is connected to the image on screen, similarly that in virtual reality that a wall has real-world properties and cannot be walked through. However, these assumptions can be either maliciously or unintentionally breached. To take a simple example, a video-conferencing system that allows someone to freeze their video streams (e.g., so that they appear to be avidly viewing the screen but instead have actually gone to make themselves a cup of tea) could produce an inaccurate appraisal of their attention within the interaction. This scenario could also produce a mismatch between the person who is actually watching the images and the assumed person receiving the data (based on the frozen image). The user's resulting behaviours can be inappropriate and the potential invasiveness of the interaction increased.

Online Learning Usability Inhibits Social Interaction and Privacy

Previous research has identified that unacceptable behaviours can unintentionally occur as a result of poor feedback, isolating users from the acceptable social norms for the situation they are in. Often this is caused by poor interface design but it can also arise from misconceptions of user perceptions by organisations and system designers (Adams & Sasse, 2001). With the increase in online learning environments supporting students throughout the world, there is an increasing variation in social and cultural norms. With this diverse population of users, the need for accurately establishing what is acceptable behaviour is becoming a crucial issue. As privacy perceptions are complicated and online environments often defy real-world assumptions, there is a need to identify users' perceptions within these environments.

Dourish (1993) argues that if a system is embedded in the organisational culture, social controls will establish a culture of use that will restrict unacceptable activities. However, many online learning systems rely on establishing a culture and associated norms purely through online interactions (Adams, 2001). We would argue that, although social controls are vital (especially in flatter, more open organisations), relying on them as the only safeguard for privacy is insufficient. It is important to understand that trust and thus social control evolves with a new technology. To nurture this the technology must not breach users' privacy assumptions, especially if those assumptions are based on social cues that are distorted by the technology.

Another important factor in perceived privacy invasions is the role of those receiving the information (Adams, 2001). Someone highly trusted may be able to view highly sensitive information but only if they are deemed, by the user, to have an appropriate role in the information's usage. A tutor viewing a student's course work may be acceptable because of their role, the trust ensured by that role and the organisational context. However although a student may highly trust a close friend (e.g., disclosing relationship details not acceptable for the tutor to know), they may not be acceptable to view their course work.

Many online systems assure users' privacy requirements by stating their privacy procedures and policies, assuming that this will set the user's mind at rest. Others use a third-party service, such as TRUSTe (Benassi, 1999), to assure users that the company keeps within certain guidelines. However, the policies are often rigid and do not allow for variations in how users perceive different types of information. The usefulness of third-party services also depends upon how much the user trusts these virtual, often unknown organisations. Reagle and Cranor (1999), however, have found that the use of brand or real-world organisational names linked to trust badges could reduce these problems. Providing users with links to real-world contacts and help lines, to ensure their privacy is actively being protected, helps to encourage trust within their virtual interaction (Adams, 2001; Preece, 2000).

Security Problems Caused by Recording and Reuse

It is important to review the permanent quality that technology can give to an interaction. When learning interaction occurs without the aid of technology, the only durable element is in the memories of the parties involved and the notes they take.

However, technology-mediated interactions, whether they are text or video controlled, can be recorded and reused. The implications of recording learning interactions should not be underestimated. Adams and Sasse (2001) found that users' perception of control is essential in building trust relationships for effective social interaction. A student's ignorance of a session being recorded or how the information was to be used could cause them great discomfort. Imagined embarrassing scenarios, which may be no less likely if the user had known of the recording, trigger students' anxiety. The important difference is the users' perception that they would have more control of the situation if they knew it was being recorded (Bellotti, 1997).

The simple act of recording users' interactions can increase the sensitivity of the data. Once an interaction is recorded it can frequently be reviewed, edited and seen by unintended and unknown recipients. All of these events can unintentionally, and without malice, become an invasive act. Adams and Sasse (1999b) detail how a presentation at a conference, which was broadcast over the Internet, was recorded initially for later viewing by students and academics. However, the recording was later shown, without the presenter's awareness, at a seminar to demonstrate the technology. The presenter was later met by a friend and told of his appearance at the seminar. The presenter was then worried about how he would appear, out of context, to an unintended audience. The essential point illustrated by this example is that it is important to consider the outcome of reusing information out of context: even if actions are not meant maliciously, they may be perceived as invasive.

Of key importance is the feedback that users are given about who is receiving their information both currently and at a later date. Ultimately, a careful balance must be maintained between developing an appropriate learning system and protecting the user's rights. It is also important to inform the students if the information is to be used for any purpose other than those previously flagged to them.

Solution: The Importance of Feedback and Control

The escalating variety of technologies available to support online learning increases the likelihood of complicated usability problems. With the use of multimedia applications, the complexity of those problems increases tenfold.

One usability problem with online learning environments arises from the control afforded students and tutors by the environments. Automatic viewing rights for tutors or other students without users' control or prior knowledge can cause problems. Similarly, monitoring and tracking users' learning interactions can be useful for tutors, but also potentially invasive if obtained and used inappropriately. For videoconferencing, Mackay (1995) and Bellotti and Sellen (1993) suggest that people should be made aware that their images are being transmitted. Ultimately users should be allowed to weigh up the information value (e.g., increased learning capabilities) against potential privacy risks involved (e.g., embarrassing slipups) prior to the interaction taking place. Users evaluating these factors prior to the interaction reduces the likelihood of these invasions occurring.

Within multimedia environments, the data transmitted is likely to be distorted and the information received completely different from that expected by the users. Within online learning situations, users can inaccurately judge the sensitivity of the information they are releasing (Adams, 2001). It is important for users receiving the data to understand how users who have transmitted it may interpret their actions with that information. In the real world, standing too close to someone or staring at them for too long would result in disapproving looks, coughs, sighs, etc. The user who enlarges a student's videoconferencing image or has their avatar standing on top of another's avatar receives no feedback of the inappropriateness of these behaviours. One solution to these problems lies in providing appropriate feedback to both users about what is being received and how distorted it is likely to be, to develop a joint understanding of the data being transmitted. A visual representation of how they are being seen, including the size of that image, is an essential aid to assessing its sensitivity. It may also be useful for users to receive instructions on where to place their cameras, with instant feedback prior to interactions taking place. Allowing the student to review potential risks involved in a multimedia interaction can also aid them in avoidance behaviours. This feedback is easier to administer within video-conferencing than virtual reality environments. Some researchers, however, have realised the importance of body cues and gestures within virtual reality environments and are seeking to replicate them (Marsh, 1998; Rime & Schiaratura, 1991). Ultimately, there is a need for accurate contextualisation of data for all parties within multimedia interactions. The more appropriate feedback parties receive about the social aspects of that interaction, the easier it will be to develop social norms for acceptable behaviours within these environments.

Finally, the implications of recording learning interactions should not be under-estimated. The simple act of recording users' interactions can increase the sensitivity of the data and the potential risks (e.g., repeated usage, out-of-context viewing, editing). Initially it is important, where possible, to obtain the user's permission to record information. If this is impractical then feedback to users who are recorded must be provided. Any later changes to those who will be viewing the information should also be provided to the user. Finally an attempt to try and contextualise data (e.g., date stamping, country of origin for transmission) should be made. For highly sensitive information, digital watermarking and watercasting should be considered. With the aid of these mechanisms, the copying and editing of multimedia data can be identified and potentially traced (Adams & Sasse, 2001; Brown, Perkins, & Crowcroft, 1999; Craver, Yeo, & Yeung, 1998). Copied multimedia data, once identified, could be traced back to its origins. However, these mechanisms are not automated and thus rely on the user trawling through data trying to find out whether their data is on public display somewhere. Furthermore, there is no mechanism that would inform the person receiving the data that it has been tampered with *against* the user's wishes.

THE FUTURE OF SECURITY FOR ONLINE LEARNING

The rapid progress in providing innovative forms of online learning is opening up many new learning opportunities. As these systems develop, the enrichment of students' learning potential throughout the world will be greatly enhanced. Students can receive information throughout the world in text, audio, video and graphic forms. A myriad of virtual worlds can mediate student interactions and support their learning capabilities. However, with these developments comes a heavy burden of responsibility. Ensuring usability in the security of these systems, their users and their data will allow them to thrive and flourish. Avoiding these issues will ultimately result in their downfall from the weight of users' distrust.

With increasing threats to online programs, security will become a high priority in the systems of the future. What is debatable, however, is how that security will be approached. Current security methods manage potential risks with restrictive, autocratic mechanisms that ignore users, their tasks and the organisational setting. The result is a dramatic decrease in the usability of online programs. Another approach is to develop security and its mechanisms for and with its users. Whichever approach is taken, security is set to be the burning issue of the future, as users trust the global online world less and the threats from unauthorised access increase.

CONCLUSIONS

We have argued that appropriate security mechanisms are essential to prevent unauthorised access to learning materials on behalf of both providers and learners. The poor usability of security mechanisms results in users' insecure behaviours and low motivation (Adams, 2001; Adams et al., 1997). These behaviours, in turn, present (to security specialists) a stereotyped user who cannot be trusted and should not be conversed with. This circle needs to be broken by improving communication between security specialists and users and providing user-centred training and design of security mechanisms. It is important to take this communication to a different level than simply security specialists dictating to their users. The future, therefore, of security design for online learning systems lies in collaboration between users and experts to develop the usable mechanisms required for the future.

The other aspect of security we have addressed in this chapter is privacy, including the need for socially acceptable behaviours in videoconferencing and virtual reality environments. Again, the need for usable and appropriate user feedback and control is essential for maintaining trust and confidence in the system (Preece, 2000). Users need rapidly to learn socially acceptable behaviours when working with systems that impose less rigid social protocols than familiar face-to-face learning situations. Care also needs to be taken over how users' images appear to others and how they may be used out of context. Designers of online learning systems must recognise that people's interpretation of images is strongly influenced by real-world experience and may therefore be inaccurate in the electronic world.

Many of these issues are related to communication and control between the providers of learning resources (at the organisational level) and the users, including both the providers of particular learning materials and the learners. The balance between these two bodies could affect users' perceptions of trust levels, confidence and legitimate use. Imposing mechanisms that circumvent communication or user control may creates perceived feelings of distrust and a lack of confidence in the providing organisation. Krull (1995) suggests that the appropriate use of authority is direction, not control, since explicit, inflexible rules undermine users' confidence. Trust is undermined by force, sending a contradictory message to people that prevents them from judging trade-offs for themselves or feeling part of the proposed solution. A future direction for security would be the development of guidelines and boundaries (but not restrictive controls) that encourage and nurture trust and allow for the natural improvement of users' secure and socially appropriate behaviours.

ENDNOTES

[1] Constructivism is a psychological theory in collaborative learning virtual environments. It highlights the importance of learning environment actions and real interactions. For further information see Vygotsky (1978).

REFERENCES

Adams, A. (1999a). The implications of users' privacy perception on communication and information privacy policies. In *Proceedings of Telecommunications Policy Research Conference* (pp. 65-67) Alexandria, VA: TPRC Press.

Adams, A. (1999b). Users' perception of privacy in multimedia communication. In *Proceedings (Extended Abstracts) of CHI'99* (pp. 53-54). Pittsburgh, PA: ACM Press.

Adams, A. (2000). Multimedia information changes the whole privacy ballgame. In *Proceedings of computers, Freedom and Privacy 2000: Challenging the assumptions* (pp. 25-32). Toronto, Canada: ACM Press.

Adams, A. (2001). Users' perceptions of privacy in multimedia communications. Unpublished doctoral thesis, University College London.

Adams, A., & Sasse, M. A. (1999a). Privacy issues in ubiquitous multimedia environments: Wake sleeping dogs, or let them lie? In *Proceedings of INTERACT'99* (pp. 214-221). Edinburgh, Scotland: Springer.

Adams, A., & Sasse, M. A. (1999b). Taming the wolf in sheep's clothing: Privacy in multimedia communications. *Proceedings of ACM Multimedia '99* (pp. 101-107). Orlando, FL: ACM Press.

Adams, A., & Sasse, M. A. (1999c). The user is not the enemy. *Communications of the ACM, 42*(12), 40-46.

Adams, A., & Sasse, M. A. (2001). Privacy in multimedia communications: Protecting users not just data. In *Proceedings of IMH HCI'01* (pp. 49-64). Lille, France: Springer.

Adams, A., Sasse, M. A., & Lunt, P. (1997). Making passwords secure and usable. In *Proceedings of HCI'97* (People & Computers XII) (pp. 1-19). Bristol, UK: Springer.

Barton, B. F., & Barton, M. S. (1984). User-friendly password methods for computer-mediated information systems. *Computers and Security, 3*, 186-195.

Bateman, B. (2000). Talking tech: Security & Passw***s. *Tech learning*. (Online Journal) CMP Media, Inc. Retrieved from http://www.techlearning.com/db_area/archives/WCE/batetek5.ht. Retrieved on June 12, 2002.

Bellotti, V. (1996). What you don't know can hurt you: Privacy in collaborative computing. In M. A. Sasse, R. J. Cunningham, & R. L. Winder (Eds.), *People and Computers XI (Proceedings of HCI'96)* (pp. 241-261). London: Springer.

Bellotti, V. (1997). Design for privacy in multimedia computing and communications environments. In P. E. Agre & M. Rotenberg (Eds.), *Technology and privacy: The new landscape* (pp. 63-98). Cambridge, MA: MIT Press.

Bellotti, V., & Sellen, A. (1993). Designing of privacy in ubiquitous computing environments. In *Proceedings of ECSCW'93, the 3rd European Conference on Computer-Supported Co-operative Work* (pp.77-92). Milano, Italy: Kluwer Academic Press.

Benassi, P. (1999). TRUSTe: An online privacy seal program. *Communications of the ACM, 42*(2), 56-59.

Bennett, C. (1997). Convergence revisited: Towards a global policy for the protection of personal data. In P. E. Agre & M. Rotenberg (Eds.), *Technology and privacy: The new landscape* (pp. 99-123). Cambridge, MA: MIT Press.

Brna, P., & Aspin, R. (1997). Collaboration in a virtual world: Support for conceptual learning. In D. Dicheva & I. Stanchev (Eds.), *Proceedings of IFIP WG3.3 working conference (Human-computer interaction and education tools*; pp. 113-123) Sofia, Bulgaria NCP ISBN 954 9582 02 7.

Brown, I., Perkins C., & Crowcroft, J. (1999, December). Watercasting: Distributed watermarking of multicast media. *Proceedings of Globecom '99*.

Carroll, J. M. (1996). *Computer security* (3rd ed.). Newton, MA: Butterworth-Heinemann.

Clarke, R. (1997). *Introduction to dataveillance and information privacy and definitions of terms*. Retrieved from http://www.anu.edu.au/people/Roger.Clarke/DV/Intro.html. Retrieved on June 12, 2002.

Cranor, L. F. (2000). Ten years of computer, freedom and privacy: A personal retrospective. In *Proceedings of Computers Freedom and Privacy 2000: Challenging the Assumptions* (pp. 11-23) ACM Press.

Cranor, L. F., Reagle, J., & Ackerman, M. S. (1999). Beyond concern: Understanding Net users' attitudes about online privacy. In *Proceedings of the Telecommunications Policy Research Conference* (September, pp. 25-27). Alexandria, VA. Retrieved on June 12, 2002, from: http://www.research.att.com/projects/privacystudy/.

Craver, S., Yeo, B., & Yeung, M. (1998). Technical trials and legal tribulations. *Communications of the ACM, 41*(7), 45-54.

Davies, S. (1997). Re-engineering the right to privacy. In P. E. Agre & M. Rotenberg (Eds.), *Technology and privacy: The new landscape* (pp. 143-166). Cambridge, MA: MIT Press.

Davis, C., & Ganesan, R. (1993). Bapasswd: A New Proactive Password Checker. In *Proceedings of the National Computer Security Conference* '93, the 16th NIST/NSA conference (pp. 1-15) Baltimore, MD.

Davis, D., & Price, W. (1987). *Security for computer networks*. Chichester, England: John Wiley & Sons.

Diffie, W., & Landau, S. (1998). Privacy on the line: The politics of wiretapping and encryption. Cambridge, MA: MIT Press.

Diotalevi, R. N. (2000). Copyright dot com: The digital millennium in copyright. *Online Journal of Distance Learning Administration, 3*(2). Retrieved on June 12, 2002 from: http://www.westga.edu/~distance/diotalevi32.html

Dourish, P. (1993). Culture and control in a media space. In *Proceedings of ECSCW'93* (pp. 125-137). Kluwer Academic Press.

Federal Information Processing Standards. (1985). *Password usage.* Federal Information Processing Standards Publication 112 May 30, 1985 (FIPSPUB112). Ford, NJ. Also available at http://www.itl.nist.gov/fipspubs/fip112.htm. Retrieved on June 12, 2002.

Fluckiger, F. (1995). *Understanding networked multimedia applications and technology.* London: Prentice Hall.

Ford, W. (1994). Computer communications security: Principles, standard protocols and techniques. NJ: Prentice Hall.

Garfinkel, S., & Spafford, G. (1996), *Practical Unix and Internet security* (2nd ed.). Cambridge, MA: O'Reilly & Associates.

Goffman, E. (1969). *The presentation of self in everyday life.* London: Penguin Press.

Granieri, J. P., & Badler, N. I. (1995). Simulating humans in virtual reality. In R. A. Earnshaw, J. A. Vince, & H. Jones (Eds.), *Virtual reality applications* (pp. 253-269). London: Academic Press.

Harris, L. & Associates, & Westin, A. F. (1998). *E-commerce & privacy: What Net users want.* Hakensack, NJ: Privacy and American Business. Hitchings, J. (1995). Deficiencies of the traditional approach to information security and the requirements for a new methodology. *Proceedings of Computers & Security, 14,* 377-383.

Hitchings. (n.d.a.) Computers and Security. 14, 5(95), 377-383.

Holmström, U. (1999). User-centered design of security software. *Proceedings of Human Factors in Telecommunications*. Retrieved on June 12, 2002, from: http://impcs3.hhi.de/HFT/HFT99/design_99.htm#5

Isaacs, E. A., & Tang, J. C., (1997). Studying bideo-based collaboration in context: From small workgroups to large organizations. In K. E. Finn, A. J. Sellen, & S. B. Wilbur (Eds.), *Video-mediated communications* (pp. 173-197). Mahwah, NJ: Lawrence Erlbaum.

Kaur, K. (1997). Designing virtual environments for usability. *Proceedings of Human-Computer Interaction* (*INTERACT'97*; pp. 636-639). Sydney: Australia: Aus, Chapman & Hall.

Kling, R. (1996). Information technologies and the shifting balance between privacy and social control. In R. Kling (Ed.), *Computers and controversy: Value conflicts and social choices*. London: Academic Press.

Krull, A. (1995). *Controls in the Next Millenium: Anticipating the IT-Enabled Future.* NY: Elsevier Science Ltd.

Mackay, W. E. (1995). 'Ethics, Lies and Videotape...' In *Proceedings of the ACM conference on Human Factors in Computing Systems* (*CHI '95*; pp. 138-145). Denver, CO: ACM Press.

Marsh, T. (1998). An iconic gesture is worth more than a thousand words. In *IEEE International Conference on Information Visualisation IV* (July 29-31, pp. 222-223) London. IEEE Computer Society, online publications: http://computer.org/proceedings/iv/8509/8509toc.htm

McAlister, M. K., Rivera, J. C., & Hallam S. F. (2001). Twelve questions to answer before offering a Web based curriculum. *Journal of Distance Learning Administration, 4*(3). Retrieved on June 12, 2002, from: http://www.westga.edu/~distance/ojdla/summer42/mcalister42.html

Needham, R. M., & Schroeder, M. D. (1978). Using encryption for authentication in large networks of computers. *Communications of the ACM, 21*(12), 993-999.

Neumann, P. G. (1995). *Computer related risks*. New York: ACM Press.

Parker, D. B. (1992). Restating the foundation of information security. In G. G. Gable & W. J. Caelli (Eds.), *IT security: The need for international co-operation* (pp. 139-151). Holland: Elsevier Science.

Preece, J. (2000). *Online communities*. Chichester, England: Wiley.

Reagle, J., & Cranor, L. F. (1999). The platform for privacy preferences. *Communications of the ACM, 42*(2), 48-55.

Reeves, B., & Nass, C. (1996). *The media equation: How people treat computers, television and new media like real people and places*. Cambridge, England: Cambridge University Press.

Rime, B., & Schiaratura, L. (1991). Gesture and speech. In R. S. Feldman & B. Rime (Eds.), *Fundamentals of nonverbal behaviour* (pp. 239-281). Cambridge, England: Cambridge University Press.

Sasse, M. A., Brostoff, S., & Weirich, D. (2001). Transforming the "weakest link": A human-computer interaction approach to usable and effective security. *BT Technical Journal*, *19*(3), 122-131.

Schneier, B. (2000). *Secrets and lies*. Chichester, England: John Wiley & Sons.

Schoeman, F. D. (1992). *Privacy and social freedom*. Cambridge, England: Cambridge University Press.

Smets, G. J. F., Sappers, P. J., Overbeeke, K. J., & Van Der Mast, C. (1995). Designing in virtual reality: Perception-action coupling and affordances. In K. Carr, & R. England (Eds.), *Simulated and virtual realities: Elements of perception* (pp. 189-208). London: Taylor Francis.

Smith, J. (1993). Privacy policies and practices: Inside the organisational maze. *Communications of the ACM*, *36*(12), 104-122.

Tromp, J. G. (1995). Presence, telepresence, and immersion: The cognitive factors of embodiment and interaction in virtual environments. *Proceedings of the FIVE conference, Frameworks for Immersive Virtual Environments*. Retrieved on June 12, 2002, from: http://www.crg.cs.nott.ac.uk/people/Jolanda.Tromp/jola2.html

Vygotsky, L. S. (1978). Mind in society: The development of higher psychological processes. Cambridge, MA: Harvard University Press.

Wacks, R. (1989). *Personal information: Privacy and the law*. Oxford, England: Clarendon Press.

Whitten, A., & Tygar, J. D. (1999). Why Johnny can't encrypt: A usability evaluation of PGP 5.0. *Proceedings of the 8th USENIX Security Symposium*. Retrieved on June 12, 2002, from: http://www.cs.cmu.edu/~alma/johny.pdf

Chapter XIX

How Useful are World Wide Web Discussion Boards and Email in Delivering a Case Study Course in Reproductive Medicine

David Cahill
University of Bristol, UK

Julian Cook
University of Bristol, UK

Julian Jenkins
University of Bristol, UK

ABSTRACT

A pilot course was carried out aiming to evaluate the relative potential of email and World Wide Web-based discussion boards to deliver an online course in reproductive medicine to 18 doctors training in obstetrics and gynecology, distributed around the South West region of England. The course organisers presented one case study per month and asked participants to comment on it by electronic means. The course was evaluated for its ability to deliver and ease of access. Tutors' and participants' views were sought. The information gathered was incorporated into the development of further Internet-based educational projects.

INTRODUCTION

Computer networks such as the Internet have been used for a number of years to enable tutors and learners in higher education to communicate at a distance (Feenberg, 1989; Mason, 1994). However, the potential of this technology to support the training of geographically spread out junior hospital doctors has only recently begun to be explored (Draycott et al., 1997). This paper describes an evaluation of World Wide Web discussion boards and email to deliver an interactive case study course in reproductive medicine from the Centre for Reproductive Medicine, University of Bristol, to doctors across the geographical South West of England and beyond. The course ran between April and August 1998.

There is a clear need for alternative approaches to both undergraduate and postgraduate training to accommodate the requirements of new curricula and increasing knowledge (Calman, 2000). New technologies such as the Internet are a vital component of this. With each year, the alterations that occur in the fabric of education technology mean that a flexible and open approach is vital so as to make best use of these advances (Harden, 2000).

BACKGROUND

Reproductive medicine is that part of gynecology which specifically relates to the process of reproduction. It encompasses such areas of medicine as infertility, miscarriage, and the failure of menstrual periods to begin or to be maintained. It is one of five areas of particular specialist training recognised by the Royal College of Obstetricians and Gynaecologists (RCOG, 2001). Hospitals capable of providing training in these areas are few, and therefore to gain exposure to these areas, doctors in training (hereinafter, trainees) must travel to or work specifically in these hospitals. The University of Bristol Centre for Reproductive Medicine is one such unit capable of providing all the requirements necessary for specialist training in reproductive medicine.

In a region such as the South West of England, it is recognised that long distances make travel to regional centres of expertise difficult for trainees to attend speciality training (RCOG, 1997). Some of the authors (Cahill and Jenkins) developed a full structured training programme for doctors in training at the Centre for Reproductive Medicine, partly through the medium of the Internet. The primary aim of this pilot training course was to test the effectiveness of the Internet to make some elements of that training programme more widely available. Would trainees be able to access the course and would they actually use such a facility in practice, how would they use it, and how could the course be designed to maximise levels of use and usefulness?

Description of the Course

Trainees were invited to enroll through an advertisement that was placed in a regional newsletter for trainees. The course took the form of a series of five monthly case studies, each covering a specific aspect of reproductive medicine. The course was free at the point of delivery for a number of reasons: It was a pilot study under formal evaluation, a pharmaceutical company funded secretarial time and a research grant funded evaluation time.

Details of the content of the course have been published earlier and are only provided here in brief (Jenkins, Cook, Edwards, Draycott, & Cahill, 2001). The text of each case study was sent out by post at the beginning of each month, along with relevant background reading and a series of questions that required a response. This information was also posted on the ReproMED Web site (www.repromed.org.uk) (Jenkins, 1999). The deadline for responses to the questions was the fifteenth of each month. The tutors undertook to return their feedback on the trainees' responses by the end of the month.

Participants submitted their responses by email or on a World Wide Web discussion board. For some months, the submission was by electronic mail (email). For other months, it was by discussion board. The method was decided in advance by the tutors. Any discussion board was within a password-protected area. This allowed a comparison of the relative effectiveness and acceptability of the two technologies. It was anticipated that the discussion board would offer an open forum where participants could see, learn from and interact with each other's contributions, but that this might also be intimidating. Email would have the advantage of being private and more personal.

Data Sources

Participants gave their consent for the evaluation that was undertaken. Data for the evaluation were collected from:
1.   Interviews with both tutors at the beginning and end of the course.
2.   Interviews with five out of 18 trainees registered on the course.
3.   Comments spontaneously exchanged between trainees by email.
4.   Questionnaires sent by email to all participants after two and six months.
5.   Messages sent to the discussion boards were analysed to examine the level of participation in the course.
6.   Logs of the activity on the server during the course were analysed to determine how many different people looked at each page of the course. Internet access figures are hard to count with watertight accuracy. They nevertheless give at least an approximate idea of the number of visitors to each page.

Participation

Eighteen trainees registered to participate in the course and 11 took an active part, by on at least one occasion replying to the questions asked in the case study and posting these on the discussion board or replying by email as appropriate. Seven took no active role in the course. The number of contributions per month measured the

Figure 1: Number of participants (of a possible 18) actively contributing by posting a response to the course in each month

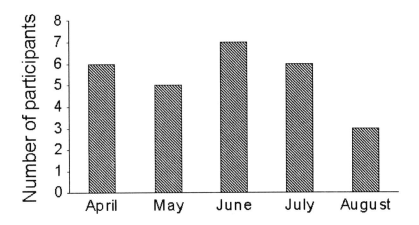

quantity of participation. The average number per month was five. Figure 1 shows the contribution by person for each month. The level of participation was fairly even across the five months of the course. However, it decreased in the last month (i.e., in August, during the summer vacation period). A breakdown of the number of contributions per trainee is given in Figure 2. Figure 3 amplifies Figure 1 by providing additional information on the extent of lurking, with data presented for those posting a response, those who viewed responses, those who looked at specimen answers and those who looked at the feedback. This is of interest as many more viewed the responses or looked at specimen answers and feedback than posted responses.

Figure 2: Number of months in which the 18 registered participants contributed to the course (maximum of five months)

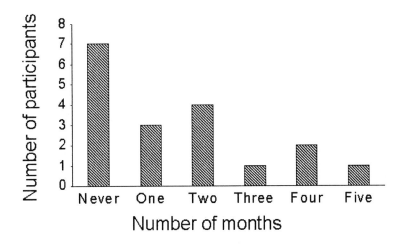

Figure 3: Number of participants (of a possible 18) actively contributing to the course in each month. Data are presented for those posting a response, viewing responses, looking at specimen answers, and looking at feedback

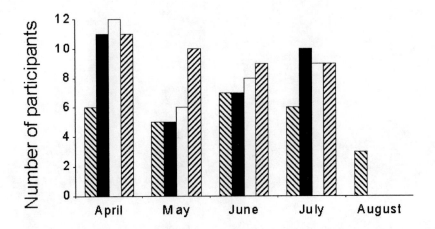

ISSUES AND THEIR RESOLUTION IN THE MODEL DESCRIBED

What were the factors that determined whether or not people participated?

Motivation

All the active participants in the course were apparently motivated by "a genuine interest in the subject matter offered," as described by one of the tutors. Where this was lacking or where this interest was satisfied elsewhere, the course provided little other incentive to take part. Non-contributors commented that a certificate awarded at the end would have increased motivation. One of the tutors believed that motivation levels might have been higher if trainees had paid for the course.

Time

Insufficient time was the most frequent reason given for nonparticipation. This factor is clearly closely tied to motivation, since where time is short, people will prioritise their activities. A large minority of the trainees agreed with the statement "I think the course is worthwhile for me but isn't a top priority at the moment."

Computer Access and Skills

Participation also depended on access to an Internet-linked computer and possession of the skills to use it. At least three trainees had some problems with PC access. For at least four trainees, lack of skills was also a barrier; in one case this prevented any participation and caused another to give up after running into technical problems (Draycott et al., 1997).

Other Factors

Participation was also influenced by the format of the course and by the characteristics of the discussion board and email environments. One commonly held view was that by the time a participant had read everyone else's responses, nothing original was left to add. This view has been reported by others when commenting on participation (Mason, 1994, p. 59). Linked to this was a lack of confidence about airing professional opinions on a discussion board. Contributions would be public (though only public within the tutor/participant environment) and in written and therefore permanent form. One trainee described this feeling: "They are going to find out I don't know anything."

However, the use of email or discussion boards did not seem to have particularly influenced the participation level, as it was similar during the months when email was available and when only the discussion boards were used. One trainee responded only to the case studies where there was an email option, possibly because they felt happier with the privacy that the medium afforded. However this was not a view expressed in the questionnaires or interviews.

How the System was Used

Most participants seemed to assume the tutors were expecting what one interviewee described as "exam-type answers." Most responses closely followed the structure implied by the questions, answering each one fairly fully and in the original order.

Interaction between participants was very low. Almost all communication took the form of tutors' questions answered by the trainees, followed by feedback from the tutors. Trainees were also reluctant to respond to the attempts of the tutors to encourage follow-up discussion. However all the data suggest that the active participants did read the other trainees' responses and found them useful.

Since only a minority of trainees posted their own contributions to the course in any given month, it is important to find out what the remainder of the registered participants was doing. Were they ignoring the course altogether or participating more passively by just looking at what others had posted (lurking)?

From the analysis of the logs of entries to the Web pages, the number who read the discussions was generally not much higher than those who posted responses. With the exception of the case study for the month of April, it seems that the proportion of the registered trainees who were *lurking* was variable and only a small section of the noncontributors. In interviews, three of the trainees confirmed that they had used the course in this way during some months. They read the background material, thought about what to submit as a response, and valued being able to compare the posted responses with what they might have written.

Level of Satisfaction

Overall satisfaction among the active participants was high. All of those who provided data said that they had enjoyed the course and found it useful. Not surprisingly, the more critical trainees were those who had not participated in the course.

Particular Positive Elements

The trainees liked the practical approach of the case study format. The background information was also thought to be useful and practical, and they also appreciated being able to get the tutors' comments online. Despite the low level of interaction observed and the comments in the following subsection, trainees felt the course and the discussion board had allowed for two-way discussions and interactivity, which they saw as a positive feature.

They valued the novelty of both the format and the subject matter. One person found it fascinating to participate in this kind of course in general. Some participants felt that the course had forced them to improve their IT skills. Moreover the online nature of the course meant that they could take part from home. Finally, because responses came from people working in different settings, this gave participants the chance to see how certain clinical routines and protocols varied between different institutions.

Dislikes

Answers on the discussion board were public and so participants considered that they risked looking stupid in front of their peers. The low participation levels exacerbated this fear as it was impossible to disappear into the crowd, which further inhibited discussion.

The problem was exacerbated by the fact that many of the trainees did not know each other beforehand. It was suggested that trainees be familiarised with the discussion board initially through some relatively lighthearted introductory communication.

There was also a perception that participants had played safe, posting what they thought would be an acceptable answer rather than saying what they really thought, and it would have been better if the communication had been more controversial and stimulated more discussion. The trainees' favourite responses were those that presented a few comments rather than a complete exam-type answer.

Participants did have some problems with the technology, either getting access to it or using it. There was some frustration caused by lost postings. Another source of frustration for some was the requirement for Internet access.

How Much Did People Learn from the Course?

Neither the pilot nor its evaluation aimed to establish objectively whether and how much people learned from this course. However, almost all the active participants in the course believed they had learned quite a lot. A similar proportion felt more confident that they were better equipped to advise couples with fertility problems as a result of doing this course.

Coping With the Technology

Of the 18 registered trainees, eight were already comfortable with the use of computers and the Internet. For a further six, the technology was unfamiliar but the course offered an opportunity to learn about it. For the remaining four, it was an insurmountable barrier that prevented participation. Some trainees found the Web site and discussion boards easy to use, while for others it was more of a problem.

Access to equipment was an impediment for a number of trainees. Some had no access at work or home. Others only had access at work that restricted the hours when they could study. However a positive outcome of the course for one trainee was that his place of work was persuaded to provide a networked computer.

Although a minority of trainees felt that email was the best medium for submitting their answers, there was a general agreement that the discussion board was the right medium for this kind of course, particularly as it enabled people to read a range of answers.

FUTURE TRENDS

Even though the level of active participation appears quite low, it was in fact comparable with those experienced by the Open University using similar technology (Mason, 1994). Nevertheless it is worth considering how participation levels may be increased. Discussion board environments might be made more familiar and friendly. Participants could be brought together physically at the beginning so that they would "see each other as human beings." Discussion boards can be set up for trainees to try out discussing subjects not directly connected with the course (Mason).

We restricted the application of the course to the use of email and discussion boards. We wanted to use methods of communication that would be instantly (or with minimal difficulty) applicable to all those participating in the study and to remove technological barriers as a reason for non-participation, having identified this previously as a deterrent (Draycott et al., 1997). We therefore deliberately kept the technology aspects simple, avoiding the difficulty of multiple system use (Jackson, 2000). The introduction to a networking environment poses interesting challenges for individuals previously unaccustomed to this, even though these were a group whose familiarity with information technology was reasonable. They also found this environment challenging and very different and had uncertainties, for instance, regarding the public and exposed status of their responses, a concern identified and discussed in other situations (Jones & Asensio, 2001). While in theory, networked environments are more flexible (Jones & Bloxham, 2001), our experience is that that flexibility can only be explored if participants are willing to be open to that.

Conferencing systems are useful methods for distance learning and communication and are probably of particular value in engendering a community spirit for learning (Conole, 2001; Garrison, Anderson, & Archer, 2000). Significant technical and technological support is required for conferencing that prevents its use in settings outside centres where such systems are regularly in place. This was not feasible within the setting we have described and, further, we have not applied its use in further courses or in our current distance learning postgraduate degree course (www.red-msc.org.uk).

Extrinsic motivation may be provided by awarding a certificate at the end of the course dependent on regular contributions. This would also encourage people to keep participating right to the end. A similar effect may be achieved by instituting points for continuing education or making the course a module of a training programme or degree course. If higher numbers of trainees were enrolled for such a course and with increased levels of participation, contributors would enjoy greater anonymity, which in turn may facilitate higher levels of participation. Although the level of participation was acceptable and the case study format proved popular, it did not exploit the discussion board's potential for facilitating the exploration of issues and developing ideas through discussion and debate. Tutors could give feedback from the outset that encourages discussion, perhaps, for example, by asking contributors to explain or expand upon their views or by inviting trainees to comment on other trainees' contributions.

An element of collaborative working may also help stimulate discussion (Klemm, 1998). Participants can be divided into subgroups, each of which uses a private discussion board to discuss and prepare a case for presentation to other groups. In this way, less-confident trainees have anonymity while learning from others, whose knowledge in turn deepens through helping and explaining to the others.

While technology remains a barrier for a number of people, the experience of this course suggests that incentive for institutions to provide access, training and support will come when there is a demand from users who perceive that the Internet contains resources that are valuable to them.

CONCLUSION

The experience of this course suggests that the Internet is a suitable medium for a course of this type. The World Wide Web, discussion boards and email can be used in conjunction for both static materials and exchanging comments and feedback.

However there are a number of issues that need to be addressed in order to optimise participation. Positive incentive to take part will be necessary for many potential participants, some users will need technical support in order to overcome problems of access, and care will need to be taken to create an environment where people will not be intimidated by its unfamiliarity.

Despite the limited participation levels and reluctance to exploit the medium to its full potential, the high level of satisfaction among those who participated actively in the course makes it clear that the basic format and content of the course was successful and the medium effective and appropriate.

The lessons we have drawn from this exercise and are applying to future courses include:

- having face-to-face contact between participants at the start of a course (introducing the element of social contact and ensuring minimal skill levels)
- having all the email responses logged, preferably into a database
- avoiding information overload for the participants
- working together in groups, such as pairs or triplets
- avoiding summer or holiday months

The techniques described will only form a part of any educational delivery, with other formats playing greater or lesser roles depending on the environment. We have maintained a steady development of these courses, and in the autumn of 2001, we launched an Internet-based distance learning MSc course (in reproduction and development)(www.ReD-MSc.org.uk) under the aegis of the University of Bristol. Much of the educational content of this new course is delivered remotely and students work at home for 70% of the course. Much of the experience from this evaluation forms the basis of the underlying structure of that course. It is also interesting to note that others, by different pathways, have reached a similar working plan for delivering and moderating education on the World Wide Web (Salmon, 2000).

Perhaps the last word on this should be from a trainee who commented that: "I am sure that this is going to be one of the ways we learn and keep up-to-date in the future and it has been a very useful exercise for me."

REFERENCES

Calman, K. C. (2000). Postgraduate specialist training and continuing professional development. *Medical Teacher, 22*, 448-451.

Conole, G. C. (2001). *External evaluation of the neonatal training in Europe project (Final report)*. Southampton, England: Leonardo da Vinci European Programme, Southampton University NHS Trust.

Draycott, T. J., Cook, J., Edwards, J., Read, M., Fox, R., Williams, J., & Jenkins, J. (1997). *The practicability of computer aided learning for training SW O&G trainees*. Paper presented at the Learning Technology in Medical Education Conference, Bristol, England (pp. 139-146) Bristol, England: CTI Medicine.

Feenberg, A. (1989). The written world: On the theory and practice of computer conferencing. In R. Mason & A. Kay (Eds.), *Mindweave: Communication, computers and distance education* (pp. 22-39) Oxford, England: Pergamon Press.

Garrison, R., Anderson, T., & Archer, W. (2000). Critical inquiry in a text-based environment: Computer conferencing in higher education. *The Internet and Higher Education, 2*(2-3), 87-105.

Harden, R. M. (2000). Evolution or revolution and the future of medical education: Replacing the oak tree. *Medical Teacher, 22*, 435-442.

Jackson, M. A. D. (2000). Computer systems for distributed and distance learning. *Journal of Computer Assisted Learning, 16*(3), 213-228.

Jenkins, J. M. (1999). The Internet, intranets and reproductive medicine. *Human Reproduction, 14*(3), 586-589.

Jenkins, J. M., Cook, J., Edwards, J., Draycott, T., & Cahill, D. J. (2001). Medical education over the Internet: A pilot training programme in reproductive medicine. *British Journal of Obstetrics and Gynaecology, 108*, 114-116.

Jones, C., & Asensio, M. (2001). Experiences of assessment: Using phenomenography for evaluation. *Journal of Computer Assisted Learning, 17*(3), 314-321.

Jones, C., & Bloxham, S. (2001). Networked legal learning: An evaluation of the student learning experience. *International Review of Law, Computers & Technology, 15*(3), 317-329.

Klemm, W. R. (1998). New ways to teach neuroscience: Integrating two teaching styles with two instructional technologies. *Medical Teacher, 20*, 364-370.

Mason, R. (1994). *Using communications media in open and flexible learning.* London: Kogan Page.

Royal College of Obstetricians and Gynaecologists. (1997). *National trainees committee survey of training: 1997 report.* London: Author.

Royal College of Obstetricians and Gynaecologists. (2001). *Subspecialisation syllabi.* Retrieved September 1, 2001, from http://www.rcog.org.uk/syllabus/background.html

Salmon, G. K. (2000). *E-moderating: The key to teaching and learning online.* London: Kogan Page.

Chapter XX

Ensuring Optimal Accessibility of Online Learning Resources

David Sloan
University of Dundee, Scotland

Lorna Gibson
University of Dundee, Scotland

Scott Milne
University of Dundee, Scotland

Peter Gregor
University of Dundee, Scotland

ABSTRACT

Online educational resources have the potential of providing enhanced access to education for everyone. To achieve this, these resources must be accessible both to the increasingly diverse range of potential users and via the diverse browsing environments now available. Legal and moral obligations also exist to ensure that disabled people are not unjustifiably denied access to education. Established accessible design guidelines and techniques exist which, if followed, help to ensure a more usable, portable and effective learning resource for all users. However, due to a lack of awareness of these amongst educational resource providers and shortcomings in courseware authoring tools, many current online learning resources may contain significant accessibility barriers.

This chapter outlines arguments for accessible design and provides a brief overview of accessible design techniques. Also discussed are strategies for ensuring accessibility of e-learning, which should include provision of appropriate support to resource providers in terms of training and guidance in accessible courseware design, as well as provision of technologies which promote creation of and access to accessible online learning resources.

INTRODUCTION

There is an increasing need for those involved in creating online education resources to ensure that such resources are accessible to the widest possible audience. There has always been a moral obligation to ensure that educational resources are accessible by people with disabilities, and there are now increasing legal responsibilities placed upon educational institutions to avoid unjustified discrimination.

Accessibility problems are not only encountered by disabled users—browsing technologies can effectively disable many users. Developments in the mobile Internet field have led to a diversification of browsing environments, and as Internet use spreads across the world, the number of users with limited bandwidth connections increases—users for whom complex or cutting-edge Web content may not be accessible.

The Web presents an unprecedented platform for innovation in teaching and learning and also offers the opportunity to widen access to education, reaching out to individuals who have previously been prevented from gaining quality and prolonged education. Unfortunately there remains a great deal of communication and information technology (C&IT) which presents many user groups with significant accessibility barriers. This "digital divide" (Waddell, 1999) frequently prevents access to Web content by the people who would benefit most from this content—ease of communication plus access to online shopping, banking and education. Sadly, the poor level of accessibility of the majority of Web content appears to be due to a lack of awareness of accessible design issues—not only in terms of the needs and requirements of disabled and other Web users, but also through misconceptions as to what accessible design does and does not require.

This chapter briefly outlines the arguments for taking accessibility into account during design and discusses strategies for ensuring that accessibility plays a core part in the design, development and maintenance of online educational material. Common accessibility problems and solutions are discussed, as is the vital issue concerning possible conflicts between pedagogical value and accessibility of Web-based teaching and learning resources.

BACKGROUND

Many reasons exist for treating Web accessibility as a vitally important issue. Primary considerations include:

- diversity of users
- diversity of browsing situations
- legal implications

Diversity of Users

In order to design an accessible Web resource, the full spectrum of potential users must be considered, including people with disabilities. There are a variety of disabilities or combination of disabilities which may result in users having problems in accessing Web content. For example, accessibility barriers may be encountered by users who are blind, visually impaired, cognitively impaired, physically disabled, hearing impaired or deaf.

There are also many users who would never consider themselves disabled but may encounter accessibility problems because of, for example, ageing, dyslexia or colour-blindness. The nature of disabilities affecting Web access may be temporary or long-term, degenerative or fluctuating, and may affect any user at any time.

There are a large number of assistive technologies available to people with disabilities, providing access to Web- and computer-based information in an accessible format. These technologies include text-to-speech devices such as screen readers and speech browsers for blind users and alternative input devices such as gesture recognition devices for manually impaired users. The success of these technologies depends on original content being provided in such a way that the assistive technology can accurately represent it in a particular format.

Therefore the onus on the Web developer is to make sure that information is provided in such a way as to ensure that it can be rendered appropriately by assistive technologies. Strategies and techniques for achieving this are discussed later in the chapter.

Diversity of Browsing Environment

As development continues into technology for accessing Web content, so the diversity of browsing environments grows. Newell and Gregor (1997) suggest that there are direct parallels between the needs of a disabled person operating C&IT in an "ordinary" environment and the needs of an able-bodied person operating C&IT in an "extraordinary" environment. In Web terms, the needs of a blind person browsing the Web using a speech browser could be considered analogous to a sighted person using an in-car browsing system where information is provided in audio format only.

New browsing technologies such as TV-based Web browsers, Internet-enabled mobile phones and personal digital assistants (PDAs) bring with them restrictions in terms of display capabilities, input devices and rate of delivery of information. Such mobile devices are also more likely to be used outdoors, perhaps in adverse weather or excessively noisy conditions. Likewise, users of legacy browsing technologies and users with restricted Internet access or low-bandwidth Internet connections may encounter similar accessibility problems.

In the above examples, the effect of browsing environments is to disable the users of these devices. Therefore designing accessible Web resources will help to ensure that not only can those resources be used by disabled people but also by able-bodied people disabled by their browsing environment.

Legal Implications

In a number of countries, there is increasingly significant legislation relating directly or indirectly to accessibility of Web resources.

In the UK, the Disability Discrimination Act (DDA) of 1995 sets out a legal obligation of goods, facilities, and service providers to ensure that users are not unjustifiably discriminated against on account of a disability. Whilst the act does not directly refer to Web sites, it has been argued (M. Sloan, 2001) that an organisation which provides a poorer service to or denies a service to a disabled person as a consequence of an inaccessible Web site is likely to be in breach of the legislation provided in the DDA. The rights of disabled people in the UK education sector are further covered by the Special Educational Needs and Disability Act (SENDA) of 2001, which places responsibilities on post-16 educational institutions to make "reasonable adjustments" to ensure that disabled students are not disadvantaged and that disabled students are not treated "less favourably" without justification.

UK disability law does not currently refer directly to Web accessibility. In Australia, however, a clear relationship between Web accessibility and disability discrimination was established in autumn 2000 when the Sydney Olympics Organisation Committee (SOCOG) was found to be in breach of Australia's Disability Discrimination Act, as significant parts of the official Olympic Games Web site could not be accessed by blind users using a Braille display (*Maguire v. SOCOG*, 2000).

In the United States, the rights of people with disabilities are defined in the Americans with Disabilities (ADA) of 1990. This has been reinforced by the revision in 1998 of Section 508 of the Rehabilitation Act, which introduced the requirement that US federal agencies make their information technology accessible to users with disabilities.

Guidelines and Resources

The World Wide Web Consortium (W3C) recognised the importance of Web accessibility through the establishment of the Web Accessibility Initiative (WAI), which has, in turn, developed the Web Content Accessibility Guidelines (WCAG) (World Wide Web Consortium, 1999). These guidelines define technical requirements of Web resources in order to ensure that no accessibility barriers are present.

The structure of the WCAG and accompanying resources is such that developers can assess existing resources for accessibility levels through checklists of guidelines. Furthermore, since the WCAG are prioritised, compliance—and therefore accessibility—can be assessed at three different levels, dependent on the significance of accessibility barriers present.

The WCAG have provided a framework for a number of automatic and semiautomatic checking tools, such as Bobby and A-Prompt (see the *Supplementary Web References* section), which provide useful validation tools for developers wishing to check for specific accessibility problems. In addition to the WCAG, the WAI has also produced separate guidelines for developers of authoring tools and for developers of browsing technology used to access Web content.

It is increasingly apparent that there is a relationship between WCAG compliance and compliance with relevant disability legislation around the world. Section 508 legislation in the US actually incorporates many of the guidelines of the WCAG directly into legislation; while during the ruling of the *Maguire v. SOCOG* case it was suggested that compliance with all Priority One checkpoints of the WCAG would ensure a Web site's compliance with the Australian DDA. M. Sloan (2001) suggests that a similar situation is likely to exist in the UK; although in the absence of a UK case at the time of writing, this remains speculation.

There are many other useful resources on accessible Web design, and the WAI provides a list of some of these (see the *Supplementary Web References* section). Supplementing the WCAG, the IMS Consortium produced guidelines specifically for accessible educational Web content (IMS Global Consortium, 2001). For Java-based Web content, IBM's Java Accessibility Checklist (see the *Supplementary Web References* section) provides Java developers with additional guidance on creating accessible resources.

Accessibility of Web content written in Java can be enhanced through the Java Accessibility API, which contains classes and programming language interfaces designed to allow information from graphical applications to be made available to assistive technologies.

ACCESSIBLE WEB CONTENT DESIGN— OVERVIEW

It should be stressed that it is beyond the scope of this chapter to provide a comprehensive guide to all accessibility problems and solutions; for more details, readers are referred to the W3C Web Accessibility Initiative's Web pages or to the many excellent Web-based resources on accessible design.

Page and Site Markup

To ensure content can be accessed satisfactorily in as many browsing environments as possible, Web content should be written in valid HTML, following specifications set by the World Wide Web Consortium (W3C). Web pages should include in the HTML code a declaration statement of the version of HTML being used, as well as a statement of the natural language of the document; any change in natural language within the page should be marked up. HTML elements should be used to reflect page structure by marking up key structural elements such as headings and lists, and special attention should also be paid to the structural markup of tables and forms.

HTML elements have been provided to allow better rendering of tables and forms in linear or non-graphic browsing environments. Elements exist to allow detailed structural markup of data tables, including row and column headings, subheadings, and groups of columns and rows, and these elements should be used to ease access of tables to users of non-graphic browsing devices. For some very complex tables, however, it may be necessary to provide a separate textual description of the data contained therein. Care should be taken when using tables for page layout purposes, to ensure page information can still be understood in browsers which linearise tables.

Similarly, for forms, elements and attributes to provide assistive technologies with more information about form structure should also be used. Additionally, all necessary components of a Web form should appear in a logical manner to people who cannot see the form, such that any instructions appear first, then input fields with associated labels, with a "submit" button as the last feature of the form. Forms must also be fully operable via the keyboard.

While Adobe's portable document format (PDF) is a useful format for providing documents on the Web which preserve appearance regardless of platform, PDF access through a screen reader is unpredictable. Despite recent advances made by Adobe in terms of accessible PDF creation, accessibility to blind and visually impaired users cannot currently be guaranteed. Therefore this file format should not be relied upon as the only way of providing information and should not be used as a replacement for HTML. The most appropriate use of PDF is to allow downloading of documents which are intended for printing (Nielsen, 2001).

Navigation

There are a number of techniques which can be applied to make navigation through Web content easier and more efficient for many users with disabilities, including blind and visually impaired users of text-to-speech browsing devices and users whose disability prevents them from being able to use a mouse.

Text of hyperlinks should clearly indicate the destination page. A poor example of hyperlink text (link text italicized) might be:

Click here to find out about the mating habits of dolphins.

A good example of hyperlink text (link text italicized) might be:
Dolphins and their mating habits.

Pages of a Web site should always have appropriate titles, and where possible hyperlink text should be consistent with the destination page titles and headings. Links should not open destination pages in separate browser windows without explicitly informing users that this will happen, and links to non-HTML documents should also be clearly indicated. To supplement navigation, a well-designed, easy to use and accurate search facility can speed up information location. Similarly, a site map, listing all pages, can also provide an accessible way for users to navigate to specific information.

Any information accessible via a mouse action must also be accessible via the keyboard. Techniques for enhancing keyboard navigation and control include ensuring that keyboard operation of forms is logical and that keyboard shortcuts are provided to important content.

Until browser support for cascading style sheets is such that they can be used to reliably specify page layout for particular browsing devices, one particularly useful interim technique, which particularly benefits users of auditory and other non-graphic browsing environments, is to provide internal page links which allow efficient access to main page content.

Client-side JavaScript should not be relied upon as the only means of providing navigational features or any other content—for example, links activated by JavaScript may mean information becomes inaccessible when JavaScript is turned off or not supported.

Page Appearance

To optimise accessibility of text on a Web page, appropriate language should be used for the context of the page, and spelling and grammar checks should be carried out as a matter of course. Wherever possible, text should be broken into lists or short paragraphs. These techniques will help users to visually locate and process information on a page and will also benefit users receiving pages aurally through a text-to-speech device.

Rather than attempt to provide a variety of different text appearance options to accommodate specific visual impairments, a sensible default text appearance should be chosen, which can be changed by users. Font size of text should be specified in relative terms, so that font size can be altered depending on eyesight and/or screen resolution.

Reasonable contrast must exist between default text and background colours; and if colour is used to distinguish information, this information should also be distinguishable by other means. Red/green colour schemes are particularly troublesome for many colour-blind people, while red/blue text and background schemes cause chromostereopsis, an unpleasant temporary visual condition (Pearrow, 2000).

The recommended way to control page appearance is through use of cascading style sheets (CSS). Here, style information is stored separately to the Web page content and can be changed by users, if necessary, through user-defined style sheets.

Given current uneven browser support for CSS, it is necessary to test pages using CSS in a variety of browsers, and it is also necessary to ensure information is still accessible when CSS are not supported at all.

Where frames are used, consideration should be taken to ensure that users of browsers which do not support frames can still access content. Frames should be given a meaningful title indicating the frame's content, and the <noframe> element should be used to present information explaining page layout and frame content.

Graphic and Multimedia Content

Use of multimedia to supplement textual information can greatly enhance online learning resources and can particularly enhance accessibility of content for those with low levels of literacy and with learning disabilities and other cognitive impairments, Unfortunately multimedia content frequently presents access barriers to many others, including blind, visually impaired, hearing impaired, and physically impaired users.

In addressing accessibility issues relating to graphics and multimedia, the core principle is to ensure as far as possible that information provided by graphical and multimedia content is provided in an alternative textual format as well. This is much to be preferred over removing multimedia content, which may be particularly beneficial to a large majority of users.

For simple graphics, HTML provides an attribute for the <img> element—the alt attribute, often referred to as "ALT Text." This attribute is displayed by non-graphic browsers and is used to provide a textual alternative for the image. The content of this alternative text must be appropriate; alternative text should provide the *same information* as the graphic—not necessarily the same as a description of the graphic.

For complex graphics which provide information, such as graphs or charts, a separate text description should be provided. For graphics which serve as navigational links, including image maps, alternative text should indicate the destination of the link. Graphics containing text should be avoided where possible; but if they are used, the alternative text should contain identical text to the graphic. Graphics which provide no information to users, usually graphics which are used to control the layout of a page, should have null alternative text here—i.e. alt=""—explicitly indicating that the image has no content value.

Provision of accessible audio/visual content presents significantly more challenges than providing accessible static graphics. Captions are required for spoken word, plus any other audio output, and textual descriptions are required of all visual content. These textual alternatives can become very complex, particularly where time-dependent information is being provided by dynamic content such as video or animated content.

It is possible to embed captions within the multimedia object, through captioning tools such as MAGpie (see the *Supplementary Web References* section), and where possible such techniques should be explored. Often, however, a compromise may have to be made, for example, by providing captions as an alternative to audio content and a separate textual transcription of the multimedia clip.

Macromedia's Flash, a proprietary file format widely used for providing dynamic audio-visual content, can greatly enhance the browsing experience. However, depending on content, Flash can also result in content which is inaccessible to many users, including those with a visual or motor impairment. In February 2002, Macromedia introduced enhanced Flash accessibility features with the launch of the Flash MX authoring environment and the Flash 6 player, providing the potential for some Flash content to be made accessible to certain screen reading technologies. Wherever possible these accessibility features should be used for creation and presentation of Flash content.

PROMOTING ACCESSIBLE DESIGN OF EDUCATIONAL WEB RESOURCES

Current Problems

Rowland (2000) describes the important role the Web has to play in postsecondary education and the challenges the sector faces in ensuring that Web-based education is accessible to disabled students. In defining solutions to accessibility problems in an educational environment, Rowland identifies six stakeholders whose involvement is key to any strategy for addressing accessibility:

1. creators of browsers
2. creators of assistive technology
3. creators of Web authoring tools
4. creators of courseware
5. resource providers
6. resource users

A lack of awareness of accessibility issues in any of these stakeholder groups will limit the effectiveness of any accessible design strategy adopted by educational institutions.

In particular, awareness in accessible design of resource providers is a current issue which must be addressed. Some may simply be unaware of the need for accessible design. Others may have misguided beliefs relating to accessibility; they may believe, for example, that accessibility is an expensive add-on which obstructs the true goals and purposes of Web sites, or that accessibility is not compatible with a visually pleasing, technologically advanced Web site.

The Web Content Accessibility Guidelines (WCAG) are an excellent resource helping designers create accessible content, and reading of the WCAG and accompanying resources suggests that the above beliefs are misguided. However, evidence (Mosier & Smith, 1987) indicates that education through the provision of design guidelines can often be ineffectual, and that there are specific usability problems with the current WCAG (Colwell & Petrie, 1999). There is therefore a clear need for the ongoing development being carried out by the W3C on the format of the guidelines and how they are presented, and the format of Version 2 of the WCAG is anticipated to be markedly different to the Version 1 format.

An additional problem is the fact that many Web design publications still pay little attention to accessible design. While a small, but increasing, number of titles discuss the topic, most notably Paciello (2000), Clark (2002) and Thatcher et al. (2002); Bingham (2001) surveyed 353 books on Web design and related topics and considered that the vast majority failed to promote accessibility.

Another challenge to the creation of accessible content relates to the nature of authoring tools increasingly used to create Web resources, from general Web authoring tools to specific courseware authoring tools. These applications allow rapid creation of feature-rich Web content by authors, many of whom have little knowledge of general HTML or other Web design techniques, let alone accessible and usable design techniques. In theory, this promotes the accessibility of the Web, by allowing easy access to Web content *contribution* by individuals without expertise in Web authoring.

Authoring tools frequently generate nonvalid HTML complete with proprietary tags and often do not promote insertion of accessibility features, such as alternative text for images, so inaccessible Web content is all too often created. The lack of awareness of many content providers in accessible design issues is therefore accentuated by the relative failure of popular authoring tools to promote the creation of accessible resources.

Fortunately, since the amendment of Section 508 of the Rehabilitation Act came into effect in the US in 2000, there has been a flurry of development of accessibility checking and retrofitting tools, and some of these are now integrated with popular authoring tools such as those from Adobe and Macromedia (Schmitt, 2002). A similar effect is noticeable in authoring tools aimed specifically at the learning technology sector, and accessibility of courseware authoring tools such as those provided by Blackboard and WebCT is now being addressed.

It is clear though that there is an increasing need to educate developers in accessible design techniques given the current constraints of the environments in which Web development takes place. In particular, accessibility must be considered a core issue throughout the life cycle of a piece of Web content, from design and development through to maintenance programs.

Often the demands on the appearance of pages by those commissioning sites, plus restrictions on time and financial, technical and human resources, result in developers working under severe constraints that, in some cases, may not be compatible with accessible design. This means that there is a real need for education and awareness in accessibility issues to be extended to administrators, policy makers, and those charged with commissioning Web content.

Strategies

How, then, does one go about ensuring that online learning technology is of optimal accessibility to the intended users, in the environment in which it is to be used? Any strategy towards accessible curricula should have two key aims:

1. Appropriate technology must be provided by educational institutions to ensure optimal accessibility of digital resources.
2. Providers of educational resources must be provided with knowledge and training on accessible design.

The first aim refers to the need for technology, such as authoring tools, which facilitates accessible design of online educational content to be made available to resource providers, and for standards-compliant browsing technology and assistive technology to be made available to allow full access to that content. Responsibility therefore lies on educational institutions to choose "off-the-shelf" Web-related technologies such as browsers and courseware with extreme care. A detailed critique of the possible technologies available to educational institutions and strategies for the provision of such technologies is, however, beyond the scope of this chapter.

In order to fulfil the second aim, to promote awareness amongst resource providers in accessible design, and to ensure that materials that are produced do meet acceptable accessibility standards, several action points are suggested:

*   Personnel involved in developing Web material must be provided with information on accessible design. This could take the form of workshops on accessible design and training in the resources and tools available to developers to evaluate resource accessibility.
*   If development of resources is taking place within virtual learning environments (VLEs), Web resource developers should be made aware of potential accessibility barriers inherent in the VLE and its authoring tools and become familiarised with techniques for overcoming or avoiding such barriers. Promotion of VLE use through staff development and training should incorporate accessibility awareness and design techniques.
*   In all development projects, accessibility must play a core role in design strategy, from initial prototypes through to testing and evaluation stages. In particular, users with disabilities should be involved throughout the development of resources, from requirements gathering to evaluation and testing.
*   All resources should comply with as many Web Content Accessibility Guidelines as possible and at a minimum with all Priority One guidelines. In-house accessibility standards, based on the Web Content Accessibility Guidelines, may help to effectively transmit the requirements contained in the guidelines to developers, and it is vital that some mechanism exists to ensure such standards are maintained.

- Where possible, Web technologies which are approved by the W3C should be used during design, in preference to proprietary technologies. Where this is not feasible or practical, techniques should be used to ensure optimal accessibility of proprietary features. In simple terms, this often requires information to be provided in an alternative format.

Accessibility Checking Techniques

It is particularly recommended that existing online educational resources are regularly reviewed for potential accessibility problems. The authors have discussed a methodology for assessing Web sites for accessibility (D. Sloan, Gregor, Rowan and Booth, 2000), and an independent expert accessibility review can help to provide an indication of the number, frequency, location and significance of accessibility barriers, and how they might be overcome. There are, though, many relatively simple steps that can be taken to check for accessibility barriers. These include:

- Utilisation of free accessibility checking tools, such as Bobby.
- Manual checks of resources: can the text size and style be adjusted by the user? Can the resource be used without a mouse?
- Testing in different browsing environments, including non-graphic browsers. This is particularly important where the resource will be used as a Web application accessible from diverse browsing environments.
- Use of the resource with assistive technologies such as screen readers or speech browsers.
- Evaluation of the resource with disabled people.

PEDAGOGICAL ISSUES

Developers of online learning technology may question the wisdom of striving to make a particular learning resource accessible to certain groups. Some may argue that the pedagogical value of the tool would be adversely affected by the adjustments which would have to be made in order to remove certain accessibility barriers.

As an example, an online learning tool assesses archaeology students by asking them to identify photographs of artefacts in order to date them. To provide all photos with alternative textual descriptions would nullify the pedagogical value of the resource. Clearly, in this example, direct implementation of accessibility guidelines is not appropriate. However, the case of the blind archaeology student still needs to be considered. How else might that student be assessed? One answer might be to provide only blind students with a limited textual description of artefacts, which can be used for identification without compromising the validity of the assessment exercise.

The above example illustrates that for educational resource providers, in practical terms, accessibility depends to some extent on the circumstances under which a resource will be used and by whom, and these factors should be of the utmost consideration throughout the design and development process.

It is important to emphasise that accessible design should not result in a "lowest common denominator" syndrome, resulting in a poorer resource for all. Accessibility of online learning is not about removing value in order to satisfy particular checkpoints on a list. Instead the aim must be to ensure that particular user groups are not denied information or services. Where possible, this can be avoided through good design, but where there is no way of making a resource accessible, the information should be provided in an alternative form.

FUTURE TRENDS

While much can be done to ensure that current Web resources are designed so as to be optimally accessible, developments in both Web development technology and assistive technology mean that, in coming years, the nature and philosophy of accessible design is likely to change. One particular decision currently related to accessible design is the debate on whether separate versions of Web resources, depending on an individual's needs, should be provided, or whether the goal of universal, inclusive design can be achieved.

In many cases, Web site providers have opted for a dual interface model—a graphic-rich site, usually with known accessibility barriers, plus a separate text-only site. Advantages in taking this approach to accessible design include the avoidance of the need to redesign a graphics-rich site with significant accessibility barriers and the relative ease of creating an "accessible" version of a site at very short notice.

There are a number of reasons why a separate text-only site should not be considered as a global solution for accessibility problems. While they may in theory be suitable for users who cannot access graphics, frequently text-only versions are generated automatically from graphical sites and consequently preserve many usability and accessibility problems from the graphical site. To avoid these problems may entail a commitment to a high maintenance cost solution of two separate sites.

As previously discussed, for many groups of users, the absence of graphics and multimedia from a Web site can greatly detract from the accessibility of information, so equating "text-only" with "accessible" is misguided. Accessibility of information to individuals with cognitive disabilities, such as attention deficit disorder or learning difficulties, can be greatly enhanced by the use of icons, pictures and sound (Jiwnani, 2001). In many other cases the provision of pictures and other multimedia can help able-bodied users to locate, identify and understand information and generally enhance the user experience.

Instead, there is undoubtedly logic in developing a single Web site which has the potential to be displayed in a variety of formats, depending on a user's display preferences, which may be based on browsing platform or personal disability. This strategy has been supported by the advent of Extensible Markup Language (XML) based Web technologies.

The use of XML along with Extensible Style Language Transformations (XSLT) gives Web authors the potential to provide additional presentational information more suited to specific user needs, such as for nonvisual representations of Web-based information. The potential of XML technologies in increasing accessibility of Web content is highlighted by Bartlett (2002), while at the same time the W3C has moved to identify the need to ensure that developers of XML-based languages are aware of accessibility implications (World Wide Web Consortium, 2002).

Other XML-based technologies, such as Scalable Vector Graphics (SVG) and Synchronised Multimedia Integration Language (SMIL), have been defined with the capability of providing increased accessibility to multimedia objects through the integrated provision of textual alternatives such as captions and descriptions.

Research has also taken place to explore ways of improving presentation at the user end of existing Web information which may contain accessibility problems. For example, methods of repurposing or transcoding current Web pages to a more accessible format for blind and visually impaired users have been discussed by Asakawa and Takagi (2000). Harper, Stevens and Goble (2001) look at how blind and visually impaired people navigate in the physical world and explore how such strategies can be supported on the Web.

While technologies are under development to allow easier creation of content which can be presented that is suitable to a user's specific access needs, the requirement remains that Web developers must follow the standards and guidelines discussed in order to ensure that these and other technologies can best display resources. As advances are made in technological developments, the potential for providing varying interfaces to Web sites based on a single source of information will increase. As an interim solution, however, in some cases discrete versions of Web pages or sites may be the only viable option as a means of addressing accessibility problems.

CONCLUSION

The need to consider accessibility as a core driver in educational Web resource development has never been greater, given current legal imperatives and the recognised advantages of widening access to as many users in as many browsing environments as possible.

To ensure optimal accessibility of online educational resources, awareness in accessible design amongst content providers is essential. Designing with accessibility in mind, through careful use of appropriate Web technologies, can greatly enhance the learning experience for all users and should result in a resource which is compatible with legacy browsers, yet is also future-looking. Through considering accessibility by training resource providers to create accessible content and providing technology which promotes online access, an environment can be created where educational resources widen access to education, instead of introducing further accessibility barriers.

REFERENCES

Asakawa, C., & Takagi, H. (2000). Annotation-based transcoding for nonvisual Web access. In *Proceedings of the 4th International ACM Conference on Assistive Technologies, ASSETS 2000* (pp. 172-179). Association for Computing Machinery.

Bartlett, K. (2002). XML as an enabling technology: Emerging developments in Web accessibility. In *Proceedings of California State University Northridge Center on Disabilities Technology and Persons with Disabilities Conference (CSUN) 2002*. Retrieved from http://www.csun.edu/cod/conf2002/proceedings/218.htm

Bingham, H. (2001). *Most Web books ignore accessibility and usability*. Retrieved on February 11, 2001 from http://www.tiac.net/users/bingham/accessbl/softpro.htm.

Clark, J. (2002). *Building Accessible Web Sites*. Indianapolis, IN: New Riders.

Colwell, C., & Petrie, H. (1999). A preliminary evaluation of the WAI guidelines for producing accessible Web pages. In C. Bühler & H. Knops (Eds.), *Assistive technology on the threshold of the new millennium* (pp. 30-41). Amsterdam: IOS Press.

Harper, S., Stevens, R., & Goble, C. (2001), Web mobility guidelines for visually impaired surfers. *Journal of Research and Practice in Information Technology*, *33*(2), 30-41.

IMS Global Consortium. (2001). *IMS accessibility guidelines for developing accessible learning applications*. Retrieved in July 2002 from http://www.imsproject.org/accessibility/accwpv0p6/imsacc_wpv0p6.html

Jiwnani, K. (2001). *Design for users with cognitive disabilities*. Retrieved in April 2001 from http://www.otal.umd.edu/UUPractice/cognition/

Maguire v. Sydney Olympics Organising Committee (SOCOG). (2000). Retrieved in August 2001 from http://scaleplus.law.gov.au/html/ddadec/0/2000/0/DD000120.htm

Mosier, J., & Smith, S. (1987). Application of guidelines for designing user interface software. *Behaviour and Information Technology*, *5*(1), 39-46.

Newell, A. F., & Gregor, P. (1997). Human computer interfaces for people with disabilities. In M. G. Helander, T. K. Landauer, & P. V. Prabhu (Eds.), *Handbook of human-computer interaction* (pp. 813-824). Amsterdam: Elsevier.

Nielsen, J. (2001, June 10). Avoid PDF for on-screen reading. *Alertbox*. Retrieved June 10, 2001 from http://www.useit.com/alertbox/20010610.html

Paciello, M. (2000). *Web accessibility for people with disabilities*. Lawrence, KS: CMP Media.

Pearrow, M. (2000). *Web usability handbook*. Rockland, MA: Charles River Media.

Rowland, C. (2000). *Accessibility of the Internet in post-secondary education— Meeting the challenge*. White paper presented at the Universal Web Accessibility Symposium 2000. Retrieved on October 31, 2000 from http://www.webaim.org/articles/meetchallenge

Schmitt, C. (2002). Accessibility and authoring tools. *A List Apart, 141*. Retrieved March 22, 2002 from http://www.alistapart.com/stories/tools/

Sloan, D., Gregor, P., Rowan, M., & Booth, P. (2000). Accessible accessibility. In J. Scholtz & J. Thomas (Eds.), *Proceedings of the Conference on Universal Usability, CUU 2000* (pp. 96-101). Association for Computing Machinery.

Sloan, M. (2001). Web accessibility and the DDA. *Journal of Information, Law and Technology, 2*. Retrieved July 2, 2001 from http://elj.warwick.ac.uk/jilt/01-2/sloan.html

Thatcher, J., Bohman, P., Burks, M., Henry, S. L., Regan, B., Swierenga, S., Urban, M., & Waddell, C. (2002). *Constructing Accessible Web Sites*. Birmingham, AL: Glasshaus.

Waddell, C. (1999). *The growing digital divide in access for people with disabilities: Overcoming barriers to participation in the digital economy*. Retrieved May 1999 from http://www.icdri.org/the_digital_divide.htm

World Wide Web Consortium. (1999). *Web content accessibility guidelines*. Retrieved May 5, 1999 from http://www.w3.org/TR/WAI-WEBCONTENT/

World Wide Web Consortium. (2002). *XML accessibility guidelines* (Working Draft). Retrieved October 3, 2002 from http://www.w3.org/WAI/PF/xmlgl

SUPPLEMENTARY WEB REFERENCES

A-Prompt Accessibility Validation Tool: http://aprompt.snow.utoronto.ca/

Bobby Accessibility Validation Tool: http://www.watchfire.com/bobby

IBM Java Accessibility Guidelines: http://www-3.ibm.com/able/accessjava.html

Media Access Generator (MAGpie): http://ncam.wgbh.org/Webaccess/magpie/index.html

W3C HTML Validation Tool: http://validator.w3.org/

Chapter XXI

Online Learning for the Visually Impaired

Mirela Arion
Babes-Bolyai University, Romania

Marius Iulian Tutuianu
SISTEC SA, Romania

ABSTRACT

At the society level, the Internet is a technological, social and cultural phenomenon, shared by the consensus of its users and not owned by anybody. It is a communication network than can, at any moment, bridge people from everywhere and can be looked at as a consequence of modernity (Giddens, 1992).

There is a growing demand and pressure coming from the technology side for adopting online learning but, in order to justify and evaluate the integration of World Wide Web techniques in education, one must attempt to answer at least *two questions:*

1. *Does the World Wide Web promote new approaches to teaching and learning?*
2. *Will the World Wide Web increase access to education?*

The case study that we had to do because of the context of learning within a special education department helped us answer these questions and understand and, more than that, appreciate online learning for the visually impaired.

INTRODUCTION

At the society level, the Internet is a technological, social and cultural phenomenon, shared by the consensus of its users and not owned by anybody. It is a communication network than can, at any moment, bridge people from everywhere and can be looked at as a consequence of modernity (Giddens, 1992). Its dynamism derives from the separation of time and space and their recombination in new forms, which permits the disembedding of social relations from local contexts of interaction and their restructuring across indefinite spans of time-space.

There is a growing demand and pressure coming from the technology side for adopting online learning but, in order to justify and evaluate the integration of World Wide Web techniques in education, one must attempt to answer *at least* two questions.

1. *Does the World Wide Web promote new approaches to teaching and learning?*

    This question can be easily answered, even if we are not trying now to identify a possible need (or not) for a new pedagogical paradigm. New approaches to teaching and learning should be able to make use of the technological change and growth in the sense of enhancing the potential strength of old values in education.

    Learning is an intellectual process of constructing knowledge. That means acquiring, processing, assimilating and integrating information and ideas through constructive social interaction. Constructivism is the philosophy of learning which states that learners make sense of their knowledge by adding new information to their existing knowledge. They must earn knowledge and participate in it, not simply be carried to it by their teachers. The Internet and its techniques seem to be the perfect media for making use of the constructivist principles. In return, constructivism seems to be a perfect starting principle for justifying and supporting the introduction of technological change to education. There is a wide spectrum of learning opportunities on and over the Internet, especially on the World Wide Web. The capacity for learners to add to the dialogue through this interactive medium provides opportunity for development, application and linkage of new knowledge; the Internet re-creates the meeting place in which knowledge is not only shared, but also created and re-created (Arion, 2001).

2. *Will the World Wide Web increase access to education?*

    This question forms the focus of our chapter.

    Technology can play an important role in increasing independence and participation through access to information and communication for everybody, including people with disabilities, but at the same time, technology can raise new barriers due to the individual differences in acquiring and using the new required skills.

    Adaptive technology makes it possible for anyone to access computers and the Internet, but simply gaining access is not enough. People with disabilities can only use the potential of the Internet if information publishers employ design features that make their sites accessible to a wide audience, including those using adaptive technology.

Because of the multimedia nature of the Web, combined with the poor design of some Web sites, many Internet users cannot make the most of it because some of them:

- cannot see graphics because of visual impairments;
- cannot hear audio because of hearing impairments; and
- use slow connections and modems or older equipment that cannot download large files.

We are going to limit the discussion further to the visually impaired because the Internet is primarily a visual medium, visual handicaps are one of the most widely suffered chronic health problems in the world today, and many of the issues regarding technological assistance are true for other handicaps. *We also think that access to the Internet and World Wide Web for the visually impaired is critical in the sense that it does not just feed a demand for change in their educational practice, but it is in many ways the only means that can give them equal access to learning.*

The case study that we had to do because of the context of learning within a special education department helped us understand and, more than that, appreciate online learning for the visually impaired. Some interface design and usability issues were identified for the educational purpose.

BACKGROUND

Usability is a key concept in human-computer interaction (HCI) and is concerned with making systems easy to learn, easy to use, easy to remember, error tolerant, and subjectively pleasing (Usability First, 2001).

The concept of *extraordinary human-computer interaction* (Edwards, 1995) underlines the link and the gap between two research and development fields that, although they share similar problems, have been separated during the years: the field for normal, ordinary users interacting with computers and the field for handicapped users. Observation shows that every human being has a set of abilities and that there is a continuum between the ordinary and the extraordinary.

As the term *Web usability* suggests, this new scientific field's goal is to investigate systematically how users interact with the World Wide Web, and typical problems subject to this investigation are: decision making during Web navigation, usage errors, learning time, etc.

Accessibility is a category of usability and it is defined relative to user task requirements and needs, as any other usability measure (Bergman & Johnson, 2001).

The World Wide Web Consortium (W3C) is the recognised standards organisation of the World Wide Web. It is a consortium led by Tim Berners-Lee, director and creator of World Wide Web, and Jean-Francois Abramatic, the chairman. It is funded by member organisations. It is vendor neutral, working with the global community to produce specifications and reference software that is made freely available throughout the world. To date, 390 organisations are members of the consortium.

Full accessibility to the Internet for persons with disabilities has been a systemic problem since the beginning of the Web. On April 7, 1997, the W3C announced the creation of the Web Accessibility Initiative (WAI). The role of WAI is to promote Web functionality for people with disabilities and to establish accessibility guidelines for use by the Web developers (W3C, 1999).

The core idea of accessibility on the Internet is the notion that there is *no standardised information consumer* and *no standardised device* being used to access the information to be found on the Internet. Not everyone is using the same type of computer or the same type of browser and not everyone can be assumed to have the same physical or sensory abilities. Variety is, in fact, what one can find on the Internet, from all points of view.

The visually impaired users' *task requirements* in the context of online education are those that can ensure them equal access to education:

- visually impaired students should have access to the same information as other students do;
- in order for that to be so, several of their *special needs* should be addressed and supported.

We believe that there is a contradiction between the two kinds of requirements, and as our work will show, we will further try to propose a best practice in Web design when it comes to the *usable* education of the visually impaired.

Universal Accessible Web Design Versus Personalised Web Design?

The best practice in Web design is to build Web sites accessible for anyone. Not only visually impaired users would benefit from it, but also many normal users, since best practice is more than just about font size or colours.

The Royal National Institute for the Blind, UK, encourages the design of Web sites that practice *universal accessible Web design, or design for all* (RNIB, 2000); that is, a single version of the Web site that is accessible to everyone, no matter how they access the Web. This is made possible by the extensive accessibility features incorporated in HTML v.4.0.

There are at least two reasons why this practice should be adopted.

1. In most circumstances, there is no need to create a separate text-only version of a Web site. Unless database content management is being used, the creation of an additional text-only version simply doubles the work involved in updating or amending the site and often leads to an increasingly useless version of the site, with time constraints resulting in the graphic version being updated regularly

while the text-only version is neglected and becomes more and more out of date. The creation of a text-only version should be seen only as a final option when all other alternatives for making the site accessible have been exhausted.

2.   Visually impaired users will have access to all the information published on the Web without having to "demand" or "expect" specially designed interfaces. That will give them *independence* to navigate and use the Web in the same way that all the users do. Independence is the most important issue in all the aspects of their life: education, social interaction, work and leisure.

For the access technologies to work properly, Web pages must be appropriately designed and must be written in valid hypertext markup language (HTML). Many sites are unusable by visually impaired people simply because they are poorly designed or they do not incorporate the World Wide Web Consortium design principles. The Web is an *information* space, but too many Web designers still think of it as a purely visual medium and are unaware even that visually impaired people *can* access the Web.

Many people with sight problems have some useful vision and read Web pages in exactly the same way as fully sighted people: with their eyes. However, the needs of people with poor sight vary considerably, depending on how their eye condition affects their vision. To accommodate everyone, Web sites should be flexible in design, enabling individual users to use their own browser to adjust the text size and colour settings to suit their own particular needs and circumstances.

People with very little or no vision, on the other hand, read Web pages with the help of access technology installed on their computer. Synthesised speech software can read the content of Web pages aloud through a speaker, while Braille software can output the same content to a retractable Braille display so that the Web page can be read by touch. Good design is essential for people accessing the Web in these ways—poor design can render a site completely inaccessible.

An accessible Web site is one that can be accessed by anyone. In this context, the essence of good design involves ensuring that a text alternative exists for every non-text element on the Web page. It is perfectly possible to produce an attractive, dynamic design that is fully accessible.

The task of the visually impaired is *the integration in the real world*, *the communication through email* and *the access to information* on the World Wide Web.

We believe that *personalised Web design* is the best practice when it comes to very well defined situations or contexts. In our view and from our experience, learning is a task that has priority in an educational context. The tools the students might use for learning should be fast and easy to use. Learning is a process of accumulating/creating information and browsing references, doing assignments and day-to-day communication between the teacher and the students. For the visually impaired students, these simple tasks can be very difficult. Building a local (university, department, etc.) Web site with all the information that is needed for their learning, designed in such a manner that it supports a *fast access* and an *easy orientation*, with *reliable* and *updated information* and *other services*, can be, in our view, a usable online learning solution for this category of students.

The *best practice* is therefore a combination between the two practices presented above. Visually impaired students should be trained to be *independent* when it comes to general aspects of their life (that means to use access technology and to ensure a universal design) and should be given the *right* to access online learning in a personalised manner for best learning outcomes.

A ROMANIAN CASE STUDY

Introduction

Babes-Bolyai University, Cluj-Napoca, Romania, is a multicultural university; the students can study here in Romanian, Hungarian or German, according to the different minority groups in our country. The university has a number of visually impaired students who practically have no access whatsoever to any form of electronic information. They are studying special education, psychology or languages. Their usual practice for learning is to tape the lectures and ask colleagues to read as much information as possible, tape them and then transcribe them in Braille format. This is an individual, slow, expensive and difficult process; the visually impaired students have not only to work a lot before they actually start learning, but they have to randomly make use of the goodwill of their peers for a right that shouldn't normally be questioned.

Current Situation

We had a pilot project running within the Centre for Educational Technology Transfer. The centre is a resource centre for online learning, offering hardware and software support for the university staff in developing and implementing online tutorials for the distance learning units within the university. Although the university has a strong distance learning department, it does not exploit the full potential of the technology and the university culture itself is still not entirely ready for this change.

We did not have any prior experience with visually impaired students in our courses: Basic Information Technology Skills (Windows, MS Office, navigation on the Internet, emailing, etc.) and Research Methods in Education (using SPSS, Statistical Package for Social Sciences).

Before the beginning of the courses (for all first- and second-year students, including the visually impaired), the students were given questionnaires in order to get information about their expertise in using computers and their IT attitude and acceptance (Cassidy & Eachus, 1997). Their expertise was found to be somewhere between "very poor" to "medium," their attitude ranged from "fear to approach" to "cool to work with," and the acceptance was more or less defined by the constraints of use and the impossibility to avoid technology in the future.

The visually impaired students did not show any fear towards computers, although their expertise was very poor. They all agreed that computers and the Web are the only things that can bring a major change into their present (learning) and future (employment) life.

An e-group was created, where all students were required to contribute, extract information about the courses and get in touch with all the events related to them. Students were also asked to keep a diary during the semester about everything that happened as far as the courses and the communication were concerned.

We started by training the first-year visually impaired students in special education to be proficient in using Windows platforms, MS Office applications, email services and Internet surfing. In time, visually impaired students from other departments joined our group.

The second-year visually impaired students were trained in research methods, using SPSS. Introducing data in SPSS and analysing it was easily done using keyboard shortcuts. Blind students quickly developed such a tutorial. The most difficult part was reading and using the results of the statistical analysis from the output SPSS results file. All the results in SPSS (including text, tables with statistics and graphics) are image type. We succeeded in exporting text and tables into Word and transforming them into text format, easily read with a Jaws screen reader.

For the two categories of students, low vision and blind, software magnifiers and screen readers were used as IT aids.

The magnifiers proved to be quite difficult to use; we tried Dolphin (UK) magnifiers and Windows accessibility options. The students preferred the Dolphin magnifier because it is obviously easier to set up compared to Windows. Still, they didn't like the fact that when they magnified the screen, the contents magnified without rearranging the text; it is like using a fixed magnifying glass, and in order to read the page, it should be moved under the magnifying glass. If the magnification is big, the students can easily lose their orientation on the page and also the orientation on the Windows desktop.

The blind students had to choose between Dolphin and Jaws (USA) screen readers. They all preferred Jaws because they heard about it from their national association before starting our courses.

The Jaws screen reader was learned very fast and used extremely well by the blind students. The screen reader can read text, and an image (graphic, video, etc.) should have a text explanation attached in order to be described for blind users. They decided to write a Jaws tutorial that will be used for the training of the new visually impaired students. This tutorial was developed as part of their assignment.

We realised that most of the information can be structured (as in normal teaching) in "taught lessons"—introducing new concepts, "references"—giving additional information and "practical work" with concrete tasks to be accomplished.

We therefore decided to try and organise the teaching of the visually impaired (beginning with the discipline Basic IT Skills and Research Methods in Education using SPSS) in the same way, using the intranet or the Internet.

The next goal was to have the tutorials in an electronic format suitable both for low-vision students and for blind students.

Changing the Current Situation

We realised that we have to teach visually impaired students having two important purposes:

- *universal accessibility*—we have to teach them to explore the information on the World Wide Web and to communicate via email, by using magnifiers or screen readers that support independence and integration into real life;
- *personalised accessibility*—we have to design a personalised interface for the learning site, in order to give them faster access to learning and easier orientation; this is an online learning solution for this category of students which supports their learning task.

We thought that locally, meaning the special education site in this case, we could publish the information in such a manner that they could have faster access to both graphics and text, better orientation within the site, and local access to commonly used Internet services.

We decided to implement magnification features within the Web site, instead of using magnifying software, for several reasons:

- the contents of the Windows desktop and the contents of the page can be rearranged; instead of magnifying the page as it is (like the magnification software does), the contents of the page will be modified, the screen won't be like a magnifying glass, everything the page will contain will be on the screen, and as a result, there will be more pages as the magnification will be bigger;
- building accessible Web sites gives visually impaired students more independence than having to rely on special tools;
- the software is rather expensive;
- the magnification software is not always compatible with the screen reader software;
- often, software for the visually impaired is operating system dedicated.

We started the design of the special education site, bearing in mind that we should have at least two Romanian versions: one for visually normal students and one for the visually impaired.

Prior to the development of the site, interviews were conducted with 12 visually impaired students with different degrees of vision loss, in order to find out their needs and the problems they encounter when searching the Web.

In the beginning, we had a set of general questions, such as What kind of visual disability do you have? Four of the students are blind, one with advanced vision loss (they all have to use screen readers), one with photophobia, and six with moderate vision loss (they can read with moderate magnifying aid).

With the next set of questions, we addressed issues such as:

- difficulty seeing small things (What font size would you be able to best read? If there was a text-magnifying option available, would you use it?). Most of them prefer bold, large font.
- difficulty seeing in conditions of low contrast (What combination of background/ foreground colours would best suit you?). The six moderate low-vision students identified sets of colours which we then used in the design of the site. We do not offer combinations of background/foreground colours in pairs; we let the user choose the desired combination (the colours were identified by the students according to their individual needs, but a larger pallet can be provided).
- difficulty in orientation on a site (Do you have problems moving to a different object? Do you have problems when a Web page contains frames?). The answers made us think that designing an experimental version with "self-speak-ability" might be a good idea.
- would they be interested in developing Web sites and how possible do they think it is to acquire the skills.
- the impact that Internet access has on their lives (the general opinion is that the Internet improves their lives).

Students were asked to participate in the development process of the sites. They had input about colours and font size and the kind of information they would like to access.

Evaluation of the Results

At that moment we thought that the best approach was to design more than one site:

- an English version for international access (for all of the following versions);
- a normal graphic version for the rest of the students;
- an accessible text version for blind and low-vision students (with the possibility of changing the font and background colours as well as the font size) which is eventually intended for access to "course" only information;
- a printable version;
- an experimental version.

The experimental version was supposed to include the characteristics of the text version. But we also thought about adding "self-speak-able" objects, with alternative long text descriptions for Jaws users and/or sound files attached which can contain ription of the content or of the function of the object (according to the principles of describing objects for the visually impaired) and an optional guided tour of the site. We believed that this version of the site would offer a better orientation for the blind students. This version would also integrate links to the most used search engines and to the most popular mail services.

All versions of the site were developed and tested with the users, while the experimental version was still in the design phase.

We soon realised that maintaining different sites containing the same information was not feasible. A new design strategy was adopted, and slowly we realised that it was possible to design one site accessible for everyone. Not only visually impaired students will benefit from it, but also the visually normal students, because the flexibility of its features makes it possible to tailor it according to the user's needs and desires.

The range of the features embedded in the interface makes learning possible for different kinds of learners (from the interface point of view):

- beginners (who can use optional features such as: description of the site, explanations of the objects and hints for orientation, all designed in fact for the visually impaired);
- more expert users (who can skip optional features);
- visually impaired (who can use optional features);
- all of the above, who can build their own user profile (with options as specified in the next paragraph).

THE NEW WEB DESIGN STRATEGY: USABILITY ISSUES

Visually impaired people do not constitute a homogenous group; they can have varying degrees of central vision, peripheral vision, and light and colour perception. Visual impairments are also unlikely to be stable, particularly for partially sighted people. Visual impairment is affected by print size, media, colour ratios, lighting, and the nature and the degree of the impairment.

All this knowledge makes it clear that there is a real need for a certain degree of personalisation and flexibility in Web design.

The WAI guideline developed by the W3C is comprehensive, long and extremely detailed and is at times quite difficult for the nontechnically inclined person to understand.

Therefore, we are going to present, further on, a summary of recommendations from W3C that we kept in mind and tried to implement in our design. The complete list of guidelines that we have considered and applied in our design, their hierarchical structure and how they can be chosen is presented in the Appendix of this chapter.

All guidelines and checkpoints referring to *priority levels 1* and *2* have been implemented to the best of our knowledge (see the Appendix).

Concluding Set of Recommendations

When we designed our Web site we used this concluding set of recommendations to ensure *good Web design* (Byrne, 2001) and a few accessibility features to *improve access* (W3C, 1999).

1.   "ALT" attributes should be provided for all graphics, and if the navigation of the site is based on the use of graphic buttons or maps, an alternative text-based navigation method should be provided. Where photographs or graphics are critical to the understanding of a page, a link should be provided which links to a description of the picture content.
2.   Style sheets should be used for presentation purposes whenever possible, and structural elements should be used in preference to presentational elements and attributes.
3.   Identify the main language used in the Web pages with the "lang" attribute. Use the ABBR and ACRONYM tags when appropriate.
4.   If you would like a frames-based layout provide an alternative version with the same information but in a more accessible format.
5.   Make the frames-based site more accessible through appropriate use of the NOFRAMES tag. Use appropriate titles for the frames, and if more information is required, use the "longdesc" or a description link.
6.   Provide an alternative "no-frames" text-based navigation method—a text navigation bar at the bottom of each page is the recommended method although this would not work with the current frames-based Web site.
7.   Use section headers (H1-H6) and paragraph tags (P) correctly to create structured documents.
8.   Provide an alternative text-based navigation method.
9.   Provide appropriate meta tag information.
10. Where it is not possible to make a page accessible as "text only," an alternative should be provided. This text page must be maintained with the same frequency as the original page.
11. It is good practice to provide a date on the bottom of each page, which indicates when the pages were last updated. It is also good practice to provide contact information at the bottom of each page.

Implementing Usability (Accessibility and Flexibility)

Besides the recommendations listed above (which ensure and improve *accessibility*), we decided to implement some *personalisation features* (which improve *flexibility*) by offering the possibility for each user to define their own *user profile*.

The Internet browsers' settings are difficult to handle by visually impaired students and beginners. Besides this, the flexibility of combining colours for background, foreground, and links and of selecting the font size is not completely implemented in the Internet browsers.

Further, we are presenting an argumentation for our choice of features.

1. Internet Explorer (IE) 5.5 offers a predefined colour table of 48 colours (8X6) and the possibility to define a custom colour from a complete range of colours and nuances. Using the keyboard (as many of the visually impaired users would do), one cannot define a custom colour unless one has knowledge about the characteristics of that particular colour (for example, how much red, green and blue is in the composition of that colour).

2. Concerning the font, IE gives the possibility to select from five different options for the size (largest, larger, medium, smaller, and smallest) and to select a font style and a type. In order to set the page features, the user can also choose to use a cascade style sheet file, but to create such a file the user has to have extended knowledge of Web design, which is not the case with most students.

3. Netscape 6.0 offers a table of 70 colours (10X7) without the possibility of defining a custom colour. It offers font size values between eight and 72.

4. In HTML, colours are expressed either as hexadecimal values (for example, #FF0000) or as colour names (red). A Web-safe colour is one that appears the same in Netscape Navigator and Microsoft Internet Explorer on both Windows and Macintosh systems when running in 256-colour mode. The conventional wisdom is that there are 216 common colours, and that any hexadecimal value that combines the pairs 00, 33, 66, 99, CC, or FF (RGB values 0, 51, 102, 153, 204, and 255, respectively) represents a Web-safe colour.

5. Testing, however, reveals that there are only 216 Web-safe colours. Internet Explorer on Windows does not correctly render the colours #0033FF (0,51,255), #3300FF (51,0,255), #00FF33 (0,255,51), and #33FF00 (51,255,0).

6. The Colour Cubes (default, Figure 1) and the Continuous Tone (Figure 2) palettes by some Web authorware tools use the 216-colour Web-safe palette (Macromedia, 2001b).

Figure 1:   Colour Cubes table

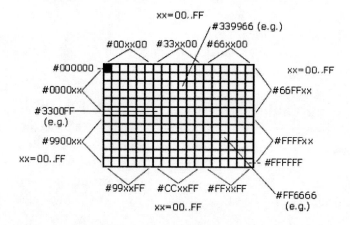

Figure 2:   Continuous Tones table

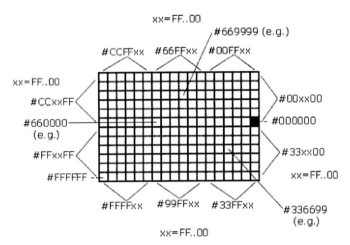

Our choice was Continuous Tones because the layout of the colours allows error when a visually impaired user is choosing a colour.

As a result of all the knowledge and experience so far, we decided that our Web site should have only two versions:

1. a normal site, accessible and flexible, that all the students can use (normal and visually impaired);
2. a printable text version which can be used again by all students, according to their needs (for the visually impaired students for a faster access to learning, for the visually normal students for printing).

The normal site has the following options for creating a user profile:

*   an input text field which, once a profile name is introduced, activates the characteristics of that specific profile; the possibility exists to alter the profile (through a link);
*   link for defining a new profile;
*   default profile: white (foreground) on black (background), font Times New Roman (generally accepted on the Web), size 14 (Figure 3).

Figure 3:   Loading profiles

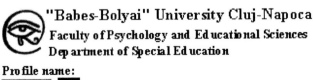

Through the profile, the following parameters can be set: background colour, foreground colour, links colour, visited links colour, active links colour, and font size; it is also possible to keep the foreground colour for the links (Figure 4).

All profiles are saved in a database with the following fields: ProfileID, BGCOLOR, FGCOLOR, LINKScolor, VISITEDlinksColor, ACTIVElinksColor, FONTsize (Figures 5 and 6).

When working with the site on a certain profile, a new profile can be chosen (from the existing profiles) or defined.

When the profile name is introduced, a connection to the database will be made; the corresponding record set for the database will be built and questioned until the introduced profile (by the name) will be found. At the end, the values that interest (background colour, foreground colour, etc.) are kept within variables.

We used:

- database: MS Access;
- the data connection defined to have no need of DNS (domain name server), which gives it portability within the Web servers type IIS;
- program code: ASP (Active Server Pages).

Within the HTML code, the database variables are used. For example: the attribute bgcolor from the Body tag gets the variable value obtained from the BGCOLOR field.

Figure 4:   Defining a new profile

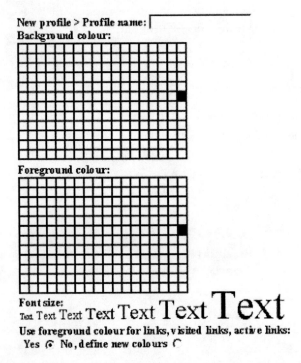

Figure 5: Part of a screen using a profile

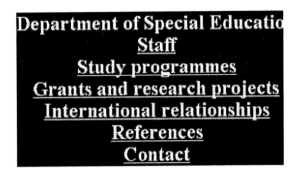

Every encountered text is defined with the Font tag; its characteristic, the size attribute, takes the value of the variable that contains that text size value set in the profile.

Usability Evaluation

The site was and will be evaluated in a few steps and using different procedures.

1. Following the first design, we decided to keep only two versions of the site, which can better address the needs of both groups of students (visually normal and impaired).
2. Tests of accessibility were run using automated and human methods (automated methods were rapid and convenient; human methods helped ensure the clarity of language and ease of navigation):
    • "Bobby," accessibility checker developed by the Centre for Applied Special Technology (CAST, 2001);

Figure 6: Part of a screen using a different profile

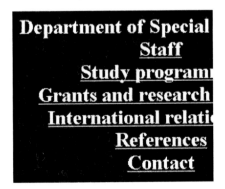

- "508 Usenet Accessibility Kit" (Macromedia, 2001a), an accessibility evaluation and repair tool, an extension for Dreamweaver Web authorware;
  - the users were involved both in the pre-design, the design and the evaluation process (through questionnaires, interviews, active testing of the site).
3. The site will be tested and evaluated with the new cohort of students in the following semester.

FUTURE WORK

We intend to further evaluate and improve the Web site and add more information about other courses.

Some of the features that we considered are not implemented yet (self-speakable objects, guided tour of the site), and new useful features were identified during the design and evaluation process.

The user profile will be included in a more general "personal page" that can support more flexibility. This page can include:
- an email account administration interface;
- a catalogue of useful links;
- a personal notes diary (notes, goals, electronic resume, finances, etc.).

There is a requirement from the visually impaired students to learn Web design. We will explore the most appropriate tools options and plan the learning strategies for developing a Web design tutorial.

CONCLUSIONS

Outcomes

There are a number of outcomes as a result of our pilot project, some of which we did not expect. All the students had changed their attitudes towards computers by the end of the semester. The bits of online learning and communication that have been introduced in the course allowed computers to be seen as useful tools.

Throughout the semester, we kept all students up-to-date with each other's progress. Visually normal students became more aware of the needs and the problems that their visually impaired peers have to face, and they were impressed with their colleagues' performance.

Visually impaired students became not only proficient in using computers, but also more involved in the social life of the entire group.

Teachers realised that the provision of complete online course materials is vital for visually impaired students.

The university management decided to offer support by setting up a Web publishing office for visually impaired students and a set of rules to be followed by the university teaching staff in order to provide electronic course-related information.

Implications

There are at least two important implications when trying to facilitate the access of visually impaired students to communication and learning:

1.   implications for the design of Web-accessible interfaces (*access usability*):
    • accessibility benefits all users, not only visually impaired;
    • accessible pages can look attractive; there is no need for them to be text-only or dull;
    • designers may use the newest features in Web design and still make a site accessible;

2.   implications for didactics (*learning usability*):
    • sometimes, online learning is the only option that visually impaired students have for learning;
    • online learning can be implemented on the Internet, on the intranet or on CD;
    • online learning creates a flexible, open environment for learning that helps them overcome communication barriers;
    • online learning supports independence and integration of visually impaired students;
    • online learning improves the social life of visually impaired students.

This chapter outlines a number of ideas about how to make a Web site accessible to visually impaired students, personalising it according to the degree and the type of impairment and to the specific context (learning situation).

Although universal access is desirable (for all the reasons that have been mentioned above), sometimes, giving equal opportunities to learners means special adaptation of the access interface. We think this is an important pedagogical message.

Looking back at HCI history, it is worth underlining the following developments.

•   It started by designing interfaces with little concern about the users or their environment.

•   User-centred design was the next step, when features of the "average user" were embedded in the interface design, but users with disabilities were not included.

•   Further on, dedicated interfaces (and hardware) were designed for users with disabilities, at high cost and thus enlarging the gap between this category and the normal users; including people with disabilities in all aspects of social life (education, work, leisure) meant having to provide them with special tools.

•   Universal design was the next step, which means "design for all"; it enhances the independence and the integration of disabled users.

- Flexible design seems to combine features of "universal design" with those of "dedicated design"; it seems to be, so far, the best practice in designing HCI.

We are not excluding situations where independence and integration require more specialised artefacts.

Our case study is an example of how improving access to education for extraordinary students leads to a whole new vision of online learning, starting with the student level, where all students can benefit from flexible design, to the university level, where a change in educational culture can be induced.

APPENDIX
How Guidelines, Checkpoints and Priorities of Work According to W3C

Web Content Accessibility Guidelines 1.0 includes 14 guidelines, or general principles of accessible design.

Each guideline includes the guideline number, the statement of the guideline, the rationale behind the guideline, and some groups who benefit from it, along with a list of checkpoint definitions.

The checkpoint definitions in each guideline explain how the guideline applies in typical content development scenarios. Each checkpoint definition includes the checkpoint number, the statement of the checkpoint, the priority of the checkpoint, and optional informative notes, clarifying examples and references to related guidelines or checkpoints.

Each checkpoint is intended to be specific enough so that someone reviewing a page or a site may verify that the checkpoint has been satisfied. In addition, each checkpoint has a priority level assigned by the working group based on the checkpoint's impact on accessibility.

There are three levels of priorities:

- *Priority 1* (the *must*)

  A Web content developer *must* satisfy this checkpoint. Otherwise, one or more groups will find it impossible to access information in the document. Satisfying this checkpoint is a basic requirement for some groups to be able to use Web documents.

- *Priority 2* (the *should*)

  A Web content developer *should* satisfy this checkpoint. Otherwise, one or more groups will find it difficult to access information in the document. Satisfying this checkpoint will remove significant barriers to accessing Web documents.

- *Priority 3* (the *may*)

A Web content developer *may* address this checkpoint. Otherwise, one or more groups will find it somewhat difficult to access information in the document. Satisfying this checkpoint will improve access to Web documents.

Guidelines, Checkpoints and Priorities We Used in Our Design for *Improving* Accessibility

Further on, we are going to mention only those checkpoints within guidelines that have *priority level 3* in order to point out what we did for *improving* accessibility.

Priority levels 1 and *2* have been implemented to the best of our knowledge.

- Guideline 1

  Provide equivalent alternatives to auditory and visual content.

  Provide content that, when presented to the user, conveys essentially the same function or purpose as auditory or visual content.

  Checkpoint 1.5

  Until user agents render text equivalents for client-side image map links, provide redundant text links for each active region of a client-side image map.

- Guideline 2

  Do not rely on colour alone.

  Ensure that text and graphics are understandable when viewed without colour.

  Checkpoint 2.2

  Ensure that foreground and background colour combinations provide sufficient contrast when viewed by someone having colour deficits or when viewed on a black and white screen.

- Guideline 4

  Clarify natural language usage.

  Use markup that facilitates pronunciations or interpretation of abbreviated or foreign text.

  Checkpoint 4.2

  Specify the expansion of each abbreviation or acronym in a document where it first occurs.

  Checkpoint 4.3

  Identify the primary natural language of a document.

- Guideline 5

  Create tables that transform gracefully.

  Ensure that tables have necessary markup to be transformed by accessible browsers and other user agents.

  Checkpoint 5.5

  Provide summaries for tables.

  Checkpoint 5.6

  Provide abbreviations for header labels.

- Guideline 9
  Design for device-independence.
  Use features that enable activation of page elements via a variety of input devices.
  Checkpoint 9.4
  Create a logical tab order through links, form controls and objects.
  Checkpoint 9.5
  Provide keyboard shortcuts to important links (including those in client-side image maps), form controls and groups of form controls.
- Guideline 10
  Use interim solutions.
  Use interim accessibility solutions so that assistive technologies and older browsers will operate correctly.
  Checkpoint 10.3
  Until user agents (including assistive technologies) render side-by-side text correctly, provide a linear text alternative (on the current page or some other) for all tables that lay out text in parallel, word-wrapped columns.
  Checkpoint 10.4
  Until user agents handle empty controls correctly, include default, placeholding characters in edit boxes and text areas.
  Checkpoint 10.5
  Until user agents (including assistive technologies) render adjacent links distinctly, include non-link, printable characters (surrounded by spaces) between adjacent links.
- Guideline 11
  Use W3C technologies and guidelines.
  Use W3C technologies (according to specification) and follow accessibility guidelines. Where it is not possible to use a W3C technology or doing so results in material that does not transform gracefully, provide an alternative version of the content that is accessible.
  Checkpoint 11.3
  Provide information so that users may receive documents according to their preferences (e.g., language, content type, etc.).
- Guideline 13
  Provide clear navigation mechanisms.
  Provide clear and consistent navigation mechanisms—orientation information, navigation bars, a site map, etc.—to increase the likelihood that a person will find what they are looking for at a site.
  Checkpoint 13.5
  Provide navigation bars to highlight and give access to the navigation mechanism.
  Checkpoint 13.6

Group related links, identify the group (for user agents), and until user agents do so, provide a way to bypass the group.

Checkpoint 13.7

If search functions are provided, enable different types of searches for different skill levels and preferences.

Checkpoint 13.8

Place distinguishing information at the beginning of headings, paragraphs lists, etc.

Checkpoint 13.9

Provide information about document collections (i.e., documents comprising multiple pages).

•   Guideline 14

Ensure that documents are clear and simple.

Ensure documents are clear and simple so they may be more easily understood.

Checkpoint 14.2

Supplement text with graphic or auditory presentations where they will facilitate comprehension of the page.

Checkpoint 14.3

Create a style of presentation that is consistent across pages.

REFERENCES

Arion, M. (2001). From Piaget to Internet—New media tools as a vehicle for bringing constructivist learning theory to life. In *Proceedings of the European Conference of the International Council for Education of People with Visual Impairment: Visions and Strategies for the New Century* (CD-ROM).

Bergman, E., & Johnson, E. (2001). *Towards accessible human-computer interaction*. Retrieved August 2001 from http://www.sun.com/access/developers/updt.HCI.advance.html

Byrne, J. (2001). *Guidelines for building an accessible Web site*. Retrieved August 2001 from http://www.ispn.gcal.ac.uk/accsites/AccessGuide.html

Cassidy, S., & Eachus, P. (1997). *Developing the computer self-efficacy (CSE) scale: Investigating the relationship between CSE, gender and experience with computers*. Retrieved March 2001 from http://www.chssc.salford.ac.uk/healthSci/selfeff/selfeff.htm

Centre for Applied Special Technology. (2001). *Bobby*. Retrieved January 2001 from http://www.cast.org/bobby/

Edwards, A. D. N. (Ed.). (1995). *Extra-ordinary human-computer interaction: Interfaces for users with disabilities*. USA: Cambridge University Press.

Giddens, A. (1992). *The consequences of modernity*. Cornwall, England: T. J. Press.

Macromedia. (2001a). *508 Usenet Accessibility Kit*. Retrieved January 2001 from http://www.macromedia.com

Macromedia. (2001b). *Using Dreamweaver 4.0.* Retrieved January 2001 from http://www.macromedia.com

Royal National Institute for the Blind. (2000). *Accessible Web design*. Retrieved March 2000 from http://www.rnib.org.uk

Usability First. (2001). *Accessibility: Principles of accessible design*. Retrieved August 2001 from http://www.usabilityfirst.com

World Wide Web Consortium. (1999). *Web content accessibility guidelines 1.0.* Retrieved March 2000 from http://www.w3.org/TR/WAI-WEBCONTENT/

About the Authors

The editor of this book, **Claude Ghaoui** (BSc, MSc, PhD, all in computer science), is a senior lecturer in computer systems (since 1995) at the School of Computing and Mathematical Sciences, Liverpool JMU, UK. Her research interests and expertise are mainly in human computer interaction, multimedia/Internet technology and their applications in education. From 1991 to 1995, she worked at the Computer Science Department of Liverpool University as a publishing director of an active R&D group of 25 staff headed by Prof. Rada, who is now at the University of Maryland, USA. This involved managing the electronic and paper publishing activities of the group, as well as pursuing research, related to European projects, and some teaching. Prior to that, she worked at IBM as a researcher and at Kuwait University as a lecturer in computing (1982-1990). She passionately promotes the use of IT for the provision of innovative and flexible learning. She has numerous publications in this area and has been invited to organize a number of international workshops since 1994. She is a UK correspondent for EUROMICRO (since 1998) and served on programme committees for several international HCI/multimedia conferences. Since 2000, she has been an advisor for eUniservity (UK-based), which promotes and provides online learning. She coedited a book on medical multimedia in 1995. A new book, by Dr. Ghaoui, called *E-Educational Applications: Human Factors and Innovative Approaches* (IRM Press, USA), is currently in progress and planned to appear in 2004.

*   *   *

From an interdisciplinary background in psychology, ergonomics and computing, **Anne Adams** has developed a wide range of research interests varying from digital libraries to security and HCI, the social impacts of technology, CSCW and qualitative methods in HCI. Her research into security and usability has reviewed authentication mechanisms and users' perceptions of privacy within multimedia applications. Previous research projects were based within a variety of organizations from industry (i.e., telecommunications and building) to clinical and academic settings. Her current research at Middlesex University, UK, extends from the effect of social structures on technology introduction to the impacts technology has on society.

David Andrew is the programme leader for the postgraduate certificate in learning and teaching and faculty coordinator in learning and teaching at the University of North London, UK.

Mirela Arion is a lecturer at the Department of Special Education, Faculty of Psychology and Educational Sciences, Babes-Bolyai University, Cluj-Napoca, Romania. She graduated with a degree in electronics and telecommunications in 1982 and worked in a research institute for computer sciences as an analyst/ programmer. Since 1990, she has lectured at the university. Most of her teaching has been concerned with information technology for special needs education and research methods in education. Her research has concentrated on psychosocial factors involved in human-computer interaction and access to education for visually impaired students. She is now finishing her PhD, concentrated on online education. She is coordinator of the Centre for Educational Technology Transfer at the university.

Sami Baffoun is a graduate student at the Computer Science Department of Université Laval, Quebec, Canada. His master's degree was codirected by Dr. Boulet and Dr. Belkhiter. He is currently a PhD candidate at the Polytechnic School in Montréal.

Nadir Belkhiter is a professor at the Computer Science Department, Faculty of Science and Engineering, Université Laval, Quebec, Canada. He received MS and PhD degrees in computer science from the Institut National des Sciences Appliquées (INSA) of Lyon, France, in 1982 and 1985, respectively. His teaching and research works concern human-computer interaction, database theory, information retrieval and decision support. Web: http://www.ift.ulaval.ca/~belkhiter

J. Bernardes is a sociologist, specialising in the study of family life, with a long-standing interest in the use of IT in teaching and learning. His textbook (*Family Studies: An Introduction*, Routledge, 1997) has recently been made available as an "ebook" (see the Taylor and Francis Web site for download). Jon uses IT to support all his current teaching and is experimenting in using IT delivery (content and assessment) at the University of Wolverhampton, UK. Current experiments include the use of streaming video for classroom exercises and exploring the use of assessment weighting to encourage online participation.

Ann Blandford is a senior lecturer at the UCL Interaction Centre, UK, and a visiting professor at Middlesex University, UK. She teaches and conducts research on usability of interactive systems. She obtained her PhD in artificial intelligence and education from the Open University in 1991. Her earlier work was on computer-based learning, particularly to support students of engineering design. More recently, her work has focused primarily on the design of usable systems; this has involved the use of both formal modelling techniques to reason about design and also empirical investigations on the use of various artefacts. Much of her current work is concerned with the design and use of digital libraries in educational, health-care and commercial settings.

Bernard Blandin holds a PhD in sociology and is senior consultant, head of the CESI-ONLINE Department and adviser to the managing director of CESI Group, France (http://www.cesi.fr). His expertise is rooted in research and evaluations of more than a hundred of open and distance learning, collaborative learning or e-learning projects funded by the French Ministry of Employment, by the European Commission within the framework of the Leonardo da Vinci programme and by the European Social Fund programmes. Since 1987, he has contributed to several books and has published a large number of papers in French and in English.

Marie-Michèle Boulet is a full professor at the Université Laval, Quebec, Canada. Since 2000, she has taught the uses of music technology for teaching and learning at the Faculty of Music. Previously, she spent several years as a full professor at the Computer Science Department. As she holds three master's degrees (MA, MMus, MBA) and a PhD, Dr. Boulet's research focuses on interdisciplinary projects. Web: http://www.mus.ulaval.ca/boulet

David Cahill is a consultant senior lecturer in obstetrics and gynaecology in the University of Bristol, UK. Appointed to that post in 1996, he had developed interests in undergraduate and postgraduate education, particularly the appropriate use of information technology and delivery of such courses. He has developed an under-graduate Web site (www.rchn.org.uk) for the University of Bristol students taking his course. With Julian Jenkins he has been involved in the growth and development of the postgraduate medical Web site (www.repromed.org.uk). He also is interested in the uptake of Web site information by students and the evaluation of undergraduate and postgraduate examination techniques.

Julian Cook works for the Learning Technology Support Service at the University of Bristol, UK, advising and training academic staff in learning technologies. Since 1996 Julian has also evaluated the role and potential of learning technologies. These include an Internet course in reproductive medicine run from the University of Bristol, and TeleDent, providing expert advice and postgraduate training to dentists through communications technologies. Most recently he has reviewed virtual and managed learning environments across UK medical education. He has authored a number of significant publications on these topics and has presented at national and international learning technology and medical education conferences.

Jacqueline Dempster is head of educational technology in the Centre for Academic Practice at the University of Warwick, UK. She has an academic background in biological sciences and has been involved in academic development and the application of educational technologies in higher education for nearly 10 years. She has been a member of executive committees of the Association for Learning Technology for five years and currently contributes to the membership committee of the Institute for Learning and Teaching, working towards professional development support and accreditation for learning technologists. She is currently project manager for three consortium-based national projects funded by HEFCE under a variety of teaching and learning programmes (TLTP3, FDTL3, JISC DNER 5/99).

Philip Duchastel received his doctorate in instructional systems and has been involved in instruction via computers since the 1970s. In the 1990s, he directed the establishment online of a series of courses providing graduate education at a distance. He was also the chief learning officer for a dot-com start-up offering services throughout Latin America. Dr. Duchastel is the director of the online Information Design Atelier, USA, where his interests center on learning theory, human-computer interfacing, and information philosophy.

Clermont Dupuis received a BS degree in mathematics and computer science from Sherbrooke University, Canada, in 1979, and MS and PhD degrees in operational research from Montreal University, Canada, in 1981 and 1984, respectively. In 1983, he joined the Faculty of Sciences and Engineering at Laval University, Quebec, Canada. He is currently teaching simulation, computer graphics and object-oriented programming. His current research interests include operational research and computer graphics. Web: http://www.ift.ulaval.ca/~dupuis

Gordon Dyer joined the Open University, UK, in 1978 as a technology staff tutor. In 1985 he was appointed deputy regional director for the East of England and tenured as senior lecturer in this post till 1999. He has taught courses offered by both the Open University Business School and Faculty of Technology and is experienced in using CMC and online methods for tuition. Now retired from full-time employment he continues with consultancy and teaching contracts with the OU. He has over 40 published papers/articles/book chapters, primarily in the field of social system design.

Giancarlo Fortino is an assistant professor of computer science in the Department of Electronics, Informatics, and Systems Science at the University of Calabria, Italy, where he is a lecturer of computer science introductory courses and information systems courses. His technical interests are mainly focused on distributed and multimedia systems. He is currently active on research projects concerning collaborative and on-demand multimedia systems over the Internet, code mobility-based middleware and frameworks for highly dynamic distributed and GRID computing. In 1997 and 1999, he worked as a visiting researcher at the International Computer Science Institute (ICSI), Berkeley, California, USA. He has a PhD in computer science from the University of Calabria. He is a member of ACM, and IEEE Computer Society.

Elizabeth Furtado holds a PhD in computer science and teaches in the master of computer science programme at the University of Fortaleza, Ce, Brazil. Her experience includes teaching HCI concepts using a distance online learning system and being the leader of the project TeleCadi, related to case-based reasoning on teacher's formation. Her research themes are the following: human-computer interaction (HCI), hypermedia and multimedia applications, intelligent user interfaces (IUI), tools for working with guidelines (TFWWG), and user interface development. She has been an invited speaker in many conferences in Brazil, an organizer of the 1st meeting of WISE1999 and IHC2002, And a reviewer of many conferences in HCI.

João José Vasco Furtado holds a PhD in computer science and teaches in the master of computer science programme at the University of Fortaleza, Ce, Brazil. His experience includes teaching knowledge acquisition and artificial intelligence. His research themes are the following: case-based reasoning methods, knowledge representation, and learning organization. He is a member of the project TeleCadi, related to case-based reasoning on teacher's formation and an invited speaker for a meeting in IBM (1991, Brazil). He has many publications, mainly in FLAIRS, 1995, SCAI-95, SIG/CR1995, FLAIRS 98, ECML98, 1998. AIDA 1999.

Floriana Grasso obtained a "laurea summa cum laude" in information science at the University of Bari, Italy, in 1993, with her final dissertation in artificial intelligence in medicine. After the thesis, she worked as a research assistant at the same university for three years before taking a research associate position at the Department of Computing and Electrical Engineering at Heriot Watt University, Edinburgh, UK. Since 1999, she has been a lecturer in the Department of Computer Science of the University of Liverpool, UK, where she is also now deputy director of the university's e-Learning Unit. Her main research interests range over two main streams: computational linguistics and cognitive modelling, with specific interests in natural language argumentation/negotiation, and modelling of cognitive aspects, personalities, emotions and other extra-rational features of believable agents.

Anders Hagström is project manager of ETH World at the Swiss Federal Institute of Technology Zurich, Switzerland. Before joining ETH he worked with continuing education and professional development at Helsinki University of Technology, the International Association for Continuing Engineering Education (IACEE), the University of Cambridge and the European Federation of National Engineering Associations (FEANI). Email: hagstroem@ethworld.ethz.ch

Following graduation from the University of Southampton Medical School in 1982, **Julian Jenkins** specialised clinically in reproductive medicine while developing an academic interest in applying information technology to medical practice, education and research. He came to the University of Bristol, UK, as a consultant senior lecturer in 1995. His past positions include codirector of the national Computers in Teaching Centre for Medicine. His current positions include membership of the Senate of the University of Bristol, chairman of the South West Region Obstetrics & Gynaecology committee, and associate medical director in information management and technology for the United Bristol Healthcare Trust.

Athanasis Karoulis has a BSc in mathematics from Aristotle University of Thessaloniki, Greece; a degree in educational technologies from the University of Macedonia, Greece; a degree in open and distance learning from the Hellenic Open University; a master's in information systems from the University of Macedonia; and a PhD in informatics, in the domain of human-computer interaction from Aristotle University of Thessaloniki. He is currently active as an instructor in educational technologies for secondary education, as a multimedia and Web project manager, and as a researcher in the domains of HCI and of distance learning, regarding the application of new technologies at the Department of Informatics at Aristotle University. He is an author of two books and coauthor of another five which are published in Greece, and he has managed more than six multimedia projects. His scientific interests are human-computer interaction, multimedia and Web design, educational technologies and distance learning.

Bridget Khursheed, senior project manager for the Technology-Assisted Lifelong Learning (TALL) group at the University of Oxford, UK, manages the diploma in computing via the Internet, the university's first online course. With qualifications from the university in both English and computing, her industrial background is in education, communication and online development. She is a well-known consultant and speaker on the Internet and education in Europe and North America and was one of the first to develop a commercial intranet. Bridget is also a poet, fisherman and salsa dancer. She lives in East Oxford with her husband and two sons.

Paul Leng has been at the University of Liverpool, UK, since 1971 and was head of the Department of Computer Science from 1991 to 1997, during which time he also co-founded the university's CONNECT Centre for Internet-related business. He is now director of the university's e-Learning Unit, which administers degree programmes that are delivered entirely online. In addition to these responsibilities, he continues to have an appointment within the Department of Computer Science, pursuing research in knowledge discovery in databases (KDD), Internet-based computing, including distributed computing on the Web, dialogue-based systems, and e-learning.

Liz Marr is a senior lecturer in the Department of Sociology at Manchester Metropolitan University, UK. Her teaching and research interests lie in the sociology of technology, communications and media. She is a founder member of KORG, Knowledge in Organisations Research Group, which conducts research into the development and implementation of technological systems in work settings.

Fernando Lincoln Mattos holds a master's in education and teaches in the pedagogy graduate programme at the University of Fortaleza, Ce, Brazil. His experiences include teaching didactics using distance online learning systems. He is a member of the project TeleCadi, related to case-based reasoning on teacher's formation and he teaches on university teacher's formation courses.

William L. Mitchell was head of the Virtual Museum Group at Manchester Metropolitan University, with a particular focus on the use of new media in museum education. He is currently a distance learning adviser at the British Council, UK.

Libero Nigro is a professor of computer science in the Department of Electronics, Informatics, and Systems Science at the University of Calabria, Italy, where he is a lecturer of computer science introductory courses and a systems programming course. His technical interests are centered on software engineering of time-dependent distributed systems. He is currently active on research projects concerned with actor/agent systems, distributed real-time systems, parallel simulation, timed Petri nets, and multimedia systems over the Internet. He is a member of ACM and IEEE Computer Society.

J. O'Donoghue's background covers a range of educational experiences. In his early career, he taught in a social priority area school, moving to postgraduate lecturing, advising and consultancy for initial teaching training to his last position as senior education officer within a large education authority. An advocate of the "global classroom," John continues to write and publish extensively on the use and exploitation of the ICT in education. In his present post as the research project manager for the UK National Centre for Education at the University of Wolverhampton, UK, he is responsible for the academic and pedagogical aspects of learning technologies.

Andreas Pombortsis received a BS degree in physics and an MS degree in electronics and communications (both from the University of Thessaloniki) and a diploma degree in electrical engineering from the Technical University of Thessaloniki. In 1987 he received a PhD degree in computer science from the University of Thessaloniki. Currently, he is a professor in the Department of Informatics, Aristotle University Of Thessaloniki, Greece. His research interests include computer architecture, parallel and distributed computer systems, and multimedia systems.

Roy Rada has the following educational credentials: BA in psychology from Yale University in 1973, MD in general medicine from Baylor College of Medicine in 1977, and a PhD in computer science from the University of Illinois in Urbana in 1980. He was virtual university academic officer at Washington State University, codirector of the Center for Distance Education at Pace University, and director of the flexible master's degree at the University of Maryland, Baltimore County, USA. He is coeditor of the journal *Interactive Learning Environments* and author of the book *Understanding Virtual Universities*.

Dave Randall is a senior lecturer in the Department of Sociology at Manchester Metropolitan University, UK, and a consultant to the Blekinge Institute of Technology, Ronneby, Sweden. His research interests center on CSCW and in particular the application of ethnomethodological insights to technology design.

Elaine M. Raybourn, who holds a PhD in communication, has a background in intercultural communication and human-computer interaction. Her research interests span simulations, games, intelligent agents, collaborative virtual environments, and interaction design. Current efforts include event-based awareness systems, adding cultural signposts to intelligent community-based systems, addressing cultural differences in agent and avatar behaviors, and designing cultural frameworks for cognitive architectures in simulations that incorporate human actors or human learning. Elaine is currently a member of Sandia National Laboratories, USA, and a National Laboratory Professor at the University of New Mexico's Department of Communication and Journalism, Institute for Organizational Communication. See http://www.cs.unm.edu/~raybourn

Joze Rugelj received BSc, MSc and PhD degrees in computer science from the University of Ljubljana, Slovenia, in 1985, 1988 and 1993, respectively. He is an associate professor of computer science at the University of Ljubljana, Faculty of Education, and a senior researcher at the Department of Digital Communications and Networks at the J. Stefan Institute, Slovenia. His research interests include group communications, computer-supported cooperative work and computer-supported collaborative learning. In the last 10 years he was a national coordinator of several international and national research projects in the field of computer-supported collaboration and collaborative learning. He is the author of more than 30 papers in international journals and conference proceedings.

Walter Schaufelberger is professor of automatic control, vice-rector for international affairs and project director of ETH World at the Swiss Federal Institute of Technology Zurich, Switzerland. He is an administrative council member and past president of the European Society for Engineering Education (SEFI) and treasurer of the International Federation for Automatic Control (IFAC). Email: ws@aut.ee.ethz.ch

Vivien Sieber is a coordinator for learning, teaching and curriculum development at the University of North London, UK, for C&IT and runs the Teaching and Learning Technology Centre. She is a discipline consultant in genetics for LTSN biology.

David Sloan, Lorna Gibson, Scott Milne, and **Peter Gregor** form the Digital Media Access Group (DMAG), an expert research and consultancy group. They are based in the Department of Applied Computing at the University of Dundee, Scotland, one of the world's leading groups researching into communication systems for disabled and elderly people. The authors' main interests lie in the accessibility and usability of digital resources, primarily Web sites, and they have researched into methodologies for reviewing and addressing resources for accessibility problems and presenting findings to customers in a pragmatic, accessible way. The authors have presented their research and given workshops at a number of international conferences. Other research interests include the involvement of children and elderly people in the design and development of accessible digital resources. Additionally, the authors have worked with several clients in the commercial, public and educational sectors, providing advice on the accessibility of major Web sites and other digital resources.

Marius Iulian Tutuianu is a last-year student at the Faculty of Mathematics and Computer Sciences, Babes-Bolyai University, Cluj-Napoca, Romania. He is currently working as a Web and WAP developer at "SISTEC," Cluj-Napoca, Romania (a certified reseller and partner of Hewlett-Packard, DTK Computers, Microsoft, Novell, Symantec). His graduation paper as well as his research is concentrating on accessible Web design and online education for visually impaired students. He is doing his research within the Centre for Educational Technology Transfer at the university.

Jean Vanderdonckt has a PhD in computer science and a postdoctorate degree in human-computer interaction (HCI) from Stanford University, USA. He is a professor at the Catholic University of Louvain (UCL), Belgium, and a leader of many projects. His research themes are: HCI, hypermedia and multimedia applications, intelligent user interfaces (IUI), and tools for working with guidelines (TFWWG). He has been an invited speaker for the first International Workshop on

Computer-Aided Generation of UI, 1993; an organizer of the meetings of the ACM Special Interest Group (SIG); a workshop chair for TFWWG'2000; a short paper and interactive cochair for ACM CHI'2001; a technical programme cochair for IHM-HCI'2001; a reviewer of many conferences; and a member of many conference programme committees in HCI.

Index

Q

quality assurance 198
quality management 198

R

real world 159
Real-Time Transport Protocol (RTP)
   48, 50
reflective learner 27
reflective questions 78
remote learning 20
representational models 299
research-based approach 128
research-led 129
resource providers 379
resource users 379
Royal National Institute for the Blind
   390

S

search engine 25
security 332
self-directed learning situation 315
seminar-based model 202
simulation 234
situated learning 111
situated usability 319
social schemata of uses 318
social-process simulation 234
software capability maturity 180
staff appointment and training 204
streamed video 20
student identity 204
student involvement 204
student-student feedback 273
student-teacher feedback 273
support structures 21
supported open-learning programme
   284

T

task requirements 390
Tele-CADI 73
TELRI (Technology-Enhanced Learning

in Research-Le 131
traditional methods 20
traditional university 199
training sessions 23
training technologies need 181
training transfer 181
transparency 91
tutor 263

U

UMBC 278
University of Liverpool 203
University of Oxford 160
URL 25
usability 88
usability heuristics 314
Usability of a CPS 42
usability of the user interface 178
usefulness 314
user interface evaluation process 177
user-centred design 314

V

validation and approval procedures 204
variety of learners 182
ViCROC system 42
videoconferencing system 332
virtual campus 1
virtual classroom 159, 238, 257
virtual environment 12, 120
virtual learning environment 26
virtual multimedia textbook 256
virtual reality 348
virtual simulation environment 239
virtual universities 238
visualization 183

W

Washington State University (WSU)
   276
Web authoring tools 379
Web navigation 376
Web page appearance 377
Web usability 389
Windows 2000 29

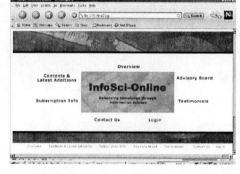

International Journal of Distance Education Technologies (JDET)

NEW!   **NEW!**

The International Source for Technological Advances in Distance Education

ISSN: 1539-3100
eISSN: 1539-3119

Subscription: Annual fee per volume (4 issues):
Individual US $85
Institutional US $185

Editors: Shi Kuo Chang
University of Pittsburgh, USA

Timothy K. Shih
Tamkang University, Taiwan

International Journal of Distance Education Technologies

INSIDE THIS ISSUE:
New network infrastructures
Distributed systems
Mobile systems
Multimedia synchronization controls
individualized distance learning

Idea Group Publishing

Mission

The *International Journal of Distance Education Technologies* (**JDET**) publishes original research articles of distance education four issues per year. **JDET** is a primary forum for researchers and practitioners to disseminate practical solutions to the automation of open and distance learning. The journal is targeted to academic researchers and engineers who work with distance learning programs and software systems, as well as general participants of distance education.

Coverage

Discussions of computational methods, algorithms, implemented prototype systems, and applications of open and distance learning are the focuses of this publication. Practical experiences and surveys of using distance learning systems are also welcome. Distance education technologies published in **JDET** will be divided into three categories, **Communication Technologies, Intelligent Technologies, and Educational Technologies**: new network infrastructures, real-time protocols, broadband and wireless communication tools, quality-of-services issues, multimedia streaming technology, distributed systems, mobile systems, multimedia synchronization controls, intelligent tutoring, individualized distance learning, neural network or statistical approaches to behavior analysis, automatic FAQ reply methods, copyright protection and authentification mechanisms, practical and new learning models, automatic assessment methods, effective and efficient authoring systems, and other issues of distance education.

For subscription information, contact:

Idea Group Publishing
701 E Chocolate Ave., Suite 200
Hershey PA 17033-1240, USA
cust@idea-group.com
URL: www.idea-group.com

For paper submission information:

Dr. Timothy Shih
Tamkang University, Taiwan
tshih@cs.tku.edu.tw